Instructor's Manual to Accompany

— PSYCHOLOGY —
Science and Application

Mark G. McGee
Brain Sciences Laboratories and
University of Colorado School of Medicine, Denver

David W. Wilson
Phillips University

Prepared by

M. Aaron Roy
Ashland College-Ohio

WEST PUBLISHING COMPANY
St. Paul   New York   Los Angeles   San Francisco

— CONTENTS —

— PREFACE —

I attempted to provide you with a functional instructor's manual, one that is closely related to the text. In the manual, there are three parts for each chapter: an outline, objectives, and multiple-choice sections. Whenever possible, phraseology and examples were taken directly from the text. This was done with the purpose of providing you with what the students are actually reading, not my interpretations of the author's work.

PART I OUTLINE

An outline summary of the chapter is presented using the first, second, and third order headings provided in the text. Each word in the text that appears in bold-face print is typed in CAPITALS along with definitional information. Each word that appears in italics in the text is presented as an underlined word. A quick reading of the outline will thus provide you with what the authors are emphasizing for the student.

PART II OBJECTIVES

Each chapter objective is printed and then answered using information in the text. Immediately after each answer, I provide one or more multiple-choice questions and/or an essay question.

PART III MULTIPLE-CHOICE QUESTIONS

There are 80-95 multiple-choice questions for each chapter. There is at least one question dealing with each word, term, or concept appearing in bold-face or in italics in the text. Miscellaneous conceptual, application, factual, and research-oriented questions complete the offering. For reference purposes, these questions are presented under the first or second level outline heading in which they were discussed in the text.

M. Aaron Roy
December, 1983

— CHAPTER 1 —

INTRODUCTION TO PSYCHOLOGY

OUTLINE

I. Introduction: Psychology Is . . . - a presentation of examples of the diverse areas that psychology studies; PSYCHOLOGY is the science of human and animal behavior; psychology is a scientific field of study, an academic discipline, and a profession

II. The Science of Psychology - psychologists use systematic methods to study behavior

    A. Research methods - SCIENCE is the observation, identification, description, experimental investigation, and theoretical explanation of natural phenomena; psychology uses the SCIENTIFIC METHOD which relies on empirical data; a variety of research methods are used
        1. Case histories - the CASE HISTORY APPROACH is a weak, but insightful approach; a discussion of a typical case history; case histories are a source of HYPOTHESES; criticisms with case histories include that they are open to a variety of interpretations, the data is obtained retrospectively, and they may lack validity
        2. CORRELATIONAL RESEARCH provides a systematic way of investigating relationships among VARIABLES; correlational analysis yields a CORRELATION COEFFICIENT which expresses the degree and type of relationship between two variables; extreme coefficients include a perfect positive correlation and a perfect negative correlation

a. observations – observations may take place either in natural, "real-life" settings or in contrived, controlled settings; there is NATURALISTIC OBSERVATION (which must include the influence on behavior of behavior settings), NONNATURALISTIC OBSERVATION and UNOBTRUSIVE OBSERVATION

b. structured interviews, surveys, and questionnaires provide information about opinions, beliefs, and other behaviors

c. tests – PSYCHOMETRIC TESTS are quantitative means for measuring psychological variables

3. Experimental research – the EXPERIMENTAL RESEARCH APPROACH is a powerful investigative method because it permits precise control over variables

a. research design – experimental research begins with a RESEARCH DESIGN or research plan that details the procedures to be followed

b. INDEPENDENT VARIABLES (IVs), including such things as person characteristics, are manipulated in the experiment to study cause

c. dependent variable – experiments observe and measure effects on the DEPENDENT VARIABLE (DV or effect)

d. EXTRANEOUS VARIABLES are held constant whenever possible so they don't influence the DV

e. experimental and control groups – minimizing the effects of extraneous variables is sometimes done through RANDOMIZATION or the random assignment of subjects to an EXPERIMENTAL GROUP or CONTROL GROUP

B. Ethical guidelines for conducting psychological research – experimenters using human subjects must safeguard the rights of participants by protecting them from harm, explaining their obligations and responsibilities, allowing them to decline participation, informing them of the nature of the study, and keeping all participants' information confidential

C. Application: An illustrative example – Does marijuana affect memory? – a nonexperimental and an experimental research approach are discussed in some detail; they are then evaluated on the basis of statistical significance, probability of results, randomization, variables that are confounded, reliability, baseline measure, and the use of a placebo

III. The Discipline of Psychology

A. Early schools of psychology – psychology evolved from philosophy in the late 1800's; groups of psychologists associated themselves with a prominent psychologist (e.g., James, Wundt) to form "schools"

1. Structuralism - using <u>introspection</u> to study <u>consciousness</u>, STRUCTURALISM studied how elements of human consciousness form the "structure" of the mind; Wundt is associated with this school
2. Personal profile: Wilhelm Wundt (1832-1920) - established the first psychology laboratory in 1879 at the University of Leipzig and is considered the "father" of experimental psychology
3. FUNCTIONALISM - advocated studying the aspects of the mind that aid the organism to function in the environment; James is associated with this school
4. Personal profile: William James (1842-1910) - the "father" of American psychology who worked at Harvard and established psychology as a practical science
5. BEHAVIORISM - a reaction to both other schools; it was primarily interested in the observation and measurement of observable behaviors; Watson is associated with this school

B. Speciality areas in psychology - what interests psychologists is reflected in the many <u>divisions</u> of the APA and in various <u>specialty areas</u>
   1. <u>Clinical and community psychologists</u> work in hospital, university, institutional, community, and private practice settings doing research and applying knowledge through treatment
   2. Developmental, personality, and social psychology - <u>developmental psychologists</u> study human growth and development through the lifespan; <u>personality psychologists</u> do research on individual differences in behavior; <u>social psychologists</u> study the interaction of individuals and how they influence each other
   3. Counseling and school psychology - <u>counseling psychologists</u> draw heavily on a range of fields in psychology; <u>school psychologists</u> work in school settings as academic and career counselors
   4. Experimental and physiological psychology - <u>experimental psychologists</u> are concerned with sensation, perception, learning, and motivation; more than two thirds do basic or applied research in colleges, universities, or research institutions; <u>physiological psychologists</u> study the biological bases of behavior
   5. Engineering, industrial, and organizational psychology - <u>engineering psychologists</u> are concerned with the <u>human factor</u> in production and with optimizing human-machine relations; <u>industrial psychologists</u> aid in personnel selection and placement, and in training programs for workers; <u>organizational psychologists</u> work on problems in leadership, worker morale, and the organization of the work environment
   6. <u>Educational psychologists</u> do research on teaching and learning, usually within college and university settings

7. Methodology and techniques - the subspecialization area of <u>psychometrics</u> is concerned with test development and the measurement of intellectual abilities and personality

8. Emerging specialty areas - <u>environmental psychologists</u> work in school, industrial, and governmental settings on such things as air and noise pollution, crime, and crowding; <u>forensic psychologists</u> work with crime prevention, jury selection, and rehabilitation programs; <u>health psychologists</u> design wellness programs for employees

C. Where psychologists work - a summary of where psychologists are most frequently employed (see Figure1-5 for specific percentages of several general areas)

D. Careers in psychology - a representative list of careers available to undergraduate majors in psychology is presented; educational requirements and representative employment positions are presented for those with master's degrees; the differences in <u>Doctor of Philosophy</u> and <u>Doctor of Psychology</u> (Psy. D.) degrees, as well as <u>psychiatrists,</u> is briefly presented

E. Plan of this book - the authors summarize the content discussed in each of the text's 20 chapters

F. Application: Getting the most out of this book - a description of the intent and use of the chapter's outline, objectives, introduction, figures and tables, personal profiles, on the horizon, summary, important terms and concepts, and suggestions for further reading sections; the journals published by the APA are listed, as are non-APA sources of information (e.g., <u>Newsweek</u> and <u>Time</u> magazines)

IV. On the Horizon: Psychology, The Future, and You - a discussion of the growth of psychology since 1920 and what the future holds: one can expect more students to earn the Psy.D.; psychology will receive more federal funding for it will be more concerned with our culture's everyday problems; the discipline will become more fractionated with new specialty areas arising; there will be a merging of professional and scientific orientations in psychology

OBJECTIVES

I.   WHAT IS PSYCHOLOGY?

Psychology is the science of human and animal behavior. It is
also a field where individuals work in many different
capacities with many different goals. As a scientific field of
study, psychology consists of the research methods and
techniques necessary for collecting, analyzing, and
interpreting new knowledge about behavior. As an academic
discipline, psychology represents a major field of study in
colleges and universities. Finally, as a profession,
psychology involves the practical application of knowledge
gained through scientific inquiry.

D   1. Psychology is considered a profession because it:

        A. is capable of promoting human welfare
        B. represents a major field of study in colleges and
           universities
        C. consists of research techniques and methods for studying
           behavior
        D. involves the application of knowledge gained through
           scientific inquiry

     2. Explain why psychology is a science, an academic discipline,
        and a profession all in one.

II.   WHAT MAKES PSYCHOLOGY A SCIENCE? WHAT MAKES IT A DISCIPLINE?

Psychology is a science because it consists of research methods
and techniques necessary for collecting, analyzing, and
interpreting new knowledge about behavior. Generally,
psychologists conduct two different kinds of research. The
purpose of basic research is the accumulation of knowledge
purely for its own sake. Applied research is aimed at using
research findings to solve practical problems or to improve the
quality of human life. As an academic discipline, psychology
represents a major field of study in colleges and universities.

B   1. When psychology consists of research methods and techniques
        for collecting and analyzing knowledge about behavior, it is
        considered a(n):

        A. research area
        B. scientific field of study
        C. academic discipline
        D. profession

C   2. Which type of research is involved in using research findings to solve practical problems?

    A. experimental research
    B. basic research
    C. applied research
    D. professional research

3. What makes psychology both a science and a discipline?

III. LIST METHODS THAT PSYCHOLOGISTS USE FOR COLLECTING, ANALYZING, AND INTERPRETING NEW KNOWLEDGE ABOUT BEHAVIOR AND MENTAL PROCESSES.

Psychologists use a wide range of techniques for gathering and understanding new knowledge about behavior. The preferred method is the experimental research approach which involves the manipulation of variables under controlled conditions that may influence behavior. However, a number of other techniques are commonly used, though potentially not without some degree of bias involved both in gathering the data and in interpreting its meaning. The weakest investigative method is the case history approach. Correlational research provides a systematic way of investigating relationships among variables, but it does not help us understand causal relationships. Systematic observations have special types reflecting the type of setting-observer relationship that are involved (i.e., naturalistic observation, nonnaturalistic observation, and unobtrusive observation). In addition, psychologists use structured interviews, surveys, questionnaires, and specialized psychometric tests. In general, all methods of investigation compliment one another with specific hypotheses used in the experimental method frequently coming from data gathered by all non-experimental approaches.

A   1. Which method of data gathering is most preferred by psychologists?

    A. experimental research approach
    B. correlational research
    C. case history method
    D. systematic observations

C   2. Which method of data gathering is least preferred by psychologists?

    A. experimental research approach
    B. correlational research
    C. case history method
    D. systematic observations

B   3. Which data gathering method used by psychologists helps us
         with predictions, but not causes, of behavior?

         A. experimental research approach
         B. correlational research
         C. case history method
         D. systematic observations

      4. Summarize the various ways that psychologists learn about
         behavior. Which methods are better than others and why?

IV.   OF WHAT VALUE ARE CASE HISTORY, CORRELATIONAL, AND EXPERIMENTAL
      RESEARCH APPROACHES? WHAT ARE THE LIMITATIONS OF EACH?

      The case history method is the least valuable because these
      reports are open to a variety of interpretations, data is
      gathered retrospectively, and the validity of the data is
      questionable. However, it is useful in that it can provide
      interesting insights into human behavior, thus providing a rich
      source of hypotheses for more systematic investigations. The
      correlational research approach provides a systematic way of
      investigating relationships among variables. Even though this
      approach is an important tool in predicting behavioral
      outcomes, it does not give us information about the causes of
      behavior. The experimental research approach is the most
      powerful research method because it allows the researcher to
      exercise precise control over conditions that might affect
      observed or measured relationships among variables, thus
      understanding cause-effect relationships.

D   1. Which method of gathering information provides psychologists
         with the best understanding of cause-effect relationships?

         A. systematic observations
         B. correlational
         C. case history
         D. experimental

D   2. What is a limitation of the case history method for
         gathering information about behavior?

         A. it collects information retrospectively
         B. its results are open to many interpretations
         C. the validity of the information is questionable
         D. all of the above

      3. What are the advantages and disadvantages of the following
         methods for gathering information about behavior: case
         history; correlational, and experimental research?

V.   WHICH SPECIALTY AREAS CURRENTLY CHARACTERIZE THE DISCIPLINE OF
     PSYCHOLOGY?

There are currently seven major specialty areas, and a few
emerging areas, which characterize the field of psychology.
They are grouped to reflect psychologists' typical work places
and activities as well as their general area of interest.
Psychologists also vary in the amount (if any) of research they
conduct.   The clinical and community psychologists work in a
variety of settings (e.g., hospitals, institutions, private
practices) doing research and applying psychological knowledge
during   the   treatment   of   psychological   disorders.
Developmental, personality, and social psychologists study
growth and developmental processes, individual differences in
behavior,   and   interactions   of   individuals, respectively.
Counseling and school psychologists perform a variety of
applied functions in schools, colleges, and universities.
Experimental and physiological psychologists typically are
found in colleges and universities doing research on such
things as sensations, perceptions, learning, motivation, and
the biological bases of behavior.   Engineering, industrial, and
organizational psychologists are all primarily concerned with
the study of people at work.   Educational psychologists do
research on teaching and learning, typically working within a
university setting. The emerging specialty areas of psychology
include environmental, forensic, and health.   These show
psychology's increasing involvement with the environment, law,
and medicine.

A   1. Which of the following is NOT considered an emerging
        specialty area is psychology?

        A. counseling
        B. environmental
        C. health
        D. forensic

     2. Describe the roles, activities, and work settings of four of
        the seven specialty areas in psychology.

VI. WHERE DO PSYCHOLOGISTS WORK?   WHAT ARE THE EDUCATIONAL
     REQUIREMENTS FOR BECOMING A PSYCHOLOGIST? WHAT ARE THE FUTURE
     EMPLOYMENT OPPORTUNITIES FOR PSYCHOLOGISTS?

Most psychologists (57%) work in colleges and universities.
The next two most prevalent work settings are hospitals,
clinics, and community centers (15%) and in private or group
practice (7%). Typically, to be a psychologist one must major
in psychology at an undergraduate college or university. Then,
many go on to do their master's work in psychology, earning a
M.S. or M.A.   Students then have a choice for their doctoral
level training.   Some earn the Ph.D. which includes extensive
training in research.   Others earn the newer Psy.D. which has
less emphasis on research experience and more on gaining

practical, clinical experience. Future employment opportunities will favor those in applied areas, especially individuals who are qualified to assist in dealing with everyday problems such as pollution, crowding, and urban decay. Even researchers are predicted to shift their emphasis to applied rather than basic research.

C   1. Where do most psychologists work?

    A. private and group practices
    B. hospitals, clinics, and community centers
    C. colleges and universities
    D. governmental agencies

    2. Where do psychologists work today and what types of future employment opportunities are foreseen for psychologists?

MULTIPLE-CHOICE QUESTIONS

INTRODUCTION: PSYCHOLOGY IS . . .

D   1. Which of the following statements about psychologists is TRUE?
    A. they study sex differences in the brain
    B. they study animal and human learning
    C. they study sleep and dreams
    D. all of the above

B   2. Psychology is defined as the science of:
    A. interpreting behavioral problems
    B. human and animal behavior
    C. interpreting and solving behavioral problems
    D. individual and group interactions

D   3. Psychology is a(n):
    A. science
    B. academic discipline
    C. profession
    D. all of the above

A   4. As a scientific field of study, psychology's main goal is to:
    A. collect and interpret new knowledge about behavior
    B. be represented in colleges and universities
    C. apply knowledge
    D. help prevent or treat abnormal behaviors

C   5. The purpose of basic research is to:
          A. study animal behavior
          B. solve practical problems
          C. accumulate knowledge purely for its own sake
          D. relate information about behavior to physical and
             chemical processes

C   6. The purpose of applied research is to:
          A. study behavior in "real-life" situations
          B. apply the knowledge gained through scientific inquiry
          C. improve the quality of human life or solve practical
             problems
          D. share information in classes at colleges and universities

B   7. The practical application of knowledge gained through
          research is associated with what area of psychology?
          A. the scientific field of study
          B. the professional
          C. the academic discipline
          D. the political

RESEARCH METHODS

A   8. One may simply define "science," as it was in Latin, as:
          A. knowledge
          B. systematic methods
          C. procedure
          D. basic understanding

D   9. Which of the following is NOT characteristic of the
          scientific method?
          A. conducting observations and experiments
          B. the interpretation of information obtained from
             experiments
          C. a reliance on empirical data
          D. the reliance on studying animal behavior

C   10. Information that can be observed and measured is called
          _____ data.
          A. basic
          B. raw
          C. empirical
          D. scientific

B   11. Which of the following is NOT characteristic of the case
          history approach in psychology?
          A. one of the oldest methods of investigation
          B. commonly used in colleges and universities
          C. one of the weakest investigative methods
          D. it provides useful insights

C   12. The real strength of the case history approach is that it:
A. can tell us about abnormal behaviors
B. is good training for young scientists
C. provides a rich source of hypotheses
D. involves dealing with people and not animals

A   13. A tentative explanation for observed phenomena that can be tested in controlled studies is a:
A. hypothesis
B. idea
C. scientific hunch
D. probability statement

A   14. Case history methods are considered to have weaknesses because their information is obtained _____, thus making it difficult to _____.
A. retrospectively ; validate
B. retrospectively ; interpret
C. unintentionally ; validate
D. casually ; interpret

D   15. The correlational research method provides a systematic way of investigating _____ among _____.
A. hypotheses ; truth
B. truth ; hypotheses
C. variables ; relationships
D. relationships ; variables

B   16. Any phenomenon that can be quantified, and therefore measured in some way, is a:
A. hypothesis
B. variable
C. unobtrusive observation
D. fact

C   17. A correlation coefficient is a mathematical expression of the degree of relationship between two:
A. validated means
B. hypotheses
C. variables
D. naturalistic observations

A   18. A perfect, positive correlation would have a correlation coefficient of:
A. −1.00
B. about −.85
C. about +.85
D. +1.00

B   19. A −1.00 correlation coefficient would signify a:
A. perfect positive correlation
B. perfect negative correlation
C. positive meaningful correlation
D. negative nonmeaningful correlation

D   20. Students who obtain high scores on midterm exams also tend
        to obtain high scores on the final exam. A correlational
        analysis would find what type of correlation for this
        relationship?
        A. +1.00
        B. -1.00
        C. between zero and -.99
        D. between zero and +.99

D   21. Jane Goodall's pioneering research on chimpanzee behavior in
        Africa is an example of:
        A. unobtrusive observation
        B. nonnaturalistic observation
        C. observations in contrived controlled settings
        D. naturalistic observation

C   22. Barker's research on people's behavior in particular
        behavior settings (such as weddings and baseball games)
        found that:
        A. an individual's behavior is consistent across settings
        B. some people are more influenced by "group pressure" than
           others
        C. behavior varies as a function of the setting in which it
           occurs
        D. the more formal the setting the more formal the behavior

A   23. A general problem with observational methods of gathering
        information is:
        A. the observer may alter the behavior being observed
        B. they usually take too long
        C. they usually cover a short time span
        D. their high cost compared to laboratory work

B   24. Gathering information on behavior which takes place in
        contrived or controlled settings (such as in schools or
        hospitals) is called _____ observation.
        A. naturalistic
        B. nonnaturalistic
        C. unobtrusive
        D. incidental

D   25. Assessing the racial attitudes of college students by noting
        how often they sat together in lecture halls was the text's
        example of _____ observation.
        A. naturalistic
        B. nonnaturalistic
        C. incidental
        D. unobtrusive

C   26. Structured interviews, surveys,   and **questionnaires** provide
         information about subjects':
         A. overt behaviors
         B. unbiased behaviors in "real-life" settings
         C. opinions and beliefs
         D. behavior in contrived, controlled settings

A   27. What types of tests measure such things as intelligence and
         abilities?
         A. psychometric tests
         B. structured interviews
         C. surveys
         D. questionnaires

B   28. Psychometric tests provide a _____ means for measuring
         psychological variables.
         A. valuable
         B. quantitative
         C. subjective
         D. naturalistic

B   29. A key characteristic of the experimental research approach
         is that it:
         A. allows the validation of case history research methods
         B. allows for precise control over conditions
         C. prevents bias by being unobtrusive
         D. studies behavior without the subject's awareness

C   30. Which of the following is NOT part of a research design?
         A. specification of procedures to be followed
         B. description of the subjects to be studied
         C. an interpretation of the obtained results
         D. specification of the hypotheses to be tested

D   31. Why are variables carefully controlled and manipulated in
         experimental research?
         A. so the experimenter can understand the results
         B. so the experimenter can interpret the results
         C. in order to compare the results to other studies
         D. in order to identify cause-effect relationships

A   32. Independent variables are those which the investigator:
         A. manipulates
         B. observes
         C. measures
         D. records

D   33. In an experiment, the behavior of interest which may or may
         not change is called the _____ variable.
         A. experimental
         B. independent
         C. extraneous
         D. dependent

B   34. In an experiment studying the effect of marijuana on memory,
         the marijuana consumed would be the _____ variable while
         the performance on the memory task would be the _____
         variable.
         A. dependent ; extraneous
         B. independent ; dependent
         C. dependent ; independent
         D. independent ; extraneous

C   35. The independent variable is synonymous with _____ while
         the dependent variable is synonymous with _____.
         A. influence ; cause
         B. effect ; influence
         C. cause ; effect
         D. result ; antecedent

A   36. Extraneous variables are those that:
         A. may influence the dependent variable
       ' B. do influence the independent variable
         C. are too difficult to manipulate
         D. are too difficult to quantify

A   37. Randomization of subjects assigned to experimental and
         control groups is done to:
         A. minimize the effects of extraneous variables
         B. have equal numbers in each group
         C. have different subjects in each group
         D. provide better statistical analyses

D   38. In an experiment, the _____ group is exposed to the
         _____ variable while the _____ group is not.
         A. control ; dependent ; experimental
         B. control ; independent ; experimental
         C. experimental ; dependent ; control
         D. experimental ; independent ; control

B   39. Cause-effect relationships concerning behavior are best
         studied with which method?
         A. psychometric tests
         B. experimental
         C. structured interviews and surveys
         D. case history method

ETHICAL GUIDELINES FOR PSYCHOLOGICAL RESEARCH

C   40. Which of the following guidelines that psychologists use
         when studying humans is perhaps the most important?
         A. protection from physical and mental harm
         B. to allow for someone to decline participation
         C. to protect confidentiality
         D. establishing a fair, clear agreement

APPLICATION: AN ILLUSTRATIVE EXAMPLE--DOES MARIJUANA AFFECT MEMORY?

A   41. An important criticism of the study by Schaeffer, et. al.,
         who used a nonexperimental approach to study marijuana's
         effect on memory, was that they:
         A. may not have used a random sample
         B. may have had subjects with previous brain damage
         C. used too many subjects to test adequately
         D. did not test them adequately

D   42. Campbell, et. al., reported that brain atrophy was due to
         marijuana use. Even though a control group was used, their
         study was criticized because the subjects were:
         A. too old
         B. all males
         C. low in intelligence level
         D. previous drug users

C   43. An experimental research approach by Darley, et. al. studied
         the effects of THC on memory. They found that marijuana
         had:
         A. no effect on memory
         B. very little effect on memory
         C. a larger negative effect with larger dosages
         D. a larger positive effect with larger dosages

B   44. Various statistical procedures are used by researchers to
         determine _____, which expresses the _____ the results
         occurred because of the independent variable.
         A. probability ; reliability
         B. statistical significance ; probability
         C. validity ; probability
         D. experimental outcome ; likelihood

B   45. A statistical term that refers to the likelihood of
         obtaining the same results if the experiment were repeated
         is:
         A. replication
         B. reliability
         C. validity
         D. statistical significance

A   46. Why would an experimenter want to have a replication of a
       study?
       A. to add confidence in the reliability of the original
          results
       B. to use different subjects with different tests
       C. to vary control groups
       D. to manipulate the independent variable more
          systematically

C   47. Why are baseline measures valuable in research?
       A. they determine reliability
       B. they make replication easier
       C. they provide a standard against which comparisons are
          made
       D. they use placebos

EARLY SCHOOLS OF PSYCHOLOGY

D   48. At about what time period were the first two laboratories
       devoted to psychological research established?
       A. around 1650
       B. around 1790
       C. early 1800's
       D. late 1800's

D   49. A method of self-examination and contemplation of one's own
       feelings and thoughts is called:
       A. consciousness investigation
       B. mental-analysis
       C. self-analysis
       D. introspection

A   50. Introspection was a key method in which psychological
       discipline?
       A. structuralism
       B. functionalism
       C. mentalism
       D. behaviorism

A   51. The study of how elements of human consciousness form mental
       processes is called:
       A. structuralism
       B. functionalism
       C. mentalism
       D. behaviorism

B   52. According to Wundt and the structuralist movement,
       consciousness consisted of which three elements?
       A. preconscious, unconscious, subconscious
       B. sensations, images, feelings
       C. reactions, beliefs, emotions
       D. functions, relationships, connections

D   53. Wilhelm Wundt:
         A. was the first psychologist
         B. was the "father" of experimental psychology
         C. established the first psychology laboratory
         D. all of the above

B   54. The school of psychology that emphasized studying mental
         processes that aid organisms in adapting to the environment
         is known as:
         A. structuralism
         B. functionalism
         C. mentalism
         D. behaviorism

C   55. The functionalists differed from the structuralists in
         whether:
         A. animals should be studied
         B. experimentation should take place
         C. the mind can be analyzed into discrete elements
         D. all of the above

A   56. The "father" of American Psychology is:
         A. William James
         B. William Wundt
         C. James Cattell
         D. John B. Watson

D   57. The study of observable behavior by objective experimental
         procedures was the goal of:
         A. structuralism
         B. functionalism
         C. mentalism
         D. behaviorism

C   58. The school of behaviorism was "led" in its early days by the
         thinking of:
         A. Wundt
         B. James
         C. Watson
         D. Skinner

SPECIALTY AREAS IN PSYCHOLOGY

B   59. One way to classify the wide range of interests that
         psychologists have is to group individuals according to
         their:
         A. academic training
         B. specialty area
         C. type of work setting
         D. type of research conducted

A   60. Which specialty area of psychology has the most
        psychologists?
        A. clinical and community
        B. counseling and school
        C. experimental and physiological
        D. educational

A   61. Which type of psychologists typically work in hospital,
        university, institutional, community, and private practice
        settings?
        A. clinical and community
        B. developmental and personality
        C. counseling and school
        D. experimental and physiological

C   62. Clinical and counseling psychologists typically:
        A. do research in mental hospitals
        B. study growth processes and treat developing organisms
        C. are interested in understanding and treating
           psychological disorders
        D. study the interaction of individuals and how they
           influence one another

D   63. Individuals who focus their research on individual
        differences in behavior are called _____ psychologists.
        A. experimental
        B. social
        C. developmental
        D. personality

B   64. What type of psychologist is most often found in a research
        setting?
        A. developmental
        B. experimental
        C. organizational
        D. educational

C   65. Those people who do applied research with the _____ in
        areas of production and human-machine relations are called
        _____ psychologists.
        A. government ; organizational
        B. laws ; industrial
        C. human factor ; engineering
        D. personality ; experimental

A   66. Those who develop educational tests and design programs for
        special children are called _____ psychologists.
        A. educational
        B. school
        C. developmental
        D. organizational

D   67. The area of psychology that is concerned with test development and the measurement of intellectual abilities and personality is called:
A. school
B. personality
C. human factors
D. psychometrics

B   68. Those who study the effects on behavior of crowding, noise, and air pollution are called _____ psychologists.
A. social
B. environmental
C. health
D. forensic

D   69. Orgainzational psychologists typically:
A. help with personnel selection and placement
B. work with law enforcement officials
C. are involved in politics and political decision making
D. deal with leadership, worker morale, and the organization of the work environment

10 CAREERS IN PSYCHOLOGY

A   70. A major difference between psychologists and psychiatrists is in their:
A. amount of research training
B. years needed for schooling
C. Psy.D.
D. clinical experience

C   71. Positions such as a high school academic counselor or a groupleader on a psychiatric ward would typically require what degree?
A. Psy.D.
B. Ph.D.
C. M.S. or M.A.
D. B.S. or B.A.

– CHAPTER 2 –

BIOLOGICAL FOUNDATIONS OF BEHAVIOR

OUTLINE

I.   Introduction: Some Effects of Disconnecting the Two Sides of the Brain – a description of the behavior of Carl who has had a split-brain operation to alleviate severe epileptic seizures and who, at times, had each hand act in incompatible ways

II. The Nervous System – the NERVOUS SYSTEM, made up of NEURONS, controls all of our movements and thoughts

   A. Neurons and the transmission of nerve impulses – glial cells and about 100 billion neurons make up the nervous system; a typical neuron is made up of a cell-body, DENDRITES which receive messages from other neurons, and AXONS that transmit impulses to other neurons, muscles and body organs. Many axons are coated with a myelin sheath which influences the speed of neural transmission
      1. Nerve impulses – the NERVE IMPULSE refers to the electrical activity that travels along the axon when the cell is stimulated; it is measured with microelectrodes inserted into the axon; the impulse results when electrically charged ions (e.g., sodium ions and potassium ions), which form a cell's resting potential, are caused to reverse their concentration on each side of the cell membrane by a stimulus, thereby generating an action potential; the exchange of ions is accomplished by the sodium-potassium pump; after an action potential

the cell enters the <u>absolute refractory period</u> when it is unable to be stimulated; following the absolute refractory period, the <u>relative refractory period</u> occurs where the cell is only responsive to a stronger than normal input; all neurons have a <u>threshold</u> that, when reached, an action potential occurs; the <u>all-or-none</u> law states that a stimulus either elicits a full-strength action potential or none-at-all; neurons carry information on the basis of the <u>rate</u> and <u>number</u> of nerve impulses that occur

2. Synaptic transmission - tiny fibers with enlarged tips called <u>terminal buttons</u> enable one neuron to communicate with one another at the SYNAPSE; NEUROTRANSMITTERS are chemicals released from the terminal buttons to activate the next neuron; SYNAPTIC TRANSMISSION is an <u>electrochemical</u> process; <u>synaptic vessicles</u> which, when ruptured by the impulse, release their stored neurotransmitters into the <u>synaptic cleft</u> or gap between the cells to change the electrical potential of the receiving neuron; <u>excitatory synapses</u> move neurons toward their thresholds while <u>inhibitory synapses</u> move neurons away from their thresholds

B. Organization of the nervous system - the nervous system is made up of bundled groups of axons called NERVES; the system is divided into the CENTRAL NERVOUS SYSTEM, made up of the brain and spinal cord, and the PERIPHERAL NERVOUS SYSTEM which is composed of all neural tissue which connects the brain and spinal cord to the rest of the body

1. The BRAIN is made up of <u>white matter</u> and <u>gray matter</u> and controls and coordinates physical and mental activities; brain growth after birth results from the build up of myelin and glial cells; <u>neurobiology</u> is the science of the nervous system; <u>neuroanatomy</u> deals with brain parts or <u>structures</u> while <u>neurophysiology</u> deals with how the brain parts operate or <u>function</u>; neuroanatomists divide the brain into three major parts

a. the FOREBRAIN is the largest and consists of the cerebrum, the limbic system, the hypothalamus, and the thalamus; the CEREBRUM is the largest portion and consists of two <u>cerebral hemispheres</u> and the <u>cerebral cortex</u>; the surface is composed of <u>gyri</u> and <u>sulci</u>; the CORPUS CALLOSUM connects the two hemispheres; the LIMBIC SYSTEM, made up of the HYPOTHALMUS and THALAMUS, is involved in emotional behavior, sexual behavior, aggression, and memory formation

b. the MIDBRAIN primarily is involved in controlling eye movements and relaying visual and auditory information to higher brain centers; the RETICULAR ACTIVATING SYSTEM is involved in arousal, attention, and sleep-waking cycles

     c. the HINDBRAIN is made up of the MEDULLA which controls heart beat, breathing, body temperature, digestion, blood pressure, and swallowing, while the CEREBELLUM governs body balance and coordination

2. The spinal cord - the SPINAL CORD receives impulses from SENSORY NEURONS (afferent neurons) and sends impulses to various parts of the body via MOTOR NEURONS (efferent neurons); the knee-jerk reflex, a behavior carried out without the brain's involvement, involves a reflex and a reflex arc; INTERNEURONS (association neurons) connect and integrate sensory and motor neuron messages; paraplegics have a severed or injured spinal cord

3. The peripheral nervous system - it is divided into the somatic and autonomic systems
   a. the SOMATIC NERVOUS SYSTEM consists of sensory neurons from sensory receptors and motor neurons from the central nervous system to the skeletal muscles
   b. the AUTONOMIC NERVOUS SYSTEM controls bodily functions considered to be automatic or involuntary; the somatic system controls smooth muscles while the autonomic system controls striated muscles; the autonomic system is divided into the SYMPATHETIC SYSTEM and the PARASYMPATHETIC SYSTEM

4. The ENDOCRINE SYSTEM consists of glands in various parts of the body that release HORMONES into the blood stream
   a. the PITUITARY GLAND in the brain releases at least eight hormones; it releases the antidiuretic hormone (ADH), oxytocin, three that act upon the gonads, another is the growth hormone
   b. the ADRENAL GLANDS release sex hormones as well as those which help the body cope with stress; two hormones released from the adrenal medulla are epinephrine (noradrenaline) and norepinephrine (adrenalin)

C. Application: Brain neurotransmitters and behavior - the first clearly identified neurotransmitter was epinephrine; now there are at least 30 known transmitters; a well understood transmitter is acetylcholine (ACh) which activates muscles; curare and botulin block ACh activity; ACh activity may also be related to Alzheimer's disease; two other classes of neurotransmitters which inhibit pain are the endorphins and enkephalins; some believe that ACUPUNCTURE triggers the release of the pain inhibiting neurotransmitters

III. The Brain and Behavior

A. Cortical areas and their functions - the brain's hemispheres are divided into four lobes (frontal lobe, parietal lobe, temporal lobe, occipital lobe)
   1. The MOTOR CORTEX of the frontal lobe controls voluntary movements of the body

  2. The SOMATOSENSORY CORTEX of the parietal lobe is involved
     in body movement and the senses of touch, heat, cold, and
     pain
  3. The AUDITORY CORTEX of the temporal lobe is specialized
     for receiving and responding to sound stimuli
  4. The VISUAL CORTEX is a portion of the occipital lobe
     specialized for receiving and responding to visual
     stimuli; the visual stimuli reach this area after
     traversing the optic nerve and the OPTIC CHIASM
  5. ASSOCIATION AREAS are portions of each lobe which are
     responsible for organizing, storing, processing, and
     integrating sensory information

B. Techniques for studying brain function - the following
   are major approaches used to study brain and behavior
   relationships
  1. Lesion and ablation studies - a LESION is an intentional
     injury of a particular area of the brain while an
     ABLATION is the removal of a part of the brain; bulimia
     and anorexia nervosa are eating disorders which may have
     a physiological basis
  2. Clinical observations - lesion and ablation studies with
     humans are made possible by studying persons with brain
     injuries (as in boxers) or those with brain damage (as in
     the case of Charles Whitman who had a tumor near his
     amygdala)
  3. Radiation techniques - the PET SCANNING TECHNIQUE, using
     positron emission tomography (PET) allows investigators
     to observe brain functioning and possibly diagnose some
     forms of mental disorder
  4. Stimulation techniques - ELECTRICAL STIMULATION OF THE
     BRAIN (ESB) uses an electrode to electrically activate or
     suppress certain brain areas
  5. Recording techniques - MICROELECTRODES can be placed
     directly into a neuron to record its activity; using the
     electroencephalograph, which measures electrical activity
     of the brain at the level of the scalp, provides an
     ELECTROENCEPHALOGRAM (EEG) of the cerebral cortex; the
     EVOKED—POTENTIAL TECHNIQUE provides a record of the
     brain's electrical activity following a specific stimulus
     in the form of an evoked potential
  6. Behavioral techniques - the DICHOTIC-LISTENING TECHNIQUE
     presents independent messages to each ear to determine
     hemispheric specialization; the TACHISTOSCOPIC TECHNIQUE
     tests the ability to recall visual information presented
     simultaneously to each eye

C. Specialization of function in the two cerebral hemispheres -
   CEREBRAL SPECIALIZATION OF FUNCTION is the hypothesis that
   certain mental faculties depend on specialized regions in
   the brain; there is considerable research support for this
   hypothesis

1. "Split-brain" studies - EPILEPSY is a disorder caused by abnormal activity of neurons in the brain; some epileptics have grand mal seizures where there is loss of consciousness and rigid limbs; severing the corpus callosum, a surgery known as the SPLIT-BRAIN TECHNIQUE, can reduce epileptic seizure frequency and severity; results of Roger Sperry's tests with various split-brain patients is presented

2. Clinical Observations and Studies of Neurologically Normal Persons - visual-spatial abilities and nonverbal information processing are associated with right hemispheric activity while the left hemisphere is specialized for verbal information processing; the brain's functions are localized asymmetrically

   a. sex-related differences in cerebral specialization of function - females generally are better on tasks requiring verbal or language abilities; males are often better on tasks requiring spatial abilities; just why these differences occur is not known - they may reflect different environmental experiences or the fact that females show more bilateral cerebral specialization which is evident as early as infancy when baby girls use their left hemisphere more often while boys tend to use their right hemisphere more often

   b. handedness and cerebral specialization of function - 90 percent of the general population is right handed which may reflect the left brain's dominance for language function; 97% of right handers show left hemisphere specialization for language while only 25% of left handers show right hemisphere language specialization; there is a disproportionately high percentage of left-handers in architectural schools and among famous painters; left handers show a better recovery rate after brain injury than do right handers

D. Application: ESB works in humans too - ESB has been applied to humans in the areas of epilepsy and chronic pain treatment, as well as in the control of narcolepsy (where permanently implanted electrodes create arousal when triggered by the individual and/or those around him)

IV. On the Horizon: Brain Implants - a project is reported which successfully implanted frontal cortical tissue from rat fetuses into the ablated frontal areas in adult rats; the subjects with grafts learned better than those ablated subjects without grafts; this project has implications for the treatment of Parkinson's disease since dopamine (which is deficient in such patients) was produced by the implanted tissue in the rat study

OBJECTIVES

I.   WHAT ARE THE BASIC COMPONENTS OF THE NEURON, OR NERVE CELL?
     HOW DO NEURONS TRANSMIT INFORMATION TO ONE ANOTHER?

     The basic components of the neuron are the cell body, the axon
     which extends from the cell body and transmits messages away
     from the cell, the branchlike dendrites which receive messages,
     and the myelin sheath which covers many axons to facilitate
     speed of conduction.   Information is transmitted between
     neurons at the synapse where two neurons come into "functional"
     contact.   Here, terminal buttons house chemicals called
     neurotransmitters in many synaptic vessicles.   One neuron
     influences another via the electrochemical process called
     synaptic transmission.   The transmitters have either an
     excitatory or inhibitory influence on the adjacent neuron after
     they are released into the synaptic cleft.

A   1. Information is conducted between neurons at the:

        A. synapse
        B. dendrites
        C. axon
        D. terminal buttons

C   2. Which part of the neuron speeds up the transmission of
        impulses?

        A. axon
        B. dendrites
        C. myelin sheath
        D. cell body

     3. Summarize how information is transmitted from one neuron to
        another.   Use a diagram if needed.

II. HOW IS THE NERVOUS SYSTEM ORGANIZED?

     The nervous system is made up of bundled groups of axons called
     nerves.   The entire nervous system is divided into the central
     nervous system (brain and spinal cord) and the peripheral
     nervous system (all neural tissue connecting the brain and
     spinal cord with other parts of the body).   The brain is
     further divided into 3 major parts (forebrain, midbrain, and
     hindbrain) with each part having specialized areas of function.
     The peripheral nervous system is divided into the somatic
     nervous system and the autonomic nervous system.   The autonomic
     system is further divided into the sympathetic and
     parasympathetic systems.

B   1. The brain and spinal cord compose the _____ nervous
        system.

        A. peripheral
        B. central
        C. somatic
        D. sympathetic

D   2. The parasympathetic nervous system is part of the _____
        nervous system.

        A. central
        B. somatic
        C. endocrine
        D. autonomic

     3. Present information stating how the nervous system is
        organized. Use either a sentence or outline format.

III. WHAT ARE NEUROTRANSMITTERS? WHY ARE THEY IMPORTANT? WHAT EFFECTS DO THEY HAVE ON BEHAVIOR?

Neurotransmitters are chemicals which are stored in synaptic
vessicles and released from the terminal buttons to diffuse
across the synapse to activate the next neuron. The first
brain neurotransmitter that was discovered was epinephrine in
1905. Today there are over 30 known transmitters with
70 more expected to be discovered. Neurotransmitters are
important for they enable the electrical nerve impulse to
traverse the synapse by means of a chemical process. The
effects of neurotransmitter substances on behavior is known to
some extent. For example, acetylcholine (ACh) activates
muscles throughout the body. Substances like curare and
botulin interfere with ACh activity and cause paralysis. ACh
may also influence the formation and maintenance of memories.
The endorphins and enkephalins are transmitters which are
believed to inhibit pain and affect emotions.

C   1. Neurotransmitters are chemicals:

        A. within the cell body
        B. within the axon
        C. released from the terminal buttons
        D. which help myelin sheath development

A   2. Which neurotransmitters are believed to inhibit pain and
        affect emotions?

        A. endorphins and enkephalins
        B. norepinephrine and acteylcholine
        C. acteylcholine and epinephrine
        D. norepinephrine and enkephalins

3. What are transmitters and how do they operate to influence our behavior?

IV. LIST THE MAJOR CORTICAL AREAS AND THEIR FUNCTIONS?

The hemispheres are divided into four major lobes. The somatosensory cortex of the parietal lobe is involved in the senses of touch, heat, cold, pain and body movement. The auditory cortex of the temporal lobe is specialized for receiving and responding to sound stimuli. The visual cortex of the occipital lobe is specialized for receiving and responding to visual stimuli. The motor cortex of the frontal lobe controls voluntary movements of the body. Association areas, located in each of the lobes, are involved in thinking and problem solving, and are responsible for organizing, storing, processing, and integrating sensory information.

D   1. The major area of the _____ lobe is called the _____ cortex.

     A. frontal ; somatosensory
     B. temporal ; motor
     C. parietal ; auditory
     D. occipital ; visual

B   2. Which is located in each of the brain lobes?

     A. motor cortex
     B. association areas
     C. visual cortex
     D. somatosensory cortex

     3. Present a summary of the four cortical lobes with the areas and different functions that are associated with each.

V.   WHAT TECHNIQUES ARE AVAILABLE FOR STUDYING BRAIN FUNCTION?

Several major approaches are used to study brain and behavior relationships. The oldest techniques for studying the brain are the lesion (an intentional injury of a particular area) and the ablation (removal of a part of the brain) techniques. Clinical observations are made on human patients suffering accidental brain damage. The pet scanning technique enables investigators to find out which brain areas are most active during particular mental and physical activities. Electrical stimulation of the brain involves inserting into the brain a tiny electrode which can activate specific brain sites to see what behavior results. The electroencephalogram provides a continuous record of cerebral cortex electrical activity by monitoring numerous scalp electrodes. Another use of scalp electrodes is in the evoked potential technique which provides a record of the brain's electrical activity following a specific stimulus. Two behavioral measures are the dichotic listening technique, which provides independent information to each ear (and hemisphere) simultaneously, and the tachistoscopic technique, which records the subject's recall of visual information presented quickly and simultaneously to each eye.

A   1. The dichotic listening and tachistoscopic techniques for studying brain functions are both _____ methods.

    A. behavioral
    B. stimulation
    C. recording
    D. radiation

C   2. A method which allows researchers to study brain activity by monitoring which area is active during certain tasks is the _____ technique.

    A. lesion
    B. electroencephalogram
    C. pet scanning
    D. electrical stimulation of the brain

    3. What are the major approaches that psychologists use to study brain functioning? Give examples for each.

VI. WHAT IS KNOWN ABOUT SPECIALIZATION OF FUNCTION IN THE TWO CEREBRAL HEMISPHERES? WHAT TYPES OF STUDIES ARE CONDUCTED TO ANSWER THIS QUESTION?

The two hemispheres have asymmetrically represented functions. The right hemisphere has areas specialized for nonverbal, visual-spatial, and nonanalytic information processing while the left hemisphere is specialized for verbal, analytic, speech, and language functions. Sex-related differences have also been found. Females generally are more bilateral than males with males generally being more right hemisphere dominant. Techniques commonly used to study hemispheric differences are the dichotic listening and tachistoscopic techniques, and the split-brain technique which involves severing the corpus callosum.

D   1. The right hemisphere is:

    A. more dominant in males
    B. involved in non-verbal activities
    C. involved in visual-spatial and nonanalytic information processing
    D. all of the above

2. What do psychologists know about how each of the brain's hemispheres function?

MULTIPLE-CHOICE QUESTIONS

INTRODUCTION: SOME EFFECTS OF DISCONNECTING THE TWO SIDES OF THE BRAIN

B   1. The story of Carl, where one hand was doing something different than the other hand, reflected an individual with:
A. epileptic seizures
B. a split-brain operation
C. a neurological disorder
D. a motor disorder of the brain's cerebrum

D   2. A split-brain operation is used to treat patients like Carl who have had:
A. brain damage
B. brain ablations
C. psychotic episodes
D. severe epileptic seizures

THE NERVOUS SYSTEM

C   3. The explanation for your ability to pick up your text, open it, and begin reading lies within the:
A. scope of consciousness
B. scope of psychology
C. nervous system
D. peripheral nervous system

A   4. The term given for the cellular network that processes input from the sense organs and regulates information flow to the muscles and body organs is the:
A. nervous system
B. central nervous system
C. peripheral nervous system
D. brain

A   5. Individual nerve cells which specialize in transmitting and
         receiving information are called:
         A. neurons
         B. axons
         C. dendrites
         D. nerves

NEURONS AND THE TRANSMISSION OF NERVE IMPULSES

C   6. Cells which support, insulate and provide neurons with
         nutrients are called:
         A. nerve cells
         B. sensory neurons
         C. glial cells
         D. axons

B   7. Short fibers that branch out around the cell body of a
         neuron to receive messages are:
         A. glials
         B. dendrites
         C. axons
         D. myelin sheaths

C   8. Which is NOT characteristic of axons?
         A. to transmit messages to other neurons or muscles
         B. many are coated by a myelin sheath
         C. clustered around the cell body like tree branches
         D. may be very short or very long

D   9. The myelin sheath serves to _____ neurons and _____ the
         transmission of impulses.
         A. protect ; regulate
         B. support ; magnify
         C. insulate ; moderate
         D. insulate ; speed

B   10. The electrical activity that travels along the axon when the
         cell body is stimulated is known as the:
         A. resting potential
         B. nerve impulse
         C. ions
         D. charge potential

A   11. The resting potential and action potential reflect:
         A. the location and flow of ions
         B. microelectrode placement in the cell body
         C. sodium-potassium pump inactivity
         D. the rate of nerve impulses

D   12. Neurons carry information on the basis of the:
        A. size of the action potentials
        B. duration of the absolute refratory period
        C. number of stimuli
        D. rate of impulses and number of neurons that fire

C   13. The period when the neuron cannot have an impulse is
        referred to as the:
        A. relative refractory period
        B. threshold
        C. absolute refractory period
        D. all-or-none law

C   14. The place in the nervous system where the nerve impulse is
        relayed by chemicals is the:
        A. sodium-potassium pump
        B. axon
        C. synapse
        D. dendrite

B   15. Chemicals released from the terminal buttons which transmit
        nerve impulses are called:
        A. electrochemicals
        B. neurotransmitters
        C. synapse impulses
        D. holonims

A   16. Synaptic transmission is a(n) _____ process.
        A. electrochemical
        B. chemical
        C. electrical
        D. photosensitive

D   17. Synapses which move neurons toward their firing thresholds
        are called _____ synapses.
        A. terminal
        B. vessicle
        C. inhibitory
        D. excitatory

ORGANIZATION OF THE NERVOUS SYSTEM

C   18. Bundled groups of axons which branch throughout the body
        carrying nerve impulses are called:
        A. glial cells
        B. dendrites
        C. nerves
        D. motor neurons

D   19. The brain and spinal cord make up the _____ nervous
         system.
         A. effective
         B. autonomic
         C. peripheral
         D. central

B   20. All neural tissue that connects the brain and spinal cord
         with other parts of the body is called the _____ nervous
         system.
         A. effective
         B. peripheral
         C. autonomic
         D. central

D   21. Which is a TRUE statement about the brain?
         A. it is made up of both myelinated and unmyelinated neurons
         B. it governs and coordinates physical movements
         C. it governs and coordinates mental activity
         D. all are true statements

A   22. Which of the following is a FALSE statement about the brain?
         A. neurons increase in number until late childhood or early
            adolescence
         B. the brain's neurons increase in size after birth
         C. there is a build up of myelin on some neurons after birth
         D. glial cells outnumber neurons in the brain by adulthood

A   23. Which of the following is not a neuroanatomical division of
         the brain?
         A. lateralbrain
         B. forebrain
         C. midbrain
         D. hindbrain

B   24. The cerebrum, limbic system, hypothalamus and thalamus are
         structures of the:
         A. lateralbrain
         B. forebrain
         C. midbrain
         D. hindbrain

C   25. Which brain structure provides a pathway for communication
         between the two hemispheres?
         A. medulla
         B. cerebellum
         C. corpus callosum
         D. thalamus

D   26. Which brain system is primarily involved in emotional and sexual behavior?
        A. somatic nervous system
        B. central nervous system
        C. reticular activating system
        D. limbic system

C   27. Which of the following behaviors is NOT regulated by the hypothalamus?
        A. eating
        B. drinking
        C. breathing
        D. sleeping

A   28. The reticular activating system is involved in:
        A. arousal, attention, and sleep-wake cycles
        B. relaying impulses from the sense organs to the cerebral cortex
        C. controlling digestion, blood flow, and breathing
        D. regulating body temperature and blood pressure

B   29. Which brain structure governs body balance and controls body coordination?
        A. cerebrum
        B. cerebellum
        C. cerebral cortex
        D. corpus callosum

D   30. Cells which carry nerve impulses to the spinal cord and brain from the sense organs are called _____ neurons.
        A. motor or efferent
        B. sensory or efferent
        C. inter or association
        D. sensory or afferent

B   31. One simple behavior pattern which involves just the spinal cord and sensory and motor neurons is the:
        A. reflex arc
        B. knee-jerk reflex
        C. yawning reflex
        D. orientation reflex

C   32. Which part of the nervous system plays a dominant role in preparing the body during times of emergency or stress?
        A. somatic nervous system
        B. central nervous system
        C. sympathetic division of the autonomic nervous system
        D. parasympathetic division of the autonomic nervous system

A   33. In the autonomic nervous system, sympathetic arousal is
         associated with _____ while parasympathetic arousal is
         associated with _____.
         A. tension ; calmness
         B. low activity ; high reactivity
         C. spontaneity ; reservation
         D. introversion ; extroversion

D   34. Which is a FALSE statement about the endocrine system?
         A. it consists of numerous glands that release chemicals
            into the blood stream
         B. its hormones influence physiological activities and
            behaviors
         C. its influence on behavior is slower than that of the
            nervous system
         D. it works independently of the nervous system

D   35. The adrenal glands secrete hormones which influence:
         A. our ability to cope with stress
         B. the body's preparation for emergencies
         C. synaptic transmission
         D. all of the above

APPLICATION: BRAIN NEUROTRANSMITTERS AND BEHAVIOR

B   36. One of the best understood neurotransmitters is:
         A. lecithin
         B. acetylcholine
         C. botulin
         D. epinephrine

C   37. What disease is believed to be influenced by the amount of
         acetycholine activity in the brain?
         A. Down's Syndrome
         B. Lou Gehrig's disease
         C. Alzheimer's disease
         D. high blood pressure

A   38. The two brain neurotransmitters which are believed to
         inhibit pain are:
         A. endorphins and enkephalins
         B. endorphins and acetylcholine
         C. epinephrine and enkephalins
         D. epinephrine and acetylcholine

C   39. The release of naturally produced "brain opiates" is one
         explanation for the effects of:
         A. relaxation therapy
         B. transcendential meditation
         C. acupuncture
         D. yoga

CORTICAL AREAS AND THEIR FUNCTIONS

B   40. Each hemisphere of the brain is divided into _____ lobes.
          A. 3
          B. 4
          C. 5
          D. 6

A   41. The control of voluntary movements of the body is located in
          the _____ cortex of the _____ lobe.
          A. motor ; frontal
          B. motor ; temporal
          C. sensory ; occipital
          D. sensory ; parietal

D   42. Sensations of touch, heat, cold, and pain are localized in
          the _____ cortex of the _____ lobe.
          A. motor ; frontal
          B. tactile ; temporal
          C. sensory ; occipital
          D. somatosensory ; parietal

B   43. Which brain area is specialized for receiving and responding
          to sound stimuli?
          A. somatosensory cortex of the temporal lobe
          B. auditory cortex of the temporal lobe
          C. auditory cortex of the occipital lobe
          D. sensory cortex of the occipital lobe

C   44. The lobe of the brain specialized for processing auditory
          information is the _____ while the lobe specialized for
          visual information is the _____.
          A. frontal ; occipital
          B. temporal ; parietal
          C. temporal ; occipital
          D. parietal ; frontal

A   45. The point at which the optic nerves from both eyes meet and
          cross is called the:
          A. optic chiasm
          B. visual area
          C. occipital lobe
          D. association area

B   46. Which of the following statements is FALSE?
          A. neural messages from the right side of each eye are
             relayed to the right occipital lobe
          B. injury to the somatosensory cortex usually blocks
             sensations permanently
          C. a large portion of the motor cortex is devoted to fine
             muscular control
          D. the left motor cortex controls movements on the right
             side of the body

C   47. The portions of each lobe which are involved in organizing, storing, processing and integrating information from the senses are _____ areas.
A. sensory
B. motor
C. association
D. somatosensory

TECHNIQUES FOR STUDYING BRAIN FUNCTION

D   48. Which of the following is NOT a major method for studying brain-behavior relationships?
A. radiation
B. electrical stimulation
C. electrical recordings
D. diet restrictions

D   49. An intentional injury of a particular brain area is called a(n):
A. tomography
B. truncation
C. ablation
D. lesion

A   50. The latest research suggests that bulimia and anorexia nervosa:
A. may have a physiological basis
B. are actually the same disorder
C. result from excessive anxiety
D. are due to transmitter problems in the amygdala

A   51. An eating disorder which involves an uncontrollable urge toward overeating is:
A. bulimia
B. satiety release
C. anorexia nervosa
D. psychological obesity

B   52. The effect of brain tumors on behavior is covered in which method of studying brain-behavior relationships?
A. lesions and ablations
B. clinical observations
C. radiation techniques
D. electroencephalography

C   53. The case of Charles Whitman who was killed in Texas after he killed and wounded many people suggests that:
A. aggressive urges are uncontrollable
B. brain lesions of the amygdala lower aggression
C. abnormal behavior may result from brain damage
D. deep breathing and relaxation could have controlled his behavior

A 54. Which technique offers great potential for diagnosing some
    mental disorders?
    A. PET scanning technique
    B. dichotic—listening technique
    C. tachistoscopic technique
    D. microelectrodes

D 55. Which of the following statements is FALSE?
    A. the PET scanning technique allows researchers to locate
       brain areas involved in ongoing mental activities
    B. ESB has been effective in rewarding rats' bar pressing
       behavior
    C. monkeys have stopped the aggressive behavior in other
       monkeys by controlling the aggressor's brain with ESB
    D. the EEG measures the electrical activity of the neuron's
       cell body

B 56. The electroencephalogram (EEG) has been quite useful in
    diagnosing which disorder?
    A. brain tumors
    B. epilepsy
    C. Alzheimer's syndrome
    D. abnormal spatial abilities

A 57. Differences in brain electrical activity between children
    with normal reading skills and those with reading
    disabilities were found using
    A. evoked potential techniques
    B. dichotic-listening techniques
    C. microelectrodes
    D. lesion and ablation techniques

C 58. Using the dichotic-listening technique, researchers have
    found that:
    A. the right temporal lobe is slightly larger than the left
    B. epilepsy tends to occur in adults more than children
    C. the left hemisphere shows a greater specialization for
       speech
    D. the amygdala is associated with aggression behavior

C 59. Which technique has been regularly used to determine which
    hemisphere processes visual information more efficiently?
    A. dichotic listening
    B. evoked potential
    C. tachistoscopic
    D. electrical stimulation

SPECIALIZATION OF FUNCTION IN THE TWO CEREBRAL HEMISPHERES

D   60. The concept which refers to the idea that certain higher
     mental faculties depend on specialized brain regions is:
     A. point-to-point specialization
     B. topical organization
     C. structural organization
     D. cerebral specialization of function

B   61. Which statement is TRUE?
     A. the human brain is fully symmetrical
     B. linguistic abilities reside mainly in the left hemisphere
     C. the left hemisphere is more important for the expression
        and recognition of emotion
     D. all are true statements

A   62. Epilepsy is caused by abnormal _____ of neurons in the
     brain.
     A. activity
     B. degeneration
     C. myelination
     D. concentrations

C   63. One with epilepsy who may fall to the ground with rigid
     limbs and lose consciousness is suffering a _____ seizure.
     A. Type A
     B. Type B
     C. grand mal
     D. petit mal

D   64. The split—brain technique severs which area in order to
     reduce epileptic seizures?
     A. optic chiasm
     B. frontal lobe
     C. amygdala
     D. corpus callosum

B   65. Individuals with split brains typically:
     A. switch their language functions to the right hemisphere
     B. are able to function normally in their daily routines
     C. are easily detected once a routine medical exam is given
     D. continue to show a "mentally retarded" right hemisphere

D   66. Which of the following is a specialized function of the left
     hemisphere?
     A. verbal
     B. analytic
     C. speech
     D. all of the above

B   67. Which is NOT a specialized function of the right hemisphere?
         A. visual-spatial
         B. language
         C. nonverbal
         D. nonanalytic

A   68. The split-brain patient is usually tested for hemispheric
         functioning by using _____ stimuli.
         A. visual
         B. auditory
         C. EEG
         D. olfactory

A   69. Research on sex-related differences in cerebral
         specialization of function have found that females in
         comparison with males:
         A. are more bilateral
         B. have a smaller corpus callosum
         C. do better at spatial ability tasks
         D. have smaller left hemispheres

C   70. Of people who are right handed, what percentage show left
         hemisphere specialization for language?
         A. 25%
         B. 50%
         C. 97%
         D. 100%

A   71. Of people who are left handed, what percentage show right
         hemisphere specialization for language?
         A. 25%
         B. 34%
         C. 75%
         D. 90%

A   72. What evidence is there to support the notion that left
         handers have better drawing and visual-spatial abilities?
         A. a disproportionately high percentage of left handers are
            found in schools of architecture
         B. many great authors are left handers
         C. left handers are more bilateral in their cerebral
            representation of both verbal and spatial functions
         D. all of the above

APPLICATION: ESB WORKS IN HUMANS TOO

D   73. ESB has been used to effectively treat which disorder?
        A. epileptic patients with the focus of abnormality
           restricted to a small area
        B. chronic pain
        C. narcolepsy
        D. all of the above

B   74. ESB testing with humans is:
        A. the third most common form of brain surgery
        B. limited to individuals with extraordinary medical need
        C. best performed with children
        D. unethical according to the APA

C   75. Controlling one's tendency to fall asleep at inappropriate
         times   by   activating   a   device   which   provided   brain
         stimulation is an example of:
        A. surgopsychology
        B. applied psychotechnology
        C. ESB
        D. brain surgery

ON THE HORIZON: BRAIN IMPLANTS

A   76. Recent research on brain implants suggests that:
        A. implanted brain cells from a donor function when put into
           the frontal cortex of another rat
        B. the left lobe is easier to transplant than the right
        C. rat cells reject transplanted tissue except in the
           cerebellum
        D. newly implanted brain cells function well, but they don't
           form connections with the old neurons

C   77. Research   on   brain   tissue   implants   suggests   a   future
         treatment for humans with:
        A. brain tumors
        B. severe brain damage resulting from accidents
        C. Parkinson's disease
        D. epilepsy

B   78. A potential ethical problem with brain implants involves the
         availability of:
        A. willing patients
        B. donor tissue
        C. trained medical staff
        D. funds for surgery with patients who can't afford to pay

– CHAPTER 3 –

SENSATION

OUTLINE

I.   Introduction: Stimulation, Above and Below the Limen:
     presentation of the potential use of subliminal anti-theft
     messages and how the sensory system receives and transmits
     sensations at the liminal level

II. The Measurement of Sensitivity: PSYCHOPHYSICS attempts to
     discover how a physical stimulus creates a SENSATION and what
     the ABSOLUTE THRESHOLD is for the sensation

     A. SIGNAL DETECTION THEORY: not concerned with absolute
        thresholds, but with the signal to noise relationship as
        determined by both the subject's sensitivity and functioning
        criterion

     B. Application: Subliminal stimulation

III. The Visual System: what is the VISUAL SYSTEM?

     A. Light: The stimulus for vision: visual sensations produced
        by reflected or emitted light energy; of the whole
        electromagnetic spectrum, the human system responds only to
        light waves which make up the VISUAL SPECTRUM; light waves
        measured in nanometers; a light wave's wavelength influences
        color sensations

B. The structure and function of the human eye: the eye
   resembles a camera
   1. Focus control: The cornea, lens, and ciliary muscles –
      light passes through the CORNEA and is bent by the action
      of the LENS and CILIARY MUSCLES; the eyeball is supported
      by vitreous humor fluid; elasticity of lens changes with
      age
   2. Aperture control: The pupil and iris – the aperture in
      human eye is called the PUPIL which is regulated by IRIS
   3. Photosensitivity: The retina – the RETINA at the back of
      the eye houses light-sensitive photoreceptive cells
      called rods and cones
      a. RODS and CONES: differ in their frequency, location,
         and sensitivity to color; the cones are concentrated
         in and around FOVEA where VISUAL ACUITY is best; the
         BLIND SPOT has neither rods nor cones; there are
         sensitivity and functional differences between the
         rods and cones; rod vision is achromatic or colorless
      b. visual adaptation: DARK ADAPTATION is increasing
         light sensitivity with increasing length in dark,
         light adaptation is the opposite; the rod-cone break
         occurs in 7–8 minutes and shows rod and cone
         sensitivity differences; how alcohol and vitamin A
         influence seeing with low illumination levels
      c. transduction: the eye and the brain – bipolar cells
         and ganglion cells are located in front of the rods
         and cones; ganglion cell axons converge at the optic
         nerve; TRANSDUCTION: electromagnetic energy is
         transformed into nerve impulses
      d. brain mechanism of vision: researchers Hubel and
         Wiesel have found FEATURE DETECTORS in brain which
         specialize in detecting specific features; three
         different types (simple cells, complex cells,
         hypercomplex cells); nerve impulses form a sensory
         code; using a microelectrode study of cat and monkey
         brains they found feature detectors for orientation,
         movement, and length of stimulus; three steps in
         seeing (receptor cell stimulation, light energy
         transduced into nerve impulses, brain cells organize
         and interpret messages)

C. Color vision: quantitative changes in stimulus leads to
   qualitative change in color sensation
   1. The dimensions of color: HUE is the name given to a
      particular color and is determined by the light wave's
      length; BRIGHTNESS refers to a color's lightness or
      brightness and is determined by light wave amplitude;
      SATURATION refers to a color's purity and is determined
      by light wave complexity; achromatic sensations (e.g.,
      black, white) have many wavelengths, are unsaturated and
      have no hue; a color solid represents all three color
      dimensions
   2. Theories of color vision: cones are primarily
      responsible for color vision

        a. TRICHROMATIC THEORY: three types of cone cells are
          most sensitive to a different color; also called
          Young-Helmholtz theory; supported by existence of
          three PHYSICAL PRIMARY COLORS (red, green, blue);
          additive mixture is when different wavelengths are
          combined (e.g., color television pictures);
          subtractive mixture results from mixing paint
          pigments; in spite of research support for theory, it
          has difficulty explaining color blindness
        b. OPPONENT-PROCESS THEORY: three different receptor
          systems (red-green, blue-yellow, black-white) have
          cells activated by light waves of different lengths;
          theory consistent with AFTERIMAGES and negative
          afterimages; theory consistent with how lateral
          geniculate body analyzes visual information

  D. Application: Measuring visual acuity - common acuity tests
     are Snellen eye chart and Landoldt rings test which evaluate
     nearsightedness (myopia) and farsightedness (hyperopia);
     color blindness is a defect compared with trichromats who
     see all colors; dichromats and monochromats

IV. The Other Senses

  A. The auditory system
    1. Hearing: AUDITION is the product of pressure changes in
      the molecules of air called sound waves; different types
      of waves include sine waves, complex sound waves,
      periodic complex sound waves, aperiodic complex sound
      waves (called noise and, if all frequencies of auditory
      spectrum, white noise)
      a. pitch and sound wave frequency: PITCH is determined
        by sound wave frequency, as expressed in Hertz;
        audible spectrum are sounds to which humans are
        sensitive
      b. loudness and sound wave amplitude: LOUDNESS refers to
        sound intensity and is determined by sound wave
        amplitude, as expressed in decibels to indicate sound
        pressure level; what is tinnitus and who is bothered
        by this hearing damage
      c. timbre and sound wave complexity: TIMBRE refers to
        each sound's perceived "voice" or quality and is
        determined by sound wave complexity; periodic sound
        waves are composed of a fundamental tone frequency and
        overtones or harmonics
    2. The structure and function of the human ear: three parts
      - outer, middle, and inner ear
      a. the outer ear is composed of pinna, auditory canal,
        and the vibrating tympanic membrane; the eustachian
        tube maintains proper pressure for tympanic membrane
      b. the middle ear is composed of the ossicles (malleus,
        incus, stapes); the stapes vibrates the oval window

      c. the <u>inner ear</u> has the <u>cochlea</u>; the <u>cochlear fluid</u>
         displaces <u>basilar membrane</u>, which vibrates the <u>organ</u>
         <u>of Corti</u> and its <u>hair cells</u>
      d. transduction: the ear and the brain - the movement of
         hair cells stimulates nerve cells that funnel into the
         <u>auditory nerve</u>
   3. Theories of hearing: the PLACE THEORY says different
      areas of basilar membrane are responsive to particular
      frequencies to generate pitch; FREQUENCY THEORY says
      pitch reflects the rate of hair cell stimulation; VOLLEY
      THEORY explains low frequency sound by the use of <u>volleys</u>
      of nerve firings

B. Smell and taste: the chemical senses - chemical substances
  are physical stimuli for CHEMICAL SENSES
  1. Smell: OLFACTION informs us about airborne substances;
     <u>receptor cells</u> are located in <u>nasal cavity</u>; nerve
     impulses travel to <u>olfactory bulb</u> and then to <u>olfactory</u>
     <u>nerve tract</u>; relevance of olfaction to human and animal
     behavior; <u>pheromones</u> for communication
  2. TASTE informs us of substances entering digestive tract;
     primary taste qualities are <u>sweet</u>, <u>sour</u>, <u>salty</u>, and
     <u>bitter</u>; main part of <u>taste system</u> are <u>taste buds</u>

C. The skin senses: SKIN SENSES produce a range of sensations
  about physical stimuli in environment through skin; older
  proposal of four primary skin senses (<u>pressure</u>, <u>pain</u>, <u>cold</u>,
  <u>warm</u>) now refered to as <u>pressure spots</u> or <u>pain spots</u>

D. The body senses: KINESTHESIS informs us of body movement by
  means of <u>kinesthetic receptor cells</u> in the muscles; the
  VESTIBULAR SENSE, or <u>equilibratory</u> sense, governs body
  orientation and position in three-dimensional space;
  vestibular organs composed of <u>semicircular canals</u>, <u>ampulla</u>,
  and <u>vestibular sacs</u>; <u>vertigo</u> and its characteristics

E. Application: Seeing with the skin senses - discussion of
  substituting one sense for a faulty one (e.g., blind people
  use touch); characteristics of effective <u>Braille</u> users.

V. On The Horizon: Seeing Without Eyes - use of a television
camera which causes a vibrator pack located in the back of a
chair or worn around the waist to stimulate the skin so that a
blind person can "see" through touch sensations

OBJECTIVES

I.   WHAT IS SENSATION?   LIST THE PHYSICAL STIMULI TO WHICH THE
     HUMAN SENSE ORGANS ARE SENSITIVE.

     Sensation describes the response of the sensory systems to
     physical stimuli. The physical stimuli to which the sense
     organs respond vary between the sense organs. In vision, the
     eyes are sensitive to a narrow range of electromagnetic
     energies called light waves. Each light wave gives us
     information about color and brightness. In audition,
     mechanical energy, or pressure changes in the molecules of air,
     stimulate the receptors. In constrast, the stimulus is a
     chemical substance in both smell and taste. Furthermore, the
     skin senses respond to contact (or near contact) with the skin
     to generate a large array of sensations. The body senses,
     kinethesis and the equilibratory sense, respond to changes
     (e.g., movement, pressure, orientation) of the internal state
     of the body

A   1. Which sense modality is sensitive to electromagnetic energy
        changes?

        A. vision
        B. audition
        C. olfactory
        D. vestibular

B   2. Which sense modality is sensitive to stimuli from within the
        body?

        A. olfactory
        B. kinesthesis
        C. skin
        D. gustation

     3. Compare and contrast the different sense modalities and the
        types of stimuli to which they react.

II. WHAT COMMON PROCESSES CHARACTERIZE THE MAJOR SENSORY SYSTEMS?

     One common process in the major sensory systems is that of
     transduction, whereby a stimulus is coded and transformed from
     one type of energy (e.g., electromagnetic in vision, mechanical
     in audition) into nervous impulses. Thus, different types and
     forms of sensory information is transformed into a single type
     of nervous system information. A second common process is the
     role of the brain. The brain, with its localization of
     function, is organized into certain areas to receive and/or
     interpret sensory information from particular sensory
     modalities.

C   1. What is one common process that characterizes the major
         sensory systems?

         A. electrical and mechanical energy
         B. simple and complex cells
         C. transduction
         D. many types of sensory cells within each modality

      2. Discuss the common process(es) which characterize(s) the
         major sense modalities.

III. HOW IS LIGHT ENERGY TRANSLATED INTO VISUAL SENSATIONS?

      The image, made up of light energy, is focused upon the retina
      which, among other types of cells, houses light sensitive
      photoreceptive cells called rods and cones. Each
      photoreceptive cell has a photoreceptive pigment which, when
      stimulated by the light energy, absorbs the light causing a
      chemical reaction in which the pigment molecules change shape.
      This photochemical reaction stimulates a release of electrical
      energy in the form of nerve impulses. These impulses then
      travel through the bipolar cells, ganglion cells, and the optic
      nerve to the visual areas of the brain where feature detectors
      organize and interpret the nerve impulse "messages."

D   1. The change from light energy to nerve impulses in the visual
         system is mediated by a:

         A. photochemical change in the ganglion cells
         B. chemical change in the optic nerve
         C. chemical change in the bipolar cells
         D. photochemical reaction in the rods and cones

C   2. The light sensitive photoreceptive cells of the retina are
         called:

         A. ganglion cells
         B. bipolar cells
         C. rods and cones
         D. simple and complex cells

      3. Describe in as much detail as possible how light energy is
         translated into visual sensations.

IV.   WHAT ROLES DO THE PHOTORECEPTOR CELLS PLAY IN PRODUCING COLOR
      SENSATIONS?

      The cones are generally considered the cells which are
      responsible for color vision. However, we are not sure exactly
      what produces color sensations. The trichromatic (or
      three-color) theory, sometimes called the Young-Helmholtz
      theory, states that there are three types of retinal cone

cells, each most sensitive to one of three different colors (red, green, and blue). These three cones then "mix together" to generate a wide variety of color sensations. The opponent-process theory assumes that there are three different color receptor systems (red-green, blue-yellow, and black-white receptors). When stimulated by a light wave of different lengths, they "excite" some cells of a particular system while "inhibiting" others. For example, some cells are excited by red but inhibited by green. These three systems then interact with one another to produce many color sensations.

B   1. The opponent-process theory of color vision makes use of which terminology?

   A. three cone types
   B. "excitation" and "inhibition" of cells
   C. physical primary colors
   D. additive and subtractive mixtures

A   2. The primary colors of red, green, and blue are particularly relevant or supportive to which color theory?

   A. trichromatic
   B. opponent-process
   C. mixture
   D. receptor "system"

3. Describe how the trichromatic and opponent-process theories explain our ability to see color.

V.   HOW CAN WE ACCOUNT FOR AUDITORY SENSATIONS AND OUR CAPACITY TO EXPERIENCE THE DIVERSITY OF SOUNDS COMPRISING THE AUDIBLE SPECTRUM?

The physical energy to which the auditory modality is sensitive is translated into nerve impulses by the hair cells located in the organ of Corti. The vibrating basilar membrane causes the hair cells to move which in turn stimulates the thousands of nerve cells to which they are connected. It is believed that different patterns of vibrations (caused by variations in pitch, loudness, and timbre) result in different nerve impulse patterns. Three theories have dealt with how this process works. The place theory says that different areas of the basilar membrane are maximally responsive to different pitches. The frequency theory states that the rate at which different hair cells are stimulated determines pitch. The volley theory states that for low frequencies (those hard to deal with by the other two theories), groups of neurons work together to generate particular frequencies. Today, many feel that components of all theories are necessary to explain human hearing.

D   1. The theory of hearing which incorporates the notion of
          groups of neurons working together for the ability to hear
          high and low frequencies is the _____ theory.

          A. Young-Helmholtz
          B. place
          C. frequency
          D. volley

       2. Describe how the three theories of audition describe our
          ability to hear sounds of many different frequencies.

VI.   WHAT ARE THE PHYSICAL ENERGIES THAT GIVE RISE TO THE SENSATIONS
       OF SMELL, TASTE, AND TOUCH?

       The physical energies that give rise to smell and taste involve
       chemical substances that stimulate receptor cells in each nasal
       cavity or on the tongue, respectively. The taste buds on the
       human tongue are sensitive to four primary taste qualities:
       sweet, sour, salty, and bitter. In contrast, physical contact
       or "touching" experiences are needed for sensations of the
       skin. Certain areas of the skin react to certain stimuli like
       pressure, pain, warmth or cold. Other sensations can be
       achieved through stimulation of these areas. For example,
       gently touching a pressure spot leads to a "tickle" sensation
       while gently and repeatedly touching a pain spot leads to an
       "itch."

A   1. A "tickle" sensation is achieved by gently coming in contact
          with a _____ spot on the skin.

          A. pressure
          B. pain
          C. "itch"
          D. "tickle"

       2. What are the physical stimuli that give rise to our
          sensations of smell, taste, and touch?

MULTIPLE-CHOICE QUESTIONS

INTRODUCTION

C   1. Subliminal auditory messages have been used with what intent
in some department stores?
A. to stimulate sales of regular priced items
B. to stimulate sales of "sale" items
C. to reduce shoplifting
D. to improve employee work habits

THE MEASUREMENT OF SENSITIVITY

B   2. An original study area of psychology which related physical
stimuli to sensations they produce is called:
A. signal detection theory
B. psychophysics
C. subliminal stimulation
D. stimulus-receptor theory

C   3. Any form of energy to which an organism is capable of
responding is a:
A. sensation
B. physical response
C. physical stimulus
D. stimulus energy

A   4. Research by psychophysicists on the minimum stimulus
intensity required to produce a sensation deals with:
A. absolute threshold
B. sensory threshold
C. response threshold
D. perception

B   5. The "absolute threshold" is the intensity of the stimulus
which is detected _____ percent of the time
A. 25
B. 50
C. 70
D. 90

C   6. Which of the following is the text's example of an absolute
         threshold in humans?
         A. two wooden matchsticks in the palm of one's preferred
            hand for touch
         B. a female whisper at 14 feet for hearing
         C. one teaspoon of sugar in two gallons of water for
            taste
         D. a flash light seen at 5 miles on a clear, dark night
            for vision

SIGNAL DETECTION THEORY

A   7. Psychophysics is concerned with sensitivity under _____
         __ situations whereas signal detection theory is concerned
         with sensitivity under _____ situations.
         A. ideal ; "noisy"
         B. quite ; loud
         C. "noisy" ; ideal
         D. relaxed ; working

D   8. The approach designed to measure someone's ability to
         correctly detect a stimulus when it is presented against
         background stimuli is called _____ theory
         A. subliminal stimulation
         B. sensitivity
         C. signal-noise
         D. signal detection

B   9. Signal detection theory states that, in addition to
         sensitivity, it is necessary to know what _____ the
         individual is operating under.
         A. mood state
         B. criterion
         C. interest level
         D. sensory modality

D   10. The terms "false alarm" and "correct rejection" pertain to
         research in:
         A. rejection theory
         B. kinesthesis
         C. subliminal stimulation
         D. signal detection theory

APPLICATION: SUBLIMINAL STIMULATION

B   11. Auditory research has shown or would suggest that:
          A. if a person is insensitive to a stimulus then it is
             subliminal
          B. weaker stimuli are less likely to produce a sensation
          C. "weak" anti-theft messages have a greater impact than
             "loud" ones
          D. weak stimuli have more influence on behavior than
             more intense ones

THE VISUAL SYSTEM

C   12. All parts of the nervous system that process information
          from the eyes are known as the _____ system
          A. perceptual
          B. sensory
          C. visual
          D. reactivity

LIGHT: THE STIMULUS FOR VISION

A   13. Most visual sensations are produced by light energy which
          is:
          A. reflected
          B. emitted
          C. released
          D. part of the mechanical spectrum

D   14. The light from a firefly or the sun is an example of _____
          light energy.
          A. natural
          B. reflected
          C. pure
          D. emitted

B   15. The electromagnetic spectrum is:
          A. physical energy from the sun
          B. physical energy transferred by radiation
          C. those wavelengths to which our sensory system is
             sensitive
          D. a discovery of signal detection theory

A   16. Electromagnetic energies to which the human visual system
          responds are called:
          A. light waves
          B. sensations
          C. sensitivity elements
          D. stimuli

C   17. Electromagnetic energies called light waves make up the:
        A. sensory spectrum
        B. electrospectrum
        C. visual spectrum
        D. reflected energy

D   18. The length of light waves in the visual spectrum
         influences our sensations of:
        A. brightness
        B. light
        C. visual
        D. color

THE STRUCTURE AND FUNCTION OF THE HUMAN EYE

A   19. The transparent outer surface of the eye is the:
        A. cornea
        B. lens
        C. pupil
        D. iris

B   20. Light rays are bent by the _____ in order to allow the eye
         to change focus.
        A. cornea
        B. lens
        C. pupil
        D. iris

C   21. Which muscles change the shape and thickness of the eye's
         lens?
        A. iris
        B. ocular
        C. ciliary
        D. extraocular

D   22. The eye's pupil is similar to a camera's:
        A. diaphram
        B. film
        C. lens
        D. aperture

B   23. Which area of the eye determines how much light enters the
         eye?
        A. pupil
        B. iris
        C. lens
        D. cornea

A   24. The lens is regulated by the _____ while the _____ is
         regulated by the iris.
         A. ciliary muscles ; pupil
         B. cornea ; pupil
         C. pupil ; cornea
         D. ciliary muscles ; cornea

C   25. The photosensitive surface at the rear of each eye is the:
         A. fovea
         B. blind spot
         C. retina
         D. visual layer

D   26. The eye's photoreceptive cells:
         A. are in the iris
         B. convert light patterns into movements
         C. control the ciliary muscles
         D. are sensitive to light waves

A   27. Rods and cones are:
         A. photoreceptors
         B. located in the pupil
         C. primarily found in the fovea
         D. lacking in most vertebrates

C   28. The eye's rods are:
         A. more common than its cones
         B. responsible for color sensations
         C. absent from the fovea
         D. more sensitive to short wavelengths

C   29. The eye's cones are:
         A. primarily responsible for black and white sensations
         B. less common than rods
         C. responsible for color sensations
         D. "color blind"

B   30. The area of the retina with the greatest visual acuity is
         the:
         A. rods
         B. fovea
         C. pupil
         D. iris

D   31. The "blind spot":
         A. is a tiny depression roughly at the center of the
            retina
         B. has primarily rods
         C. is an area of moderate visual acuity
         D. has neither rods nor cones

D   32. Which is a characteristic of cone functioning?
         A. active in nighttime vision
         B. account for achromatic vision
         C. lower absolute threshold than rods
         D. sensitive to bright, high-intensity light

A   33. What accounts for our increased sensitivity to light when we
         enter a darkened movie theater?
         A. dark adaptation
         B. light adaptation
         C. a decrease in our absolute threshold
         D. accommodation

B   34. During the rod-cone break:
         A. rods adapt first, then the cones
         B. cones adapt first, then the rods
         C. the rods become more sensitive to visual stimuli
         D. the cones become more sensitive to visual stimuli

C   35. Experiments on dark adaptation have found that:
         A. cones primarily do the functioning
         B. alcohol speeds up the rate of dark adaptation
         C. vitamin A helps rod functioning
         D. it is complete in about 20 minutes

D   36. The connections between the eyes and the brain are the:
         A. rods and cones
         B. biopolar cells
         C. ganglion cells
         D. optic nerves

B   37. The process whereby light energy is absorbed by
         photosensitive pigments in the rods and cones which then
         stimulates a release of electrical energy in a neuron is
         called:
         A. light transmission
         B. transduction
         C. reduction
         D. adaptation

A   38. Cells in the visual cortex which specialize in detecting
         patterns of visual stimulation are:
         A. feature detectors
         B. ganglion cells
         C. biopolar cells
         D. transductory cells

C   39. Hubel and Wiesel call cells in the visual cortex which
         respond to the length of a visual stimulus _____ cells.
         A. simple
         B. complex
         C. hypercomplex
         D. none of the above

COLOR VISION

A 40. In color vision, _____ changes in the length of light
    waves gives rise to _____ changes in color sensations.
    A. quantitative ; qualitative
    B. qualitative ; quantitative
    C. small ; quantitative
    D. large ; quantitative

A 41. A light wave's length determines its color or _____.
    A. hue
    B. brightness
    C. saturation
    D. additive mixture

B 42. A light wave's amplitude, or intensity, determines its:
    A. hue
    B. brightness
    C. saturation
    D. achromatic sensations

D 43. Saturation refers to a color's degree of:
    A. intensity
    B. hue
    C. brightness
    D. purity

A 44. Which of the following is an achromatic sensation?
    A. seeing gray or black
    B. a color solid
    C. an owl's visual system
    D. seeing red or green

C 45. The trichromatic or Young-Helmholtz theory of color vision
    assumes that there are three:
    A. primary colors
    B. stages or processes for seeing color
    C. types of retinal cone cells
    D. chromatisms present in the visual cortex

B 46. The opponent-process theory of color vision assumes the
    existence of:
    A. two physical primary colors
    B. three different color receptor systems
    C. three different color cone types
    D. rod-cone interactions

A 47. A problem with the trichromatic theory of color vision is in
    explaining:
    A. color blindness
    B. night blindness
    C. subtractive and additive mixtures
    D. the blind spot

B 48. The physical primary colors are:
  A. red and yellow
  B. red, green, and blue
  C. red, yellow, and blue
  D. blue and yellow

D 49. What is the principle used to produce color television
  pictures?
  A. color solid
  B. opponent-process
  C. subtractive mixture
  D. additive mixture

D 50. Sensory impressions that persist after removal of the
  stimulus that caused them are called:
  A. complex images
  B. opponent-processes
  C. aftersensations
  D. afterimages

D 51. If one stares at the color red, and then looks at a white
  piece of paper, one sees "green." This exemplifies a _____
  __ afterimage.
  A. lateral
  B. color
  C. positive
  D. negative

APPLICATION: MEASURING VISUAL DEFECTS

C 52. The Snellen eye chart and Landoldt rings test measure:
  A. night blindness
  B. color blindness
  C. visual acuity
  D. visual sensitivity

C 53. Nearsightedness, or myopia, is caused by:
  A. too few cones in the fovea
  B. a retina too close to the lens
  C. the image to be focused falls short of the retina
  D. vitamin A depletion

B 54. Dichromats typically see:
  A. all but the basic colors
  B. all colors but red and green
  C. only shades of gray and white
  D. all colors but red and blue

A   55. Which are the least common?
       A. monochromats
       B. dichromats
       C. trichromats
       D. hyperats

THE AUDITORY SYSTEM

A   56. Unlike vision, audition is the product of:
       A. mechanical energy called sound waves
       B. electrical energy called sound waves
       C. physical energy called sine waves
       D. physical energy called pure tones

D   57. Noise is produced by hearing:
       A. pure tones
       B. sine waves
       C. periodic complex sound waves
       D. aperiodic complex sound waves

C   58. Psychological experience that accompanies variations in
       sound wave frequency is called:
       A. auditory spectrum
       B. audible spectrum
       C. pitch
       D. loudness

B   59. A psychological experience corresponding to changes in sound
       wave amplitude is called:
       A. audible spectrum
       B. loudness
       C. Hertz
       D. timbre

D   60. Pitch is to sound wave _____ as loudness is to sound wave
       _____.
       A. frequency ; complexity
       B. amplitude ; frequency
       C. complexity ; amplitude
       D. frequency ; amplitude

C   61. Decibels are the auditory measure of sound:
       A. complexity
       B. frequency
       C. intensity
       D. harmonics

D   62. Which of the following statements is FALSE?
        A. the audible spectrum for humans is from 20 to 20,000
           Hertz
        B. tinnitus is a ringing or buzzing sensation in the ears
        C. dogs can hear things humans can't hear due to a different
           audible spectrum
        D. most sounds that humans hear are pure tones

A   63. Two musical instruments sound the same note, but are
        perceived as different due to harmonic differences. This is
        explained by:
        A. timbre
        B. pitch
        C. decibels
        D. aperiodic complex sound waves

C   64. Which part of the outer ear moves as a function of sound
        waves hitting it?
        A. pinna
        B. auditory canal
        C. tympanic membrane
        D. eustachian tube

D   65. The actual receptors for hearing, the hair cells, are
        located in the:
        A. basilar membrane
        B. eustachian tube
        C. stapes
        D. organ of Corti

A   66. Auditory research by Békésy has demonstrated that sounds
        differing in pitch, loudness, and timbre result from
        different:
        A. vibration patterns in the basilar membrane
        B. locations of stimulation in the middle ear
        C. types of hair cells
        D. pressure changes in the cochlear fluid

C   67. The hearing theory that says pitch depends on the exact
        location the basilar membrane is maximally displaced is the
        _____ theory.
        A. volley
        B. frequency
        C. place
        D. sound pressure

B   68. The hearing theory that says pitch depends on the rate at
        which the hair cells are stimulated is called the _____
        theory.
        A. volley
        B. frequency
        C. place
        D. sound pressure

A   69. Which hearing theory helps explain the transduction of low
         frequency sounds between 1000 and 4000 cycles per second?
         A. volley
         B. frequency
         C. place
         D. sound pressure

SMELL AND TASTE: THE CHEMICAL SENSES

A   70. Smell and taste are commonly called the _____ senses.
         A. chemical
         B. basic
         C. electrical
         D. primary

D   71. Information about chemical substances in the air around us
         result from:
         A. gustation
         B. pheromones
         C. taste
         D. olfaction

C   72. Which of the following statements is FALSE?
         A. for most of us smell is not necessary for survival
         B. chemicals released for olfactory communication that
            cause specific reactions are pheromones
         C. the brain area for the sense of smell is in the
            olfactory bulb
         D. our recognition of foods comes from both smell and taste
            sensations

B   73. The most potent pheromone known in animals controls which
         behavior?
         A. alarm
         B. sexual
         C. attack
         D. eating

B   74. Sweet, sour, salty, and bitter make up:
         A. our four types of taste buds
         B. the primary taste qualities of humans
         C. sensations only found in humans
         D. our basic taste system

THE SKIN SENSES

C   75. Which of the following senses is composed of a broad range
        or large array of sensations?
        A. taste
        B. audition
        C. skin
        D. vision

D   76. Attempts to map skin sensations have been successful for:
        A. tickles
        B. itching
        C. vibration
        D. temperature

THE BODY SENSES

A   77. Kinesthesis informs us about body:
        A. movement
        B. balance and position
        C. orientation
        D. pressure and pain

B   78. Which sense serves to monitor the motion of the body as a
        whole?
        A. kinesthesis
        B. vestibular
        C. hormonal
        D. skin

C   79. The semicircular canals, located in the inner ear, are
        maximally sensitive to changes in:
        A. pitch
        B. pitch and amplitude
        C. rotations of the body, expecially the head
        D. muscle movements

D   80. The disorder known as "vertigo" is particularly detrimental
        to:
        A. dentists
        B. artists
        C. teachers
        D. pilots

ON THE HORIZON

B   81. A current procedure used to enable some blind individuals to
        interact more efficiently with their environment is:
        A. the use of trained monkeys
        B. a television camera which, through an electrical
           system, causes vibrators to stimulate the skin
        C. a television camera which translates visual information
           into auditory information passed through miniture
           earphones
        D. a magnifying glove which doubles the reading rate for
           people who know Braille

FURTHER READING SUGGESTIONS

Boynton, R. M. (1979). Human color vision. New York: Holt,
    Rinehart and Winston.

Goldstein, E. B. (1980). Sensation and perception. Belmont, C.A.:
    Wadsworth.

Gregory, R. L. (3rd ed.) (1977). Eye and brain. New York:
    McGraw-Hill.

Levine, M. W. & Shefner, J. M. (1981). Fundamentals of sensation
    and perception. Reading, Mass.: Addison-Wesley.

Marr, D. (1982). Vision. San Francisco: Freeman.

Melzack, R. (1973). The puzzle of pain. New York: Basic Books.

— CHAPTER 4 —

PERCEPTION

OUTLINE

I. Introduction: Reading Records and Recording Sensations — a description of someone who can visually "read" record grooves and tell what song is recorded; PERCEPTION is how the brain interprets sensations

II. Perceptual Processes

    A. Gestalt psychology: Perceptual organization and form perception — GESTALT PSYCHOLOGY, obtaining its name from the German word <u>gestalt</u>, is concerned with patterns or the "whole" of perception; four <u>principles of perceptual organization</u> were **described by Gestalt psychologists**
       1. FIGURE AND GROUND deals with object-background relationships; presentation of common reversible figure-ground relationships
       2. Principles of grouping: with PERCEPTUAL GROUPING we perceive meaningful wholes; there are organization subsets
          a. SIMILARITY deals with the appearance of stimuli (e.g., color, shape)
          b. PROXIMITY deals with location
          c. CONTINUATION pertains to the "smoothest path" that lines or contours should take
          d. CLOSURE deals with the proper perception of physically incomplete objects

3. The importance of contours in form perception: CONTOURS give shape and meaning to objects; to camouflage an object reduces contours and perception of the object; subjective contours occur without physical boundries to objects

4. The importance of context in form perception: a CONTEXT, influenced by past experiences and adaptation level, determines our perceptions of individual objects, especially ambiguous ones

5. SHAPE CONSTANCY states an object's perceived shape is constant in spite of different retinal images

B. Depth perception: our ability to have DEPTH PERCEPTION results from the use of both BINOCULAR DEPTH CUES and MONOCULAR DEPTH CUES

1. Binocular depth cues: STEREOSCOPIC VISION, or seeing with two eyes, results in BINOCULAR DISPARITY because each retinal image angle is different; this cue is good for objects less than 100 meters away

2. Monocular depth cues: depth perception using a single eye; there are seven separate cues

   a. LINEAR PERSPECTIVE deals with parallel lines converging in the distance (e.g., railroad tracks)

   b. AERIAL PERSPECTIVE pertains to closer objects being seen more clearly than distant objects (e.g., "on a clear day you can see forever")

   c. INTERPOSITION states that the object obstructing the view of another object is judged to be closer (e.g., a complete card appears closer than a card with a section missing)

   d. TEXTURE GRADIENTS states that closer objects have more detail and texture (e.g., a cobblestone street becomes less detailed in the distance)

   e. LIGHT AND SHADOW pertains to darker areas appearing farther away; based upon an assumption that light comes from above (e.g., reversing orientation of photos changes our perceptions)

   f. RELATIVE SIZE pertains to distant objects using less of the visual field and being judged farther away

   g. pictorial depth: pictorial depth cues (another name for monocular depth cues) are regularly used by artists

   h. MOTION PARALLAX deals with the apparent motion of distant objects when the observer is actually moving

3. Accommodation and convergence: depth cues from eye muscles are ACCOMMODATION, due to the ciliary muscles bending the lens, and CONVERGENCE, due to the extraocular muscles moving the entire eye; these cues effective only for objects 10 feet from the observer

C. The perception of size: familiarity with objects helps with SIZE CONSTANCY, where different retinal images of the same object are judged to be the same size; ambiguous depth cues may cause perceptual illusions of size; various ILLUSIONS have studied to see what and how perceptual distortions can be induced

1. Ames room illusion demonstrates that size is perceived as varying as a result of alterations in depth cues and physical context; the visual angle or size of the retinal image changes

2. The moon illusion: the moon appears larger near the horizon than at its zenith in the moon illusion; it is explained by the apparent distance theory which incorporates terrestial depth cues as inducing the illusion

3. Other illusions of size
   a. the Muller-Lyer illusion is attributed to misapplied size constancy
   b. the PONZO ILLUSION in which the perception of identical horizontal lines is influenced by a background containing depth cues

D. The perception of movement and motion: REAL MOTION of an object provides cues for motion perception; these cues involve changes in the angle of light reaching the eye and the stimulation of movement detectors on the retina; one explanation for motion perception involves the image-retina system and the eye-head system

1. APPARENT MOTION is motion perceived without real movement of an object; there are three types of apparent motion
   a. AUTOKINETIC MOVEMENT: a stationary light "moves" about in a dark room
   b. INDUCED MOVEMENT: a stationary object "moves" from moving a larger background
   c. STROBOSCOPIC MOVEMENT: movement is perceived between two stationary lights that are flashed on and off in sequence

E. Application: Movement in cinema and television - Wertheimer, experimenting with stroboscopic movement, created the phi phenomenon or perceptual movements resulting from numerous still pictures being flashed on and off; the apparent movement seen in movies is created this way

III. Perceptual Development: PERCEPTUAL LEARNING involves perception as a result of experience with the environment; psychologists today are concerned with how innate (nature) and learned (nurture) factors contribute rather than how much each contributes

A. Infant perceptual development: infants are born with a highly developed visual system; numerous examples of visual capabilities are presented

   1. Form perception in human infants: Visual scanning
      studies - research by both Salapatek and Fantz have shown
      visual scanning ability improves rapidly during the first
      four months, both for simple forms and human facial
      features
   2. Depth perception in human infants: Visual cliff studies
      - research by Gibson and Walk, using the visual cliff
      apparatus, has shown that depth perception is present
      when human infants and young animals of different species
      are mobile; results favor innate depth perception
      abilities; recent studies suggest that depth perception
      is learned

B. Experience and perceptual development: recent researchers
   suggest that learning and experience may be more important
   than innate factors in depth perception; studies show only
   subjects capable of self-produced movement are wary of
   heights, not those that are prelocomotor
   1. The importance of self-produced movement: research by
      Held and Hein with a "kitten carousel" found that
      actively-moving kittens, but not passively-moving kittens
      showed normal perceptual development inspite of identical
      visual stimulation
   2. The importance of visual stimulation: Deprivation studies
      a. chimpanzees reared in total darkness functioned as if
         blind
      b. Blakemore and Cooper found kittens reared in total,
         and then partial, darkness showed several defects in
         perceptual development
      c. deprivation studies not only induce perceptual defects
         but also defects in neurological development
      d. kittens reared with goggles showing one type line only
         recognized objects with that line orientation when the
         goggles were removed
      e. "enriched" rearing environments promote neurological
         development
   3. The effects of restored vision: two cases where vision
      was restored following surgery; both showed retarded
      visual functioning which improved slowly if at all

C. Application: Attention and perception - our ATTENTION is
   based on selective perception; demonstrated in the cocktail
   party phenomenon where we hear our name mentioned in the
   midst of distracting and loud sounds; factors which
   influence our attention are characteristics of the stimuli
   (intensity, novelty, movement, repetition) and
   characteristics of the person (motives, needs)

IV. On The Horizon: Extrasensory Perception: EXTRASENSORY
    PERCEPTION (ESP), perceptions without normal sensory input, are
    studied by parapsychologists; three types of ESP are
    clairvoyance, telepathy, precognition; a discussion and
    evaluation of Uri Geller

OBJECTIVES

I.   WHAT IS PERCEPTION?

Perception is the term psychologists use to describe the brain's interpretation and analysis of sensory information (nerve impulses) from the various sense modalities.

A   1. Perception is concerned with:

A. the brain's analysis and interpretation of nerve impulses coming from sense organs
B. the flow of nerve impulses to the brain
C. how a sensory system codes information that it sends to the brain
D. "making something out of relatively little"

2. Define and give a few examples of the term "perception."

II. HOW DOES THE BRAIN ORGANIZE SENSATIONS INTO MEANINGFUL PERCEPTIONS?

Gestalt psychologists believe that perception depends on the brain's tendency to organize pieces of sensory information into wholes whose significance differs from the mere sum of the parts. Gestalt is a German word meaning "pattern" and Gestalt psychology is concerned with the whole perception rather than individual sensations. According to Gestalt psychologists there are four primary principles of perceptual organization: figure and ground, grouping (e.g., similarity, continuation, proximity, closure), contours, and context

B   1. Gestalt psychology is primarily concerned with:

A. individual sensations
B. whole perceptions
C. European psychology
D. illusions

B   2. The Gestalt principle of perceptual organization which deals with the similarity and proximity of stimuli is:

A. figure and ground
B. grouping
C. contour
D. context

3. Describe how the Gestalt psychologists felt the brain organized sensations into meaningful perceptions.

III. WHAT ARE THE PROCESSES INVOLVED IN PERCEPTUAL ORGANIZATION, AND IN FORM, DEPTH, SIZE, AND MOVEMENT PERCEPTION?

The processes involved in various types of perceptions are different and too detailed to present here. Thus, only generalities are given. The four general principles of perceptual organization are figure and ground, grouping (with the four sub-principles of similarity, continuation, proximity and closure), contours, and context. These also apply to form perception. In addition to these four principles contributing to our ability to see forms, the principle of shape constancy states that objects remain the same in spite of differing retinal images. Depth perception involves making inferences about three-dimensional objects on the basis of two-dimensional retinal images. These inferences are made on the basis of binocular depth cues (stereoscopic vision, binocular disparity) or monocular depth cues (linear perspective, aerial perspective, interposition, texture gradients, light and shadow, relative size, and motion parallax). Two additional, non-retinal cues are accommodation and convergence. Size perception is based on the principle of size constancy. Movement perception is based upon the stimulation of actual movement detectors across the retina or upon changes in the angle at which light from the moving object strikes the retina.

1. Discuss the processes involved in one of the following: the perception of form, depth, size, or movement.

IV. HOW HAVE PSYCHOLOGISTS LEARNED ABOUT PERCEPTUAL PROCESSES THROUGH THE STUDY OF PERCEPTUAL ILLUSIONS?

The study of various perceptual illusions (such as the Ames room, the Muller-Lyer, and Ponzo that were discussed in the text) enables psychologists to appreciate how the perception of an object is distorted by the context in which the object appears. All of the illusions which were discussed in the text showed how an object's or a line's perceived size can be modified by the actual presence or mere expectation of depth cues in the background.

D   1. The study of various illusions has demonstrated the importance of _____ on size perception.

    A. color
    B. shape
    C. motivation level
    D. real or expected depth cues

2. What have psychologists learned about perception through the study of visual illusions?

V.   WHAT CAN NEWBORN BABIES SEE?   HOW CAN DEPTH AND FORM PERCEPTION
     IN HUMAN INFANTS BE TESTED?

Research has shown that newborns can see and appreciate much
more than has been expected in the past. As young as two hours
of age, neonates can follow a moving light. Newborns also show
signs of boredom to repetitive stimulation. Infants also
prefer the color red. Visual acuity and visual scanning
abilities improve rapidly after birth. For example, at one
month infants tend to only look at one peak of a triangle but
by two months the entire triangle is scanned (see Figure 14).
By four months of age, infants prefer faces with normally
arranged features as compared to faces with reorganized
features.   The study of infant depth and form perception
requires special apparati that utilize infant motor responses
(rather than the verbal or written responses commonly used with
older subjects).   Visual scanning is used by monitoring eye
movements and depth perception has made use of crawling on a
visual cliff apparatus.

C   1. Infant visual acuity and visual scanning abilities:

        A. remain the same during the first year
        B. actually get worse for a few months after birth
        C. improve rapidly the first few months
        D. have not been adequately studied

B   2. Researchers measure what kind of behavior in human visual
        cliff studies?

        A. walking
        B. crawling
        C. crying
        D. eye movements

     3. Summarize, with examples, some of the visual capabilities
        that infants show.

VI. WHAT   EFFECT   DOES   VISUAL   DEPRIVATION   HAVE   ON   PERCEPTUAL
     DEVELOPMENT?

Visual deprivation which begins at an early age and which
continues for some length of time results in retarded
perceptual development.   Chimpanzees reared in darkness for
their first 16 months of life behaved as if they were blind.
Kittens, reared in the dark for their first two weeks of life
but then given five hours of light each day for the next five
months, were not blind. However, their head movements were
jerky, they tried to paw distant objects, and they bumped into
objects when walking.   Kittens reared with goggles which
presented stripes of a particular orientation only responded to
things in the same orientation when the goggles were removed.

Humans who have been visually deprived but then, at an advanced age, had their sight restored surgically report a slow and sometimes incomplete recovery to normal visual functioning.

D   1. Which of the following statements is FALSE?

A. Chimpanzees reared in darkness acted as if they were blind
B. Kittens reared with limited amounts of light each day did not develop normal vision
C. Kittens reared with access that was limited to a certain orientation only recognized objects in that orientation
D. Humans, with few exceptions, see fairly well after their sight has been restored

2. What have visual deprivation studies in animals found out about perceptual development?

MULTIPLE-CHOICE QUESTIONS

INTRODUCTION: READING RECORDS AND RECORDING SENSATIONS

D   1. "Reading" records with one's eyes is a strange, but not altogether unrepresentative, example of:
A. unusual touch sensitivity
B. unusual visual sensitivity
C. extrasensory perception
D. human perception

B   2. The term we use to describe the brain's interpretation of nerve impulses sent to it is:
A. cortical analysis
B. perception
C. sensation
D. cortical interpretation

GESTALT PSYCHOLOGY: PERCEPTUAL ORGANIZATION AND FORM PERCEPTION

A   3. Gestalt psychologists believe that the brain organizes sensory information:
A. in ways that go beyond individual sensations
B. in the simplist fashion
C. in the most economical manner
D. none of the above

C   4. The study of patterns, or the whole perception, is the
       focus of:
       A. empiricists
       B. rationalists
       C. Gestalt psychology
       D. perceptual psychology

D   5. Which of the following is NOT one of the principles of
       perceptual organization in Gestalt psychology?
       A. grouping
       B. contour
       C. context
       D. illusion

A   6. The fact that most seen objects tend to stand out from a
       background is suggested by:
       A. figure-ground relationships
       B. familiarity grouping
       C. continuation
       D. closure

B   7. Organizing subsets of stimuli into meaningful forms on the
       basis of similarity and closure is an example of:
       A. sensory organization
       B. perceptual grouping
       C. good figure
       D. the principle of contour

C   8. Objects or stimuli of like appearance are grouped together
       because of what Gestalt principle?
       A. grouping
       B. proximity
       C. similarity
       D. constancy

B   9. The principle of proximity states that objects or stimuli
       are grouped together on the basis of their:
       A. similarity
       B. nearness
       C. color
       D. shape

A   10. When a number of dots are grouped together so that they
        "make" a smooth path or line, it is an example of which
        principle of grouping?
        A. continuation
        B. closure
        C. similarity
        D. contour

D   11. A strong tendency to perceive whole forms even if they are
        not complete (perceiving a "square" out of hash marks)
        demonstrates the principle of:
        A. good continuation
        B. proximity
        C. similarity
        D. closure

C   12. Camouflage is an effective way of hiding an object or animal
        because:
        A. the context is hidden
        B. similarity is diminished
        C. contours are diminished
        D. shape constancy is made easier

B   13. Perceiving an "upright triangle" where none exists
        physically merely because of the surrounding configuration
        demonstrates:
        A. camouflage
        B. subjective contours
        C. closure
        D. overriding contours

D   14. Our perceptions of particular stimuli are highly influenced
        by the context in which they appear. This results from:
        A. our emotional level
        B. the principle of proximity
        C. the principle of similarity
        D. past learning experiences

D   15. Our strong tendency to perceive the correct physical shapes
        of objects even though their retinal images are not correct
        demonstrates the principle of:
        A. context and contour
        B. adaptation level
        C. retinal constancy
        D. shape constancy

DEPTH PERCEPTION

C   16. Our ability to perceive three dimensions even though an
        object's image falls upon the two-dimensional surface of the
        retina is explained by:
        A. object perception
        B. perceptual reorganization
        C. depth perception
        D. adaptation

A   17. Which of the following is NOT a monocular depth cue?
         A. stereoscopic vision
         B. linear perspective
         C. texture gradients
         D. motion parallax

A   18. Stereoscopic vision is a valuable depth cue because each
         eye:
         A. receives a slightly different view of the world
         B. has an optic nerve
         C. sends impulses to the brain
         D. perceives depth by itself

B   19. Which of the following is a FALSE statement about binocular
         dispairty?
         A. it is based upon stereoscopic vision
         B. it is a monocular depth cue
         C. there is more of it with distant rather than close
            objects
         D. it functions with comparatively near objects (100 meters
            or less)

C   20. Which is perhaps our most important cue for depth?
         A. linear perspective
         B. light and shadow
         C. binocular disparity
         D. interpositioning

D   21. Clearly seen objects appear closer than they actually are
         according to the principle of:
         A. binocular dispairty
         B. interpositioning
         C. convergence
         D. aerial perspective

A   22. The principle of aerial perspective helps explain why:
         A. distant mountain peaks appear closer on clear days then
            on hazy days
         B. the moon is larger near the horizon
         C. railroad tracks seem to converge in the distance
         D. a green piece of paper is seen as closer than a red one

D   23. When one object obstructs the view of another and the object
         that is entirely in view is judged to be closer, it is due
         to the principle of:
         A. size constancy
         B. relative size
         C. light and shadow
         D. interposition

B   24. When looking down a cobblestone street, the distant
        cobblestones are perceived as being finer and less detailed.
        This is explained by the depth cue of:
        A. aerial gradients
        B. texture gradients
        C. relative size
        D. linear gradients

B   25. The depth cue known as "light and shadow" functions because:
        A. both our eyes have rods for brightness sensitivity
        B. we normally expect light to come from above
        C. we can see the contours of dark objects better than light
           ones
        D. disparity of retinal images

C   26. Which of the following pictorial depth cues is NOT commonly
        used by artists?
        A. overlap
        B. texture
        C. apparent motion
        D. light and shadow

A   27. As you move about, nearby objects appear to move farther
        than do more distant objects. This is due to:
        A. motion parallax
        B. relative area
        C. aerial perspective
        D. movement induced perceptions

A   28. Binocular depth cues involve:
        A. the use of both eyes
        B. the use of one eye only
        C. unlearned or innate responses
        D. secondary perceptual information

D   29. Accommodation refers to:
        A. the way our eyes look inward or outward
        B. the ability to perceive movement in the distance
        C. a distortion in depth perception
        D. changes in shape of the lens the eyes make to focus
           objects at various distances

B   30. Accommodation and convergence provide depth information for
        objects within about _____ of the observer.
        A. 100 meters
        B. 10 feet
        C. 5 feet
        D. 5 meters

C   31. Convergence and accommodation supply depth information as
        the result of changes in:
        A. corneal curving
        B. lens curving
        C. eye muscles
        D. intraocular fluid density

THE PERCEPTION OF SIZE

A   32. An object's perceived size remains constant regardless of
        the object's distance from the observer. This is known as
        the principle of:
        A. size constancy
        B. distance constancy
        C. size accommodation
        D. relative size

A   33. A distortion in perception that contradicts objective
        reality is called a(n):
        A. illusion
        B. perceptual error
        C. error in perception
        D. context error

D   34. The Ames room illusion results from differences in the
        _____ of the people being looked at.
        A. actual distance
        B. clothing texture
        C. body position
        D. visual angle

B   35. In the moon illusion, the moon looks _____ when it is

        _____.
        A. gigantic ; a full moon
        B. gigantic ; near the horizon
        C. larger ; partially covered by clouds
        D. larger ; viewed through a partial fog

B   36. The moon illusion "disappears" when one:
        A. shuts one eye
        B. views the horizon moon through a peep hole
        C. looks through a concave mirror
        D. looks through a convex mirror

C   37. When "Vs" and arrowheads are added to two equal line
        segments, the perceived length of each line changes. This
        is called the
        _____ illusion.
        A. Ames
        B. Gregory
        C. Muller-Lyer
        D. Ponzo

C   38. The Muller-Lyer illusion has been explained on the basis of:
        A. misapplied depth perception
        B. accommodation errors
        C. misapplied size constancy
        D. adaptation errors

A   39. Two identical horizontal lines appear to differ in length
         when shown against a background that contains depth cues.
         This is known as the _____ illusion.
        A. Ponzo
        B. Gregory
        C. Muller-Lyer
        D. Ames

D   40. The Ponzo illusion occurs because the background contains:
        A. many objects of different sizes
        B. no objects
        C. stereoscopic visual cues
        D. depth cues

THE PERCEPTION OF MOVEMENT AND MOTION

B   41. A change in an object's position in space refers to:
        A. motion perception
        B. real motion
        C. perceptual motion
        D. illusionary movement

A   42. Which of the following is a visual cue for motion
         perception?
        A. changes in the angle at which light from the moving
           object strikes the retina
        B. movement receptors in the ciliary muscles
        C. actual movements in each eye
        D. none of the above

A   43. Movement detectors, or cells sensitive to the movements of
         objects, are located in the:
        A. retina
        B. ciliary muscles
        C. optic nerve
        D. skin

C   44. Which system is responsible for detecting object movements
         when the eyes are stationary?
        A. eye - retina
        B. eye - head
        C. image - retina
        D. retinal firing

B   45. Which system for motion perception is responsible when the
        object's retinal image remains stationary?
        A. eye - retina
        B. eye - head
        C. image - retina
        D. retinal firing

D   46. The vestibular sense as well as muscles needed for head
        movement help provide signals for the _____ system of
        motion perception.
        A. retinal firing
        B. eye - retina
        C. image - retina
        D. eye - head

D   47. Apparent motion is when there is:
        A. slow real movement in the visual field
        B. more than one kind of real movement
        C. movement faster than real movement
        D. perceived movement without the physical motion of objects

C   48. Which of the following is NOT an example of apparent
        movement?
        A. induced movement
        B. stroboscopic movement
        C. perceptual movement
        D. autokinetic movement

A   49. Autokinetic movement is exemplified by:
        A. the "wandering" glowing end of a cigarette in a dark room
        B. a bouncing ball appearing to go faster than it is
        C. the movement of the moon near the horizon
        D. motion pictures

B   50. Autokinetic movement is accounted for by:
        A. retinal movement detectors
        B. eye muscles and tiny head movements
        C. less than optimum brain cell nerve firings
        D. the "overlap" in brain cell nerve firings

D   51. The moon appears to race across the sky on a cloudy night
        because of _____ movement.
        A. autokinetic
        B. inherent
        C. stroboscopic
        D. induced

C   52. Induced movement occurs because we generally:
        A. move our heads slightly
        B. move our eyes slightly
        C. assume smaller objects move and larger objects remain
           stationary
        D. assume large objects move slower than smaller objects

C   53. Movement perceived between two stationary lights flashing on
        and off is called:
        A. the Ponzo illusion
        B. ESP
        C. stroboscopic movement
        D. autokinetic movement

APPLICATION: MOVEMENT IN CINEMA AND TELEVISION

B   54. Two pictures of a single line in slightly different
        locations, when flashed in sequence, give the appearance
        that the line moves. This is called the _____ phenomenon.
        A. perceptual
        B. phi
        C. Gregory
        D. Wertheimer

A   55. The most familiar example of stroboscopic effect is movement
        created by:
        A. television and cinema
        B. flying in an airplane
        C. driving late at night with high beam lights on
        D. jugglers and magicians

A   56. What can producers of movies do to reduce "jerky" movements?
        A. use more pictures or frames per second
        B. increase the time interval between frames or pictures
        C. make each frame or picture less similar to each other
        D. make each frame larger in size

PERCEPTUAL DEVELOPMENT

B   57. The ability to extract information from stimuli in the
        environment as a result of practice, training, or experience
        is called:
        A. perception
        B. perceptual learning
        C. stimulus grouping
        D. stimulus categorization

D   58. Currently, psychologists are more concerned with _____
        nature and nurture contribute to perception rather than
        _____ each contributes.
        A. how much ; when
        B. how ; when
        C. how much ; how
        D. how ; how much

INFANT PERCEPTUAL DEVELOPMENT

C   59. Various experiments in infant perceptual development have
          shown that infants:
          A. see little because they have poor focusing abilities
          B. are born with a relatively underdeveloped visual system
          C. have a highly developed visual system at birth
          D. perceive more than they actually see

D   60. Which of the following statements is FALSE concerning infant
          perceptual capacities?
          A. newborns two hours old can follow a moving light
          B. boredom is shown when the same stimulus is repeatedly
             presented
          C. increasing brain complexity parallels increasing visual
             acuity
          D. infants show a marked preference for the color blue

B   61. Fantz has demonstrated that babies prefer looking at normal
          faces rather than faces with rearranged features at how many
          months of age?
          A. 2
          B. 4
          C. 6
          D. 8

A   62. The apparatus used by Gibson and Walk to study whether depth
          is perceived in human infants is called the:
          A. visual cliff
          B. visual scanning test
          C. perceptual drum
          D. depth perception "carousel"

C   63. Gibson and Walk's research on depth perception in young
          organisms found that:
          A. infants can discern depth by 4 months of age
          B. lambs and chicks tended to go to the deep side for a day
             or so after birth or hatching
          C. human infants perceive depth as soon as they can crawl
          D. rearing in darkness retards the development of depth
             perception in chicks

EXPERIENCE AND PERCEPTUAL DEVELOPMENT

C   64. Relatively recent research has suggested that fear of
          heights in human infants is:
          A. innate
          B. learned
          C. not necessarily innate as Gibson and Walk have reported
          D. is more innate than learned

D   65. Relatively recent research on depth perception in infants
          has shown those _____ are afraid of heights.
          A. with strong maternal attachments
          B. who are older
          C. who show good early visual scanning abilities
          D. capable of self-produced movement

B   66. The experiments conducted by Held and Hein found that only
          those kittens that experienced _____ showed normal
          perceptual development.
          A. passive movement
          B. self-produced movement
          C. visual stimulation
          D. no visual deprivation

A   67. The research by Held and Hein with the "kitten-carousel"
          suggests what to be important for normal perceptual
          development?
          A. active movement
          B. passive movement
          C. visual stimulation
          D. visual and tactual stimulation

D   68. Visual deprivation studies with both chimpanzees and kittens
          have shown that:
          A. if deprived long enough, the subjects behaved as if they
             were blind
          B. when deprived for a few months, kittens could still see,
             but they had perceptual defects
          C. when deprived for a few months, kittens' head movements
             were jerky and they bumped into things
          D. all of the above

A   69. A major flaw in the early visual deprivation studies was the
          fact that the deprivation experience:
          A. also impaired development of the visual system
          B. impaired development of the motor system
          C. was often too short
          D. was often too long

C   70. The adverse affect of visual deprivation on brain-cell
          growth and perception development was demonstrated by
          having:
          A. chimpanzees wear bifocal glasses
          B. subjects reared in continual bright light
          C. kittens wear goggles
          D. subjects kept in isolation cages

B   71. Which of the following statements is TRUE?
         A. brain cells in cats reared without horizontal stripes
            still responded to horizontal stripes
         B. rats reared in "enriched" environments have a more
            developed visual cortex than those reared in isolation
         C. poor depth perception abilities are usually due to a
            lack of learning and experience in isolated **rats**
         D. all of the above

D   72. Patients who have had their vision restored following
         operations:
         A. show surprisingly good but not perfect vision
         B. have perfect vision
         C. are essentially blind
         D. have poor depth perception and other deficits

APPLICATION: ATTENTION AND PERCEPTION

C   73. The process which allows us to selectively focus on some
         stimuli and filter out others is called:
         A. perception
         B. selection
         C. attention
         D. focus selection

A   74. The cocktail party phenomenon is a good demonstration of:
         A. the selective nature of perception
         B. perception at low volume
         C. perception at high intensity
         D. **repetition** of stimulation

B   75. Which characteristic of stimuli do advertisers NOT generally
         use to gain our attention?
         A. intensity
         B. shape
         C. novelty
         D. movement

D   76. Television commercials commonly gain our attention through
         the use of:
         A. novelty
         B. intensity
         C. repetition
         D. all of the above

D   77. Which personal characteristics are important influences on
         attention?
         A. age and education
         B. gender (sex) and age
         C. socioeconomic status and age
         D. motives and needs

ON THE HORIZON: EXTRASENSORY PERCEPTION

C   78. Extrasensory perception refers to perceptions that
         purportedly do not depend on:
         A. extra sensory input
         B. above threshold stimulation
         C. normal sensory input
         D. sub-threshold stimulation

D   79. Researchers interested in extrasensory perception are
         typically called:
         A. extrasensory researchers
         B. illusionary psychologists
         C. Gestalt psychologists
         D. parapsychologists

A   80. Which of the following is NOT an example of ESP?
         A. palm reading
         B. clairvoyance
         C. telepathy
         D. precognition

A   81. The purported ability to perceive future events is called:
         A. precognition
         B. telepathy
         C. clairvoyance
         D. palm reading

D   82. Uri Geller, the famous "psychic," is thought by critics to
         be (a):
         A. parapsychologist
         B. clairvoyant
         C. telepathic personality
         D. fraud

− CHAPTER 5 −

STATES OF
CONSCIOUSNESS

OUTLINE

I.   Introduction: From the depths of consciousness − the use of hypnosis to aid victims or witnesses of crimes in their recall of details needed to solve the crime

II. The Nature of Consciousness: What is CONSCIOUSNESS and the characteristics of <u>waking consciousness</u>

   A. Modes and levels of consciousness: <u>passive</u> vs. <u>active consciousness</u> and the differences between Freud's <u>four levels</u> of consciousness (CONSCIOUS, NONCONSCIOUS, PRECONSCIOUS, and UNCONSCIOUS)

   B. Hypnosis and consciousness: HYPNOSIS and its beginning with Mesmer's <u>animal magnetism</u>
      1. How is hypnosis done − achieving the hypnotic state with four directions
      2. Who can be hypnotized − use of the <u>Stanford Hypnotic Susceptibility Scale</u> to determine responsive individuals
      3. The experience of being hypnotized − a personal description with general characteristics

   C. Application: hypnosis as a clinical tool: the advantages and limitations of hypnosis in police work and <u>hypnotherapy</u> in surgery and childbirth

III. Sleep and Dreams

    A. Sleep: who needs it and how much do they need
        1. The function of sleep
           a. a comparison of three theories of sleep - ENERGY
              CONSERVATION THEORY, BEHAVIORAL ADAPTIVE THEORY, and
              BIOLOGICAL RHYTHM THEORY
           b. the role of CIRCADIAN RHYTHMS in the biological rhythm
              theory
        2. Sleep deprivation
           a. divergent reactions of two people to extended <u>sleep</u>
              <u>deprivation</u>
           b. three common consequences of prolonged wakefulness
           c. daytime napping to shorten nighttime sleep
           d. what is <u>natural sleep length</u> and how to find it
        3. The measurement of sleep
           a. sleep states as determined by the <u>electroencephalogram</u>
              (EEG), ELECTROMYOGRAM (EMG), and ELECTROOCULOGRAM
              (EOG)
           b. two kinds of sleep - REM SLEEP (with dreaming) and
              NREM SLEEP
           c. three characteristics of each kind of sleep
           d. five <u>sleep stages</u> and characteristics of common <u>sleep</u>
              <u>cycles</u>

    B. Dreams: three characteristics of <u>dreams</u>
        1. The importance of dreaming
           a. use of <u>dream deprivation</u> studies
           b. no dreaming leads to <u>rem rebound</u>
        2. The interpretation of dreams
           a. Freud discussed the <u>manifest content</u>, <u>latent content</u>,
              and <u>function</u> of dreams
           b. dream content varies between individuals and genders

    C. Application: Diagnosis and treatment of sleep disorders
        1. Nightmares and night terrors
           a. characteristics of, and differences between,
               NIGHTMARES and NIGHT TERRORS
           b. night terrors and SOMNAMBULISM
         2. Insomnia
           a. characteristics of INSOMNIA and its treatment with
               sleep medications
           b. traditional and behavioral treatment for
               <u>drug-dependency insomnia</u>
        3. Hypersomnia - causes of HYPERSOMNIA and <u>excessive daytime</u>
           <u>sleepiness</u> (EDS)
        4. Sleep apnea
           a. the relationship of SLEEP APNEA to hypersomnia and
               insomnia
           b. sleep apnea in children and its relation to SUDDEN
               INFANT DEATH SYNDROME (SIDS)
           c. treatment with a <u>tracheotomy</u>

5. Narcolepsy
   a. characteristics of NARCOLEPSY include hypersomnia and cataplexy
   b. treatment limitations
6. Sleep disorders in perspective: use of treatment and research centers for dealing with sleep disturbances, bruxism, and enuresis

IV. Drug-induced Alterations in Consciousness: a comparison of LICIT and ILLICIT drugs and how they pertain to drug use and drug abuse. The five uses of drugs: experimental, recreational, circumstantial, intensive, and compulsive. Drug misuse as it relates to TOLERANCE, PHYSICAL DEPENDENCE (and withdrawal symptoms), and PSYCHOLOGICAL DEPENDENCE.

A. Narcotics: historical use and characteristics of three NARCOTIC DRUGS (opium, morphine, and heroin); medical treatment and the withdrawal reaction associated with narcotic dependence

B. Sedatives: SEDATIVE DRUGS depress the nervous system
1. Barbiturates - the different effects created by different dosage levels and the treatment of physical dependence make barbiturates interesting
2. Alcohol
   a. alcohol depresses the nervous system
   b. relationship between six levels of alcohol consumption and both blood alcohol level and behavior
   c. statistics on alcohol misuse in America

C. Stimulants: STIMULANT DRUGS that arouse the nervous system include caffeine and nicotine
1. Amphetamines
   a. uses of commonly prescribed amphetamines
   b. case history about country singer Johnny Cash's addiction
   c. methedrine and its resulting amphetamine psychosis
2. Cocaine
   a. source and domestic uses of cocaine
   b. intranasal ingestion and growth of cocaine use in America
   c. addictive vs. non-addictive properties of cocaine

D. Hallucinogens: the HALLUCINOGENS, also called psychedelics which, like mescaline and psilocybin, produce hallucinations
1. Lysergic acid diethylamide or LSD - effects at small and large doses
2. Phencyclidine or PCP and its dramatic effects
3. Marijuana
   a. source and active ingredient of THC in marijuana
   b. hashish is similar but more potent
   c. decriminalization
   d. consequences of use

E. Application: Self-regulation   with   meditation   —   three
   self-regulation techniques used in place of drugs are
   MEDITATION,   transcendental meditation,   and   PROGRESSIVE
   RELAXATION

V.   On the Horizon: Consciousness, physiology, and longevity — a
     discussion of the research conducted with practioners of
     Transcendetal Meditation to determine what effects it has on
     basic physiological mechanisms and the aging process

OBJECTIVES

1. TO WHAT DOES THE TERM CONSCIOUSNESS REFER?

Consciousness refers to an immediate awareness of both the
external environment, and internal events, such as thoughts,
fantasies, and daydreams. Specific states of consciousness
vary with respect to content, sensory impressions, alertness,
attention, and volition. There is waking consciousness (e.g.,
recall the past, plan for the future, make decisions), passive
consciousness (e.g., open awareness of surroundings, relaxed
enjoyment of daydreaming, listening to music) and active
consciousness (e.g., planning decision making, and initiating
actions.)

C   1. Passive consciousness includes which activity?

    A. dreaming
    B. sleeping
    C. listening to music
    D. decision making

A   2. "Waking" consciousness is most similar to which of the
       following levels of consciousness?

    A. conscious
    B. nonconscious
    C. preconscious
    D. unconscious

3. Discuss what consciousness is, and differentiate between waking, passive, and active types of consciousness.

2. HOW IS HYPNOSIS DONE? WHAT IS IT LIKE TO BE HYPNOTIZED?

For those that agree that hypnosis is a unique, altered state of consciousness, it is said to involve relaxation, suggestion, restriction of attention, and intense concentration. A person being hypnotized is encouraged to 1) focus his or her attention on what is being said, 2) to relax and feel tired, 3) to accept suggestions, and 4) to use a vivid imagination. People that are hypnotized may feel that they are free to do as they please, but they still follow the hypnotist's suggestions. When deeply hypnotized, one generally 1) sits passively without initiating activity, 2) has a more selective attention, 3) can concentrate better, 4) accepts consciousness uncritically, and 5) can "act" out past experiences.

D   1. Which is a characteristic of the hypnotic state?

     A. generalized attention
     B. concentration weakness
     C. insincerity
     D. relaxation

A   2. People who are hypnotized may feel:

     A. they can concentrate better that in an ordinary
        waking state
     B. guilty afterward
     C. uneasy about their current thoughts
     D. more emotional toward the opposite sex

     3. Present and discuss the four instructions typically given by a hypnotist.

     4. Summarize what individuals have reported about their feelings and thinking while hypnotized.

3. HOW IS IT POSSIBLE TO STUDY SLEEP AND DREAM STATES? WHAT IS KNOWN ABOUT STAGES OF SLEEP?

Sleep states are studied by recording ongoing brain activity, muscle activity, and eye movements. Dream states occur during REM periods of high brain activity, body immobility, and rapid eye movements. Each of the five stages of sleep has a characteristic type of brain wave activity. The first four stages are associated with NREM periods (relative brain inactivity, active body movements, little eye movements) while the fifth stage is the REM period. Sleep cycles consist of all five stages and vary from 70 to 110 minutes during each full period of sleep.

B   1. Which is NOT associated with the dreaming state?

      A. high brain activity
      B. shallowness of breath
      C. body immobility
      D. rapid eye movements

D   2. Research has discovered _____ stages of sleep.

      A. 2
      B. 3
      C. 4
      D. 5

C   3. A sleep cycle refers to:

      A. the period between two dreams
      B. a progression from sleep stages 1 to 4
      C. one NREM and one REM period
      D. the actual period of sleep without dreaming

    4. What are the different techniques used to study sleep and dream states, and what do they measure?

    5. Discuss what reasearchers have discovered about each stage of sleep.

4. HOW IS WAKING CONSCIOUSNESS ALTERED BY SLEEP, DREAMS, AND DRUGS?

Sleep deprivation studies have found that some, but not all, people who undergo prolonged wakefulness may develop psychotic thoughts and have difficulty separating reality from "waking nightmares." Some researchers using dream deprivation studies have found that when permitted, we typically make-up for our prior lack of dreaming. Thus, for many individuals both sleep and dream states are important and even a necessity for normal waking consciousness. Drugs can modify waking consciousness. All drugs directly influence the central nervous system.

D   1. Some individuals who are deprived of sleep develop:

      A. physical ailments
      B. long lasting personality changes
      C. increased sensitivity to drugs
      D. psychotic thoughts while awake

    2. How do humans alter their state of waking consciousness with a) sleep, b) dreams, c) drugs?

5. WHAT DO THE MOST WIDELY USED CONSCIOUS-ALTERING DRUGS HAVE IN COMMON?

They have the potential for being abused and misused. Whether a drug (licit or illicit) is abused or misused depends upon tolerance and dependence. Tolerance exists when a drug becomes less effective due to repeated use, thereby requiring larger and more frequent doses to achieve the desired effect. Dependence also results from increased drug use; it may be either physical (where bodily processes are modified so that the system needs the drug) or psychological (where the drug is needed to produce pleasure or avoid emotional discomfort.)

B   1. What do the consciousness-altering drugs NOT have in common?

A. potential for tolerance
B. they are all illicit drugs
C. potential for physical dependence
D. they can produce psychological dependence

2. Present and discuss the three common characteristics of conscious-altering drugs.

3. Compare and contrast psychological drug-dependence and physical drug-dependence.

6. WHAT TECHNIQUES ARE AVAILABLE AS ALTERNATIVES TO DRUGS FOR ACHIEVING CONTROL OVER MENTAL AND PHYSIOLOGICAL PROCESSES?

The traditional technique of meditation is said to heighten powers of concentration, an altered sense of consciousness, and personal enlightment. A popular Westernized form of meditation and self-regulation is transcendental meditation, or TM, a technique which can alter bodily feelings and subjective feelings. A technique called progressive relaxation is said to be able to decrease muscle tension, heart rate, blood pressure, and rate of breathing. Long-term achievements include deep levels of relaxation and a sense of control.

B   1. A Westernized form of self-regulation which can alter bodily feelings and subjective feelings is called:

A. meditation
B. transcendental meditation
C. yoga
D. mantra

2. Describe three self-regulatory procedures for altering mental and physiological processes and discuss what they are said to accomplish.

MULTIPLE-CHOICE QUESTIONS

INTRODUCTION

C   1. In California, a school bus driver who had been kidnapped
       was hypnotized so that he could:
       A. remember the color of the kidnapper's car
       B. reduce his own anxiety feelings
       C. remember the kidnappers license plate
       D. remember who killed the three children

THE NATURE OF CONSCIOUSNESS

MODES AND LEVELS OF CONSCIOUSNESS

A   2. The state of immediate awareness to both the external
       environment and internal events such as thoughts, refers
       to:
       A. consciousness
       B. volition
       C. passive consciousness
       D. active consciousness

A   3. Which of the following activities is NOT associated with
       "active" consciousness?
       A. listening to music
       B. planning
       C. decision making
       D. initiating actions

B   4. The level of consciousness that includes such activities as
       electrical brain patterns and hormone changes is the:
       A. conscious
       B. nonconscious
       C. preconscious
       D. unconscious

C   5. The level of consciousness which deals with memories of
       important events that may be brought to awareness is the:
       A. conscious
       B. nonconscious
       C. preconscious
       D. unconscious

A   6. The level of consciousness which contains undesireable
       memories or feelings is the:
       A. unconscious
       B. preconscious
       C. nonconscious
       D. conscious

HYPNOSIS AND CONSCIOUSNESS

C   7. An altered state of awareness which is sometimes called a
        "trauce" is called:
        A. preconscious
        B. animal magnetism
        C. hypnosis
        D. passive consciousness

B   8. Mesmer's system of healing during the 1700's which included
        current elements of hynosis was called:
        A. primal therapy
        B. animal magnetism
        C. trancetation
        D. hypnotic susceptibility

C   9. A device which is used to identify a person's chances of
        being hypnotized is called the:
        A. Hypnosis Scale
        B. Western Hypnosis Test
        C. Stanford Hypnotic Susceptibility Scale
        D. Morgan Hypnotic Scale

D   10. Only about _____ out of 10 persons can be hypnotized.
        A. 2
        B. 4
        C. 6
        D. 8

APPLICATION: HYPNOSIS AS A CLINICAL TOOL

D   11. Hypnosis is being used increasingly by _____ to help
        crime victims recall past events.
        A. public defenders
        B. prosecuting attorneys
        C. social workers
        D. police

A   12. Hypnotherapy is being used by physicians to aid them in:
        A. delivering babies and surgery
        B. finding out the psychological causes of some diseases
        C. reducing how many drugs they prescibe
        D. diagnosing terminal illnesses

D   13. Hypnosis is limited in its usefulness because:
        A. "pseudomemories" may be produced
        B. major surgery usually requires chemical anesthesia
        C. several states ban police from hypnotic questioning
        D. all of the above

SLEEP AND DREAMS

SLEEP

A   14. Which theory believes that sleep serves as a time period
         when energy is restored to the organism?
         A. energy conservation
         B. behavioral adaptive
         C. biological rhythm
         D. neurological benefit

B   15. Which theory incorporates the notion that sleep patterns
         were shaped by environmental pressures over time?
         A. energy conservation
         B. behavioral adaptive
         C. biological rhythm
         D. neurological benefit

C   16. One who believes sleep is a natural rhythm governed by
         one's biological clock accepts the _____ theory of sleep.
         A. energy conservation
         B. behavioral adaptive
         C. biological rhythm
         D. neurological benefit

C   17. Circadian rhythms or daily cycles are especially relevant
         to which theory of sleep?
         A. energy conservation
         B. behavioral adaptive
         C. biological rhythm
         D. neurological benefit

B   18. Sleep researchers call the time between when you go to bed
         sleepy and wake up rested as your _____ sleep length.
         A. common
         B. natural
         C. ideal
         D. healthy

D   19. The measure of muscular activity near the chin during sleep
         is the:
         A. electroencephalogram
         B. electrocardiogram
         C. electrooculogram
         D. electromyogram

C   20. During sleep, an electrical recording of one's eye
         movements is the:
         A. electroencephalogram
         B. electrocardiogram
         C. electrooculogram
         D. electromyogram

D   21. One consequence of going for long periods without sleep is:
        A. long term psychosis with hallucinations
        B. an inability to engage in vigorous physical exercise
        C. memory loss for the time spent awake
        D. a "catch-up" period of about one night's sleep when one
           does go to sleep

C   22. A common way to reduce the length of time you sleep each
        night is to:
        A. go to bed earlier
        B. go to bed later
        C. take naps in the day
        D. eat a small meal before going to bed

B   23. Which is NOT a characteristic of NREM sleep?
        A. the brain is relatively inactive
        B. there is a minimum of eye movement
        C. the body is immobile and without reflexes
        D. nondream-like thoughts

B   24. Which is NOT a characteristic of REM sleep?
        A. the brain is quite active
        B. there are few eye movements
        C. the body appears to be paralyzed
        D. detailed dream images

C   25. There are _____ sleep stages that characterize a typical
        night's sleep.
        A. 3
        B. 4
        C. 5
        D. 6

B   26. Dreams most often occur during:
        A. the beginning of sleep
        B. REM sleep
        C. NREM sleep
        D. sleep with delta waves

DREAMS

A   27. Dream research has found that:
        A. all people dream
        B. dreams last about 10 seconds
        C. most people have two dreams per night
        D. women dream twice as often as men

D   28. Research on "dream deprivation" has found that:
        A. dreams in color are remembered better
        B. we increase our dreams about sexual matters
        C. people tend to sleep longer
        D. a certain amount of dreaming is a necessity

B   29. Freud believed that by interpreting dreams he could expose
         the dream's:
         A. manifest content
         B. latent content
         C. function
         D. purpose

D   30. Which is NOT true about dream content?
         A. color appears in about one-third of all dreams
         B. most dreams involve two or more people
         C. men's dreams have more aggression and hostility than
            women's
         D. female's dreams are more achievement oriented than
            male's

APPLICATION: DIAGNOSIS AND TREATMENT OF SLEEP DISORDERS

A   31. Bad dreams that generally occur toward morning are:
         A. nightmares
         B. night terrors
         C. somnambulisms
         D. insomniacs

D   32. Which is NOT a characteristic of night terrors?
         A. they occur during NREM sleep
         B. the sufferer returns to sleep without waking
         C. they usually occur during the first few hours of sleep
         D. the sufferer clearly remembers the episode

B   33. Somnambulism, or sleepwalking, often accompanies:
         A. insomnia
         B. night terrors
         C. nightmares
         D. sleep deprivation

B   34. About _____ of all 3-8 year old children have nightmares
         and night terrors.
         A. one-third
         B. one-fourth
         C. one-half
         D. two-thirds

B   35. Sleeping too little or not being able to fall asleep, both
         prevalent sleep disorders, are called:
         A. somnabulism
         B. insomnia
         C. enuresis
         D. hypersomnia

A   36. A questionnaire study of adults over 30 years of age found
         that as many as _____% of those females studied had
         problems with insomnia.
         A. 14
         B. 23
         C. about 33
         D. 50

C   37. Drugs which, at least initially, help with problems of
         insomnia are:
         A. various aspirins
         B. tranquilizers
         C. barbiturates
         D. narcotics

A   38. Drug-dependency insomnia is frequently found in people who:
         A. habitually use sleep medications
         B. drink excessively on weekends
         C. are taking pain relief medications
         D. use "street" drugs

B   39. Withdrawal from the habitual use of sleep medications is
         often complicated by:
         A. excessive weight gain
         B. intensified insomnia
         C. shorter periods of sleep
         D. longer periods of sleep

B   40. Excessive daytime sleepiness, or _____ usually involves
         sleeping too much or continuous fatigue.
         A. insomnia
         B. hypersomnia
         C. sleep apnea
         D. narcolepsy

D   41. Which is a characteristic of sleep apnea?
         A. it mostly affects overweight females
         B. it is related to psychological depression
         C. only hypersomniacs have it
         D. effective treatments exist

A   42. Sleep apnea involves an inability to:
         A. breathe and sleep at the same time
         B. fall asleep quickly
         C. sleep without breathing heavily
         D. sleep and dream at the same time

A   43. Severe sleep apnea, commonly known as "crib death," is
         properly known as:
         A. Sudden Infant Death Syndrome (SIDS)
         B. narcolepsy
         C. bruxism
         D. enuresis

D   44. It is not uncommon for some sleep apnea patients to wake up
         _____ times per night in an effort to breathe.
         A. 50
         B. 100
         C. 250
         D. 500

C   45. Which is NOT a characteristic of narcolepsy?
         A. excessive daytime drowsiness
         B. loss of muscle control
         C. develops in later adulthood
         D. sufferers fall asleep at inappropriate moments

B   46. Falling asleep while making love or driving a car may mean
         you have:
         A. hypersomnia
         B. narcolepsy
         C. cataplexy
         D. sleep apnea

C   47. Most patients with narcolepsy will, by the time they are
         40, be:
         A. cured
         B. adjusted to their new life style
         C. partially or completely disabled
         D. sleeping very little each night

D   48. Sleep disorders such as apnea and narcolepsy are disabling
         conditions that:
         A. usually are treated successfully
         B. are diagnosed by adulthood
         C. occur more frequently in children
         D. often go undiagnosed

DRUG-INDUCED ALTERATIONS IN CONSCIOUSNESS

D   49. Licit drugs are:
         A. not usually promoted or advertised
         B. always prescribed by a physician
         C. more powerful than other types
         D. legal and sanctioned by a particular culture

D   50. Illicit drugs are:
         A. rarely abused
         B. used primarily for experimental use
         C. used by everyone
         D. typically have dangerous or undesirable side effects

A   51. Experimental use of drugs is motivated by:
          A. curiosity
          B. pleasure
          C. vocational problems
          D. performance demands

C   52. The use of stimulants at work or drugs to relieve boredom
          represent _____ use of drugs.
          A. experimental
          B. recreational
          C. circumstantial
          D. intensive

A   53. When a drug needs to be given in larger doses with repeated
          use, what is said to have occurred?
          A. tolerance
          B. physical dependence
          C. psychological dependence
          D. it has become a narcotic

B   54. When bodily processes are modified due to continued drug
          usage, _____ dependence is said to have occurred.
          A. illicit
          B. physical
          C. biological
          D. psychological

A   55. Which is a false statement about psychological dependence?
          A. it follows physical dependence
          B. it is associated with both illicit and licit drugs
          C. it is associated with increased drug use
          D. it represents misuse of a drug

NARCOTICS

C   56. Narcotic drugs:
          A. are uncommon today
          B. are sometimes sold "over the counter"
          C. numb the senses and produce euphoria
          D. are also called stimulants

D   57. Which of the following is NOT a narcotic drug:
          A. opium
          B. morphine
          C. heroin
          D. alcohol

B   58. Which narcotic drug was once sold legally in drug stores?
          A. morphine
          B. opium
          C. heroin
          D. methedrine

B   59. A narcotic drug which relieves pain, was widely used during
         the civil war, and which is still prescribed today is:
         A. opium
         B. morphine
         C. heroin
         D. methedrine

C   60. A strong narcotic which can produce a expanding tolerance
         after using it only 2 or 3 weeks is:
         A. opium
         B. morphine
         C. heroin
         D. methedrine

SEDATIVES

D   61. Drugs which have a tranquilizing or calming effect by
         depressing the activity of the central nervous system are:
         A. narcotics
         B. stimulants
         C. amphetamines
         D. sedatives

A   62. Barbiturates are interesting in their pharmacologic
         activity in that they:
         A. produce a euphoric "lift" or depression depending on the
            dosage
         B. are non-addictive
         C. are long lasting
         D. are more potent than LSD

C   63. Physical dependence on barbiturates is _____ difficult to
         produce than narcotic drugs, and withdrawal symptoms are _
         ____ dangerous.
         A. less ; more
         B. less ; less
         C. more ; more
         D. more ; less

D   64. Alcohol is a(n) _____ drug which acts as a central
         nervous system _____.
         A. licit ; stimulant
         B. illicit ; stimulant
         C. illicit ; depressant
         D. licit ; depressant

B   65. The outcome of drinking six (6) ounces of 90 proof whiskey
         is:
         A. relaxation and loss of inhibition
         B. slurred speech and overconfidence
         C. distorted sensations and drowsiness
         D. loss of conscious control over movements

C   66. Consumption of six (6) ounces of 90 proof whiskey leads to
        a _____ percent blood alcohol level.
        A. .05
        B. .10
        C. .15
        D. .20

D   67. An estimated _____ million Americans have a severe
        drinking problem.
        A. 2 to 3
        B. 5 to 8
        C. 6 to 10
        D. 12 to 15

A   68. Which of the following facts was NOT provided in the 1978
        Presidential report on alcohol related problems?
        A. alcoholism was the leading cause of deaths the past 25
           years
        B. there has been a shift from public to private drinking
           the last 30 years
        C. about 38% of state mental patients have a diagnosis of
           alcoholism
        D. for those who have committed homicides, as many as 86%
           were using alcohol at the time

STIMULANTS

A   69. The most widely used stimulant drugs are found in:
        A. coffee and tobacco
        B. pills prescribed by physicians
        C. foods with lots of salt
        D. cough medicines

B   70. Caffeine is commonly found in:
        A. tobacco products
        B. soft drinks and coffee
        C. sleeping pills
        D. birth control pills

D   71. Excessive use of caffeine and nicotine can lead to:
        A. tolerance
        B. physical dependency
        C. psychological dependency
        D. all of the above

C   72. Stimulant drugs, such as dexedrine and benzedrine, are:
        A. sedatives
        B. hallucinogens
        C. amphetamines
        D. narcotics

B   73. The text used Johnny Cash's attempt to deal with fatigue as
        an illustration of _____ addiction.
        A. alcohol
        B. amphetamine
        C. nebutal
        D. cocaine

B   74. The most dangerous amphetamine is:
        A. preludin
        B. "speed" or methedrine
        C. nebutal
        D. LSD

A   75. A state characterized by paranoid delusional thinking,
        induced by "speed" addiction, is called:
        A. amphetamine psychosis
        B. drug overdose
        C. withdrawal symptoms
        D. drug psychosis

D   76. One disturbing aspect of the misuse of amphetamines is that
        they:
        A. are relatively inexpensive
        B. build up a quick tolerance
        C. are easily obtained
        D. often are initially prescribed by a physician

B   77. Cocaine may be characterized as:
        A. an experimentally used drug
        B. a drug which can lead to severe psychological dependence
        C. a general depressant
        D. a licit drug

B   78. Available statistics from 1980 suggest that _____ use has
        grown most rapidly in the last 20 years.
        A. methedrine
        B. cocaine
        C. LSD
        D. PCP

D   79. Cocaine is typically consumed by:
        A. "speed balling"
        B. swallowing pills
        C. injection
        D. intranasal ingestion

A   80. It is now believed that excessive cocaine use can lead to
        _____, but that a _____ will not develop.
        A. psychological dependence ; tolerance
        B. physical dependence ; tolerance
        C. tolerance ; psychological dependence
        D. physical dependence ; psychological dependence

HALLUCINOGENS

D   81. Drugs which produce alterations in perception, thinking, and emotions, and are sometimes called psychedelics are:
A. amphetamines
B. stimulants
C. narcotics
D. hallucinogens

A   82. A commonly used hallucinogen is:
A. marijuana
B. cocaine
C. speed or methedrine
D. all of the above

A   83. The most powerful psychedelic drug is:
A. LSD
B. PCP
C. marijuana
D. hashish

B   84. Visual hallucinations which occur days or even weeks after drug use are associated with which drug?
A. "speed"
B. LSD
C. "angel dust"
D. hashish

D   85. Which is NOT a characteristic of phencyclidine (PCP or "angel dust") use?
A. dissociation from surroundings
B. uninhibited actions
C. pain insensitivity
D. large doses are needed for an effect

C   86. Which hallucinogen is considered a "mild" substance, yet it has the most regular users?
A. LSD
B. PCP
C. marijuana
D. hashish

B   87. Hashish has what in common with mariujuana?
A. "flashbacks"
B. tetrahydrocannabinol (THC)
C. mescaline
D. psilocybin

C   88. Marijuana usage leads to:
         A. aggressive behavior
         B. antisocial behavior
         C. dreamy, euphoric state
         D. rapid psychological dependence

APPLICATION: SELF-REGULATION WITH MEDITATION

D   89. A type of self-regulation technique used as an alternative
         to drugs is known as:
         A. meditation
         B. transcendental meditation
         C. progressive relaxation
         D. all of the above

B   90. Which of the following statements is FALSE?
         A. meditation has been practiced for at least seven
            centuries
         B. those people under a true trancendental meditation
            state have supernatural powers
         C. transcendental meditation is a westernized form of
            meditation
         D. meditation can lead to heightened powers of
            concentration and personal enlightenment

C   91. A newer technique (compared to TM) used to improve
         self-regulation is called:
         A. transcendental meditation
         B. TM
         C. progressive relaxation
         D. combination thinking

ON THE HORIZON

C   92. A study by Wallace, et. al. (1982) to evaluate the
         relationship between the TM technique and aging found that:
         A. there was no relationship
         B. that TM may enhance the biological aging process
         C. that TM may retard the biological aging process
         D. that one's psychological age was younger with TM use

FURTHER READING SUGGESTIONS

Benson, H. (1976). The relaxation response. New York: Avon Books.

Dement, W. C. (1976). Some must watch while some must sleep. Stanford, CA: Stanford Alumni Association.

Ornstein, R. E. (Ed.) (1974). The nature of human consciousness. New York: Viking.

Ray, O. S. Drugs, society, and human behavior. (2nd ed.). St. Louis, Mo.: C. V. Mosby.

Smith, S. (1973). ESP and hypnosis. New York: Macmillan.

Tart, C. T. (Ed.) (1972). Altered states of consciousness. New York: Doubleday.

- CHAPTER 6 -

CONDITIONING AND LEARNING

OUTLINE

I. Introduction: Pathological Gambling - the personal and professional life of a pathological gambler whose behavior centers around obtaining more money for gambling

II. Classical and Instrumental Conditioning

A. Classical (respondent) conditioning - a basic form of LEARNING called CLASSICAL CONDITIONING is based upon REFLEX and RESPONDENT (REFLEX) BEHAVIOR being elicited by stimuli
   1. Pavlov's contribution to the psychology of learning - his original work with a salivating dog incorporating neutral stimulus, orienting reflex and the concept of HABITUATION; stimuli and responses associated over trials; the LAW OF CLASSICAL (RESPONDENT) CONDITIONING with the terms UNCONDITIONED STIMULUS (UCS), UNCONDITIONED RESPONSE (UCR), CONDITIONED STIMULUS (CS), and CONDITIONED RESPONSE (CR); conditioned indicates an association
   2. Personal profile: Ivan P. Pavlov (1849-1936) - Russian researcher's lab activities and contributions
   3. Acquisition of classically conditioned responses - the acquisition stage is quantified by amplitude and/or latency of conditioned response

    4. Timing and conditioning – the stimulus and response
       related in <u>temporal contiguity</u>; four such relationships –
       <u>standard pairing procedure</u>,   <u>delayed pairing procedure</u>,
       <u>simultaneous conditioning</u>, <u>backward conditioning</u>; newer
       thought favors <u>predictive contingency</u> as the basis of
       conditioning rather than contiguity
    5. Watson's interpretation of learning – He believed all
       learning occured by classical conditioning

B. Instrumental (operant) conditioning – an operant behavior or
   response is <u>instrumental</u> on environment; LAW OF INSTRUMENTAL
   (OPERANT) CONDITIONING says REINFORCEMENT strengthens
   response; DISCRIMINATIVE STIMULUS offers <u>cue</u> or <u>signal</u> value
   for response; behavior is <u>controlled</u> by <u>contingent</u>
   reinforcement
    1. Thorndike's contribution to the psychology of learning –
       one of the first Americans to study instrumental
       conditioning; generated the <u>law of effect</u> where the S–R
       association is stamped in because of <u>effects</u> that
       followed response
    2. Skinner's contribution to the psychology of learning –
       his work with pigeons in Skinner box; instrumental
       conditioning is a <u>discrete-trial procedure</u> while operant
       conditioning is a <u>free-responding procedure</u>
    3. Personal profile: B. F. Skinner (1904-   ) – American
       who applied operant conditioning principles to both
       missile firings and rearing his daughter; author of <u>The</u>
       <u>Behavior of Organisms</u>, <u>Walden Two</u>, and <u>Beyond Freedom and</u>
       <u>Dignity</u>
    4. Acquisition of operantly conditioned responses – operant
       behavior is measured by RATE OF RESPONDING and is
       recorded on a <u>cumulative record</u>; the <u>operant level</u>
       (before any conditioning) changes with <u>operant</u>
       <u>conditioning</u>

C. Application: Extinction of conditioned responses –
   EXTINCTION weakens or eliminates responses; SPONTANEOUS
   RECOVERY describes the brief recurrance of response; <u>phobias</u>
   and <u>school phobias</u> are effectively treated with <u>systematic</u>
   <u>desensitization</u> and <u>counterconditioning</u>; the treatment of
   <u>enuresis</u> is presented

III. Principles of Learning and the Interaction of Classical and
    Instrumental Conditioning – shows how classical and
    instrumental conditioning interact to produce complex behavior

   A. Operant conditioning of respondent behavior – conditioning
      of autonomic responses supports respondent and operant
      interaction; discusses how <u>biofeedback</u> influences
      "involuntary" behavior

B. Principle of reinforcement: a <u>reinforcer</u> increases or maintains response rate; two types of reinforcing stimuli – UNCONDITIONED (PRIMARY) REINFORCING STIMULI such as food and water are unlearned while CONDITIONED (SECONDARY) REINFORCING STIMULI such as money and praise are learned; POSITIVE REINFORCERS work by their presentation while NEGATIVE REINFORCERS work by their withdrawal – thus there is an <u>unconditioned positive reinforcing stimulus</u>, an <u>unconditioned negative reinforcing stimulus</u>, a <u>conditioned positive reinforcing stimulus</u>, and a <u>conditioned negative reinforcing stimulus</u>; accidental reinforcement may cause SUPERSTITOUS BEHAVIOR

C. Reinforcement schedules: there are three general types of <u>schedules of reinforcement</u> – CONTINUOUS REINFORCEMENT, CONTINUOUS NONREINFORCEMENT, PARTIAL REINFORCEMENT SCHEDULES; two main classes of partial or intermittent reinforcement schedules are based on the passage of time (<u>interval</u>) or the number of responses (<u>ratio</u>), yield four separate schedules – FIXED-INTERVAL (FI) SCHEDULES , VARIABLE-INTERVAL (VI) SCHEDULES, FIXED-RATIO (FR) SCHEDULES, and VARIABLE-RATIO (VR) SCHEDULES; the greater <u>resistance to extinction</u> under partial inforcement schedules is known as the PARTIAL REINFORCEMENT EFFECT

D. Stimulus control of behavior: a discriminative stimulus, or S^D , sets the occasion for response while $S^\triangle$ sets the occasion for nonreinforced responding
   1. STIMULUS GENERALIZATION, when the response occurs to other than originally conditioned stimulus; shows a <u>generalization gradient</u> representing the degree of stimulus similarity
   2. STIMULUS DISCRIMINATION involves making a distinction among stimuli and is obtained by DIFFERENTIAL REINFORCEMENT
   3. Shaping complex chains of behavior – reinforcing successive approximations (SHAPING) leads to the final behavior; can shape to create a CHAIN OF BEHAVIOR; examples with animals and humans are provided
   4. Biological constraints on shaped learned behaviors: learning without response – contingent reinforcement (AUTOSHAPING) is influenced by a <u>species-specific response</u> which is fixed and universal for a species; species-specific response as an aide or hinderance to learning; PREPAREDNESS principle says the learner may be <u>prepared</u>, <u>unprepared</u>, or <u>contraprepared</u> to learn

E. Aversive control of behavior: PUNISHMENT reduces response probability; punishment versus negative reinforcement
   1. Escape and avoidance conditioning: in ESCAPE TRAINING a response terminates an aversive stimulus while in AVOIDANCE TRAINING a response enables learner to <u>avoid</u> shock

      2. LEARNED HELPLESSNESS, or failure to respond appropriately in a new situation following uncontrollable aversive stimuli, may explain maladaptive human behaviors

      3. Punishment: An evaluation of its effects - discussion of the value of spanking and other physical punishments as they eliminate or suppress a behavior

F. Application: Behavior modification and self-control techniques - growth of BEHAVIOR MODIFICATION techniques by professionals and nonprofessionals to control the behavior of others; a technique called SELF-CONTROL enables individuals to change their own behavior by <u>changing the stimulus conditions</u>, <u>self-reinforcement</u>, <u>self-punishment</u>, or <u>alternative response training</u>; examples of self-control

IV. Cognitive Learning - a change of intellectual processes (rather than simple S-R associations) is called COGNITIVE LEARNING

A. LATENT LEARNING - learning without any obvious change in behavior at the time of learning; Tolman and his use of a <u>cognitive map</u> in rats

B. INSIGHT LEARNING - learning resulting from sudden perception or grasp of a problem's solution; Kohler and chimpanzee stick problems

C. Application: Learning through observation - Bandura's use of OBSERVATIONAL LEARNING to explain learning through observation without direct reinforcement; example of learning aggressive responses through observation

V. On the Horizon: Behavior Technology in the Coming Years - the widespread use of behavior modification has started the early stages of a <u>behavioral technology</u>; the use of PROGRAMMED INSTRUCTION in education emphasizes the <u>knowledge of results</u> and progression at an individual rate; programmed instruction and computers have created <u>computer assisted instruction</u> to teach reading; a discussion of the future applications of behavior technology

OBJECTIVES

I.   WHAT IS LEARNING?

Learning is defined as any relatively permanent change in behavior that can be attributed to experience or practice. Two major perspectives on learning are (1) the associative, stimulus

- response type which interprets learning as a connection between sensory stimuli and responses, and (2) the cognitive approach which emphasizes the mental activities such as thinking, reasoning, and remembering which change during learning

A 1. The two major perspectives on learning are the:

    A. associative and cognitive
    B. behavioral and mental
    C. permanent and temporary
    D. intentional and unintentional

C 2. Learning is defined as any relative _____ change in behavior that can be attributed to _____.

    A. temporary ; experience or practice
    B. temporary ; rewards or punishments
    C. permanent ; experience or practice
    D. permanent ; rewards or punishments

3. How do the associative and cognitive approaches differ in their interpretation of learning?

II. LIST THE ESSENTIAL CHARACTERISTICS OF CLASSICAL (RESPONDENT) CONDITIONING.

Initially, a stimulus (UCS) elicits a reflexive response (UCR) prior to any learning. Then, a neutral, yet noticeable, stimulus (US) is repeatedly paired with the UCS in a short temporal contiguity. After a number of these US and UCS pairings, or trials, the US begins to elicit a conditioned response (CR) similar to the original UCR. Stimuli are viewed as eliciting responses or, put in another way, the organism responds to its environment. Little if any conditioning (or associating an "old" response with a "new" stimulus) occurs when the UCS precedes the presentation of the US.

D 1. Which of the following is a characteristic of classical conditioning?

    A. the UCS should precede the CS for optimum learning
    B. the CS and UCS should be presented with the CR for best conditioning
    C. the reflexive response elicits the non-neutral stimulus
    D. a CS and UCS should be repeatedly paired with each other

C   1. Classical differs from instrumental conditioning on which of
       the following characteristics?

       A. the use of stimuli to explain learning
       B. the use of responses to explain learning
       C. whether the learner is passive or active
       D. whether the learner is capable of thinking

D   2. Classical and instrumental conditioning are similar in that
       they both:

       A. use rewards
       B. use conditioned stimuli
       C. are cognitive examples of learning
       D. view responses and stimuli as being connected

    3. Present the similarities and differences between classical
       and instrumental conditioning.

V. WHAT ARE THE DIFFERENCES BETWEEN PRIMARY AND SECONDARY
    REINFORCERS? BETWEEN POSITIVE AND NEGATIVE REINFORCEMENT? HOW
    DOES PARTIAL REINFORCEMENT AFFECT LEARNING?

    Primary (or unconditioned) reinforcers, abbreviated S^R, have
    the ability to change the probability of a response without any
    prior learning. Examples include food, water, and sleep.
    Secondary (or conditioned) reinforcers, abbreviated S^r, change
    response probability because of their prior association with a
    primary reinforcing stimulus. Almost any stimulus can become a
    secondary reinforcer, and common examples are praise, money,
    the voice of a dog's master, and even stock market quotations.
    Partial (or intermittent) reinforcement influences behavior in
    many ways: (1) speed of acquisition, (2) rate of responding,
    and (3) resistance to extinction. As compared to continuous
    reinforcement, partial reinforcement leads to slower
    acquisition, more variable rates of responding (depending on
    the particular schedule of partial reinforcement) and more
    resistance to extinction.

A   1. Primary and secondary reinforcers differ on the basis of
       their:

       A. ability to reinforce with or without prior learning
       B. ease of consumption by the learner
       C. ability to be beneficial to the learner
       D. presentation before or after the response

D   2. When does little, if any, learning occur during classical conditioning?

   A. when the CS is stronger than the UCS
   B. if the CR is more complex than the UCR
   C. when the learner is young
   D. when the CS follows the UCS during conditioning trials

   3. What are four of the essential characteristics of classical conditioning?

III. WHAT ARE THE BASIC FEATURES OF INSTRUMENTAL (OPERANT) CONDITIONING?

When an operant response (R) is followed by a reinforcing stimulus (S^R), or desirable consequence, then the probability that the R will occur again is increased. Reinforcing stimuli are called positive or negative reinforcers. When a R is followed by an aversive or negative event, then the probability that the R will occur again is reduced. This is called use of punishment. The organism learns that it can control the stimulus consequences in its environment by behaving in particular ways. Sometimes a discriminative stimulus (S^D) precedes the R and serves as a cue or signal that if the R is made, then a S^R or an aversive event will occur.

B   1. In instrumental conditioning, the operant is said to:

   A. react to the environment
   B. control or change the environment
   C. lead to the discriminative stimulus
   D. follow the reinforcing stimulus

   2. Discuss how stimuli and responses are said to influence each other under instrumental (operant) conditioning.

IV. IN WHAT WAYS ARE CLASSICAL AND INSTRUMENTAL CONDITIONING DIFFERENT? IN WHAT WAYS ARE THEY SIMILAR?

Respondent behavior is involuntary, it is elicited by particular stimuli, it is based upon the pairing of two stimuli, and the learner is relatively passive. In contrast, operant behavior is voluntary, it is emitted in the presence of particular stimuli, it is based upon the relationship of a response and a stimulus, and the learner is active by causing changes in the environment. In classical conditioning, behavior is a function of preceding events whereas in instrumental conditioning, behavior is a function of its consequences. Classical and instrumental conditioning are similar in that they are both examples of the associative perspective of learning where stimuli and responses are viewed as being connected to account for learning.

C   2. Which is a characteristic of partial schedules of
          reinforcement?

          A. they lead to low rates of responding
          B. they are more relevant to understanding animal behavior
          C. they can lead to high rates of responding
          D. the responses they influence are less resistant to
             extinction

       3. Differentiate between, and then give examples of, primary
          and secondary reinforcers.

       4. Describe how partial schedules of reinforcement influence
          both the rate of responding and resistance to extinction.
          Give examples whenever possible.

VI.   WHAT DISTINGUISHES COGNITIVE LEARNING FROM ASSOCIATIVE
       LEARNING?

       Associative learning is considered the connecting of
       stimulus-response associations. In contrast, cognitive
       learning involves a consideration of the intellectual
       (cognitive) process, such as thinking, reasoning, and memory.
       In both animals and humans, learning is considered the
       formation of categories, the construction of intricate mental
       maps of the world, and various processes of reasoning. One of
       the first scientists to question associative learning and to
       support a more cognitive type of learning was Tolman, whose
       work on latent learning and the formation of cognitive maps
       (mental pictures of a maze) in rats presented learning as
       occurring without any direct reinforcement.

B   1. Which is a process under a cognitive theory of learning?

          A. formation of categories after S-R associations
          B. construction of mental maps of the environment
          C. specific responses to a particular stimulus
          D. behavioral shaping and chains of behavior

D   2. Tolman, who pioneered the study of latent learning in rats,
          referred to rats as using _____ to solve maze problems.

          A. S-R associations
          B. observational learning
          C. insight
          D. cognitive maps

       3. In what ways does cognitive learning differ from
          associative, stimulus-response learning? Give examples when
          possible.

MULTIPLE-CHOICE QUESTIONS

INTRODUCTION

C 1. To obtain money for his pathological gambling activity, Charlie K. had to:
   A. borrow from his friends
   B. steal from his employer
   C. use scams to cheat people out of their money
   D. sell his home and car

B 2. Any relatively permanent change in behavior that can be attributed to experience or practice is called:
   A. respondent behavior
   B. learning
   C. maturation
   D. associative acquisition

C 3. Associative, stimulus-response approaches view learning as:
   A. a more elementary form characteristic of lower animals
   B. occurring faster than cognitive approaches
   C. a connection between responses and stimuli
   D. a longer lasting form as compared to cognitive types

C 4. Which of the following is an example of a cognitive approach to learning?
   A. operant
   B. shaping
   C. insight
   D. respondent

CLASSICAL (RESPONDENT) CONDITIONING

D 5. A basic form of learning that takes place when a neutral stimulus is repeatedly paired with a stimulus that already elicits a reflexive response is called:
   A. instrumental conditioning
   B. respondent learning
   C. reflex learning
   D. classical conditioning

A 6. An unlearned reaction to a specific stimulus is called a:
   A. reflex
   B. behavior arc
   C. conditioned response
   D. innate arc

B   7. A response made by humans and animals that is <u>elicited</u> by
        environmental stimuli is known as a(n):
        A. learned component
        B. respondent behavior
        C. stimulus-response behavior
        D. S-R association

C   8. A simple form of learning that involves a change in behavior
        (such as when an orienting reflex disappears) is called:
        A. fatigue
        B. saturation
        C. habituation
        D. classical conditioning

B   9. Which law of conditioning states that when two stimuli are
        paired, and one causes a reflex response, a new reflex is
        created when the previously neutral stimulus comes to elicit
        the response?
        A. habituation
        B. classical (respondent)
        C. instrumental
        D. associative

D   10. What person's name is associated with formulating the basic
        concepts of classical conditioning?
        A. Watson
        B. Thorndike
        C. Skinner
        D. Pavlov

A   11. In the text's example of respondent conditioning, the tone
        was the _____ while the food was the _____.
        A. CS ; UCS
        B. UCS ; UCR
        C. CS ; UCR
        D. UCS ; CS

D   12. Any stimulus that initially brings forth an unconditioned
        response is called a(n) _____ stimulus.
        A. previous
        B. eliciting
        C. conditioned
        D. unconditioned

A   13. What is the name given to the response that is elicited by a
        UCS?
        A. unconditioned
        B. learned
        C. secondary
        D. conditioned

C   14. Any stimulus that elicits a conditioned response is called
         a(n) _____ stimulus.
         A. eliciting
         B. unconditioned
         C. conditioned
         D. previous

D   15. Any response elicited by a conditioned stimulus is called
         a(n) _____ response.
         A. secondary
         B. learned
         C. unconditioned
         D. conditioned

B   16. Which statement is FALSE about classical conditioning?
         A. the CS and CR are associated during the acquisition stage
         B. the amplitude of the CR decreases with conditioning
         C. each pairing of the tone and food is called a trial
         D. the CS can be viewed as predicting the UCS, thus giving
            information to the learner

C   17. Classical conditioning typically occurs most rapidly with
         which type of pairing between the CS and UCS?
         A. simultaneous
         B. delayed
         C. standard
         D. backward

C   18. The experiment conducted by Watson and Rayner with infant
         Albert primarily demonstrated:
         A. the ease of conditioning in children
         B. the predictive contingency relationship between the CS
            and UCS
         C. how emotional responses such as fear may be conditioned
         D. children's unlearned fears of white rats and monkeys

INSTRUMENTAL (OPERANT) CONDITIONING

D   19. Which statement is TRUE about instrumental or operant
         conditioning.
         A. behavior is involuntary
         B. the learner is relatively passive
         C. it is based on the pairing of two stimuli
         D. the learner operates on the situation by the response it
            emits

A   20. Which law of conditioning states that if an operant response
       is followed by a reinforcing stimulus, the probability of
       the response occurring again is increased?
       A. instrumental
       B. classical
       C. respondent
       D. associative

B   21. The basic element of instrumental or operant learning can be
       diagramed which way?
       A. $S_{food} \longrightarrow R$
       B. $R \longrightarrow S^R$
       C. $S \longrightarrow R$
       D. IL = S + R

C   22. The term given to a stimulus consequence that strengthens a
       preceding response is:
       A. operant conditioning
       B. discriminative stimulus
       C. reinforcement
       D. positive aftereffect

A   23. A cue or signal which indicates that a response is likely to
       be followed by a reinforcement is called a _____ stimulus.
       A. discriminative
       B. reinforcing
       C. instrumental
       D. conditioned

D   24. A critical element in instrumental (operant) conditioning is
       that the reinforcement is said to be _____ upon the
       response.
       A. relied
       B. based
       C. conditioned
       D. contingent

B   25. What idea is at the core of instrumental or operant
       conditioning?
       A. the learner does not have to think about the consequences
       B. behavior is a function of its consequences
       C. this form of learning is the easiest for the organism
       D. stimuli elicit responses

A   26. Thorndike's research with cats in a "puzzle-box" led him to
       generate his instrumental conditioning law of _____.
       A. effect
       B. parsimony
       C. contingency
       D. reaction

B   27. Unlike   classical   conditioning,   behavior   in   operant
        conditioning is most often measured in terms of the
        _____ of responding.
        A. volume
        B. rate
        C. strength
        D. magnitude

APPLICATION: EXTINCTION OF CONDITIONED RESPONSES

B   28. An operant or conditioned response may be weakened or
        eliminated through a process called:
        A. elimination
        B. extinction
        C. forgetting
        D. termination

C   29. One characteristic of extinguishing an operant response is
        the fact that it:
        A. decreases rapidly and evenly
        B. decreases slowly at first, but then very rapidly
        C. may increase in frequency or forcefulness before
           decreasing
        D. may remain present without any reinforcement

A   30. The situation where there is a spontaneous and brief
        recurrence of a response following extinction is known as:
        A. spontaneous recovery
        B. relearning
        C. end of fatigue
        D. habituation

A   31. According to the text, systematic desensitization has been
        used to effectively treat _____ through conditioning
        principles.
        A. school phobias
        B. stealing hub caps
        C. vomiting
        D. poor school performance

PRINCIPLES OF LEARNING AND THE INTERACTION OF CLASSICAL AND INSTRUMENTAL CONDITIONING

C   32. Recent developments in the study of learning have found that:
A. respondent conditioning is better than operant
B. classical conditioning typically follows instrumental
C. respondent and operant conditioning frequently occur together
D. classical conditioning is limited to the activity of the autonomic nervous system

OPERANT CONDITIONING OF RESPONDENT BEHAVIOR

B   33. The operant conditioning of respondent behavior has been demonstrated in research by Miller and DiCara with:
A. running speeds in monkeys
B. heart rate changes in rats
C. key pressing rates in pigeons
D. weight gain in humans

PRINCIPLE OF REINFORCEMENT

D   34. A stimulus which has the ability to reinforce without prior learning is called a _____ stimulus.
A. desirable
B. necessary
C. secondary (conditioned) reinforcing
D. primary (unconditioned) reinforcing

C   35. A stimulus which has the ability to reinforce because of its prior association with a primary reinforcing stimulus is called a _____ stimulus.
A. desirable
B. necessary
C. secondary (conditioned) reinforcing
D. primary (unconditioned) reinforcing

C   36. Which of the following is a secondary reinforcer?
A. food
B. water
C. money
D. sleep

C   37. Which of the following is a primary reinforcer?
A. the voice of a dog's master
B. stock market quotations
C. sleep
D. verbal praise

A   38. The stimuli whose presentation is reinforcing are called
         ____ reinforcers.
         A. positive
         B. negative
         C. needed
         D. desirable

B   39. The stimuli which serve as reinforcers when they are
         withdrawn or removed are called _____ reinforcers.
         A. positive
         B. negative
         C. unneeded
         D. undesirable

D   40. When a rat presses a bar to turn off a buzzer (which was
         previously paired with shock), the termination of the buzzer
         is a _____ reinforcing stimulus.
         A. unconditioned positive
         B. unconditioned negative
         C. conditioned positive
         D. conditioned negative

B   41. A student insists on sitting at a particular desk or wearing
         certain clothes while taking an exam is showing what kind of
         behavior?
         A. conditioned
         B. superstitious
         C. accidental
         D. non-reinforced

REINFORCEMENT SCHEDULES

A   42. A reinforcement schedule where each response that is emitted
         is reinforced is called:
         A. continuous
         B. partial
         C. regular
         D. maximum

D   43. When no response is rewarded in instrumental conditioning,
         it is known as:
         A. regular nonreinforcement
         B. partial reinforcement
         C. continuous reinforcement
         D. continuous nonreinforcement

C   44. In partial schedules of reinforcement, the response
         consequences are said to be:
         A. maximizing
         B. irregular
         C. intermittent
         D. optimum

A   45. A salaried worker whose behavior is maintained by weekly
        paychecks is reinforced under which reinforcement schedule?
        A. fixed interval
        B. variable interval
        C. fixed ratio
        D. variable ratio

B   46. An instructor who gives "pop-quizzes" for extra credit is
        reinforcing the student's studying under a _____ schedule
        of reinforcement.
        A. fixed interval
        B. variable interval
        C. fixed ratio
        D. variable ratio

C   47. A shirtmaker who is paid on the basis of how many buttons
        are sewed on is rewarded under a _____ schedule of
        reinforcement.
        A. fixed interval
        B. variable interval
        C. fixed ratio
        D. variable ratio

D   48. A constant, high rate of sustained responding is achieved
        with which reinforcement schedule?
        A. fixed interval
        B. variable interval
        C. fixed ratio
        D. variable ratio

B   49. A ratio schedule of reinforcement is based upon the
        _____ of responses made by the organism.
        A. interval
        B. number
        C. forcefulness
        D. length

D   50. Which of the following is a FALSE statement?
        A. slot-machine gambling is rewarded under a ratio schedule
           of reinforcement
        B. behaviors rewarded under partial schedules are resistant
           to extinction
        C. the two main schedules of intermittent reinforcement are
           called interval and ratio
        D. intermittent reinforced behaviors extinguish most rapidly

C   51. The partial reinforcement effect refers to what general
        issue?
        A. ease of learning
        B. high levels of responding
        C. resistance to extinction differences
        D. a major difference between classical and operant
           conditioning

STIMULUS CONTROL OF BEHAVIOR

B   52. The tendency for stimuli other than the one that was
         originally conditioned to now evoke the conditioned response
         is referred to as:
         A. stimulus variability
         B. stimulus generalization
         C. the generalization gradient
         D. the spreading effect

B   53. Stimulus discrimination is learning to:
         A. choose the best stimulus
         B. make distinctions among stimuli
         C. choose between positive and negative reinforcers
         D. detect the most prominent stimulus

D   54. A pigeon learns to peck at a blue key. Later, it will peck
         at a decreasing rate to blue keys of a different hue or
         brightness. This demonstrates a(n):
         A. equivalent stimulus
         B. stimulus control
         C. stimulus discrimination
         D. generalization gradient

A   55. In operant conditioning, the reinforcing of some responses
         but not others is called:
         A. differential reinforcement
         B. shaping
         C. chaining behavior
         D. response discrimination

A   56. One can "mold" the behavior of another by selectively
         reinforcing correct responses and not reinforcing incorrect
         ones. This is called:
         A. shaping
         B. response approximation
         C. chaining behavior
         D. response discrimination

D   57. The example of Barnabus, the rat, who was taught a series of
         different behaviors to earn food, was used to demonstrate
         what shaping technique?
         A. delay of gratification
         B. autoshaping
         C. differential reinforcement
         D. chain of behavior

D   58. Which of the following was used by the text as an example of shaping a complex chain of behaviors?
A. teaching pigeons to tell the difference between red and orange
B. training dogs to salivate to a circle but not an elipse
C. students attending four years of college
D. teaching a mute patient to talk

C   59. What is said to occur when learning occurs "automatically," without response-contingent reinforcement, such as when a pigeon learns to peck a key on its own.
A. self-control
B. reflexive learning
C. autoshaping
D. operant conditioning

D   60. Which of the following was NOT given in the text as an example of a species-specific response?
A. humans talking
B. pigeons pecking a target when food is present
C. dogs circling before reclining
D. horses circling to their left in an arena

A   61. An important characteristic of species-specific responses and their consequences is that they:
A. can prevent reinforcement from controlling behavior
B. are primarily limited to humans
C. are learned very rapidly
D. do not show a generalization gradient

C   62. Under what principle of learning do biological constraints influence what is learned, and how quickly it may be learned?
A. genetic
B. learning-biological
C. preparedness
D. predestination

A   63. A rat pressing a bar is an example of a behavior that it is _____ to learn.
A. unprepared
B. prepared
C. contraprepared
D. ultraprepared

AVERSIVE CONTROL OF BEHAVIOR

A   64. When behavior is influenced by presenting a negative event
         or removing a positive event, we say _____ has occurred.
         A. punishment
         B. aversive control
         C. avoidance conditioning
         D. negative conditioning

D   65. Psychologists define an event as punishment if it:
         A. involves pain
         B. is disagreeable to the one giving the punishment
         C. is partially reinforcing
         D. reduces the probability of a preceding response

C   66. What is an example of a punishment?
         A. turning off a loud television after entering a room
         B. avoiding oncoming traffic when walking across streets
         C. giving a traffic ticket to a speeder
         D. taking off a sweater when the room gets too warm

B   67. What kind of training has occurred when a rat learns to
         press a bar to terminate a shock to its paws?
         A. punishment
         B. escape
         C. avoidance
         D. learned helplessness

B   68. Avoidance and escape training differ in what important way?
         A. the magnitude of the shock used
         B. how often the learner is shocked
         C. the use of an escape area
         D. how rapidly learning occurs

B   69. Maier and Seligman studied dogs that could or could not
         control aversive stimuli. Those that could not, when later
         shocked in a new situation,:
         A. barked more
         B. sat passively and accepted shock
         C. learned faster
         D. learned a new escape behavior

A   70. What is said to result from exposure to aversive stimuli
         that cannot be controlled and that leads to failure to
         behave appropriately in another situation?
         A. learned helplessness
         B. escape training
         C. avoidance training
         D. excessive use of punishment

B   71. Punishment is so popular with parents for modifying
        children's behavior because it:
        A. is better than positive reinforcement
        B. is reinforced by the child's response
        C. is painful
        D. satisfies parents' unconscious aggressive urges

D   72. One example of when punishment has a positive role in
        acquiring a new behavior is in learning to:
        A. drive a car
        B. multiply and add
        C. train a dog to "shake hands"
        D. stay away from hot stove burners

APPLICATION: BEHAVIOR MODIFICATION AND SELF-CONTROL TECHNIQUES

C   73. Techniques for controlling and modifying behavior that use
        principles of learning are collectively called:
        A. learning approaches
        B. conditioning
        C. behavior modification
        D. therapy

D   74. Which behavior modification technique is used when a student
        selects a quiet corner in the library for studying rather
        than the dorm room?
        A. self-reinforcement
        B. self-punishment
        C. self-discipline
        D. self-control

B   75. Which of the following is NOT a technique for achieving
        self-control?
        A. changing the stimulus conditions
        B. response flooding
        C. self-reinforcement
        D. alternate response training

A   76. Examples of self-reinforcement or self-punishment to control
        one's own behavior that were used by the text include:
        A. meeting or dating females and overeating
        B. playing basketball and racketball
        C. golfing and swimming
        D. applying for a job and driving carefully

D   77. A limitation of self-control techniques is that:
        A. they are too time consuming
        B. you must be above average in intelligence
        C. they are hard to learn
        D. you may not adhere to the response contingencies

COGNITIVE LEARNING

A   78. A consideration of the intellectual processes (rather than simple S-R associations) such as reasoning and memory that are involved in learning is referred to as:
   A. cognitive learning
   B. thinking
   C. perceptual learning
   D. latent learning

C   79. Pigeons initially trained to peck at a picture of a person later pecked at pictures of other people without further training. This was the text's example of _____ learning.
   A. purposeful
   B. insight
   C. cognitive
   D. latent

LATENT LEARNING

B   80. Learning that occurs when mental expectations about stimulus relationships develop without a change in overt behavior is called:
   A. passive organization
   B. latent learning
   C. unintentional acquisition
   D. cognitive development

B   81. Tolman's use of the term "cognitive map" to explain maze learning by rats is relevant to:
   A. insight learning
   B. latent learning
   C. learned helplessness
   D. observational learning

INSIGHT LEARNING

A   82. What type of learning is said to involve a sudden perception or grasp of a problem that leads to the problem's solution?
   A. insight
   B. cognitive
   C. observational
   D. latent

C   83. A child who rote-memorizes the multiplication tables, but later recognizes that there are meaningful patterns among the numbers, is demonstrating what form of learning?
A. latent
B. observational
C. insight
D. mathematical

APPLICATION: LEARNING THROUGH OBSERVATION

D   84. Learning without direct reinforcement and perhaps without any overt change in behavior at the time of learning is referred to as _____ learning.
A. latent
B. insight
C. cognitive
D. observational

A   85. Which of the following is a FALSE statement about observational learning:
A. it occurs faster when positive rewards are given regularly
B. much social learning occurs using teachers and peers as models
C. it is similar to latent learning since no immediate behavior change may occur
D. aggressive responses may be learned in this manner

ON THE HORIZON

B   86. Learning to proceed by small steps with knowledge of results provided immediately is a major consideration in:
A. observational learning
B. programmed instruction
C. insight learning
D. psychological therapy

A   87. Computer assisted instruction has been used to teach:
A. children how to read
B. handicapped individuals to walk again
C. pilots how to fly better
D. basic mathematical skills at all ages

— CHAPTER 7 —

MEMORY AND INFORMATION PROCESSING

OUTLINE

I.   Introduction: The Frailties of Human Memory — two examples are given to demonstrate poor human memory (e.g., recognition of a common U.S. coin and an incorrect eyewitness identification); in contrast, human memory can be very good

II. The Nature of Memory — one may separate <u>processes</u> of memory from the <u>structure</u> of memory

  A. Information processing and memory — memory processes can be divided into three categories (encoding, storage, retrieval); the INFORMATION PROCESSING MODEL is first encoded, then stored, and then retrieved; ENCODING involves putting information into memory via a <u>memory code</u>; a STORAGE process holds the information in memory; RETRIEVAL involves the use of stored information

  B. The structure of memory — one model involves three types of memory (sensory memory, short-term memory, long-term memory); REHEARSAL is the conscious repetition of material in short-term memory
     1. Sensory memory — the first storage area where almost all information can be kept for 1-2 seconds is SENSORY MEMORY; ICONIC STORE refers to a visual sensory memory while ECHOIC STORE refers to a sound-oriented sensory memory
     2. Information not lost from sensory store or not removed by incoming information goes to SHORT-TERM MEMORY, which is

the storage of information that is currently being
attended to; the information is forgotten in 15-20
seconds unless it is actively rehearsed

   a. the capacity of short-term memory - a <u>memory-span</u>
<u>procedure</u> tests the <u>capacity</u> of short-term memory;
short-term memory can hold a "magic number" of 7 ± 2
items or chunks; a CHUNK is any meaningful unit of
information; one can't increase the capacity of short
term memory but the amount of material in each chunk
can be increased; thus, the 5 digit but not the 9
digit zip codes can be easily kept in short-term
memory; DISPLACEMENT refers to a new item taking the
place of another in a short-term memory at capacity

   b. how is short-term memory information encoded? -
information is represented mainly in auditory form,
while semantic codes based on <u>meaning</u> are also used

   c. retrieving short-term memory information - it is not
clear if we retrieve information from short-term
memory with a sequential, item-by-item search as many
suggest

3. Long-term memory - the largest part of the memory system
that stores information for indefinite periods is
LONG-TERM MEMORY; the longer an item remains in
short-term memory the more likely it will be placed in
long-term memory; simple repetition or MAINTENANCE
REHEARSAL may transfer information from short-term to
long-term memory; rehearsal which elaborates on the
information and/or uses images and memory aids, called
ELABORATIVE REHEARSAL, helps retention of information in
long-term memory

   a. encoding, storage, and retrieval of LTM information -
long-term memories are most often coded <u>semantically</u>
or by <u>meaning</u>, but also by the way the information
looks, sounds, smells, and tastes; we organize
information in long-term memory in a meaningful way;
CLUSTERING, or "subjective organization" is the
tendency to organize or group items during recall;
RETRIEVAL CUES help us check different parts of
long-term memory while searching for a particular item
of information

   b. measuring retrieval - retrieval is usually measured by
recognition or recall; RECALL involves reproducing
information with the help of retrieval cues;
RECOGNITION involves the correct identification of
some specific item of information and the rejection of
others; multiple-choice tests require recognition;
recognition tasks are easier than recall tasks

C. Short-term and long-term memory: One or two memory systems?
  - the DUAL MEMORY THEORY says that short- and long-term
memory are two distinct systems

1. A dual memory - support for this theory comes from various areas; following electroconvulsive therapy there is the chance of RETROGRADE AMNESIA (forgetting of events just before the shock) which is believed to result from the lack of CONSOLIDATION, or the time consuming process where the memory becomes solidified and durable; sometimes "mental shock" from traumatic events can cause retrograde amnesia; ANTEROGRADE AMNESIA, produced by removal of part of the hippocampus, results in impaired memory for new events but not for older information; FREE RECALL, the recall of learned material in any order, has shown that some information is recalled best; the RECENCY EFFECT describes the recall of newer information best while the PRIMACY EFFECT describes the improved recall of older information (intermediate information, such as items in the middle of a list, is recalled to a lesser degree)

2. The levels-of-processing view - in contrast to the dual memory theory, the LEVELS-OF-PROCESSING VIEW conceptualizes memory as one system composed of a hierarchy of processing levels with "deeper" processing corresponding to better retention

D. The fallibility of reconstruction - since we can't remember every fact about some event, we may show REFABRICATION or the building of a memory from bits and pieces of truth; the refabrication may then become a memory; repeated story telling from one individual to another may result in the shortening of the story (leveling) and/or some features becoming dominant (sharpening); Bartlett's thinking and research suggest that memory is more a process of reconstruction than it is of recollection

E. Application: Eyewitness testimony--psychology goes to court - a series of interesting studies are presented which evaluate the reliability of eyewitness testimony when subjects, through the type of questions asked or the amount and type of external information that was provided, are asked to recall events; the studies clearly show the fallibility of eyewitness accounts by the presentation of misinformation after an event; Loftus suggests that jurors be made to understand the dangers of eyewitness testimony

III. Forgetting

A. Theories of forgetting
   1. Interference theory - this theory says that we forget information when something else we have learned blocks or interferes with recall; in PROACTIVE INTERFERENCE something previously learned interferes with an ability to recall newly learned material; RETROACTIVE INTERFERENCE refers to the fact that learning additional information interferes with the recall of information learned earlier; three factors affect retroactive interference

2. Decay theory - DECAY THEORY assumes that a memory "trace" or change in neural tissue fades or decays from disuse
3. Retrieval failure - the RETRIEVAL FAILURE hypothesis says that "forgotten" information is only temporarily inaccessible because an appropriate retrieval cue is lacking
    a. context-dependent memory - context may serve as a retrieval cue in that recalling something in the same context in which it was learned improves recall; the authors discuss how this pertains to learning in college and preparing for essay and multiple-choice exams
    b. state-dependent memory - retention is improved when one's mood or "state" is the same on occasions of learning and testing
    c. the TOT phenomenon - the TIP-OF-THE-TONGUE (TOT) PHENOMENON refers to our feeling that we know something, that it is on the "tip of the tongue," and with the correct retrieval cue it would surface
4. Motivated forgetting - forgetting something because we "want to" is called MOTIVATED FORGETTING; this poorly understood process may be related to Freud's concept of <u>repression</u> which involves <u>unconsciously</u> motivated <u>forgetting</u>
5. Storage failure - some apparent "forgetting" is due to the fact that the information was never stored in the first place

B. Application: The problem of getting "permanent" information out of memory - examines evidence on permanence of memories
    1. Brain stimulation - Penfield concludes that memories are highly stable while other interpretations of the same data suggest otherwise
    2. Hypnosis - there is no evidence to support the view that hypnotically-induced memories are any more accurate or complete than ordinary, waking memories
    3. Psychoanalysis - it does not seem that all memories are potentially recoverable with <u>psychoanalysis</u>

IV. Improving Memory

A. Organization and memory - the key to effective retrieval from long-term memory is organization; MNEMONIC DEVICES are organizational devices which relate new material to existing, well-learned information; the NARRATIVE-CHAINING METHOD weaves the new information into a story so that they are somehow tied together; the "first-letter-technique" and rhymes are also effective mnemonic devices
    1. Imagery, encoding, and mnemonics - IMAGERY, or forming a mental representation of something that is not physically present, is used to link or associate terms to be remembered

a. the METHOD OF LOCI is a mnemonic device that involves associating new information with a series of specific physical locations (loci) that are already firmly established in memory

b. the KEYWORD METHOD, especially helpful in learning a foreign language vocabulary, associates an English "keyword" (that sounds like some part of the foreign word) with the entire foreign word

B. Elaboration and encoding: The role of meaning - an efficient strategy for encoding material is to elaborate it or give it meaning

C. The role of context in memory - an efficient strategy when the external context is unavailable is to re-create the context mentally

D. Additional memory aids - distributed practice is better than massed practice; other strategies include practicing retrieval and paying more attention to the material initially

E. Application: The SQ3R method - remembering what you've read - the SQ3R method aids in organizing and giving meaning to information as well as in practicing retrieval; the five sequential steps are Survey, Question, Read, Recite, and Review

V. On the Horizon: Memory control - memory control is an issue in George Orwell's 1984 (written in the 1940's); in reality, there is some "memory restructuring" going on in therapy with clients having a history of an unhappy childhood; from a research standpoint, vasopressin has enhanced learning and memory in human subjects, and its application with electroconvulsive therapy patients and with elderly people is being suggested; in contrast, oxytocin impairs retention in animals

OBJECTIVES

I. WHAT ARE THE CORE DISTINCTIONS BETWEEN SENSORY MEMORY, SHORT-TERM MEMORY, AND LONG-TERM MEMORY? HOW IS INFORMATION PROCESSED THROUGH THESE THREE SYSTEMS?

The structure of the memory system is viewed as three separate stores or "boxes," each representing three types of memory: (sensory memory, short-term memory, and long-term memory). Sensory memory holds virtually all the information reaching a sense organ, but it does so only for a short time (1-2 seconds) before the information is lost or is transferred into short-term memory. There is a sensory memory for each sense modality. Short-term memory is that part of memory that holds the contents of one's attention. Whatever one is thinking about remains in short-term memory as long as they think about it. Without a conscious effort at retention, information is lost within 15-20 seconds. The capacity of short-term memory is 5 to 9 items or "chunks." Information is coded mainly in auditory form in short-term memory. Long-term memory, the largest part of the memory system, stores information for indefinite periods. Memories are coded here on the basis of semantics, as well as on the basis of their sensory characteristics. The information processing model states that there are three sequential activities involved in our memory system. Initially, the information is encoded or put into memory when each sensory input is transformed into a memory code. Then the information is stored through processes that hold the memory overtime. Finally, one retrieves and uses the stored information.

B   1. The dominant encoding form in short-term memory is _____ while in long-term memory it is _____.

     A. visual ; semantic
     B. auditory ; semantic
     C. semantic ; auditory and visual
     D. semantic ; auditory

C   2. According to the information processing model, information is processed in which sequence?

     A. storage - encoding - retrieval
     B. storage - retrieval - encoding
     C. encoding - storage - retrieval
     D. encoding - retrieval - storage

     3. Discuss the differences in sensory memory, short-term memory, and long-term memory.

II. WHAT IS THE DUAL MEMORY VIEW?   DESCRIBE THE EVIDENCE FOR IT? WHAT IS THE COMPETING POSITION?

     The dual memory theory, based on considerable research, states that short-term memory and long-term memory are two distinct memory systems. Evidence in support of it is found in activities dealing with retrograde amnesia, anterograde amnesia, and free recall. Electroconvulsive therapy, which induces retrograde amnesia (events immediately preceding the therapy), is said to interfere with memory consolidation (or transfer into long-term memory). Anterograde anmesia, produced by removal of the hippocampus, results in an inability to transfer information between short- and long-term memories.

Studies using free recall of previously learned materials show that different parts of the material are recalled better (e.g., as a result of the recency and primacy effects). In contrast to the dual memory theory is the levels-of-processing view, which states that information processing takes place within a hierarchy of different levels. Here, memory is believed to be a function of how "deeply" and "elaborately" the material is processed (e.g., shallow, simple processing will make memories weak and forgetting rapid).

A   1. Which of the following does NOT support the dual memory theory?

        A. tip-of-the-tongue phenomenon
        B. retrograde amnesia
        C. anterograde amnesia
        D. free recall

    2. Compare and contrast how the dual memory theory and levels-of-processing view interpret our memory system.

III. IN WHAT WAY IS MEMORY MORE A PROCESS OF RECONSTRUCTION THAN RECOLLECTION? WHAT ARE THE IMPLICATIONS OF THIS FOR EYEWITNESS TESTIMONY?

We cannot seem to remember every single fact about some event. As a result, we show refabrication or the building of memory from bits and pieces of the truth. Some believe that, in turn, a refabrication becomes a "fact" when put into long-term memory. Work by Bartlett favors the reconstruction interpretation of memory since memories become increasingly shorter (leveling) and some features become dominant (sharpening) with repetition. The implications for eyewitness testimony are important. Judges and jurors tend to weight heavily the testimony from an eyewitness. However, since this testimony is based upon memories, then one's testimony (no matter how sincere the individual is) may be distorted and/or incorrect.

D   1. What factor or process tends to undermine the reliability of one's eyewitness testimony?

        A. refabrication
        B. leveling
        C. sharpening
        D. all of the above

    2. Why do some say we reconstruct (in contrast to recollect) our memories and, assuming they are correct, what are the implications for eyewitness testimony?

IV.   WHY DO WE SOMETIMES FORGET INFORMATION WE HAVE LEARNED?   IS ALL
      INFORMATION IN LONG-TERM MEMORY PERMANENTLY STORED? EXPLAIN.

      Psychologists offer at least five reasons why we forget.
      Interference theory states that we forget information when
      something else we have learned interferes with our recall.   In
      proactive interference something previously learned interferes
      with our ability to recall newly learned material.   In
      retroactive interference some new learning interferes with the
      recall of information learned earlier.   Decay theory suggests
      that a memory "trace" in the nervous system fades or decays
      with disuse.   Others believe that "forgotten" information is
      only temporarily inaccessible because an appropriate retrieval
      cue is lacking.   The failure in retrieval cues is shown in
      context-dependent memory, state-dependent memory, and the
      tip-of-the-tongue phenomenon.   Motivated forgetting pertains to
      the intentional loss of some memories (as in Freud's concept of
      repression).   Many believe that memories are permanently stored
      in long-term memory.   However, research involving brain
      stimulation, hypnosis, and psychoanalysis does not support this
      position.

C   1. Which of the following offers support for the retrieval
         failure idea of forgetting?

         A. retroactive interference
         B. memory "traces" in the brain
         C. tip-of-the-tongue phenomenon
         D. all of the above

A   2. A neurological explanation for failure to recall memories is
         found in:

         A. decay theory
         B. motivated forgetting
         C. proactive interference
         D. context-dependent memories

      3. How do psychologists explain the fact that we sometimes
         forget information we have learned?

V.   HOW CAN MEMORY BE IMPROVED?   WHAT ARE MNEMONIC DEVICES?   HOW DO
      THEY WORK?

      There are various "keys" to improve our memories.   One is to
      learn the material during distributed rather than massed
      practice sessions.   During practice, one can then facilitate
      later retrieval by organizing the information to be learned.
      To do so there are various mnemonic devices which organize the
      material by relating it to existing, well-learned information.
      Mnemonic devices include the narrative-chaining method (items
      are woven into a story so that they are tied together), the
      "first letter technique" (compose a word or sentence of the

first letter of each word to be learned); rhymes made up of the
necessary facts; the method of loci (which involves associating
new information with a series of specific physical locations
which are easily remembered); and the keyword method (where a
known keyword is associated with each new item to be learned).
Also influencial in many mnemonic devices is the use of imagery
(where one forms a mental representation of something that is
not physically present). Mnemonic devices all tend to provide
better organization of the material and, to some extent, more
visual imagery, both of which facilitate retrieval of the
stored memories. Another way of facilitating our memories,
regardless of how well organized and meaningful they are, is to
practice retrieval.

B   1. Which of the following mnemonic devices would NOT likely use
        imagery?

        A. narrative chaining
        B. rhymes
        C. method of loci
        D. keyword method

     2. Present and explain at least 5 ways that memory can be
        improved.

VI. WHAT IS THE SQ3R METHOD? WHY DOES IT HELP IMPROVE MEMORY?

The SQ3R method is is a well-known study technique emphasizing
organizing and giving meaning to information, as well as the
practicing of retrieval. There are five steps in the process.
Initially, one is to survey the assignment followed by (as in
the case of text book material) turning each topic heading in
the text into a question. These steps focus on content and
increase interest. The third step is to read the material.
The fourth step is to recite or answer the questions that one
created in the second step. The final step, called review, is
to again recite the answers to the questions generated from the
chapter headings. As a result, this is the Survey, Question,
Read, Recite, and Review method. It helps one to organize the
material, to be an active reader, to give meaning to the
material, and to practice retrieval.

A   1. The SQ3R technique is used to improve:

        A. learning ability
        B. motivation level
        C. interpersonal relationships
        D. use of mnemonic devices

     2. Describe the SQ3R learning method and discuss how it is
        designed to improve our memory for text material.

MULTIPLE-CHOICE QUESTIONS

INTRODUCTION: THE FRAILTIES OF HUMAN MEMORY

A   1. Research by Nickerson and Adams on the identification of penny drawings from memory found how many subjects to be correct?
       A. fewer than half
       B. about half
       C. a little more than half
       D. almost 85 percent

C   2. Eyewitness testimony in a trial may be incorrect due to:
       A. faulty perceptions
       B. conflicting motives
       C. memory distortions
       D. slanted questions offered by the lawyer

THE NATURE OF MEMORY

D   3. Memory processes refer to mental activities used to:
       A. put information into memory
       B. keep information in memory
       C. remove information from memory
       D. all of the above

B   4. Which of the following does NOT pertain to the structure of memory?
       A. how information is organized in memory
       B. the process used to put information into memory
       C. how long information stays in our memory
       D. the representation of information in memory

INFORMATION PROCESSING AND MEMORY

C   5. The information processing model of memory suggests that the system works:
       A. within a six stage process
       B. in a way that all information is relabeled
       C. much like a computer
       D. in a fairly random fashion

B   6. Which is the proper sequence of the information processing
         model?
         A. storage – structure – retrieval
         B. encoding – storage – retrieval
         C. storage – encoding – retrieval
         D. structure – storage – retrieval

A   7. When information is put into memory according to the
         information processing model, it is transformed into:
         A. a memory code
         B. chunks
         C. an echoic store
         D. a memory trace

D   8. Which of the following processes is said to involve the use
         of stored information?
         A. structure
         B. encoding
         C. storage
         D. retrieval

THE STRUCTURE OF MEMORY

A   9. What does the term storage refer to according to the
         information processing model?
         A. the persistence of information over time
         B. the final information processing activity
         C. a memory coding process which facililates retrieval
         D. all of the above

C   10. Current thinking about the structure of our memories views
         the memory system as a:
         A. group of expanding and condensing "balloons"
         B. large number of "chunks"
         C. series of separate stores or "boxes"
         D. revolving "merry-go-round" effect

B   11. Which process serves to maintain material within the memory
         system?
         A. iconic store
         B. rehearsal
         C. echoic store
         D. memory-span procedure

D   12. Which of the following is NOT a characteristic of sensory
         memory?
         A. information fades very quickly
         B. information is lost if not transferred
         C. almost all information reaching a sense organ is held
            here
         D. information is transferred to long-term memory

A   13. How long is information believed to stay in sensory memory?
        A. 1-2 seconds
        B. 7 seconds
        C. less than 60 seconds
        D. 1-2 minutes

C   14. Iconic store refers to _____ sensory memory.
        A. auditory
        B. tactual
        C. visual
        D. gustatory

C   15. Sound-oriented sensory memory is called _____ store.
        A. iconic
        B. ohconic
        C. echoic
        D. audoconic

D   16. Information does not remain in sensory memory because it:
        A. fades
        B. is transferred into short-term memory
        C. is replaced by incoming information
        D. all of the above

B   17. The contents of one's attention is believed to be held in:
        A. sensory memory
        B. short-term memory
        C. long-term memory
        D. the chunks

A   18. Unless one attends to information in short-term memory, it
        will be lost within _____ seconds.
        A. 15 to 20
        B. 10 to 30
        C. 30 to 45
        D. 60 to 90

B   19. Remembering a phone number you just looked up is a function
        of _____ memory.
        A. sensory
        B. short-term
        C. long-term
        D. maintenance rehearsal

D   20. The memory-span procedure is used to determine the _____
        of short-term memory.
        A. functioning
        B. preferences
        C. duration
        D. capacity

C   21. The typical capacity of short-term memory is about _____
         items.
         A. 2 to 4
         B. 4 to 6
         C. 5 to 9
         D. 10 to 15

A   22. Any meaningful unit of information in short-term memory is
         called a:
         A. chunk
         B. bit
         C. aggregate
         D. span

B   23. How can one improve his or her short-term memory?
         A. increase one's capacity through practice
         B. increase the size of chunks
         C. use mnenomic strategies
         D. expand one's sensory store

D   24. A major cause of forgetting in short-term memory is due to:
         A. retrieval failure
         B. clustering
         C. age
         D. displacement

D   25. Information in short-term memory is represented mainly in
         _____ form.
         A. symbolic
         B. visual and auditory
         C. visual
         D. auditory

C   26. Short-term memory is associated with what type of thought?
         A. subconscious
         B. unconscious
         C. conscious
         D. preconscious

A   27. Which memory structure enables us to benefit from past
         experiences or to communicate?
         A. long-term memory
         B. short-term memory
         C. sensory memory
         D. iconic and echoic store

A   28. Which of the following statements is FALSE?
         A. rehearsal guarantees the storage of information in long-
            term memory
         B. long-term memory stores information for an indefinite
            period
         C. the largest part of the memory system is long-term memory
         D. the longer an item exists in short-term memory the more
            likely it will reach long-term memory

B   29. Which of the following is an example of maintenance
         rehearsal?
         A. learning a mnenomic device
         B. the transfer of a phone number from short- to long-term
            memory
         C. chunking
         D. studying for a cumulative final exam

D   30. Which of the following is NOT a technique that may be used
         during elaborative rehearsal?
         A. embellish or elaborate on information
         B. form images or use memory strategies
         C. organize the information
         D. simply repeat information a few times

C   31. Long-term memories are most often coded by:
         A. recency
         B. proximity
         C. meaning
         D. similarity

B   32. The tendency to organize or group items during recall is
         known as:
         A. retrieval
         B. clustering
         C. free recall
         D. recognition

A   33. Seniors in college, when asked to write the names of their
         faculty members, tended to group them according to their
         departments. This demonstrates _____ in recall.
         A. clustering
         B. retrieval cues
         C. long-term memory
         D. refabrication

D   34. Which would NOT likely be a retrieval cue when trying to
         remember the name of your first pet dog?
         A. "animal"
         B. "pet"
         C. "dog"
         D. "first"

C   35. Which of the following would be a test of memory recall?
         A. pointing to the crime suspect from the witness stand
         B. identifying a crime suspect in a police lineup
         C. describing a crime suspect to police
         D. choosing the correct answer on a multiple-choice exam

B   36. Which type of retrieval is easier?
         A. production
         B. recognition
         C. recall
         D. refabrication

SHORT-TERM AND LONG-TERM MEMORY: ONE OR TWO MEMORY SYSTEMS?

B   37. The dual memory theory suggests that:
          A. memories are stored on the basis of what is important
             (primary) or unimportant (secondary)
          B. short- and long-term memory are two distinct systems
          C. there are two memory "banks" in long-term memory
          D. all of the above

C   38. Memory loss is a major side effect of:
          A. improper clustering
          B. brain surgery
          C. electroconvulsive therapy
          D. retrograde interference

A   39. Retrograde amnesia refers to the loss of memories for events
          _____ the shock in electroconvulsive therapy.
          A. just before
          B. just after
          C. during
          D. all of the above

D   40. Which term explains the retention of memories for events
          occurring well-before electroconvulsive therapy?
          A. rehearsal
          B. imagery
          C. displacement
          D. consolidation

D   41. Loftus and Burns' research on "mental shock" as it
          interferes with the recall of information following a
          traumatic event questions the reliability of:
          A. childhood memories
          B. past memories in general
          C. neutral observers
          D. eyewitness testimony

B   42. When memory for new events is impaired, but older
          information is recalled normally, it is called _____
          amnesia.
          A. retrograde
          B. anterograde
          C. partial
          D. selective

C   43. The recall of information in any order in memory is named
          _____ recall.
          A. unclustered
          B. available
          C. free
          D. random

A   44. When items toward the end of a learning list are remembered
        best, it is called the _____ effect.
        A. recency
        B. primacy
        C. short-term
        D. saturation

B   45. The primacy effect refers to one's ability to remember:
        A. childhood events better than adolescent events
        B. the first part of a learning list better than the later
           parts
        C. the most important information best
        D. the information that is the basis or foundation for
           future learning

D   46. Which of the following supports a short-term versus
        long-term memory distinction?
        A. primacy and recency effects
        B. anterograde amnesia
        C. retrograde amnesia
        D. all of the above

C   47. Which of the following is NOT a characteristic of the
        levels-of-processing view of memory?
        A. there are multiple processing levels instead of "boxes"
        B. there is a hierachy of processing levels
        C. semantic processing tends to occur at shallow levels
        D. information is remembered longer when the depth of
           processing is greater

THE FALLIBILITY OF RECONSTRUCTION

A   48. The process occurring when we tend to fill in our memories
        with things that may have been true is called:
        A. refabrication
        B. fabrication
        C. processing levels
        D. imagery

A   49. A series of individuals pass around a story that one tells
        another verbally. When the story becomes increasingly
        shorter with repetition, it is called:
        A. leveling
        B. reduction
        C. memory short-cutting
        D. consolidation

B   50. When a story is told repeatedly by different individuals and
        in the process certain features of the story become
        dominant, it is called:
        A. highlighting
        B. sharpening
        C. peaking
        D. none of the above

D   51. Bartlett, a researcher in the area of the fallibility of
        memory, concludes that memory is more a process of:
        A. rethinking than it is recalling
        B. recalling than it is rethinking
        C. recollection than it is reconstruction
        D. reconstruction than it is recollection

APPLICATION: EYEWITNESS TESTIMONY--PSYCHOLOGY GOES TO COURT

C   52. A series of research projects by Loftus and colleagues
        studied eyewitness testimony.   One could summarize their
        results as:
        A. females are better at remembering important details than
           are males
        B. such testimony can be improved with practice
        C. eyewitness accounts are far from infallible
        D. crimes or accidents which result in physical harm to
           the innocent one(s) are remembered in more detail

D   53. Loftus' research on eyewitness testimony found out what
        about the presentation of misinformation or additional
        information?
        A. the type of questions asked can enhance the eyewitness'
           memory
        B. the introduction of misleading information during
           questioning can cause the recall of something that
           didn't happen
        C. a warning prior to the presentation of misinformation
           makes people more resistant to it
        D. all of the above

A   54. As a result of research on the fallibility of eyewitness
        testimony, Loftus suggests that:
        A. jurors should be made to understand the dangers of
           eyewitness testimony
        B. eyewitness testimony should not be given to jurors or
           judges
        C. eyewitness testimony should only be given to qualified
           experts for evaluation
        D. all of the above

THEORIES OF FORGETTING

B   55. The interference theory of forgetting assumes that recall is
        poor because of interference from:
        A. our emotions
        B. other experiences or learned information
        C. our motivations
        D. current conscious activities

C   56. When something previously learned interferes with our
        ability to recall newly learned material it is called
        _____ interference.
        A. retrieval
        B. retroactive
        C. proactive
        D. recall

C   57. The failure to remember a friend's new phone number because
        of interference from having learned the old number is due to
        _____ interference.
        A. retrieval
        B. retroactive
        C. proactive
        D. recall

A   58. In general, proactive interference _____ as the amount of
        previously learned material _____.
        A. increases ; increases
        B. increases ; decreases
        C. decreases ; increases
        D. decreases ; decreases

D   59. What would be a way to lessen proactive interference?
        A. overlearn the first material learned
        B. increase the semantics of the old material
        C. avoid the use of memory strategies
        D. spend extra time learning the new material

B   60. When the learning of additional material interferes with the
        recall of material learned earlier, it is called _____
        interference.
        A. retrieval
        B. retroactive
        C. proactive
        D. recall

D   61. Which of the following factors affect retroactive
        interference?
        A. the similarity of the two learning materials
        B. the extent the new material is learned
        C. the amount of rehearsal of the old material
        D. all of the above

C   62. The fading of memory "traces" through disuse is part of the
          _____ theory of memory.
        A. refabrication
        B. retrieval
        C. decay
        D. shifting

B   63. Decay theory is hard to experimentally test because:
        A. no one has defined what is meant by "decay"
        B. forgetting may actually be due to interference since
           interfering activities always occur
        C. research with lower animals is difficult to evaluate
        D. the brain's chemical make-up changes too rapidly

D   64. The retrieval failure hypothesis to memory:
        A. deals with "forgotten" material that "pops" into your
           head at a later date
        B. pertains to memories that are temporarily inaccessible
        C. is based on a lack of appropriate retrieval cues
        D. all of the above

B   65. A study by Tulving and Pearlstone where subjects were given
        a list of category names (e.g., professions) and a list of
        items within each category (e.g., engineer) demonstrated
        the:
        A. problem with overlearning
        B. importance of retrieval cues on memory
        C. problem with proactive interference
        D. importance of recognition as a valid test for memory

B   66. Research by Smith and others who tested subjects in rooms
        that were or were not similar to the room in which the
        learning took place found that:
        A. learning was facilitated
        B. altering context impaired memory performance
        C. the difference-context group did better than the same-
           context group
        D. refabrication was better under similar conditions

C   67. Memory that is influenced by the mood or emotion that was
        present during both learning and testing is referred to as
        _____ memory.
        A. TOT
        B. context-dependent
        C. state-dependent
        D. retrieval-dependent

A   68. The tip-of-the-tongue phenomenon may be summarized as:
        A. bit-by-bit retrieval
        B. context-dependent memory
        C. state-dependent memory
        D. clustering

D   69. You recognize someone, you know where you met them, you like
         them, but you can't remember their name although you "feel
         that you know it." This is the:
         A. motivated forgetting phenomenon
         B. difference with long-term and short-term storage
         C. problem with inappropriate state-dependent memories
         D. tip-of-the-tongue phenomenon

B   70. Forgetting something because we "want to" is known as:
         A. intentional relapse
         B. motivated forgetting
         C. emotional clouding
         D. motivational clouding

B   71. Motivated forgetting resembles:
         A. anterograde amnesia
         B. Freud's process called repression
         C. proactive interference
         D. retroactive interference

A   72. What would be a good explanation as to why many of us have
         difficulty recognizing a correct U.S. coin?
         A. storage failure
         B. inappropriate retrieval cues
         C. retroactive interference
         D. retrieval failure

APPLICATION: THE PROBLEM OF GETTING "PERMANENT" INFORMATION OUT OF
MEMORY

D   73. Support for memory permanence comes from:
         A. brain stimulation
         B. hypnosis
         C. psychoanalysis
         D. none of the above

B   74. Results of research with brain stimulation, hypnosis, and
         psychoanalysis suggest that:
         A. childhood memories are permanent
         B. not all of our memories are permanently stored
         C. permanent memories can be recalled with the proper
            techniques
         D. hypnosis is the best technique for recalling permanent
            memories

ORGANIZATION AND MEMORY

A   75. The one key word for improving memory is:
     A. organization
     B. practice
     C. motivation
     D. attention

D   76. Which of the following is NOT a mnemonic device?
     A. narrative chaining method
     B. the "first letter technique"
     C. rhymes
     D. clustering

C   77. The mnemonic device which involves using the items to be
         learned in a story is called:
     A. the key-word method
     B. imagery
     C. the narrative-chaining method
     D. the method of loci

C   78. Which of the following is an example of imagery to
         facilitate remembering?
     A. "i" before "e" except after "c"
     B. ROY G. BIV
     C. milk pouring onto a soggy loaf of bread
     D. none of the above

B   79. The method of loci used to enhance remembering involves:
     A. placing things in alphabetical order
     B. associating new information with physical locations
        already in memory
     C. forming a mental link or image between two objects
     D. placing things in numerical order

A   80. A mnemonic device especially useful in learning a foreign
         language vocabulary is the _____ method.
     A. keyword
     B. loci
     C. narrative chaining
     D. imagery

ADDITIONAL MEMORY AIDS

D   81. Which of the following can improve one's memory?
     A. learn the material with distributed practice
     B. practice retrieval
     C. pay attention to the material
     D. all of the above

APPLICATION: THE SQ3R METHOD--REMEMBERING WHAT YOU'VE READ

C   82. How many "steps" are involved in the SQ3R method?
       A. 3
       B. 4
       C. 5
       D. it is really up to the individual learner

B   83. The first "step" in the SQ3R method of learning is:
       A. study
       B. survey
       C. search
       D. select

ON THE HORIZON: MEMORY CONTROL

A   84. What might the future hold if we want to improve or
       interfere with our memories?
       A. "memory doctors" and "memory clinics"
       B. electrical brain stimulation
       C. memory pills implanted under our skins
       D. radio wave "hook-ups" with our home computers

C   85. The hormone _____ has been shown to improve learning and
       memory while the hormone _____ seems to have the opposite
       effect.
       A. oxytocin ; epinephrine
       B. epinephrine ; vasopressin
       C. vasopressin ; oxytocin
       D. norepinephrine ; epinephrine

D   86. Individuals are speculating that in the future vasopressin
       may:
       A. reverse retrograde amnesia after electroconvulsive
          therapy
       B. treat patients with Alzheimer's disease
       C. retard some characteristics of aging
       D. all of the above

– CHAPTER 8 –

LANGUAGE AND THOUGHT

OUTLINE

I. Introduction: The Story of Genie - a description of the language development of a girl who was raised in near isolation by her parents until 13 1/2 years of age and then treated for four years by professionals; LANGUAGE and THINKING as they relate to humans and nonhumans

II. Language

A. The development of language - the same sequence of three stages for persons in all cultures (<u>prelinquistic stage</u>, <u>first words</u>, and <u>first sentences</u>)
   1. The prelinquistic stage: The emergence of phonemes - the first 10-12 months of life where crying, cooing, and babbling occur; one's language PHONEMES are learned here; BABBLING begins around 6 months and seems to be a maturational development
   2. The first words stage: The emergence of morphemes - MORPHEMES are begun to be uttered around 12-18 months of age; the first word stage is also known as the <u>holophrastic stage</u> since many HOLOPHRASES are used
   3. The first sentences stage: The emergence of syntax - two word sentences first appear about 18 months of age; rules of SYNTAX and GRAMMAR are acquired; sentences during this period are absent of INFLECTIONS and GRAMMATICAL MORPHEMES and thus referred to as TELEGRAPHIC SPEECH because their context is important; OVERREGULARIZATION is common at this stage

a. more on syntax – during this stage construction of <u>phrases</u> and their <u>interrelationships</u> are learned, something called <u>phrase structure</u>; SURFACE and DEEP STRUCTURE deal with the actual words or the underlying meaning, respectively, of sentences; TRANSFORMATION RULES are syntactic rules; AMBIGUOUS SENTENCES have more than one deep structure; <u>context</u> is a cue to aid comprehension; psychologists distinguish between one's <u>competence</u> in grammar identification and one's daily <u>performance</u>

B. Theories of language acquisition
   1. Social learning theory: The role of imitation – though many believe <u>imitation</u> contributes to language acquisition, it has difficulty explaining creative sentences and the learning of grammar
   2. Reinforcement theory – adults use <u>reinforcement</u> to <u>shape</u> the child's language; this theory has difficulty explaining creativity and complex grammatical constructions which are not shaped
   3. Innate theory – the INNATENESS HYPOTHESIS of Chomsky supports an inborn, genetic potential for creating and understanding language; this theory has the most support; Lenneberg believes a <u>critical period</u> for language development occurs during the period from 2 to 12 years

C. Language and chimpanzees – a discussion of Washoe's and Koko's learning of American Sign Language and Lana's use of colored plastic shapes in an effort to understand language learning abilities in apes; Terrace's work with Nim Chimsky suggests chimps don't learn a language but only are conditioned to make certain signs without knowing what they mean

D. Relationship between language and thought – does language control perception and thinking?
   1. Linguistic relativity – Whorf's LINGUISTIC RELATIVITY HYPOTHESIS says perceptions and thought are influenced by language, but there is a lack of research support for this model
   2. Other language and thought relationships – language may facilitate one's thinking and communicating about a subject (e.g., knowing more terms about baseball enables one to make finer discriminations); language also positively affects problem solving; however, as shown by deaf children, <u>spoken language</u> is not essential for thought or problem solving

   3. Language disorders: Aphasias - language disorders caused
      by brain injuries are APHASIAS; victims are called
      aphasics; anterior aphasia, or BROCA'S APHASIA, shows
      difficulty in speaking but not comprehending; Broca's
      area is in the anterior part of the left hemisphere;
      posterior aphasia, or WERNICKE'S APHASIA, shows a serious
      impairment in thought and the comprehension of speech;
      Wernicke's area is located at the back of the left
      hemisphere; the arcuate fasciculus sends information to
      Broca's area

   E. Application: Facilitating language development in young
      children - researchers have suggested eight ways that
      parents can serve as facilitators of language development

III. Thought - it has been suggested that thinking involves three
     broad categories (concept formation, problem solving, and
     decision making)

   A. Concept formation - a CONCEPT is a symbol representing a
      class of objects or events having common properties;
      concepts lend stability and regularity to our environment;
      attributes and rules are two critical features of concepts;
      individuals learn concepts by hypothesis-testing; there are
      both CONJUNCTIVE RULES and DISJUNCTIVE RULES for combining
      conceptual attributes
      1. Factors affecting concept formation - there are three
         factors
         a. the type of positive or negative examples which are
            used
         b. the number of relevant versus irrelevant attributes
         c. the abstractness versus concreteness of a concept
         d. RELATIONAL CONCEPTS are the most difficult to learn;
            e.g., large, small, north, south
      2. Applying principles of concept formation - two ways of
         improving concept learning are to generate many examples
         of the concept and to make relevant features as
         distinctive as possible

   B. Problem solving
      1. Stages of problem solving - a series of three (perhaps
         four) definable stages called preparation, production,
         judgment (and incubation)
         a. preparation is when we study a problem and arrive at
            some understanding of it.
         b. production is when we generate one or more potential
            problem solutions while rejecting those not feasible;
            solution strategies involve ALGORITHMS and HEURISTICS;
            different general heuristics include PLANNING PROCESS,
            MEANS-END ANALYSIS (with the use of subgoals), and
            WORKING BACKWARD

    c. judgment is when the adequacy of potential solutions
     is evaluated and compared with previously selected
     solution criteria
    d. incubation is where no active work is done on an
     unsolved problem with the intent of a solution coming
     "out of the blue"; the incubation effect may occur due
     to both reduced mental fatigue and frustration and the
     shedding of inappropriate thoughts about the problem
   2. Problems in solving problems - previous experience can
    both help and hinder current problem solving
    a. SET refers to the tendency to approach a problem the
     same way each time; an example with obtaining water
     quantities is given
    b. FUNCTIONAL FIXITY refers to the tendency to perceive
     objects as having only the uses for which they were
     originally designed; the traditional tac, candle and
     matches example is given

  C. Application: Some tips on solving problems--four practical
   aids are presented: broaden your knowledge, look for new
   ways of structuring the problem, describe the problem to
   someone, and set the problem aside.

IV. On the Horizon: Programming Intelligent Computers - the goal
  of the science of ARTIFICIAL INTELLIGENCE is to program
  computers to behave intelligently; artifical intelligence is
  already aiding in medical diagnosis where logic and an
  infallible memory for symptoms and past cases is a main
  advantage when assisting physicians

OBJECTIVES

I. HOW DOES LANGUAGE DEVELOP AS THE CHILD GROWS? WHAT ARE SOME OF
 THE IMPORTANT FEATURES OF EACH STAGE OF DEVELOPMENT?

 Language development seems to occur for persons in all cultures
 in three sequential stages: a prelinguistic stage, first
 words, and first sentences. The prelinguistic stage (the first
 10-12 months of life) is characterized by crying, cooing, and
 babbling. During this stage the child can emit about 100
 distinguishable phonemes. The "first words" stage begins
 around 12-18 months of age and is characterized by the
 emergence of learned morphemes which are part of the child's
 particular language and holophrases. It is not until the third

stage that children combine words into sentences, a behavior typically shown at about 18 months of life. During this "first sentence" stage, the child begins to demonstrate a knowledge of both syntax and grammar. Inflections grammatical morphenes, telegraphic speech, and overregulation are also common in this stage.

A   1. Language development is shown in all cultures as:

     A. a sequence of three basic stages
     B. different dependent on the number of phonemes to learn
     C. different dependent on the number of morphenes to learn
     D. dependent on whether rules of syntax or grammar are
        mastered first

C   2. Grammar and syntax rules are mastered during which stage of
        language development?

     A. prelinquistic
     B. first words
     C. first sentences
     D. social interchange

     3. What are the important characteristics in each of the three
        basic stages of language development?

II. HOW CAN WE ACCOUNT FOR THE CHILD'S ACQUISITION OF LANGUAGE?
     HOW DO THEORIES OF LANGUAGE ACQUISITION DIFFER?

     There are three theories of language acquisition: social learning theory, reinforcement theory, and the innateness hypothesis. Social learning theorists believe that imitation contributes to language learning. The reinforcement theory suggests that adults shape a child's language behavior by giving and withholding reinforcement. Neither of these theories adequately explain the acquisition of grammatical constructions or the creative nature of children's sentences. The innateness hypothesis suggests that children have an inborn, genetic potential for creating and understanding language that results from a "language acquistion device" in the brain which sorts and applies rules to sounds. The innateness hypothesis has the most support of the three theories of language acquisition.

B   1. Which statement is FALSE concerning language acquisition?

     A. The social learning theory emphasizes the role of
        imitation
     B. Complex grammatical constructions are often shaped
        by parental rewards
     C. The reinforcement and social learning theories favor
        environmental influences
     D. Most evidence supports the innateness hypothesis

2. Compare and contrast the three theories of language acquisition.

III. WHAT EVIDENCE EXISTS THAT LANGUAGE AND THOUGHT ARE OR ARE NOT RELATED?

Whorf has suggested in the linguistic relativity hypothesis that language affects both thinking and perceptions. Support for this are the examples of where some people have more words for objects than we do (i.e., Eskimos when describing snow). Research evidence, however, does not support this hypothesis. Even though a Stone Age people in New Guinea only have two color terms, they still can perceive all eleven basic colors. Even though research suggests that language does not greatly affect thinking and perception, language and especially one's vocabulary, can facilitate thinking, communication, and problem solving.

C   1. Since Eskimos have more words for snow than do Americans, some believe that Eskimos then perceive and think differently about snow. This example supports which theory?

         A. perception-language
         B. innate hypothsis
         C. linguisitic relativity
         D. cognitive-perceptual

D   2. Which process does language NOT typically influence?

         A. thinking
         B. communicating
         C. problem solving
         D. using sign language

     3. How are language and thought related?

IV. WHAT ARE CONCEPTS? WHAT IS THEIR SIGNIFICANCE IN EVERYDAY LIFE? WHAT AFFECTS THE LEARNING OF CONCEPTS?

Concepts are verbal or nonverbal symbols which represent a class (or group) of objects or events having common properties. Examples are "dog," "magazine," and "sports cars." Concepts lend a certain sense of stability and regularity to our interactions with our environment. They also permit us to apply general rules to specific situations, thus discriminating between groups of stimuli (e.g., poisonous vs. nonpoisonous snakes). Some have said that concepts are fundamental aspects of our knowledge and cognitive abilities. There are three well-known factors affecting concept formation. One is whether the examples are positive or negative. Faster learning occurs with positive instances. Another factor is how many relevant or irrelevant attributes are present. Faster concept formation

occurs with more relevant and fewer irrelevant attributes.   A
final factor is whether the concept is concrete ("house" or
"dog") or abstract ("circle" or "rectangle").   Concrete
concepts are most easily acquired.

B   1. When are concepts most readily formed?

            A. when they have many attributes
            B. when they are concrete
            C. if they pertain to colored objects
            D. if negative instances are provided

D   2. Which of the following is a concept?

            A. large
            B. south
            C. dog
            D. all of the above

        3. How do concepts help us in dealing with our environment?

V.   LIST THE STAGES OF PROBLEM SOLVING.   WHAT IS INVOLVED IN EACH
        STAGE?

        There are three necessary stages of problem solving:
        preparation, production, and judgment.   Some believe that a
        fourth sometimes exists.   It is incubation.   In the preparation
        stage, a problem is studied and we arrive at some understanding
        of it.   The ease of finding solutions is affected greatly by
        how one initially structures the problem.   In the production
        stage, one or more potential problem solutions are generated
        while unrealistic solutions are rejected.   Strategies common
        during this stage are algorithms and heuristics.   In the
        judgment stage, the problem solver evaluates the adequacy of
        potential solutions by comparing them to the solution criteria
        generated earlier.   During the incubation stage the problem
        solver does not actively work on an unsolved problem, but takes
        time off for other matters with the goal of having the solution
        to the original problem come "out of the blue."

A   1. Which stage is NOT said to be a necessary part for problem
           solving?

            A. incubation
            B. preparation
            C. judgment
            D. production

C   2. During which stage of problem solving do we typically
         compare potential solutions with solution criteria generated
         in an earlier stage?

         A. incubation
         B. preparation
         C. judgment
         D. production

      3. Present and summarize characteristics in each stage of
         problem solving.

VI.   NAME SOME FACTOR THAT CAN INHIBIT EFFECTIVE PROBLEM SOLVING.

      Two phenomena known as set and functional fixity can hinder
      effective problem solving. Set refers to the tendency to
      approach a problem the same or habitual way each time.
      Functional fixity refers to the tendency to perceive objects as
      having only the uses for which they were originally designed.
      It interferes with the solution to a problem which requires a
      novel use of a familiar object. Both of these phenomena can
      blind us to fresh and new ways of exploring problems.

A   1. What are two factors that inhibit effective problem
         solving?

         A. set and functional fixity
         B. set and means-end analysis
         C. functional fixity and incubation
         D. means-end analysis and functional fixity

      2. Describe, with examples the two factors that inhibit
         effective problem solving.

                    MULTIPLE-CHOICE QUESTIONS

INTRODUCTION: THE STORY OF GENIE

C   1. Genie, the girl raised in near isolation, developed:
         A. near normal speech without training
         B. near normal speech with training
         C. less than normal speech even with training
         D. normal speech with training

D 2. An arbitrary system of symbols that allows individuals to understand and communicate with one another is called:
A. species communication
B. thinking
C. social understanding
D. language

A 3. Human language is said to be different than most animal communication because it is used:
A. creatively
B. more regularly
C. spontaneously
D. with forethought

B 4. An inherent ability to mentally manipulate symbols and concepts to organize information is called:
A. abstract reasoning
B. thinking
C. non-abstract reasoning
D. conceptualization

THE DEVELOPMENT OF LANGUAGE

B 5. What characterizes the prelinguistic stage of language development?
A. learning how to talk
B. cooing and babbling
C. some language skills
D. first sentences

C 6. The prelinguistic stage of language development encompasses approximately the age _____ months.
A. 0 - 6
B. 0 - 8
C. 0 - 10 to 12
D. 6 - 12

D 7. The basic sounds of any language are called:
A. morphemes
B. babbling
C. words
D. phonemes

C 8. Which is a FALSE statement about phonemes?
A. humans produce about 100 different ones
B. the English language has about 45
C. French and German use all of the phonemes
D. most phonemes, by themselves, have no meaning

A   9. The unsystematic use of a wide variety of speechlike sounds
        is called:
        A. babbling
        B. cooing
        C. phonetics
        D. morphetics

A   10. Babbling is considered to be a(n):
        A. type of vocal play
        B. early effort at language
        C. behavior resulting from learning and experience
        D. necessary behavior before acquiring words and sentences

D   11. The average child says its first word between _____ months
        of age.
        A. 6 - 8
        B. 8 - 10
        C. 6 - 10
        D. 12 - 18

B   12. A morpheme is:
        A. a language's basic sound
        B. the smallest meaningful unit in a language
        C. any word with 3 or less letters
        D. any word with 2 or less letters

C   13. Morphemes include:
        A. words and short phrases
        B. suffixes and short phrases
        C. words, suffixes, and prefixes
        D. only words

A   14. Single words that often communicate an entire idea or
        thought are known as:
        A. holophrases
        B. phonemes
        C. elementary grammar
        D. syntax errors

D   15. The single-word phase of language development is referred to
        as the _____ stage.
        A. elementary
        B. syntax
        C. prelinguistic
        D. holophrastic

D   16. The rules for combining words into sentences is called:
        A. native language
        B. holophrases
        C. grammar
        D. syntax

B   17. Grammar refers to the rules relating to:
A. syntax
B. syntax, phonemes, and morphemes
C. syntax and phonemes
D. syntax and morphemes

B   18. Grammatical markers such as "ing" and "ed" are called:
A. inclusions
B. inflections
C. modifiers
D. grammatical morphemes

C   19. Saying "where Papa" instead of "where is Papa" is an example of:
A. missing grammatical morphenes
B. pre-syntax speech
C. telegraphic speech
D. a holophrase

A   20. The tendency for children to take grammatical rules and inappropriately generalize them to instances where they do not apply is called:
A. overregularization
B. telegraphic speech
C. misrepresentation
D. rule transformation

D   21. An example of overregularization is saying:
A. "doggie" instead of "dog"
B. "Papa work" instead of "Papa is at work"
C. "Mommy sock" instead of "Mommy's sock"
D. "Daddy goed" instead of "Daddy went"

B   22. The actual words and their organization within a sentence refers to the sentence's _____ structure.
A. deep
B. surface
C. transformational
D. spoken

C   23. Which of the following is NOT a characteristic of a sentence's deep structure?
A. underlying meaning
B. what the speaker really intends to convey
C. unconscious motives
D. it can be expressed by different surface structures

A   24. What rules explain how a single underlying meaning can be expressed in different surface forms?
A. transformation rules
B. ambiguous rules
C. rules of context
D. rules of structure

A   25. The sentence "They are flying planes" could be about planes
        or about people. This sentence exemplifies:
        A. ambiguous sentences
        B. dual surface structures
        C. transformation rules
        D. context errors

THEORIES OF LANGUAGE ACQUISITION

D   26. Which of the following is a criticism of the role of
        imitation in language learning?
        A. it doesn't explain grammar acquisition
        B. it can't explain the creative nature of children's
           sentences
        C. when children imitate an adult, they modify the grammar
           to conform to their own level
        D. all of the above

C   27. The biggest problem with the reinforcement theory in its
        explanation of language learning is that:
        A. adults shape performance by reinforcement
        B. syntax rules are ignored
        C. parents do not seem to shape complex grammatical
           constructions
        D. all of the above

B   28. The "language acquisition device" is used in which theory of
        language acquisition?
        A. social learning theory
        B. innateness hypothesis
        C. reinforcement theory
        D. imitation hypothesis

A   29. The innateness hypothesis for human language use and
        understanding is partially supported because:
        A. deaf children begin to create sign language on their own
        B. animals communicate
        C. we automatically imitate our parents and older siblings
        D. we are a social species

D   30. Lenneberg believes that a critical period for language
        development occurs between:
        A. 12 - 24 months
        B. 12 - 36 months
        C. 2 - 4 years
        D. 2 - 12 years

C   31. Which theory of language use and learning is best supported
         today?
         A. social learning theory
         B. reinforcement theory
         C. innateness hypothesis
         D. imitation hypothesis

LANGUAGE AND CHIMPANZEES

C   32. The most frequent subjects in animal language studies are:
         A. parrots
         B. rats
         C. chimpanzees
         D. bottlenose dolphins

B   33. Language capabilities have been studied in both "Washoe" and
         "Koko" by using:
         A. simple words
         B. American Sign Language
         C. facial movements and configurations
         D. a computer

C   34. Language research with "Washoe" who learned many words and
         sentences suggests that chimps:
         A. are more intelligent than gorillas
         B. are better "talkers" than parrots
         C. can master some vocabulary and simple sentence
            construction
         D. are not as intelligent as we once thought

D   35. An interesting approach to language useage was performed by
         Premack and the chimp Lana using:
         A. a talking computer
         B. ASL
         C. hand and facial gestures
         D. colored plastic shapes

RELATIONSHIP BETWEEN LANGUAGE AND THOUGHT

D   36. The linguistic relativity hypothesis deals with the notion
         that:
         A. we understand only what we want to
         B. different cultures think differently
         C. Western languages are more complex than Eastern languages
         D. our language affects how we think and perceive the world

B   37. A major problem with the linguistic relativity hypothesis is
       its:
       A. emphasis on short sentences
       B. lack of experimental research support
       C. lack of understanding of "3rd World" languages
       D. simplicity

A   38. Which statement is FALSE?
       A. spoken language is essential for thought and solving
          problems
       B. language affects problem solving ability
       C. an appropriate vocabulary can facilitate thinking
       D. a complex vocabulary does not necessarily improve our
          perceptions

B   39. Language disorders caused by brain injuries are called:
       A. language traumas
       B. aphasias
       C. aphixias
       D. arcuates

D   40. Nearly all aphasics have an injury to the:
       A. parietal lobe
       B. occipital lobe
       C. right hemisphere
       D. left hemisphere

C   41. Individuals who have difficulty speaking but no difficulty
       comprehending language have _____ aphasia.
       A. Wernicke's
       B. Chomsky's
       C. Broca's
       D. posterior

C   42. Which is TRUE about an anterior aphasia?
       A. grammatically correct speech
       B. impairment in thinking and reasoning
       C. halting and labored speech
       D. all of the above

D   43. Wernicke's aphasia signifies:
       A. disturbed thinking
       B. fluent speech
       C. poor understanding of words
       D. all of the above

A   44. Which area of the brain is believed responsible for
       interpreting information and producing meaningful sentences?
       A. Wernicke's area
       B. Broca's area
       C. the arcuate fasciculus
       D. the anterior lobe

APPLICATION: FACILITATING LANGUAGE DEVELOPMENT IN YOUNG CHILDREN

B   45. A good way to refer to parents is as _____ of language
          development.
          A. perpetuators
          B. facilitators
          C. signalers
          D. imitators

B   46. Which of the following was not discussed as a useful
          parental strategy to use in children's language development?
          A. talk with children at their own level
          B. use many hand gestures when talking
          C. encourage good listening and attention skills
          D. encourage words as a substitute for action

C   47. An effective parental strategy to use when a child uses an
          unclear word or inexact terminology is to:
          A. criticize the child immediately
          B. have the child write and then say the correct word or
             phrase
          C. correct the speech error but avoid being critical
          D. ignore them because the child will grow out of them with
             time

CONCEPT FORMATION

D   48. A verbal or nonverbal symbol representing a class or group
          of objects or events having common properties is called a:
          A. verbal grouping
          B. norm
          C. rule
          D. concept

D   49. Which statement is FALSE concerning concepts?
          A. each object in a concept has one or more common
             characteristics
          B. they help in the stability and regularity of our
             environmental interactions
          C. they aid our memories
          D. we use them to apply specific rules to general statements

A   50. What two critical features are found in concepts?
          A. attributes and rules
          B. laws and characteristics
          C. rules and laws
          D. attributes and features

B   51. Psychologists believe that individuals learn concepts by a
         process of:
         A. imitation
         B. hypothesis-testing
         C. behavior sampling
         D. attribute sampling

C   52. Another term used to describe multidimensional-concept
         learning is _____ learning.
         A. attribute
         B. law
         C. rule
         D. hypothesis

A   53. Concepts such as "living things," "justice," and "economy
         cars" have what in common?
         A. more than one dimension
         B. conjunctive ruling
         C. disjunctive ruling
         D. plurality of symbols

D   54. Which of the following is the text's example of a concept
         that is NOT based on the conjunctive rule for combining
         attributes?
         A. animals
         B. good quality
         C. sports cars
         D. person

B   55. The logical relation used by a disjunctive rule for
         combining conceptual attributes is:
         A. "and"
         B. "or"
         C. "when"
         D. "if"

D   56. What factor makes it difficult to learn a new concept?
         A. when negative instances or examples are provided
         B. when many irrelevant attributes are present
         C. when concepts are abstract
         D. all of the above

C   57. Concepts are easier to learn if they are:
         A. taught through negative instances
         B. made up of more than one irrelevant attribute
         C. concrete
         D. given to children who are very young

A   58. Which concepts are based on some dimension other than the
         presence or absence of an attribute?
         A. relational
         B. conjunctive
         C. disconjunctive
         D. extrasensory

B   59. An example of a typically difficult concept to learn is:
        A. "dogs"
        B. "left" and "right"
        C. "animals"
        D. "circle" vs. "triangle"

B   60. According to the text, a good thing to do when one is
        learning a new concept is to:
        A. apply it to an old concept
        B. think of many examples of the concept
        C. study the concept early in the morning
        D. think of 2 or 3 irrelevant attributes for that concept

PROBLEM SOLVING

D   61. The stage of problem solving which involves studying a
        problem and arriving at an understanding of it is called the
        _____ stage.
        A. incubation
        B. judgment
        C. production
        D. preparation

C   62. Algorithms and heuristics are associated with which stage of
        problem solving?
        A. incubation
        B. judgment
        C. production
        D. preparation

A   63. Methods that will guarantee a solution to a problem if they
        are correctly applied are known as:
        A. algorithms
        B. heuristics
        C. planning processes
        D. means-end analyses

A   64. Which is a FALSE statement about heuristics?
        A. they will always generate a solution
        B. they are "rules of thumb" or educated guesses
        C. they increase our chances of success
        D. they may lead to quick solutions

C   65. Preparing for a test by studying only lecture notes while
        ignoring the reading material is an example of which type of
        problem solving?
        A. subgoals
        B. algorithms
        C. heuristics
        D. means-end analysis

D   66. A human problem solving strategy called "planning process"
         typically involves simplifying the problem by:
         A. looking for a common concept
         B. resorting to a well-known formula
         C. generating 3 or 4 good hunches before starting
         D. ignoring some details

B   67. A problem solving strategy which involves reducing but not
         increasing differences between existing and desired states
         is called:
         A. planning process
         B. means-end analysis
         C. working backwards
         D. incubation

A   68. An example of a "means-end analysis" for problem solving
         that was presented in the text is:
         A. how to keep warm outside during the winter
         B. calculating how far and fast birds fly
         C. traveling from New York to San Francisco
         D. moving one's belongings to a new house

A   69. Playing chess, solving mathematical proofs, or plotting
         one's vacation route are problems that can commonly be
         solved by:
         A. working backward
         B. incubation
         C. means-end analysis
         D. algorithms

C   70. The third step in problem solving, where the adequacy of
         potential solutions is evaluated, is called:
         A. preparation
         B. production
         C. judgment
         D. incubation

D   71. Taking time off from the problem, only to have the solution
         come to you "out of the blue" exemplifies which problem
         solving stage?
         A. preparation
         B. production
         C. judgment
         D. incubation

D   72. Why might the "incubation effect" to problem solving occur?
         A. one may overcome mental fatigue
         B. inappropriate ways of thinking about the problem may be
            shed
         C. frustration may dissipate
         D. all of the above

C   73. The text's example of problem solvers who used a formula to
        obtain quantities of water in jars demonstrated that one's
        _____ may interfere with new ways of exploring problems.
        A. solving attitude
        B. functional fixity
        C. set
        D. judgment

B   74. A tendency to approach a problem the same way each time
        because of habitual types of solutions is known as:
        A. functional fixity
        B. set
        C. response bias
        D. negative savings

A   75. Functional fixity may interfere with problem solving
        whenever:
        A. a new and creative use of an object is required
        B. two correct solutions are possible
        C. set is evident
        D. all of the above

A   76. The text's example of using a candle, matches, and a box of
        tacks to solve a problem of properly mounting the burning
        candle demonstrated:
        A. functional fixity
        B. set
        C. response bias
        D. incubation

C   77. Both set and functional fixity can impede effective problem
        solving because of:
        A. lower intelligence levels
        B. attempts to solve a problem too quickly
        C. one's previous experience
        D. high levels of mental fatigue

APPLICATION: SOME TIPS ON SOLVING PROBLEMS

B   78. Which of the following was NOT suggested in the text as a
        tip on solving problems:
        A. broaden your knowledge
        B. don't stop thinking about the problem
        C. look for new ways of structuring the problem
        D. describe the problem to someone

ON THE HORIZON: PROGRAMMING INTELLIGENT COMPUTERS

B   79. The goal of artificial intelligence is to:
         A. help in our use of robots
         B. program computers to behave intelligently
         C. improve our study techniques
         D. improve our defense capabilities in time of war

B   80. One area where artificial intelligence has already made a
         breakthrough is in:
         A. education
         B. medical diagnosis
         C. manufacturing
         D. exploration for oil and gas

A   81. The main advantage of the use of computers and artifical
         intelligence in medicine is a(n):
         A. infallible memory for past symptoms and diseases
         B. rapid diagnosis time
         C. exact science of the machine
         D. less than 1% error rate in diagnosis

— CHAPTER 9 —

MOTIVATION AND EMOTION

OUTLINE

I.   Introduction: The "Subway Samaritan" - presents the story of a
     bystander who spontaneously rescues an elderly man who has
     fallen onto subway tracks to emphasize the role motives play on
     behavior; some are <u>altruistically</u> or <u>egotistically</u> motivated;
     an EMOTION consists of <u>feelings</u>, <u>internal bodily reactions</u>, and
     <u>observable expressions</u>; MOTIVATION refers to forces acting on
     or within an organism that initiate and direct behavior

II. Theories of Motivation

     A. Instinct theory - an INSTINCT is an innate, unlearned,
        goal-directed, species-specific behavior; early theorists
        postulated an unending list of human instinctive motives;
        ETHOLOGISTS have revitalized traditional instinctive theory
        1. Modern instinct theory of the ethologists - gives an
           example of the behavior of the stickleback fish using
           such terms as <u>reaction-specific energy</u>, <u>sign stimulus</u>,
           and <u>innate releasing mechanism</u>; IMPRINTING, a specific
           type of instinctive activity, deals with early
           attachments
           a. an extension to humans? - <u>sociobiology</u> studys the
              biological (and instinctive) basis for human social
              behaviors

     B. Drive theory - replaced the "instinct" concept in the
        1930's; the body attempts to maintain its HOMEOSTASIS; NEEDS
        are any <u>physiological</u> deviations from homeostatic balance

C. Incentive theory - whereas drives are viewed as <u>internal</u> conditions which <u>impel</u> organisms, INCENTIVES refer to <u>external</u> objects or stimuli which <u>attract</u> organisms

D. Arousal theory - AROUSAL THEORY proposes that individuals seek an "optimal" level of arousal by increasing or decreasing stimulation

E. Cognitive theories - COGNITIVE THEORIES assume individuals are motivated to evaluate the consistency or accuracy of their knowledge about the world or themselves
   1. Social comparison theory - Festinger proposed that humans are motivated to evaluate the correctness of their opinions and appraisals of their abilities in the SOCIAL COMPARISON THEORY
   2. Cognitive consistency theories - the COGNITIVE CONSISTENCY THEORIES maintain that humans have a need for consistency in their thoughts and will alter their cognitions or their behavior to achieve consistency

F. Competence and control
   1. Self-actualization - Carl Rogers believes all humans are innately motivated to achieve SELF-ACTUALIZATION, a state of "wholeness" and "full-functioning"
      a. Maslow's hierarchy of needs - this HIERARCHY OF NEEDS deals with the sequential satisfaction of needs ranging from biological to self-actualization; these needs are <u>physiological needs</u>, <u>safety needs</u>, <u>belongingness and love needs</u>, <u>esteem needs</u>, and <u>self-actualization needs</u>.
   2. Personal profile: Abraham Maslow (1908-1970) - the important events in his life that influenced his theory were his marriage and the birth of his first child
   3. Competence and intrinsic motivation - Robert White believes our striving for <u>competence</u> determines our EFFECTANCE MOTIVATION; Edward Deci believes our behavior is motivated by <u>intrinsic</u> needs for competence, self-determination, and feelings we control our environment (i.e., INTRINSIC MOTIVATION refers to performing activities for their own sake)

G. Application: Intrinsic motivation, rewards, and threats - research has shown that intrinsic motivation can be undermined by extrinsic reasons for performing or not performing an activity; examples are given for child-rearing, the use of discipline, and cheating on exams

III. Types of Motives - motives are classified as being either <u>biological</u>, <u>stimulus seeking</u>, or <u>acquired</u>

A. Biological motives - motives related to survival of the individual or of the species are BIOLOGICAL MOTIVES

1. Hunger - damage to the <u>ventromedial hypothalamus</u> (VMH) induces extreme overeating or HYPERPHAGIA whereas damage to the <u>lateral hypothalamus</u> (LH) stops eating; the GLUCOSTATIC THEORY states that the hypothalamus regulates eating by means of <u>glucoreceptors</u> that monitor blood glucose levels; <u>stretch receptors</u> in the stomach also control food intake; the SET-POINT THEORY says the body has a normal weight, or "set-point," which the hypothalamus works to maintain

2. The problem of obesity - OBESITY, found in 30% of all American adults, is defined as body weight which exceeds ideal weight by 20% or more

   a. Responsiveness to external cues - some believe obesity occurs in those who are overly responsive to external cues (e.g., sights, smells) of food

   b. set-point theory - this position says obese people are biologically programmed to have elevated set-points, this position is consistent with the thought that the number of fat cells is fixed at birth

   c. restrained eaters - some studies suggest that chronic dieters risk becoming overweight or even more obese because in the long run chances of overeating are increased due to the loss of self-control

   d. consequences of obesity - certain consequences of obesity serve to maintain obesity; for example, obesity lowers <u>basal metabolism rate</u> and decreases activity rate

   e. some conclusions about obesity - six ways of conquering a weight problem are presented

3. Thirst - a dry mouth is not a primary factor in thirst regulation; two more important mechanisms exist; one regulates <u>intracellular thirst</u> through <u>osmoreceptors</u> in the hypothalamus that detect reductions in <u>volume of cells</u> due to water loss by OSMOSIS; one regulates <u>extracellular thirst</u> by detecting a reduced <u>volume of extracellular fluid</u>; receptors sensitive to lower extracellular fluid also cause <u>renin</u> to be secreted by the kidneys

4. Sex - this motive involves no bodily deficit and is not necessary for survival; thus, sexual motivation is analyzed according to <u>external stimulation, physiological processes, beliefs and expectations, emotion and attitudes, fantasy and imagination</u>; external cues in animals and possibly humans are <u>sex pheromones</u>; in many animal species sexual behavior is <u>periodic</u> and influenced by <u>estrogens, testosterone,</u> and <u>androgens</u>; imagination may be one of the strongest sources of human sexual arousal, though beliefs and expectations are also important

B. Stimulus-seeking motives - STIMULUS-SEEKING MOTIVES, having as their goal the seeking of stimulation, do not appear to be directly related to physiological needs or to learning

1. Exploration and stimulus-seeking — children find exploration of novel stimuli <u>intrinsically motivating</u>; phenomena of exploration, manipulation, and stimulus-seeking are often labeled "curiosity"
   a. sensory deprivation — sensory deprivation studies show the importance of stimulation in our daily lives
2. Sensation seekers — the <u>Sensation Seeking Scale</u> identifies people high and low in sensation seeking; high and low sensation seekers differ in four basic ways (<u>thrill and adventure seeking</u>, <u>boredom susceptibility</u>, <u>disinhibition</u>, <u>experience seeking</u>)

C. Acquired motives — ACQUIRED MOTIVES are thought to be based on learning and experience; two well-researched motives are the need for affiliation and the need to achieve
   1. Need for affiliation — those who prefer social contact and establishing friendships have a strong NEED FOR AFFILIATION; situations are discussed which alter this need state
   2. Need for achievement — the need to strive for success and excellence is called the NEED FOR ACHIEVEMENT
      a. measuring the achievement need — the most popular means has been the <u>Thematic Apperception Test</u>
      b. the development of achievement motivation — though early research found that <u>independence training</u> and <u>achievement training</u> fostered achievement motivation in children, recent research questions this broad conclusion
      c. characteristics of high achievers — they tend to have high IQ's and school grades, to be better users of their time and better at planning ahead, to be able to delay immediate gratification, and they are more likely to cheat
      d. what about females? — most research has been with males; FEAR OF SUCCESS, a learned motive to avoid success for fear of its negative consequences, is found in both females and males

D. Application: Achievement motivation and achievement behavior — the <u>Work and Family Orientation Questionnaire</u> assesses three components of achievement motivation (mastery, work orientation, and competitiveness); competitiveness tends to limit high achievement

IV. Emotion

   A. Defining emotions - experiencing an emotion produces a
      subjective feeling; Izard suggests there are 10 fundamental
      emotions: <u>interest-excitement</u>, <u>joy</u>, <u>surprise</u>, <u>distress</u>,
      <u>anger</u>, <u>disgust</u>, <u>contempt</u>, <u>fear</u>, <u>shame</u>, and <u>guilt</u>; others
      such as <u>anxiety</u> may reflect a combination of these basic
      motives; emotion is also defined by bodily changes, usually
      those mediated by the autonomic nervous system; others not
      mediated by the ANS include specific facial expressions,
      posture, and verbal behavior

   B. How do emotions occur?
      1. The James-Lange theory - this older theory states that a
         stimulus leads to internal bodily changes which then
         leads to the subjective experience of emotion; thus,
         <u>perception</u> of bodily changes leads to the subjective
         experience of an emotion
      2. Schachter's cognitive-physiological theory - the
         modification of the James-Lange theory which added a
         cognitive or "thinking" component to the physiological
         component of emotions; thus, external situations can also
         influence our emotional states
      3. Lazarus' cognitive appraisal theory - emotions arise from
         the evaluations (e.g., cognitive activity, thoughts) we
         make of environmental stimuli; physiological changes are
         not necessary for emotions to occur
      4. Izard's differential emotions theory - believes that
         basic emotions result from facial feedback to the brain
         which is made conscious as a specific emotional feeling;
         innate neural programs are involved
         a. the FACIAL FEEDBACK HYPOTHESIS states that facial
            expressions regulate emotional experiences both in the
            type and intensity of felt emotion
         b. the innateness of facial expressions - cross-cultural
            research suggests some expressions are innate;
            however, learning can influence when these emotions
            are expressed; DISPLAY RULES are norms regarding the
            expected management of facial appearance; further
            support for innate facial expressions is found in the
            fact that very young children show emotions expressed
            in the same fashion as adults

   C. How emotions affect us - many examples of how emotions
      influence a wide range of behaviors are presented; the
      YERKES-DODSON LAW discusses how arousal level and task
      complexity interact to influence performance level

   D. Application: Lie detectors - the POLYGRAPH measures a
      number of bodily changes associated with emotion to assess
      truthfulness; the growing use of polygraph testing in
      private industry is a concern since many "false-positives"
      are associated with this test; a discussion of how and why a
      truthful individual can be labeled a "liar" is presented

V.   On the Horizon: Anorexia Nervosa – an eating disorder
     involving self-starvation and weight loss is called ANOREXIA
     NERVOSA; it is sometimes associated with BULIMIA which refers
     to intense, recurrent episodes of excessive eating
     (binge-eating) followed by depression, self-deprecating
     thoughts, and self-induced vomiting; some speculate lowered
     levels of catecholamines are involved in anorexia; both
     anorexia and bulimia are growing in frequency

OBJECTIVES

I.   HOW DO EACH OF THE MAJOR THEORIES OF MOTIVATION ACCOUNT FOR
     BEHAVIOR?

     The instinct theory assumes that much human behavior is
     instinctual and that we are born with certain motivational
     instincts. The drive theory, which replaced instinct theory as
     the dominant motivational concept in the 1930's, assumes that
     drives (as different from needs) result from specific
     biological needs for food, water, and the like. In this
     approach, needs give rise to the "psychological tensions"
     called drives. In contrast to drive theory which believes
     internal conditions impel organisms to engage in particular
     behaviors, incentive theory emphasizes the role that external
     objects or stimuli attract organisms. Arousal theory preposes
     that individuals seek an optimal level of arousal by either
     behaving in a way to decrease or increase external stimulation.
     Cognitive theories are closely associated with social
     psychology. They assume that individuals are motivated to
     evaluate the consistency or accuracy of their knowledge about
     the world or themselves. Finally, the theories of
     self-actualization by Rogers and the hierachy of needs by
     Maslow are competence and control types of theories. They
     believe we strive for a sense of control or a belief that we
     can affect the world around us.

C   1. Which of the general types of motivational theories
        empasizes external factors?

        A. instinctive
        B. drive
        C. incentive
        D. competence and control

     2. Summarize the explanations that the major motivational
        theories offer for our behavior.

II.   WHAT FACTORS EXPLAIN THE BIOLOGICAL MOTIVES OF HUNGER, THIRST, AND SEX? DESCRIBE SOME OF THE PROBLEMS AND THEORIES ASSOCIATED WITH OBESITY.

Both hunger and thirst are said to be based on physiological mechanisms and bodily deficits, while sex is not. The glucostatic theory states that the hypothalamus regulates eating by monitoring glucose levels with the use of glucoreceptors. The hypothalamus is also believed to monitor stored fat levels to eat enough to maintain an individual's set-point. At least two mechanisms are offered to explain the primary reason why we drink. One theory says that osmoreceptors in the hypothalamus detect reductions in the volume of cells due to water loss. Another theory deals with extracellular thirst. We are believed to drink because of a reduction in the volume of extracellular fluid. In contrast to biological explanations, our sexual motivation is believed to be influenced by a wide range of interacting factors - external stimulation, physiological processes, beliefs and expectations, emotions and attitudes, and fantasy and imagination. People who are obese have a higher incidence of hypertension and diabetes, they are viewed more negatively than those with normal weight, and they tend to be more unhappy. Various explanations for obesity include individuals being more responsive to external cues associated with eating, an elevated set-point, and a history of chronic dieting.

A   1. Which of the following motives is NOT primarily physiological in origin?

      A. sex
      B. thirst
      C. hunger
      D. breathing

D   2. Which of the following was NOT discussed in the text as a contributor to, or cause of, obesity?

      A. a history of chronic dieting
      B. a higher set-point
      C. an individual more responsive to external cues for eating
      D. personality problems associated with self-confidence

      3. What factors explain the biological motives of hunger, sex, and thirst?

III. WHAT ARE STIMULUS-SEEKING MOTIVES? WHAT EVIDENCE SUPPORTS THE EXISTENCE OF SUCH MOTIVES? HOW CAN THEY BEST BE EXPLAINED?

Stimulus seeking motives, like our sex motive, cause the organism to show an initial increase in tension. They include such motives as exploration, manipulation, and curiosity. These motives serve to increase our stimulation level, and they do not appear to be directly related to physiological needs nor do they seem to be learned. Evidence used to support the existence of such motives can be found in many behaviors regularly shown by some humans. These include driving fast, parachute jumping, seeking unusual friends, frequent traveling, drug taking, gambling, and/or sexual variety. These motives can be best explained by the theories of optimal-level-of-arousal or in terms of our desire to achieve competence and control over the environment.

B   1. Stimulus seeking motives are somewhat different from other motives because they:

    A. are not controlled by the hypothalamus
    B. lead to behavior which increases tension
    C. are learned
    D. only motivate adult behaviors

B   2. Which type of theory would best explain the presence of stimulus seeking motives?

    A. incentive theory
    B. arousal theory
    C. cognitive appraisal theory
    D. biological theory

    3. What are the stimulus-seeking motives and in what ways are they explained by psychologists?

IV.   WHAT ARE ACQUIRED MOTIVES? IN WHAT WAYS ARE NEEDS FOR AFFILIATION AND ACHIEVEMENT EXPRESSED?

Acquired motives are thought to be based on learning and experience, e.g., the need for social approval, the need to achieve, the need to dominate others, the need to affiliate, the need for recognition, and the need for nurturance. These needs are purely psychological. The expression of these needs occurs in a variety of ways. Individuals with a strong need for affiliation are more likely than others to seek social contact, to attempt to establish friendships, and to initiate conversations with strangers. Individuals with a high achievement motive tend to have higher IQ scores and school grades, but they are also more likely to cheat. Furthermore, high achievers prefer challenging tasks, they are better able to delay immediate gratification, and they are more concerned with planning ahead and using their time wisely.

C   1. What is a negative or undesirable characteristic found in
          those with a high achievement motive?

          A. high blood pressure
          B. sarcasm
          C. a tendency to cheat
          D. treating friendships lightly

       2. What are acquired motives? Give examples of how they may be
          expressed?

V.   WHAT ARE EMOTIONS? HOW ARE THEY EXPRESSED?

       Emotions consist of subjective feelings (e.g., "I am happy")
       accompanying internal bodily reactions in the brain, nervous
       system and internal organs, and observable expressions,
       expecially in the face. The bodily changes involve activity of
       the autonomic nervous system which include increases in heart
       rate, respiration, blood flow to muscles, and adrenaline
       secreted by the adrenal glands. Other bodily changes involve
       inhibition of digestion, a dry mouth, dilation of the pupils,
       and a decrease in the GSR. Specific facial expressions (e.g.,
       frown, smile, laugh, crying), posture, and verbal behavior are
       among the body's outward, visible signs of emotions.

D   1. Emotions are made up of:

          A. bodily changes
          B. subjective feelings
          C. observable expressions
          D. all of the above

B   2. Which is NOT a bodily change associated with emotions that
          is mediated by the autonomic nervous system?

          A. increase in heart rate
          B. increase in salivation
          C. decrease in GSR
          D. inhibition of digestion

       3. What are emotions and in what general ways are they
          displayed in humans?

VI.   HOW DO THE VARIOUS THEORIES OF EMOTION EXPLAIN THE SUBJECTIVE
       EXPERIENCE OF EMOTION? HOW DO EMOTIONS AFFECT US?

       The James-Lange theory assumes that our subjective experiences
       of an emotion actually follow our internal bodily changes in
       response to some stimulus, i.e., our perceptions of bodily
       changes contribute to our subjective experience of an emotion.
       Schachter's cognitive-physiological theory is a modification of
       the James-Lange theory. This theory add's a cognitive

component which allows us to evaluate or interpret our physical arousal on the basis of external cues. Lazarus' cognitive appraisal theory says that cognitive activity in response to the stimulus is a necessary as well as sufficient condition of emotion, and that physiological changes are not necessary. Izard's differential emotion theory states that our basic emotions result from facial feedback to the brain which is made conscious as a specific emotional feeling. This theory tends to rely on innate components to emotional reactivity. Emotions affect us in numerous ways. The book presents in a later section a number of ways emotions affect our body, perceptions, cognitions, actions, and sexual behavior. The Yerkes-Dodson law states that arousal interacts with task complexity to influence performance level.

A   1. The Yerkes-Dodson law states that _____ interacts with _____ to influence performance level.

     A. arousal ; task complexity
     B. emotions ; motivations
     C. motivations ; personality
     D. arousal ; rewards available

D   2. Which theory of emotion tends to rely on innate components to explain emotional reactivity?

     A. the James-Lange theory
     B. Schachter's cognitive-physiological theory
     C. Lazarus' cognitive appraisal theory
     D. Izard's differential emotions theory

     3. What are the four major theories of emotion and how does each explain our subjective experiences?

MULTIPLE-CHOICE QUESTIONS

INTRODUCTION: THE "SUBWAY SAMARITAN"

B   1. Andrews jumps into a dangerous situation to save a man who desperately needs help. Those psychologists who study motivation are interested in:
     A. why didn't someone else help
     B. what motivated Andrews
     C. how the two were related
     D. the cognitive processes that influenced Andrews perception of the situation

C   2. Someone who behaves altruistically is said to:
       A. be trying to relieve his or her own discomfort
       B. be afraid of behaving in another manner
       C. empathize with the victim's suffering
       D. welcome added excitement and stimulation

D   3. The person who behaves in order to relieve his or her own
       discomfort is said to be _____ motivated.
       A. personally
       B. altruistically
       C. socially
       D. egoistically

A   4. Which of the following is NOT considered to be part of our
       emotions?
       A. perceptions
       B. feelings
       C. internal bodily reactions
       D. observable expressions

INSTINCT THEORY

A   5. Forces acting on or within an organism that govern the
       intensity of behavior are known as:
       A. motivation
       B. judgments
       C. emotions
       D. unconsciousness

D   6. Which term is NOT characteristic of an instinct?
       A. innate
       B. unlearned
       C. species-specific
       D. simple

C   7. A major problem with early instinct theory was that the list
       of instincts:
       A. was poorly explained
       B. dealt more with reflexive behavior
       C. became too long
       D. was not adequately tested

B   8. Ethologists are those who:
       A. test instinct theory
       B. study animal behavior in its natural habitat
       C. say only animals are instinctive
       D. all of the above

B 9. Ethologists postulate that behind each instinctive act is a reservoir of:
  A. emotions
  B. reaction-specific energy
  C. motivations
  D. altruistic behavior

D 10. In order for an instinctive act to occur, a specific _____ must be present.
  A. motivation
  B. emotion
  C. situation
  D. sign stimulus

D 11. Imprinting:
  A. is a specific type of instinctive activity
  B. occurs when an animal becomes socially attached to an object
  C. tends to occur during a critical period
  D. all of the above

A 12. A new field studying the biological basis for social behaviors, called _____, explains many social behaviors on the basis of _____.
  A. sociobiology ; altruism
  B. sociobiology ; imprinting
  C. ethology ; altruism
  D. ethology ; imprinting

DRIVE THEORY

C 13. What term some years ago replaced "instinct" as the dominant motivational concept in psychology?
  A. needs
  B. emotion
  C. drive
  D. motive

B 14. The tendency known as homeostatis pertains to:
  A. instinct regulation
  B. an optimal physiological balance
  C. any physiological deviation
  D. reducing underlying needs

A 15. Any physiological deviation from homeostatic balance is called a:
  A. need
  B. instinct
  C. drive
  D. emotion

D   16. Drives are another term for _____ tensions.
         A. physiological
         B. unlearned
         C. instinctive
         D. psychological

C   17. What according to learning theorist Hull is reinforcing?
         A. a need
         B. the environment
         C. actions that generate drive-reduction
         D. homeostasis

INCENTIVE THEORY

B   18. The drive concept suggests that _____ conditions _____
         organisms to engage in particular behaviors.
         A. internal ; shape
         B. internal ; impel
         C. external ; impel
         D. external ; shape

A   19. An external object or stimulus to which an organism is
         attracted is called a(n):
         A. incentive
         B. drive
         C. need
         D. motive

C   20. Motivation can best be understood in many cases as an
         interaction of:
         A. drives and needs
         B. incentives and needs
         C. drives and incentives
         D. emotions and drives

AROUSAL THEORY

D   21. One weakness of drive theory is that it:
         A. doesn't explain animal behavior very well
         B. doesn't explain human behavior very well
         C. is hard to study experimentally
         D. has difficulty explaining why organisms seek stimulation
            or arousal

B   22. The explanation as to why individuals with too little
         stimulation engage in activities to increase arousal is
         found in _____ theory.
         A. drive
         B. arousal
         C. incentive
         D. cognitive

A   23. Which characteristic of a stimulus is NOT associated with
         how arousing it is?
         A. size
         B. complexity
         C. novelty
         D. intensity

COGNITIVE THEORIES

C   24. Individuals are believed to be motivated to evaluate the
         consistency or accuracy of their knowledge about the world
         or themselves according to which theory of motivation?
         A. drive
         B. need
         C. cognitive
         D. arousal

C   25. Social comparison theory believes that people:
         A. have two basic social drives
         B. have four basic social drives
         C. evaluate opinions and abilities by comparison with others
         D. are different socially than animals

D   26. Cognitive consistency theories maintain that people:
         A. behave in a way to obtain things they think they need
         B. behave in a way to obtain things they actually need
         C. act on the basis of a hierarchy of social motives
         D. alter their cognitions or their behaviors so that they
            match

B   27. The cognitive theories of motivation are closely associated
         with:
         A. ethology
         B. social psychology
         C. psychoanalysis
         D. physiological psychology

COMPETENCE AND CONTROL

B   28. A state that all humans are innately motivated to achieve
         because it represents "wholeness" and "full-functioning" is
         called:
         A. matra
         B. self-actualization
         C. niruana
         D. cognitive enrichment

A   29. Whose name is closely associated with self-actualization and
         hierachy of needs?
         A. Maslow
         B. Bolles
         C. Festinger
         D. Hull

C   30. Which statement is FALSE concerning the idea of a hierarchy
         of needs?
         A. needs range from basic biological motives to the motive
            for self-actualization
         B. the stronger, basic needs must be satisfied first
         C. humans become partially self-actualized at each stage of
            the hierarchy
         D. malnourished people are rarely concerned with
            self-actualization

A   31. Which of the following needs is NOT one of Maslow's
         hierarchy of needs?
         A. awareness
         B. belongingness and love
         C. esteem
         D. safety

D   32. Which need according to Maslow might be fulfilled through
         marriage or friendship?
         A. safety
         B. esteem
         C. self-actualization
         D. belongingness and love

D   33. A striving for competence according to White satisfies
         _____ motivation.
         A. altruistic
         B. intrinsic
         C. personal
         D. effectance

B   34. Intrinsic motivation refers to:
         A. the ability to deal effectively with one's surroundings
         B. performing activities for their own sake
         C. a desire to obtain socially mediated rewards
         D. none of the above

APPLICATION: INTRINSIC MOTIVATION, REWARDS, AND THREATS

C   35. Research on what happens when there is threatened punishment
        (extrinsic reasons) for cheating on an exam (performing an
        unattractive activity) has found that:
        A. the punishment is viewed lightly
        B. the punishment is accepted if the grade change is
           considerable
        C. cheating was likely in another situation
        D. cheating behavior decreased in a range of situations

A   36. Research suggests that to keep people from cheating,
        engaging in crime, or other undesirable behaviors, it is
        best to:
        A. use extrinsic constraints moderately
        B. emphasize the severity of the outcome
        C. rely on their effectance motivational system
        D. reduce the potential rewards for such activities

BIOLOGICAL MOTIVES

D   37. Motives related to survival of the individual or of the
        species are called _____ motives.
        A. basic
        B. intrinsic
        C. effectance
        D. biological

B   38. Damage to a specific area of the hypothalamus, known as the
        ventromedial hypothalamus, causes:
        A. overeating without weight gain
        B. hyperphagia
        C. excessive weight loss
        D. none of the above

A   39. The hypothalamus regulates _____ levels according to the
        _____ theory.
        A. blood sugar ; glucostatic
        B. blood pressure ; glucostatic
        C. blood sugar ; set-point
        D. blood pressure ; set-point

D   40. What has been found to influence eating behavior?
        A. the ventromedial hypothalamus
        B. the lateral hypothalamus
        C. stomach stretch receptors
        D. all of the above

C   41. Set-point theory pertains to:
        A. satisfying the glucoreceptors
        B. reducing body fat levels gradually
        C. maintaining a normal weight
        D. the brain-behavior relation in moderating drinking

B   42. Obesity is defined as body weight which exceeds one's ideal
        weight by _____ percent or more.
        A. 15
        B. 20
        C. 25
        D. 30

C   43. What percentage of all Americans are considered obese?
        A. 20
        B. 25
        C. 30
        D. 35

A   44. Which of the following statements is FALSE?
        A. obese people tend to be overweight as a result of their
           unhappiness
        B. one theory of obesity is that some are overly responsive
           to external cues
        C. dieting may actually increase one's chances of overeating
           and becoming overweight
        D. obesity tends to lower the basal metabolism rate

D   45. One explanation for how we regulate drinking involves
        _____ which incorporates the process called _____.
        A. the hypothalamus ; dehydration
        B. extracellular thirst ; osmosis
        C. osmoreceptors ; expansion
        D. intracellular thirst ; osmosis

C   46. The mechanism dealing with extracellular thirst says we
        drink because of a(n) _____ of extracellular fluid.
        A. heightened volume
        B. increase in osmosis
        C. reduced volume
        D. decrease in osmosis

B   47. Which of the following statements is FALSE?
        A. chemical substances known as sex pheromones influence
           animal sexual behavior
        B. like eating and drinking, sex is necessary for individual
           survival
        C. sexual interest and activity are not aperiodic in humans
        D. imagination may be one of the strongest sources of human
           sexual arousal

A   48. The main source of sexual interest in both human males and
        females seems to be the:
        A. androgens
        B. estrogens
        C. testosterone level
        D. sex pheromones

STIMULUS-SEEKING MOTIVES

D   49. The biological motives such as hunger and thirst fit which
        type of motivational model?
        A. emotional
        B. effectance
        C. stimulus-seeking
        D. drive-reduction

C   50. Exploration,   manipulation,   and   curiosity   are   _____
        motives.
        A. drive reduction
        B. biological
        C. stimulus-seeking
        D. acquired

B   51. Sensory deprivation studies, such as that by Heron, show the
        importance of _____ to our lives.
        A. perception
        B. stimulation
        C. social contacts
        D. rational thinking

A   52. According to Zuckerman's research using the Sensation
        Seeking Scale; _____ desire more stimulation than _____.
        A. males ; females
        B. females ; males
        C. children ; adults
        D. adults ; children

A   53. According to Zuckerman, which of the following does NOT
        differ in high and low sensation seekers?
        A. emotional sophistication
        B. disinhibition
        C. boredom susceptibility
        D. thrill and adventure seeking

C   54. Which of the following is NOT an activity likely to be found
        in high sensation seekers?
        A. parachute jumping
        B. keeping unusual friends
        C. an activity that is repetitious, routine, and boring
        D. gambling

ACQUIRED MOTIVES

D   55. Acquired motives are:
         A. purely psychological
         B. based on learning and experience
         C. used synonymously with the term needs
         D. all of the above

B   56. Individuals who prefer social contacts and establishing
         friendships are said to have a strong need for:
         A. social approval
         B. affiliation
         C. nurturance
         D. domination

B   57. The need to strive for success and excellence is the need
         for:
         A. attainment
         B. achievement
         C. dominance
         D. recognition

A   58. The Thematic Apperception Test is a popular means of
         assessing:
         A. achievement
         B. emotional states
         C. sensation seeking
         D. intrinsic motivation

D   59. Which factors have been associated with high achievement
         motivation in adults?
         A. independence training by parents
         B. severity of toilet training in childhood
         C. scheduling of infant feeding
         D. all of the above

C   60. Which of the following is a characteristic of high
         achievers?
         A. they prefer challenging tasks that have a high
            probability of failure
         B. a negative relationship exists between high achievers
            and their actual school grades
         C. they are more likely to cheat
         D. all of the above

C   61. A learned motive to avoid success for fear of its negative
         consequences is known as:
         A. apathy
         B. inhibition
         C. fear of success
         D. attainment loss

D   62. When is fear of success particularly likely to influence
       one's behavior?
       A. if one is a middle-aged, female excutive
       B. if one is a young female excutive
       C. after one has had a traumatic social experience
       D. when the behavior is "out of role" for one's gender

APPLICATION: ACHIEVEMENT MOTIVATION AND ACHIEVEMENT BEHAVIOR

B   63. The Work and Family Orientation Questionnaire measures
       achievement motivation in all but which area?
       A. mastery
       B. personal goals
       C. work orientation
       D. competitiveness

A   64. Which characteristic according to research by Spence and
       others tends to limit high achievement?
       A. competitiveness
       B. mastery
       C. personal goals
       D. work orientation

DEFINING EMOTIONS

C   65. Which statement is FALSE?
       A. some emotions reflect combinations of other emotions
       B. experiencing an emotion produces a subjective feeling
       C. each of us experience 5 fundamental emotions
       D. three of the fundamental emotions are surprise, joy, and
          guilt

B   66. Emotions are typically associated with which bodily change?
       A. somatic nervous system activity
       B. activity of the autonomic nervous system
       C. blood flow away from the muscles
       D. increased salivation

D   67. Which of the following is NOT associated with a "positive"
       emotion?
       A. crying
       B. smiling
       C. a lot of eye contact
       D. frowning

A   68. Which outward sign of emotion gives observers the best clue
       as to the emotion being experienced?
       A. facial expressions
       B. posture
       C. verbal behavior
       D. activity level

HOW DO EMOTIONS OCCUR?

C   69. A central theme in the James-Lange theory of emotion is
       that:
       A. there are no more than 5 basic emotions
       B. subjective emotional experiences precede internal bodily
          changes
       C. internal bodily changes precede our subjective emotional
          experiences
       D. true emotions do not overlap with one another

B   70. Schachter's theory of emotions modified the James-Lange
       theory by:
       A. deemphasizing bodily changes
       B. adding a thinking component
       C. emphasizing physiological changes
       D. having emotional experiences occur before physiological
          changes

B   71. A study by Schachter and Singer (1962) where epinephrine was
       injected into subjects to produce a strong autonomic arousal
       found that the emotions experienced were:
       A. different in the laboratory
       B. influenced by situational cues
       C. influenced by cognitive appraisals
       D. subjectively different than "real" emotions

D   72. Which theory tends to view emotions as arising from thought,
       and thought only?
       A. James-Lange
       B. Schachter's Cognitive-Physiological
       C. Izard's Differential Emotions Theory
       D. Lazarus' Cognitive Appraisal Theory

A   73. Izard's differential theory of emotions believes basic
       emotions result from:
       A. facial feedback to the brain
       B. one's cognitive evaluation of the situation
       C. neurotransmitter differences in the hypothalamus
       D. learned display rules

D   74. The innateness of facial expressions (of emotions) is
        supported by the fact that:
        A. emotional intensity varies with the type and degree of
           facial expression
        B. individuals living in remote areas of the world use
           expressions similar to Americans
        C. facial expressions are shown by very young children
        D. all of the above

C   75. Display rules are defined as:
        A. innate facial patterns in humans
        B. social and courtship activities in humans and animals
        C. norms regarding the expected management of facial
           appearance
        D. consistent facial patterns shown by individuals in all
           cultures

HOW EMOTIONS AFFECT US

A   76. The Yerkes-Dodson law deals with:
        A. arousal level and performance
        B. physiological reaction and emotions
        C. emotional level and cognitive awareness
        D. optimal level of arousal for normal living conditions

B   77. The optimal level of arousal for _____ tasks is a(n)
        _____ level.
        A. complex ; high
        B. complex ; low
        C. intermediate ; high
        D. simple ; low

APPLICATION: LIE DETECTORS

C   78. An instrument that measures a number of bodily changes
        associated with _____ is called the _____.
        A. motivation ; polygraph
        B. motivation ; GSR
        C. emotion ; polygraph
        D. emotion ; Lie Control Test

D   79. Which statement about "lie detector tests" is TRUE?
        A. they were originally used in private industry
        B. they can detect the specific emotion of guilt about 77%
           of the time
        C. it is difficult to be found guilty of lying if you are
           telling the truth
        D. the validity of the test is questionable

ON THE HORIZON: ANOREXIA NERVOSA

A   80. Anorexia nervosa, an eating disorder, is:
         A. associated with distorted body images
         B. found more often in lower socio-economic classes
         C. an exaggerated bulimia
         D. all of the above

B   81. Which of the following characteristics is NOT associated
         with bulimia?
         A. depression and self-deprecating thoughts
         B. self-starvation
         C. self-induced vomiting
         D. recurrent episodes of excessive eating

– CHAPTER 10 –

EARLY DEVELOPMENT

OUTLINE

I. Introduction: A Baby is Born – a story about the expected
    birth of a deformed child and how the parents reacted before
    and after its delivery; DEVELOPMENTAL PSYCHOLOGY is the
    scientific study of the determinants of human growth and
    development, the underlying processes of change, and the hows
    and whys of alterations in behavior; it has three goals; the
    PRENATAL PERIOD includes the nine months of growth that precede
    birth; the baby's heredity is fully determined at conception,
    but the environment is involved in a continuous interaction
    with heredity

II. Prenatal Growth and Development

    A. The beginning of life – human development begins at
       CONCEPTION when a female's egg cell or ovum and a male's
       sperm cell are united; the fertilized egg is a zygote with
       chromosomes; the zygote undergoes cell division or mitosis

    B. Phases of prenatal development – there are three phases
       1. The period of the ovum – the PERIOD OF THE OVUM lasts
          from 1-14 days and includes the time between
          fertilization and when the zygote (or blastocyst) is
          firmly implanted in the uterine wall; the placenta and
          umbilicus are then formed

   2. The period of the embryo - the PERIOD OF THE EMBRYO, or
      embryo phase, lasts from 15-56 days and is characterized
      by rapid development; internal organs, sex organs,
      nervous system, circulatory system, and external
      characteristics are beginning to form; the embryo phase
      is a particularly <u>critical</u> or <u>sensitive developmental
      period</u>
   3. The period of the fetus - the PERIOD OF THE FETUS,
      lasting from 57-280 days, is marked by development of
      bone cells, the functioning of major organ systems, the
      sex of the fetus becoming apparent, and motor behavior
      becoming more complex

  C. Application: Factors   that   influence   the   prenatal
     environment
   1. Diet during pregnancy - poor maternal nutrition
      (deficiencies in calcium, iodine, vitamins, and protein)
      may lead to fetal malformations and mental retardation
      not only in the offspring but also in the offspring's
      offspring
   2. Emotional state during pregnancy - maternal emotional
      states may activate the autonomic nervous system, in turn
      hormones can cross the <u>placental barrier</u>; maternal stress
      is associated with a more difficult labor and delivery,
      an increased probability of premature birth, and lower
      birth weight
   3. Use of drugs during pregnancy - the use of the sedative
      <u>thalidomide</u> produced physical deformaties and the
      antimiscarriage drug <u>stilbestrol</u> is associated with
      cancer in female offspring; the FETAL ALCOHOL SYNDROME is
      associated with chronic, heavy drinking by pregnant
      women; infants born to heroin addicts suffer withdrawal
      symptoms and are at high risk for a variety of
      psychological disturbances
   4. Other factors influencing the prenatal environment -
      these include exposure to radiation during the embryo
      phase and maternal diseases which include hepatitis,
      chicken pox, and especially rubella; about one-half of
      babies of mothers who had rubella during the first month
      of pregnancy suffer <u>birth defects</u>

III. The World of the Newborn - the NEONATAL PERIOD encompases the
     first month of life

  A. The newborn baby - newborns "tune out" or show <u>habituation</u>
     to many types of stimulation, or they may show an
     involuntary, sleep response to shut out stimuli
   1. The newborn's sensory reactions and reflex behaviors -
      there are some major <u>milestones</u> of hearing development
      and <u>reflexes</u> present in the newborn include the
      <u>withdrawal reflex</u>, the <u>rooting reflex</u>, and the <u>Moro
      reflex</u>

2. Motor development - the rate of MOTOR DEVELOPMENT varies for individual babies, but its order is similar for children in all cultures
3. Vocalization and the influence of early stimulation - there are major milestones of vocal and speech development; the rate at which babies develop speech varies somewhat, but the sequence remains basically the same across cultures; environmental stimulation can influence the frequency and type of speech sounds, e.g., American infants vocalize more than Guatemalen infants because American infants receive more vocal "play"
4. Behavioral states of the newborn and differences in temperament - Brazelton's Neonatal Behavioral Assessment Scale distinguishes six BEHAVIORAL STATES or levels of alertness and consciousness; there are two sleep states (deep and light sleep) and four awake states (drowsy, alert, active, and crying); Brazelton details differences among average babies, quiet babies, and active babies; TEMPERAMENT refers to the newborn's predispositions in mood and behavior; three major temperaments are activity level, responsiveness, and irritability

B. Developmental and birth complications - about 1 in 12 infants in the United States are born with a BIRTH DEFECT or an abnormality of structure, function, or metabolism; structural defects affect the body's physical shape or size; functional defects ·involve one or more body parts not working properly; inborn errors of metabolism an inability to convert certain chemicals into others
1. Genetic and chromosomal abnormalities - the LESCH-NYHAN SYNDROME affects mostly males and its symptoms include spastic movements, abnormal posture, speech difficulties, and self-destructive behavior; PHENYLKETONURIA (or PKU) is due to a defect in enzyme production resulting (if not treated with a low-protein diet) in mental retardation; a PKU screening test at birth measures phenylpyruvic acid in the urine; CRETINISM resulting from an insufficiency of thyroxine will lead to mental retardation if not given thyroid hormone therapy; DOWN'S SYNDROME, due to an extra chromosome as determined by karyotype analysis, is characterized by both physical abnormalities and mental retardation.

2. Hemorrhaging and anoxia – birth complications that can have life-long consequences; HEMORRHAGING refers to the breaking of blood vessels that may be caused by excessive pressure on the fetus' head during delivery; ANOXIA refers to a lack of oxygen resulting from failure to breathe properly or hemorrhaging; anoxia results in defects in motor behavior while hemorrhaging is likely to impair intellectual development; cerebral palsy refers to a variety of motor deficits, frequently associated with anoxia at birth; mild oxygen deprivation may lead to minimal brain damage which may lead to hyperkinesis and impulsivity

3. Prematurity – one out of 10 babies in the United States is born with a complication of PREMATURITY, defined medically by preterm birth and low birth weight; prematurity is related to various psychological problems, though the problems may in fact relate more to early illness and/or prolonged hospitalization

C. Application: Diagnosing   developmental   and   birth complications – three techniques are used; AMNIOCENTESIS, drawing amniotic fluid and analyzing fetal cells, is best done during the 14th to 16th weeks of pregnancy; ULTRASOUND directs sound waves to the womb and when they reflect off of the fetus they form an image; AFP SCREENING measures the amount of alphafetoprotein in the mother's blood

IV. On   The   Horizon: Genetic Counseling and the Prevention of Developmental and Birth Complications – prospective parents are increasingly using prenatal screening and genetic counselors to help them determine and react to prenatal and birth complications; in GENETIC COUNSELING there is an emphasis on giving information to help parents and family understand, choose intelligently, take action, and make the best possible adjustment to a birth defect; genetic counselors may take a directive or non-directive strategy; Tay-Sachs disease is associated with mental deterioration and death between the ages of 3 to 5; people using genetic counseling are those who already have a child with a birth defect or who have no children but have misgivings about possible abnormality in their offspring

OBJECTIVES

I.   WHAT IS DEVELOPMENT?   HOW DO PSYCHOLOGISTS STUDY IT?

Development involves the normal and abnormal changes in behavior with increasing age as well as individual differences in behavior during particular developmental periods. It starts at conception and ends at death. Psychologists try to understand human development by studying hereditary factors, environmental factors, and the continuous interaction of heredity and environmental factors.

1. What is development and how do psychologists study it?

II. WHAT ARE THE GOALS OF DEVELOPMENTAL PSYCHOLOGY?

Developmental psychology is the scientific study of the determinants of human growth and development, the underlying processes of change, and the hows and whys of alterations in behavior. Its three goals are the description, measurement, and explanation of (1) universal, age-related changes in behavior; (2) individual differences in behavior during particular developmental periods; and (3) malformations or disruptions in development.

B   1. Which of the following is NOT something that developmental psychologists typically describe, measure, and explain?

A. universal, age-related changes in behavior
B. ways of treating young abnormal individuals
C. individual differences during particular developmental periods
D. malformations or disruptions in development

2. Discuss the three major goals of developmental psychology.

III. WHAT ARE THREE MAJOR PHASES OF PRENATAL DEVELOPMENT?   WHAT
     BEHAVIORS CHARACTERIZE EACH PHASE?

There are three major phases of prenatal development. The
period of the ovum lasts from 1-14 days. No behavior, per se,
characterizes this stage when the developing zygote or
blastocyst implants in the uterine wall. The period of the
embryo (extending from 15-56 days) is characterized by six
weeks of rapid growth where the internal organs, the nervous
system, and external features begin to form and function to
some degree. The period of the fetus (from 57-280 days) is
when the major organ systems begin to function, including
respiration, digestion, and excretion. By 16 weeks, motor
behavior becomes more complex and the mother can feel fetal
movement.

C   1. The major organ systems begin to function during the period
        of the _____.

        A. ovum
        B. embryo
        C. fetus

C   2. During what period can the mother feel fetal movement?

        A. ovum
        B. embryo
        C. fetus

A   3. Which period of prenatal development is the shortest?

        A. ovum
        B. embryo
        C. fetus

     4. What are the three major phases of prenatal development and
        what characterizes development during these periods?

IV. TO WHAT EXTENT DO FACTORS SUCH AS DIET, DRUG USE, AND GENERAL
     HEALTH AFFECT THE PRENATAL ENVIRONMENT, AND THE UNBORN BABY'S
     DEVELOPMENT?

Since almost everything a woman eats, drinks, injects, or
inhales reaches the baby through the placenta, almost any of
these things may affect the unborn baby's development. For
example, diets deficient in calcium, iodine, and various
vitamins are associated with higher than average rates of fetal
malformations and mental retardation in humans. Animal work
with protein-deficient mothers found that both first and second
generation offspring are underweight and learning-disabled.
Hormones can cross the placental barrier. Thus, a variety of
emotional states (rage, fear, anxiety) which activate the
autonomic nervous system may affect the fetus. Research has

shown that emotional stress during pregnancy is related to delivery difficulties, an increase probability of premature birth, and lower birth weight. The previous use of the sedative thalidomide and the antimiscarriage drug stilbestrol have been associated with severe physical deformities and female cancer in offspring. Heavy cigarette smokers during pregnancy have lower-than-average offspring birthweights. The well-documented fetal alcohol syndrome is associated with heavy (but not moderate) drinking by pregnant women. Infants born to heroin addicts suffer withdrawal symptoms which may last up to six months after birth. Maternal diseases contracted during pregnancy (e.g., hepatitis, chicken pox, and especially rubella) can cause a range of physical and mental deficiencies.

A   1. Why does a mother's emotional state affect her unborn baby?

    A. the autonomic nervous system is activated to produce hormones
    B. emotional mothers are more active
    C. they tend not to eat a well-balanced diet
    D. all of the above

D   2. What can adversely affect the development of the unborn child?

    A. heavy use of alcohol
    B. both prescription and "street-drug" consumption
    C. poor maternal diets
    D. all of the above

    3. Discuss the range of factors that may influence prenatal development, including the specific consequences of certain factors.

V.   WHAT ARE THE CAPACITIES OF THE NEWBORN? WHAT TYPES OF STIMULATION ARE MOST LIKELY TO AID THE DEVELOPING INFANT?

Historically, psychologists believed babies existed in a "buzzing confusion." Today, we know that the newborn enters the world with sophisticated sensory and reflex capacities. They can hear, see, as well as smell, taste, and feel at, or soon after, birth. In fact, many early capacities are fairly well developed. A number of reflexes are also present in the newborn, notably the withdrawal reflex, a rooting reflex, and the Moro reflex. The unfolding of infant motor behavior is nearly complete by the age of 13 or 14 months. There is also an unfolding of vocal and speech development. Both speech and motor development show a rate of development which varies between individuals but an order of development that is similar for children of all cultures.

1. Discuss as specifically as possible the capacities of the
   newborn child.

VI. HOW DO COMPLICATIONS DURING BIRTH RELATE TO LATER DIFFICULTIES
    IN DEVELOPMENT? WHAT PRENATAL SCREENING PROCEDURES ARE
    AVAILABLE TO ENABLE EARLY DIAGNOSIS, AND POSSIBLE PREVENTION,
    OF DEVELOPMENTAL AND BIRTH COMPLICATIONS?

There are a variety of birth complications that can have
life-long consequences. Two of these are hemorrhaging and
anoxia. Hemorrhaging refers to the breaking of blood vessels
in the brain which may result from excessive pressure on the
fetus' head during prolonged labor and delivery. It is likely
to cause impairments in intellectual development. Anoxia
refers to a lack of oxygen. It may occur due to hemorrhaging
or failure of the infant to breath properly. Oxygen
deprivation during birth is most likely to damage the
brainstem, thus causing defects in motor behavior. For
one-third of cerebral palsy patients there is evidence of
anoxia at birth. Mild oxygen deprivation is associated with
minimal brain damage, hyperkinesis, and impulsivity. Prenatal
screening procedures for developmental and birth complications
include amniocentesis (analysizing fetal cells obtained from
drawn amniotic fluid), ultrasound (sound waves reflected from
the fetus form an image of the fetus), and AFP screening
(measuring maternal blood for high levels of alphafetoprotein).
AFP screening is the newest technique and can be used to
determine if the other two procedures are warranted.

A   1. Which of the following is NOT a screening procedure for
       developmental and birth complications?

       A. x-irradiation
       B. ultrasound
       C. amniocentesis
       D. AFP screening

    2. What are two common birth complications shown in humans and
       what screening techniques are available to diagnose and
       prevent these and other developmental complications?

MULTIPLE-CHOICE QUESTIONS

INTRODUCTION: A BABY IS BORN

B   1. The scientific study of the underlying processes of changes
           in growth and the "hows" and "whys" of alterations in
           behavior is called _____ psychology.
           A. child
           B. developmental
           C. adolescent
           D. personality

C   2. The goals of developmental psychology are to _____
           behavior.
           A. explain and control
           B. describe and study
           C. describe, measure, and explain
           D. study, measure, and control

D   3. Which of the following is a major interest area of
           developmental psychology?
           A. age-related changes in behavior
           B. individual differences in behavior
           C. malformations or disruptions in development
           D. all of the above

A   4. The nine months of growth that precede birth is called the
           _____ period.
           A. prenatal
           B. neonatal
           C. prebirth
           D. embryonic

C   5. What guarantees that any one baby will be a unique
           individual?
           A. the prenatal period
           B. its developmental history
           C. heredity
           D. age-related changes in behavior

D   6. The key to understanding development is:
           A. child rearing practices
           B. heredity
           C. the environment
           D. interaction between heredity and environment

THE BEGINNING OF LIFE

A   7. The term which describes when a female's egg cell is united
         with a male sperm cell is:
         A. conception
         B. gestation
         C. union
         D. pairing

B   8. Mitosis is another name for:
         A. zygotes
         B. cell division
         C. chromosomes
         D. hereditary instructions

PHASES OF PRENATAL DEVELOPMENT

B   9. The phase of prenatal development which immediately precedes
         birth is the period of the:
         A. ovum
         B. fetus
         C. embryo
         D. neonate

A   10. The period of the ovum extends from _____ days.
         A. 1-14
         B. 15-56
         C. 1-56
         D. 57-280

C   11. The major event of the period of the ovum is:
         A. fertilization of the egg
         B. the embryo begins to take shape
         C. implantation of the zygote
         D. all of the above

D   12. The period of the embryo is characterized by:
         A. rapid development
         B. the head and body begin to take shape
         C. a primitive heart begins to beat
         D. all of the above

B   13. By the end of the second month, the embryo is about _____
         inch(es) long.
         A. one-half
         B. one
         C. one and one-half
         D. two

C   14. The development of bone cells mark the period of the
_____.
A. ovum
B. embryo
C. fetus
D. neonate

C   15. The sex of the fetus becomes apparent during the period of
the _____.
A. ovum
B. embryo
C. fetus
D. neonate

D   16. Which statement is FALSE concerning the period of the fetus?
A. it is marked by the development of bone cells
B. major organ systems begin to function
C. motor behavior becomes more complex
D. the sex organs are beginning to form

APPLICATION: FACTORS THAT INFLUENCE THE PRENATAL ENVIRONMENT

A   17. Researchers found that _____ mother rats had offspring (as
well   as   their   offsprings'   babies)   that   were
learning-disabled and underweight.
A. protein-deficient
B. calcium-deficient
C. vitamin-enriched
D. salt-enriched

B   18. Which of the following does NOT appear to be related to
emotional stress during pregnancy?
A. a more difficult labor and delivery
B. an irritable neonate
C. an increased probability of premature birth
D. lower birth weight

D   19. When taken during pregnancy, the drug _____ has been
associated with _____ in offspring.
A. alcohol ; cancer
B. stilbestrol ; retarded mental development
C. nicotine ; cancer
D. thalidomide ; physical deformities

A   20. Stilbestrol, an antimiscarriage drug, has been associated
with:
A. cancer in female offspring
B. children with severely deformed arms and legs
C. lowered birth weight in offspring
D. retarded physical development in children

C   21. Thalidomide, a sedative given during pregnancy, is
        associated with:
        A. withdrawal symptoms
        B. mental retardation
        C. physical deformities
        D. all of the above

D   22. Which of the following has an adverse affect on fetal growth
        and development?
        A. alcohol
        B. heavy cigarette smoking
        C. medicines
        D. all of the above

B   23. Which characteristic has NOT been associated with the fetal
        alcohol syndrome?
        A. sleep disturbances
        B. alcoholism in adulthood
        C. premature birth
        D. retarded physical and mental development

C   24. Which of the following statements is FALSE?
        A. fetal heartrate increases as the mother smokes
        B. the fetal alcohol syndrome is not associated with
           moderate drinking
        C. surprisingly, children of narcotic-addicted mothers are
           not at risk for psychological disturbances
        D. hormones may influence the fetus by crossing the
           placental barrier

A   25. Which is one of the most seriously disruptive viral disease
        during pregnancy?
        A. rubella
        B. chicken pox
        C. hepatitis
        D. rabies

B   26. Approximately _____ of all babies born to mothers who had
        rubella during the _____ month(s) of pregnancy show birth
        defects.
        A. one-half ; first four
        B. one-half ; first
        C. one-third ; first
        D. one-third ; first four

D   27. Which of the following is NOT a common characteristic of
        babies exposed to rubella during gestation?
        A. deafness
        B. blindness
        C. mental retardation
        D. physical malformations

THE WORLD OF THE NEWBORN

A   28. The neonatal period of development encompasses the first
         _____ of life.
         A. month
         B. three months
         C. six months
         D. eight months

THE NEWBORN BABY

C   29. One explanation for a newborn's ability to withstand various
         disturbances and insults from the environment is that it:
         A. has a limited stimulus threshold
         B. associates little meaning to the environmental stimu-
            lation
         C. makes an involuntary, sleep response
         D. has a short attention span

A   30. Babies are able to differentiate sounds during the _____
         week of life.
         A. 1st
         B. 2nd
         C. 3rd
         D. 4th

D   31. Researchers have reported that infants averaging _____
         hours old visually discriminated among a live model's happy,
         sad, and surprised facial expressions.
         A. 18
         B. 20
         C. 24
         D. 36

A   32. Babies tested as soon as _____ after birth demonstrate a
         capacity to detect differences in smell and taste.
         A. 1 or 2 days
         B. 2 to 3 months
         C. 3 to 5 months
         D. 5 to 6 weeks

A   33. The Moro reflex in newborns is elicited by:
         A. sudden changes in head position
         B. pricking the foot
         C. tickling the side of the mouth
         D. pushing against the palm of the hand

C   34. The orderly emergence of active movement skills is called
         _____ development.
         A. physical
         B. motoric
         C. motor
         D. sequence

B   35. Even though the _____ of motor development varies for
         individual babies, its _____ is similar for children in
         all cultures.
         A. order ; speed
         B. rate ; order
         C. sequence ; rate
         D. order ; sequence

D   36. Which activity precedes "sits without supports" according to
         the typical sequence of motor development?
         A. walks holding on to furniture
         B. stands alone well
         C. stands holding on to furniture
         D. rolls over

D   37. The average child walks alone around _____ months of age.
         A. 9
         B. 10
         C. 11
         D. 12

A   38. The Neonatal Behavioral Assessment Scale is used to
         distinguish:
         A. levels of alertness and consciousness
         B. mental retardation
         C. physical retardation
         D. vocal ability

C   39. The Neonatal Behavioral Assessment Scale differentiates
         _____ sleep states and _____ awake states.
         A. 3 ; 3
         B. 4 ; 2
         C. 2 ; 4
         D. 2 ; 5

B   40. Levels of alertness and consciousness are called:
         A. emotional states
         B. behavioral states
         C. reactivity levels
         D. responsivity

B   41. Which·of the following terms is NOT used by Brazelton to
         describe babies' behavioral states?
         A. average
         B. neutral
         C. quiet
         D. active

D   42. The newborn's predispositions in mood and behavior are
        referred to as its:
        A. personality
        B. reactivity range
        C. heritability
        D. temperament

A   43. Which of the following is NOT a major dimension of infant
        temperament as reported by recent studies?
        A. emotional softness
        B. activity level
        C. irritability
        D. responsiveness

DEVELOPMENTAL AND BIRTH COMPLICATIONS

C   44. According to the National Foundation March of Dimes the rate
        of children born in the United States with some type of
        birth defect is:
        A. 1 in 20
        B. 1 in 15
        C. 1 in 12
        D. 1 in 8

C   45. The nation's most serious child health problem is related
        to:
        A. inherited disorders
        B. poor family rearing practices
        C. prenatal and birth complications
        D. infectious diseases

B   46. An abnormality of structure, function, or metabolism in
        children is known as a(n):
        A. anomaly
        B. birth defect
        C. developmental hindrance
        D. behavioral retardation

D   47. Self-destructive behavior is a common symptom in which
        disorder?
        A. phenylketonuria
        B. cretinism
        C. Down's Syndrome
        D. Lesch-Nyhan Syndrome

A   48. In which of the following disorders is mental retardation
        NOT a major symptom?
        A. Lesch-Nyhan Syndrome
        B. PKU
        C. cretinism
        D. Down's Syndrome

C   49. The retardation associated with cretinism can be reversed
         with:
         A. genetic services
         B. simple dietary regulation
         C. thyroid therapy
         D. early special education classes

A   50. Phenylketonuria is caused by:
         A. an enzyme production deficiency
         B. too little thyroxine
         C. chromosomal abnormalities
         D. brain damage associated with birth

D   51. Down's Syndrome:
         A. occurs in people with 47 chromosomes
         B. is associated with faulty cell division
         C. is more common in children born to women over age 45
         D. all of the above

B   52. Karyotype analysis is most commonly used to detect which
         disorder?
         A. cretinism
         B. Down's Syndrome
         C. PKU
         D. Lesch-Nyhan Syndrome

D   53. Two useful clinical symptoms for diagnosing Down's Syndrome
         are:
         A. a flat face and at least one malformed ear
         B. flat feet and mouth corners turning downward
         C. a fold of skin over each eye and flat feet
         D. a protruding tongue and slanted eyes

C   54. Hemorrhaging, which can lead to brain damage, is likely to
         result from:
         A. chromosomal abnormalities
         B. a poor prenatal maternal diet
         C. excessive pressure on the head during birth
         D. none of the above

B   55. Anoxia refers to:
         A. low protein intake during pregnancy
         B. a lack of oxygen
         C. increased blood supply to the brain
         D. apathy in newly born children who are retarded

A   56. Developmental defects in motor behavior are likely to result
         from _____ while impaired intellectual development is
         likely a result of _____.
         A. anoxia ; hemorrhaging
         B. anoxia ; prematurity
         C. hemorrhaging ; anoxia
         D. hemorrhaging ; chromosomal abnormalities

D   57. Mild oxygen deprivation is associated with:
         A. minimal brain damage
         B. hyperkinesis
         C. impulsivity
         D. all of the above

D   58. There is evidence of anoxia at birth in about one-third of
         _____ patients.
         A. Lesch-Nyhan Syndrome
         B. PKU
         C. Down's Syndrome
         D. cerebral palsy

D   59. Prematurity is defined medically by:
         A. preterm birth
         B. low birth weight
         C. preterm birth and physical complications
         D. low birth weight and preterm birth

C   60. Prematurity is NOT related to which psychological or
         physical problem?
         A. cerebral palsy and hyperkinesis
         B. lower measured intelligence
         C. stuttering
         D. learning disabilities during the early school years

APPLICATION: DIAGNOSING DEVELOPMENTAL AND BIRTH COMPLICATIONS

B   61. Amniocentesis is used to detect:
         A. cerebral palsy
         B. genetic and chromosomal abnormalities
         C. neurological impairments
         D. all of the above

A   62. Withdrawing amniotic fluid for analysis of fetal cells is
         called:
         A. amniocentesis
         B. ultrasound
         C. AFP screening
         D. genetic analysis

B   63. The optimium time for amniocentesis is between the _____
         weeks of pregnancy.
         A. 10th to 12th
         B. 14th to 16th
         C. 16th to 17th
         D. 18th to 20th

A   64. A recent technique used to form an image of the unborn baby
         within the womb is called:
         A. ultrasound
         B. x-rays
         C. AFP screening
         D. amniocentesis

C   65. AFP screening has been used to detect birth defects before
         the use of ultrasound and amniocentesis by analyzing:
         A. x-rays
         B. urine samples
         C. blood samples
         D. heart beat patterns of the fetus

ON THE HORIZON: GENETIC COUNSELING AND THE PREVENTION OF
DEVELOPMENTAL AND BIRTH COMPLICATIONS

D   66. Information as to whether a fetus has, or is expected to
         have, a birth defect is now being provided by:
         A. delivery-room physicians
         B. family physicians
         C. psychiatric nurses
         D. genetic counselors

C   67. The importance of genetic counseling is demonstrated by
         studies which showed that about _____ of parents with PKU
         children did not know it was inherited.
         A. 10%
         B. 25%
         C. 60%
         D. 85%

B   68. Most genetic counseling is done in a:
         A. directive manner
         B. non-directive manner
         C. home setting
         D. hospital setting

A   69. The disorder which first causes mental deterioration and
         then death, usually between the ages of 3 to 5 years, is
         called:
         A. Tay-Sachs disease
         B. PKU
         C. cretinism
         D. Lesch-Nyhan Syndrome

- CHAPTER 11 -

LIFE-SPAN DEVELOPMENT

OUTLINE

I.   Introduction: The Parent's Role In Child Development — an example of how a baby's crying influences its mother and how different maternal reactions to crying may influence social development.

II. Infancy and Childhood: what ages correspond to INFANCY, EARLY CHILDHOOD, and LATE CHILDHOOD; most research is conducted with infants

   A. Developmental tasks of infancy and childhood: what are DEVELOPMENTAL TASKS and how are they influenced by maturation and learning.

   B. Cognitive development: what is COGNITION (and thus cognitive development) three views of cognitive development (EMPRICISM, RATIONALISM, and interactionism which incorporate the influence of nurture and nature).
      1. Piaget's theory of cognitive development: Piaget's schemata are present at birth and change through the processes of ASSIMILATION and ACCOMMODATION to account for cognitive development.
      2. Stages of cognitive development: there are four stages; A STAGE THEORY OF COGNITIVE DEVELOPMENT stresses mastering of skills in order.
         a. SENSORIMOTOR STAGE (birth to 2 years) — the egocentric infant interacts through sensory perception and motor action; an important task is OBJECT PERMANENCE

        b. PREOPERATIONAL STAGE (2 to 7 years): pre-logical operations; two substages of preoperational thought – preconceptual substage (2 to 4) with preconceptual thought and intuitive substage (4 to 7) with some CONSERVATION being mastered.

        c. CONCRETE OPERATIONAL STAGE (7 to 12 years): limited logical thought following the four rules of <u>identity</u>, <u>associativity</u>, <u>reversibility</u>, and <u>combinativity</u>.

        d. FORMAL OPERATIONAL STAGE (12 years to adult): final stage that not all adults reach.

    3. Summary: how children at each stage of cognitive development would play Monopoly game.

    4. Personal profile: Jean Piaget (1896-1980): His life, training, and contributions to education

C. Psychosocial development: Erikson's theory of PSYCHOSOCIAL DEVELOPMENT pertains to psychological and social interactions; conflicts at each of 8 stages establish basic virtue (e.g., <u>trust</u> vs. <u>mistrust</u> establishes basic trust; <u>autonomy</u> vs. <u>doubt</u> establishes autonomy; <u>initiative</u> vs. <u>guilt</u> establishes initiative; <u>industry</u> vs. <u>inferiority</u> establishes industry; SOCIALIZATION, with <u>milestones of socialization</u>, contribute to task mastery.

D. Social attachments: social development a function of ATTACHMENT to caregiver; <u>critical periods of development</u> as they relate to <u>imprinting</u> and <u>social attachment</u>; CRITICAL PERIODS of development (also <u>sensitive periods</u> or <u>optimal periods</u>) relate to human <u>bonding</u>.

    1. The development of attachment: Bowlby and Ainsworth present <u>phases</u> of attachment (<u>preattachment</u>, <u>attachment-in-the-making</u>, <u>clear-cut attachment</u>, <u>goal-corrected partnership</u>).

    2. Consequences of attachment for later development: <u>maternal deprivation</u> and <u>social deprivation</u> impair early relationships, as shown in Spitz's term <u>hospitalism</u>.

        a. attachment and separation in infant monkeys: Harlow's subjects reared with <u>surrogate</u> mothers who were <u>physiologically</u> but not <u>phychologically</u> equivalent; various negative consequences of this type of rearing.

        b. attachment and separation in human infants: the <u>strange situation procedure</u> for research showed <u>secure attachment</u>, <u>ambivalent attachment</u>, and <u>avoidant infants</u>; stimulation and caregiver attention is the most important developmental factor.

E. Families, children, and social change: statistics related to current family characteristics (e.g., divorces, single-parent families).

    1. Working mothers: positive and negative consequences; <u>quality of care</u> at day-care centers and <u>quality and quantity of interactions</u> between mother and child when together.

2. Separation and divorce: research and statistics on the effects on children.
3. The father's role: little available information

F. Application: Child-rearing practices, I: Styles of parenting - child-rearing practices change over time; research rated parent-child relationships on dimensions (maturity demands, parent-child communication, parental nurturance) correlated to children's social competency.

III. Adolescence: ADOLESCENCE as influenced by Hall.

A. Maturation and physical development during adolescence.
1. PUBERTY (or pubescence) as it occurs in the normative population; physical changes in girls (e.g., menarche) and boys.
2. Adolescent growth spurt: boys about 2 years behind
3. Individual differences in physical development: statistics for each gender.

B. Developmental tasks of adolescence: there are four
1. Adjustment to physical changes: early vs. late maturation; characteristics for each in both genders.
2. Achieving independence from parents: Erikson's conflict of role identity vs. role confusion.
3. Developing mature peer relations: interactions with same-sex peers; sexual activity and unwanted pregnancy.
4. Development of social responsibility and morals: Kohlberg's six stages of moral development; two PRECONVENTIONAL STAGES OF MORAL DEVELOPMENT, two CONVENTIONAL STAGES OF MORAL DEVELOPMENT, two POSTCONVENTIONAL STAGES OF MORAL DEVELOPMENT with the first showing MORAL INTERNALIZATION; the Moral Judgement Scale measures moral maturity; example of ethical conflict and how each stage would react.

C. Application: Child rearing practices, II: Fostering moral judgment development - characteristics of children raised by power-assertive, (authoritarian) and non-power-assertive authoritative parents.

IV. Adulthood and Later Maturity: a new stage for late teens and early 20's called youth?

A. EARLY ADULTHOOD (18 to 35 years) with particular developmental tasks (e.g., Erikson's INTIMACY vs. ISOLATION)

B. MIDDLE AGE (35 to 65 years) with certain developmental tasks (e.g., Erikson's GENERATIVITY vs. SELF ABSORPTION)

C. LATER MATURITY (after age 65) with particular developmental tasks (e.g., Erikson's INTEGRITY vs. DESPAIR).
1. Personal profile: Erik Erikson (1902-   ): His life, training, and academic positions.

D. Application: Charting life-span development - summary of Erikson's basic virtues (<u>drive</u> and <u>hope</u> from basic trust; <u>self-control</u> and <u>willpower</u> from autonomy; <u>purpose</u> and <u>direction</u> from initiative; <u>competence</u> from role identity; <u>affiliation</u> and <u>love</u> from intimacy; <u>production</u> and <u>care</u> from generativity; <u>wisdom</u> from integrity); table summarizing Erikson's 8 stages for age, basic virtue, child's needs, and parent's appropriate responses is presented.

V.   On the Horizon: Death and Dying - a presentation of the Karen Ann Quinlan case and the ethical dilemma it presented for her parents, doctors, lawyers, and our society as a whole; Elizabeth Kubler-Ross' five phases of dying are presented (<u>denial</u>, <u>anger</u>, <u>bargaining</u>, <u>depression</u>, <u>acceptance</u>); HOSPICE and <u>bereavement counseling</u>

OBJECTIVES

I.   WHY DO PSYCHOLOGISTS STUDY COGNITIVE DEVELOPMENT IN INFANTS AND CHILDREN? HOW IS SUCH DEVELOPMENT STUDIED?

Psychologists study cognitive development in young humans because, as in many areas of development, infancy and childhood provide a special foundation for later development. Cognitive development has generated considerable research as a result of Piaget's pioneering work which demonstrated that humans progress through four stages of cognitive development, each stage with its own characteristics and, at times, limitations. Piaget's interpretation of cognitive development is one of an interactionist (versus an empirical or rational) where innate "schematas" are molded and reorganized by the environment. Thus, it is important to understand the cognitive characteristics and limitations of youngsters and study how they change through interactions with their environment. The standard way to study cognitive development is to verbally give a child a series of simple tasks to see if the child can solve each task and, if so, how the solution is reached (see figure 5 in the text).

A   1. The pioneering studies in cognitive development were conducted by:

A. Piaget
B. Harlow
C. Erikson
D. Havighurst

B   2. Current and prominent interpretations of cognitive
          development favor a(n) _____ view.

          A. Empirical
          B. Rational
          C. Interactional
          D. Generative

       3. How do psychologists study cognitive development and what
          differences have been discovered in children at different
          developmental stages?

II.   HOW DOES THE SPECIAL BOND OF ATTACHMENT BETWEEN INFANT AND
       CAREGIVER DEVELOP?   WHAT ARE THE CONSEQUENCES OF EARLY
       ATTACHMENT FOR LATER DEVELOPMENT?

       Bowlby and Ainsworth have described various phases of
       attachment.   (1) The initial, preattachment phase is
       characterized by an infant who is unable to tell one person
       from another and thus responds favorably to all.   (2) The
       attachment-in-the-making phase begins when the infants can
       discriminate their primary caregivers from others (as well as
       one familiar person with another) and then the infant directs
       proximity-seeking actions toward the caregiver.   (3) The
       clear-cut attachment phase is characterized by maintenance of
       proximity to a particular caregiver with both locomotion and
       signals.   (4) The fourth phase is where the child is able to
       make inferences about the primary caregiver's feelings and
       motives.   The benefits of early attachment has been studied in
       both humans and animals with deprivation and separation types
       of studies.   Infants deprived of early attachments, or removed
       from objects of attachment, develop a wide range of physical,
       social, and emotional deficits.

D   1. A strong attachment is typically formed with an infant's:

          A. mother
          B. father
          C. sibling
          D. primary caregiver

C   2. Infants deprived of strong early attachments:

          A. grow faster
          B. become more independent
          C. show social behavior deficits
          D. are physically, but not emotionally, healthier

       3. Summarize the various phases of attachment presented by
          Bowlby and Ainsworth.

III. DESCRIBE THE COURSE OF PHYSICAL DEVELOPMENT DURING ADOLESCENCE. HOW DO BOYS AND GIRLS DIFFER WITH RESPECT TO THE RATE OF MATURATION AND PHYSICAL DEVELOPMENT?

Maturational changes occur in both genders during physical development. There is rapid acceleration of physical growth (the growth spurt), changing bodily dimensions, hormonal changes which among other things increase the sexual drive, and development of primary and secondary sex characteristics. Girls generally mature physically about two years earlier than boys. For girls, puberty brings an enlargement of the ovaries, uterus, breasts, vagina, as well as the appearance of pubic hair and menarche. For boys, puberty is associated with enlargement of the penis and testes, the growth of pubic and other body hair, and the lowering of the voice.

C   1. Which characteristic do boys but not girls show at puberty?

      A. secondary sex characteristics
      B. growth spurt
      C. growth of body hair
      D. increase in sexual drive

     2. What are the primary and secondary sex characteristic changes which occur in boys and girls during adolescence?

IV. WHAT DEVELOPMENTAL TASKS CHARACTERIZE THE TRANSITION FROM CHILDHOOD TO ADULTHOOD?

The text discusses four developmental tasks of adolescence. (1) Adjustment to physical changes deals with every adolescent as accepting their physique and using their body effectively in physical activity. This is especially relevant to early- vs. late-maturers. (2) Achieving independence from parents concerns emotional independence which can only occur if they have some idea of "who they are" and "where they are going." (3) Developing mature peer relations with same-sex peers (age-mates) will serve as models for later adult relationships in various settings. (4) Developing social responsibility and morals requires a knowledge of right and wrong, good and bad. Morality occurs gradually.

A   1. The developmental task of adolescence which concerns emotional independence and knowing "where you are going" is known as:

      A. achieving independence from parents
      B. developing mature peer relations
      C. adjusting to physical changes
      D. developing social responsibility

D   2. The development of morality is associated with which developmental task of adolescence?

      A. achieving independence from parents
      B. developing mature peer relations
      C. adjusting to physical changes
      D. developing social responsibility

      3. Present and discuss the four developmental tasks that the text says characterize adolescence.

V.   WHAT DEVELOPMENTAL TASKS CHARACTERIZE ADULTHOOD AND LATER MATURITY?

The developmental tasks of adulthood are divided into those for early adulthood (ages 18 to 35) and middle age (ages 35 to 65). The tasks of early adulthood range from selecting and learning to live with a marriage partner, starting and rearing a family, getting started in a career, and taking on civic responsibility. During middle age, adults become truly concerned about doing something useful with their lives. The tasks include achieving adult civic and social responsibility, establishing and maintaining satisfactory performance in an occupation, relating successfully to one's spouse, and adjusting to one's own and one's parents' increasing age. The developmental tasks of later maturity (after age 65) include adjusting to decreasing physical strength, establishing satisfactory living arrangements and relationships with same-age peers, and coping with a spouse's death.

C   1. During what stage do people become truly concerned about doing something useful with their lives?

      A. adolescence
      B. early adulthood
      C. middle age
      D. later maturity

D   2. Establishing satisfactory living arrangements and relationships with same-age peers is a developmental task of what stage?

      A. adolescence
      B. early adulthood
      C. middle age
      D. later maturity

      3. How are the developmental tasks of later maturity, middle age, and early adulthood different concerning one's relation to his or her spouse?

VI.   DESCRIBE ERIKSON'S STAGES OF PSYCHOSOCIAL DEVELOPMENT.   WHAT
      CAN PARENTS DO TO BETTER MEET THEIR CHILDRENS' NEEDS AT EACH
      STAGE OF PSYCHOSOCIAL DEVELOPMENT?

      Erikson's theory of psychosocial development states that the
      individual develops through eight stages, from infancy to
      old age.   A conflict must be resolved at each age, and each
      conflict is closely tied to social relationships.   The tasks
      or conflicts are believed to be accompained by basic virtues
      which appear to emerge from generation to generation (e.g.,
      drive and hope emerge from basic trust).   A complete list of
      these eight stages, with their corresponding ages, basic
      virture, and both the child's needs and appropriate parental
      responses are summarized in a table near the end of this
      chapter.

   1. Discuss any 3 of Erikson's eight stages of psychosocial
      development.   Include in your answer the ages and basic
      virtues associated with each stage as well as the child's
      needs and how parents may respond appropriately to these
      needs.

                    MULTIPLE-CHOICE QUESTIONS

INTRODUCTION

A   1. As demonstrated in the text by the cases of Toby's and
        Sharon's crying, one can conclude that picking up a crying
        baby:
        A. does not spoil the baby
        B. will cause it to cry more the next time
        C. will cause it to cry louder the next time
        D. has little long term effect on its behavior

INFANCY AND CHILDHOOD

A   2. Which type of subject has been most extensively studied in
        developmental psychology?
        A. infants
        B. children
        C. adolescents
        D. adults

B   3. Infancy spans what period of development?
         A. conception to birth
         B. the first 18 months of life
         C. conception to roughly age 5
         D. from birth to the beginning of the teen years

C   4. Early childhood extends from:
         A. one month to 1.5 years
         B. one month to 5 years
         C. 1.5 to 5 years
         D. 1.5 to about 8 years

C   5. Which developmental period immediately precedes adolescence?
         A. infancy
         B. early childhood
         C. late childhood
         D. early adulthood

B   6. Which two developmental periods do researchers consider
         especially important for later development?
         A. infancy and adolescence
         B. infancy and childhood
         C. childhood and adolescence
         D. late childhood and adolescence

DEVELOPMENTAL TASKS OF INFANCY AND CHILDHOOD

D   7. Which is the term given to particular behavior skills that
         characterize different stages of development?
         A. maturational stages
         B. behavioral markers
         C. milestones
         D. developmental tasks

B   8. Biological maturation is exemplified by:
         A. unorderly, fairly random changes
         B. learning to walk
         C. mental growth influencing physical capacities
         D. mastering reading and writing

COGNITIVE DEVELOPMENT

C   9. The process by which infants come to know their world and
         acquire knowledge is called:
         A. maturation
         B. socialization
         C. cognitive development
         D. psychosocial development

B   10. Two key terms in development that are associated with
         empiricism are:
         A. tabula rasa and nature
         B. tabula rasa and nurture
         C. nature and nurture
         D. environmentalism and nature

A   11. The view that the source of all knowledge, the intellect, is
         present at birth is:
         A. rationalism
         B. empiricism
         C. cognition
         D. interactionism

A   12. Piaget considers schemata to be:
         A. "building blocks" of knowledge
         B. learned by age one
         C. motor activities used in development
         D. the first stage of cognitive development

D   13. The process of modifying new information to make it fit
         existing schemata or knowledge is known as:
         A. knowledge through action
         B. accommodation
         C. cognition
         D. assimilation

D   14. When a child's cognitive structures are changed by
         experience, Piaget would say _____ has occurred.
         A. cognitive growth
         B. cognitive development
         C. assimilation
         D. accommodation

C   15. The critical feature of Piaget's stage theory of cognitive
         development is the:
         A. notion that one's age determines one's stage
         B. belief that very bright children can skip stages
         C. belief that the stages are attained in the same order
         D. assumption that all stages are attained by over 99.5% of
            us

B   16. The stage of cognitive development where knowledge is
         primarily acquired through sensory perception and motor
         action is the _____ stage.
         A. object permanence
         B. sensorimotor
         C. egocentric
         D. preoperational

D   17. A child who has recently mastered object permanence will:
    A. behave as if its schemata were prewired
    B. know the difference between yesterday and tomorrow
    C. judge 5 pounds of feathers and 5 pounds of stone
       to weigh the same
    D. "know" that an object exists even if it can't be
       seen

B   18. The preoperational stage of cognitive development typically
       covers what ages?
    A. birth to 2 years
    B. 2 to 7 years
    C. 7 to 12 years
    D. 7 to 15 years

B   19. Which is a characteristic of the intuitive substage of
       preoperational thought?
    A. children can identify broad classes of objects, such
       as houses and dogs
    B. visual impressions dominate thought
    C. rules and operations necessary for logic are present
    D. conservation is mastered in numerous areas

C   20. A child who judges an elongated piece of clay equal to an
       identical amount of clay shaped into a ball has mastered:
    A. preconceptual thought
    B. object permanence
    C. conservation
    D. cognitive development

D   21. The concrete operational stage is shown by:
    A. mastery of conservation tasks
    B. logical thought applied to concrete objects
    C. logical thought applied to situations
    D. all of the above

C   22. Piaget's rule of logic which says that a clay ball can be
       shaped and reshaped to look the same is called:
    A. identity
    B. associativity
    C. reversibility
    D. combinativity

D   23. Conservation of area is generally achieved around _____
       years.
    A. 3 to 4
    B. 5 to 6
    C. 7 to 8
    D. 9 to 10

A   24. The formal operational stage of cognitive development:
         A. shows problem solution following hypothesis
            testing
         B. is reached about 18 years of age
         C. is found in most adolescents and all adults
         D. shows conservation based upon concrete
            operations

C   25. Research has demonstrated that training can facilitate
         development of:
         A. object permanence
         B. logical thought
         C. conservation of number and length
         D. egocentrism

B   26. Children playing Monopoly who are in the preoperational
         stage would likely:
         A. put dice in their mouth
         B. make up their own rules
         C. have no trouble arranging mortgages
         D. all of the above

B   27. Piaget's theory of cognitive development has had a major
         impact on:
         A. computer development
         B. education
         C. business
         D. child-rearing practices

PSYCHOSOCIAL DEVELOPMENT

D   28. Each of Erikson's stages of psychosocial development
         involve:
         A. using different cognitive abilities
         B. reaching optimum social growth
         C. establishing basic trust
         D. resolving a conflict

A   29. The first of Erikson's eight stages of psychosocial
         development is:
         A. trust vs. mistrust
         B. autonomy vs. doubt
         C. initiative vs. guilt
         D. industry vs. inferiority

B   30. During the autonomy vs. doubt stage of psychosexual
         development, doubt will be fostered by parents who:
         A. are controlling
         B. are overcritical
         C. are too demanding
         D. are too lenient

A   31. The conflicts in Erikson's theory of psychosocial
        developmental are closely tied to:
        A. social relationships
        B. physical maturation rate
        C. psychological advances
        D. cognitive advances

C   32. The psychosexual stage which involves initiative vs. guilt
        appears during the:
        A. first year
        B. years 2 to 3
        C. years 3 to 5
        D. years 6 to 11

C   33. A sense of industry is fostered in Erikson's fourth stage
        when children are:
        A. left alone
        B. told to initiate activities
        C. encouraged to "make" and "create"
        D. encouraged to work outside of the house

A   34. When individuals gradually acquire the behaviors, beliefs,
        and motives that are valued by both their family and the
        community, it is called:
        A. socialization
        B. development
        C. maturation
        D. psychosocial growth

C   35. Which of the following is a milestone of socialization for
        infants under one month of age?
        A. says things like "Da-Da" and "Ma-Ma"
        B. shows fear of strangers
        C. emits expression of discomfort
        D. is toilet trained

SOCIAL ATTACHMENTS

D   36. Another name for the social attachment shown by infants is:
        A. love
        B. affection
        C. clear-cut attachment
        D. bonding

B   37. A social attachment in animals that develops quickly during
        an early critical period is called:
        A. bonding
        B. imprinting
        C. socialization
        D. love

C   38. A time when the organization of certain behaviors is most
         easily affected by the environment is called a(n) _____
         period.
         A. effective
         B. open
         C. critical
         D. imprinting

D   39. Research by Klaus and Kennell demonstrated that human
         bonding was encouraged by:
         A. a warmer room
         B. hungry babies
         C. the presence of fathers in the room
         D. physical contact after birth

A   40. Which phase of attachment begins when the infant can
         distinguish their primary caregiver from others?
         A. attachment-in-the-making
         B. preattachment
         C. clear-cut attachment
         D. goal-oriented attachment

A   41. Which two types of deprivation are potentially irreversible
         if they occur during the first two years of life?
         A. maternal and social
         B. paternal and sibling
         C. paternal and social
         D. none of the above

B   42. Spitz used the term "hospitalism" to refer to
         orphanage-reared infants who showed:
         A. increased physical development
         B. apathy and withdrawal
         C. increased mental development
         D. fewer psychological problems

D   43. Which of the following statements is FALSE about research
         with young monkeys conducted by Harlow and others?
         A. bodily contact with a cloth covered surrogate
            was preferred over a wire surrogate with food
         B. maternal separation altered body temperature
            and sleep patterns
         C. deprivation of peer relations led to
            increased aggression and poor play behavior
         D. mental development can be enhanced with the
            proper stimulation

C   44. Infants who wanted to be close to their mothers during the
         "strange situation procedure" were described as having a __
         ___ attachment.
         A. natural
         B. ambivalent
         C. secure
         D. avoidant

A   45. Mothers of avoidant infants who did not seek contact during
         the "strange situation procedure" were found to:
         A. be less promoting of physical contact
         B. be older
         C. be from lower socio-economic classes
         D. have more children on the average

B   46. Research has shown that the important factor underlying
         secure infant attachments was:
         A. the mother's previous experience with
            other infants
         B. the amount of stimulation and attention
            given the child
         C. how much the mother worked outside the home
         D. both the mother's and father's caring for the
            child

FAMILIES, CHILDREN, AND SOCIAL CHANGE

C   47. Which statistic characterizes the "family" of the mid-1970's
         compared to families of an earlier era?
         A. fewer divorces are occuring
         B. the number of single-parent families is
            decreasing
         C. adults are increasingly unavailable to
            children
         D. the birth rate among unmarried women is
            decreasing

B   48. Which statistic characterizes working mothers?
         A. the fastest growing segment of the work
            force are those with teenagers
         B. more than half with school-aged children
            work outside the house
         C. liscensed day-care capacity does exist
            for all of their children
         D. the percentage who worked is decreasing
            slightly

A   49. The effects of day-care primarily depend on:
         A. the quality of care given by both the
            staff and the mother when she is at home
            with the child
         B. the total time the child spends in centers
            each day
         C. the total time the child spends in centers
            each week
         D. the presence of the child's father to assist
            the mother when she is at home

B   50. One reason why maternal employment has little apparent
         negative effect on children's psychological development is:
         A. the presence of fathers
         B. maternal compensation when with the child
         C. the hiring of quality baby-sitters
         D. extra money for children's entertainment

D   51. Research has shown that a major cause of problems for
         developing children is (the):
         A. mother's psychological well-being
         B. father's psychological well-being
         C. separation and divorce of the parents
         D. parental conflict

C   52. The fact that only _____ percent of children from divorces
         live with their father suggests more potential problems for
         the development of _____.
         A. 20 ; boys
         B. 10 ; girls
         C. 10 ; boys
         D. 20 ; girls

APPLICATION: CHILD-REARING PRACTICES, I: STYLES OF PARENTING

D   53. The fact that children still live and function after being
         raised in very different rearing styles demonstrates that
         children are:
         A. young
         B. curious
         C. mini-adults
         D. adaptable

B   54. The extent to which parents reason with children and
         consider their opinions and feelings is a dimension of
         parent-child relationship called:
         A. maturity demands
         B. parent-child communication
         C. parental nurturance
         D. expressionism

D   55. Research has found that children of nursery school age who
         were mature and competent had parents who were rated high
         in:
         A. maturity demands
         B. parental-child communication
         C. parental nurturance
         D. all of the above

ADOLESCENCE

C   56. The "father" of the study of adolescence in America is:
    A. Kohlberg
    B. Ainsworth
    C. Hall
    D. Bowlby

A   57. Contemporary scientific investigation of adolescence by
    psychologists began around:
    A. 1900
    B. 1915
    C. 1925
    D. 1940

MATURATION AND PHYSICAL DEVELOPMENT DURING ADOLESCENCE

D   58. The biologically-determined phase when sexual maturation
    becomes apparent is called:
    A. adolescence
    B. adolescence growth spurt
    C. menarche
    D. puberty

A   59. Which of the following statements is TRUE?
    A. the average age at menarche is quite variable
       across cultures
    B. in America, the average age at menarche has
       dropped about 4.2 years since the 19th century
    C. puberty and sexual maturation is accompanied
       by attainment of formal operational thought
    D. there is surprisingly little variation
       between boys in the onset of puberty

C   60. Normal males are about _____ years behind normal females
    in their growth spurt.
    A. 1.0
    B. 1.5
    C. 2.0
    D. 2.5

DEVELOPMENTAL TASKS OF ADOLESCENCE

C   61. Which is a typical characteristic of early maturing boys and
    girls?
    A. lacking in self-confidence and security
    B. boisterous and loud
    C. accepting
    D. restless and bossy

B   62. According to Erikson the challenge facing adolescents is
        developing a sense of:
        A. mature peer relationships
        B. role identity
        C. independence from parents
        D. social awareness

B   63. One of the most disturbing aspects of adolescent sexuality
        is:
        A. direct sexual contact
        B. the continuing increase in adolescent
           pregnancies
        C. the increase in teen marriages
        D. the spread of venereal disease

A   64. During Kohlberg's preconventional stages of moral
        development, the child is said to develop:
        A. a sense of "good" and "bad"
        B. behavior that pleases or helps others
        C. conformity to rules
        D. self-questioning of poor governmental laws

B   65. Learning to conform to rules when there is ample opportunity
        to break them is an example of:
        A. moral judgment
        B. moral internalization
        C. social internalization
        D. conscience development

C   66. Which stage of moral development suggested by Kohlberg is
        possible only with the attainment of formal operational
        thought?
        A. preconventional
        B. conventional
        C. postconventional
        D. none of the above

D   67. Kohlberg devised the Moral Judgment Scale to evaluate a
        person's level of moral _____.
        A. retardation
        B. understanding
        C. internalization
        D. maturity

D   68. Kohlberg's theory of moral development has been criticized
        because it is:
        A. too simplistic
        B. culturally biased
        C. hard to differentiate between some stages
        D. all of the above

APPLICATION: CHILD-REARING PRACTICES, II: FOSTERING MORAL
JUDGMENT DEVELOPMENT

C   69. Probably the most important influence in determining whether
        the child or adolescent has a strong conscience is the role
        played by:
        A. early experiences
        B. peers
        C. parents
        D. school teachers

D   70. The non-authoritarian pattern of parental behavior:
        A. emphasizes obedience to authority
        B. promotes adolescents who lack self-esteem
        C. encourages behavior influenced by external
           rewards and punishments
        D. promotes the development of internalized
           moral standards

B   71. Available research suggests that the internalization of
        moral standards is fostered by:
        A. parental discipline and punishment
        B. parental discipline and affection
        C. peer affection and support
        D. both peer and parental affection

ADULTHOOD AND LATER MATURITY

B   72. The period during the late teens and early 20's is called
        the _____ stage of development.
        A. transition
        B. youth
        C. ado-adult
        D. reality

C   73. Early adulthood is said to encompass the years 18 to _____.
        A. 25
        B. 30
        C. 35
        D. 40

B   74. The challenge of early adulthood according to Erikson is
        developing a sense of intimacy vs. isolation. This involves
        forming close and mature relationships with:
        A. parents
        B. peers
        C. brothers and sisters
        D. children

C   75. Which of the following is a developmental task for middle
         age according to Havighurst?
         A. learning to live with a marriage partner
         B. striving for civic and social responsibility
         C. guiding the next generation
         D. developing appropriate part-time experiences

A   76. Erikson considers the proper concerns of mature, middle-aged
         adults to be a conflict between:
         A. generativity vs. self-absorption
         B. integrity vs. despair
         C. morality vs. fairness
         D. self-satisfaction vs. other-satisfaction

C   77. Later maturity is said to begin at:
         A. retirement
         B. the time the youngest child permanently
            leaves home
         C. age 65
         D. age 65 for men and 70 for women

D   78. Which of the following is an important concern of the
         elderly individual?
         A. adjusting to retirement and reduced income
         B. establishing satisfactory living arrangements
            with peers
         C. coping with the death of a spouse
         D. all of the above

APPLICATION: CHARTING LIFE-SPAN DEVELOPMENT

B   79. According to Erikson, the virtues of _____ are believed to
         emerge from _____.
         A. drive and hope ; competence
         B. self-control and willpower ; autonomy
         C. purpose and direction ; integrity
         D. affiliation and love ; basic trust

ON THE HORIZON: DEATH AND DYING

C   80. The case of Karen Quinlan who, after an accident, was
         maintained mechanically illustrates the difference between:
         A. life and death
         B. right from wrong
         C. biological and psychological death
         D. death vs. dying

A   81. Which of the five phases of dying identified by Kubler-Ross
        do we reach first?
        A. denial
        B. anger
        C. depression
        D. bargaining

FURTHER READING SUGGESTIONS

Bowlby, J. (1969). Attachment and loss: Vol. 1. Attachment. New
     York: Basic Books.

Bowlby, J. (1973). Attachment and loss: Vol. 2. Separation:
     Anxiety and anger. New York: Basic Books.

Bowlby, J. (1980). Attachment and loss: Vol. 3. Loss: Sadness and
     depression. New York: Basic Books.

Byrne, D., & Fisher, W. A. (Eds.) (1983). Adolescents, sex, and
     contraception. Hillsdale, N.J.: Erlbaum.

Conger, J. J., & Petersen, A. C. (1983). Adolescence and youth:
     Psychological Development in a changing world. (3rd edition).
     New York: Harper & Row.

Lamb, M. R. (Ed.) (1981). The role of the father in child
     development (2nd edition). New York: Wiley.

Maccoby, E. E. (1980). Social development: Psychological growth
     and the parent-child relationship. New York: Harcourt Brace
     Jovanovich.

Mussen, P. H. (Ed.) (1983). Handbook of child psychology. (4th ed.)
     New York: Wiley.

- CHAPTER 12 -

INTELLIGENCE AND THE MEASUREMENT OF INDIVIDUAL DIFFERENCES

OUTLINE

I.   Introduction: Autistic Savants -- A Puzzle Unsolved - a description of the behaviors of AUTISTIC SAVANTS and how this term is related to autism and savant

II. Measurement of Human Intelligence - Binet offers his view of INTELLIGENCE which emphasizes judgement; Wechsler's definition is also given; intelligence is composed of both a general and some specific mental abilities

A. History of mental testing - Galton and Cattell developed early "mental tests" based primarily on sensory and motor functioning; in 1895 Binet proposed a more fruitful measure of intelligence that was related to school performance
1. Stanford-Binet Intelligence Scale - this test was a translation of Binet's test into English by Terman at Stanford; it was age-standardized which led to the INTELLIGENCE QUOTIENT (IQ); the IQ is a relation between mental age (MA) and chronical age (CA)
2. The Wechler intelligence scales - Wechsler's DEVIATION IQ compared one with others of the same age; two Wechsler tests are the Wechsler Adult Intelligence Scale (WAIS) and the Wechsler Intelligence Scale for Children (WISC); these tests are divided into a verbal scale and a performance scale which generates three measures of intelligence (verbal IQ, performance IQ, and full scale IQ)

B. Types of mental tests - the Stanford-Binet and Wechsler tests are individually administered, others like the Army Alpha and Army Beta Tests are for groups; ACHIEVEMENT TESTS measure what has been learned while APTITUDE TESTS measure one's capacity to learn; the Scholastic Aptitude Test (SAT) is an aptitude test

C. Characteristics of good psychological tests - we assess tests on their reliablility, validity, and standardization
   1. Reliability - TEST RELIABILITY, the consistency of scores by the same individual across different occasions, is obtained by the test-retest, alternate-forms, and split-half methods.
   2. Validity - TEST VALIDITY refers to whether the test measures what it claims to measure; three types of validity are CONTENT VALIDATION, CRITERION-RELATED VALIDATION, and CONSTRUCT VALIDATION; construct validation refers to whether the test measures a construct or TRAIT; intelligence is a trait
   3. STANDARDIZATION occurs when a test is given to a large standardization or norm group to which individual scores are then compared
   4. The normal distribution - a NORMAL PROBABILITY DISTRIBUTION or normal curve is a bell-shaped curve; the two most important statistics for describing a distribution are the mean and standard deviation

D. Testing for intelligence over the life span
   1. Stability and change in IQs - no relationship between tests scores at 18-24 months and age 18 exists, but there is a highly predictive relationship between ages 5-7 and age 17 and 18
   2. The special case of infant intelligence - Gesell developed tests for intellectual processes in infants 1-24 months and obtained a DEVELOPMENTAL QUOTIENT (DQ); the DQ is related to later IQ test performance
   3. The growth of intellectual abilities - early CROSS-SECTIONAL RESEARCH DESIGNS showed an age-related IQ decline, but LONGITUDINAL RESEARCH DESIGNS have found little or no decline in IQ with age.

E. Application: Testing your own IQ - Mensa, the international high IQ society, a special IQ self-test

III. Distribution of IQ Scores

A. Mental retardation - retardates' role in society determined largely by the quality of training society provides
   1. Definition, diagnosis, and classification - MENTAL RETARDATION pertains to significantly subaverage intellectual functioning existing concurrently with deficits in adaptive behavior and manifested during a developmental period.

      a. intellectual functioning - an IQ cutoff of 70 is used; most are <u>mildly</u> retarded (80%), 12% is <u>moderately</u> retarded, 7% is <u>severely</u> retarded, 1% is <u>profoundly</u> retarded.

      b. ADAPTIVE BEHAVIOR refers to various duties and social roles appropriate to age

      c. age of onset - mental retardation is used if symptoms occur prior to age 18, <u>dementia</u> after 18; most with mental retardation live outside of institutions

   2. Two broad classes of retardation - there are many <u>etiologies</u>, but two broad classes

      a. ORGANIC RETARDATION, due to chromosomal and genetic abnormalities, accounts for 25% of the cases

      b. CULTURAL-FAMILIAL RETARDATION, due to cultural disadvantage and/or one's family environment, accounts for 75% of all cases

   3. Treatment and prevention - more knowledge is needed to prevent and treat optimally; the prognosis is best for cultural-familial retardation

B. Genius, giftedness, and creativity - a discussion of intellectual precocial youngsters, including Francis Galton; a personal profile of Galton is given, including his views on inheritable characteristics in humans

   1. Studies of geniuses - a GENIUS is defined by three areas (public achievements, major impact on other's thinking, peer recognition); all geniuses are considered to be intellectually gifted

   2. Giftedness - Terman's longitudinal study of GIFTEDNESS found gifted persons to enroll in college more often, graduate with more honors, and to publish and write more regularly

   3. CREATIVITY is not synonymous with a high IQ but means a quality of thought that leads to unexpected problem solving; two separate abilities in creative thinking are DIVERGENT THINKING and CONVERGENT THINKING

C. Application: Identifying creative talent - a study conducted by U. of California's Institute of Personality Assessment and Research (IPAR) has reported on creative individuals using the <u>California Personality Inventory</u>; a creative architect is discussed

   1. Predicting creativity and identifying the academically gifted - unlike IPAR's <u>retrospective</u> approach, Guilford's <u>Plot Titles Test</u> is a <u>prospective</u> device where creative individuals generate clever titles to a standard short story

   2. Factors that block the development of creative thinking - three ways to suppress creative thinking in children are to eliminate fantasies in play, restrict curiosity, and overemphasize sex roles

IV. Genetic and Environmental Determinants of Intellectual Development

A. HUMAN BEHAVIORAL GENETICS - A field which studies the contribution of heredity to behavior
   1. A brief history of behavioral genetics - Darwin offered his theory of NATURAL SELECTION; Galton expanded it to eugenics; geneticists distinguish between GENOTYPE and PHENOTYPE; one's genotype limits the REACTION RANGE while a restricted environment or enriched environment influences where the phenotypes occur
   2. Methods of human behavioral genetics - ways of determining the relative influence of genetic and environmental factors on intelligence
      a. twin studies - the twin-study method evaluates monozygotic twins and dizygotic twins reared together.
      b. adoption studies - twins reared apart so that genetic and environmental factors can be separated
      c. family studies evaluate similarities between parents, brothers and sisters
   3. Summary of results from twin, adoption, and family studies - correlations for twins reared in various ways are given; a presentation of HERITABILITY; some research concludes that 70% of the variation in human intelligence is due to genetic factors

B. Controversies in behavioral genetics - an overview of Jensen's position and his major works
   1. IQ and SOCIOECONOMIC STATUS (SES)--there is a positive relationship between higher status and higher IQ scores; some believe this relationship is spurious
   2. Racial - ethnic group differences in IQ - some research has shown racial-ethnic group differences in cognitive ability with whites scoring an average of 15 points higher; the reason for the difference is not clear; Japanese outperform both American whites and blacks on IQ tests
   3. Sex-related differences in mental abilities - males are generally better on spatial ability tasks while females generally do better on verbal ability tasks; why these sex-related cognitive differences exist is unclear

C. Family configuration and intellectual development - Zajonc suggests that one's FAMILY CONFIGURATION, as defined by family size, birth order, and sibling separation significantly influences intellectual development
   1. The theory of family configuration - the value of the intellectual environment (VIE) can be calculated; research shows that early children in the smallest families tend to have the highest IQs
   2. Evaluation of the family configuration theory - critics suggest that the supporting studies are cross-cultural and biased; longitudinal studies are needed

D. Environmental enrichment programs - preschool enrichment programs don't lead to any long term IQ gains

1. The head start program - PROJECT HEAD START does not foster long term IQ gain, but does generate increases in other broader goals (e.g., health, social and emotional adjustment, community support)
2. Early enrichment programs: Summary and evaluation - research suggests that programs are effective in a number of areas, especially in increased school success

E. Application: Enrichment through nutrition - research suggests intellectual functioning can be enhanced with improved childhood nutrition; Sampson, a "soft-drink" fortified with protein, minerals, and vitamins is being touted by a Coca-Cola excutive as an answer to poor nutrition world-wide

V. On the Horizon: Engineering Human Intelligence - a discussion of the current technique of artificial insemination using sperm from Mensa members and Nobel Laureates

OBJECTIVES

I. WHAT IS INTELLIGENCE? HOW IS IT MEASURED?

Binet, who developed an early intelligence test in France, assumed intelligence to include a basic ability called judgement (good sense, practical sense), adaptable to circumstances. Wechsler, who has developed intelligence tests in America, considers it to be "the aggregate or global capacity of the individual to act purposefully, to think rationally, and to deal effectively with the environment." Even though many say there is a "general intelligence," some argue that there are also specific mental abilities that are relatively independent of one another. Early tests of intelligence by Galton and by Cattell were not related to school performance. More recent tests (e.g., Stanford-Binet Intelligence Test, WAIS, WISC) assess a wide range of attributes such as information, comprehension, arithmetic, similarities, attention, vocabulary, object sorting and manipulation, story understanding. Performance in these areas is grouped, as in the Wechsler tests, into verbal scales and performance scales which provide a verbal IQ, a performance IQ, and then a full scale IQ which is an average of the other two.

All current intelligence tests are given individually through the interview, simple task completion process or in groups through the paper-pencil process (e.g., Army Alpha and Army Beta Tests). The individual tests compare one's mental age against either one's chronological age (as in the Stanford-Binet) or scores of other's of the same age (as in the Wechsler tests).

C   1. Early intelligence tests were criticized because they:

    A. were too long
    B. could not be used with retardates
    C. were unrelated to school performance
    D. did not test verbal abilities

A   2. Which of the following is NOT a common intelligence test in America?

    A. Binet-Illinois
    B. WAIS
    C. WISC
    D. Stanford-Binet

B   3. Intelligence is said to be made up of:

    A. general abilities
    B. specific and general abilities
    C. specific abilities
    D. general abilities and intuition

    4. Discuss how the trait "intelligence" is measured.

II.   LIST   THE   CHARACTERISTICS OF GOOD PSYCHOLOGICAL TESTS.

Good psychological tests, as with tests in general, will yield meaningful results if they are valid, reliable, and standardized. Test reliability refers to the consistency of scores obtained when the same persons take the same test on different occasions. Three methods of obtaining reliability are the test-retest, alternate-forms, and split-half. Test validity refers to whether a test actually measures what it claims to measure. Three types of validity are content validity, criterion-related validity, and construct validity. Standardization involves administering the test to a large group or population to obtain a reference group's performance to which individual scores are later compared. Furthermore, tests are designed so that results from a large sample of individuals will yield a normal probability distribution.

A   1. Which characteristic of tests deals with whether the results are similiar when an individual takes the test more than once?

A. test reliability
B. test validity
C. standardization
D. normal probability distribution

D   2. Administering a test to a large group of individuals so that they may be used as a reference group is called:

A. testing
B. test validation
C. test reliability
D. standardization

3. Name and discuss the four ways which make a psychological test "good."

III. HOW CAN THE RANGE OF INDIVIDUAL DIFFERENCES IN INTELLIGENCE BEST BE DESCRIBED?

The best way to discuss the range of differences in intelligence is to use the normal probability distribution. When a very large sample of individuals is tested, their scores will yield a symmetrical, bell-shaped curve which is sometimes called a normal curve. In actuality the normal probability distribution is a mathematical ideal, yet it is a good way to describe intelligence ranges. With this distribution, we assume that the majority of scores will fall around the center (or mean) of the distribution, but that scores of others will spread out away from the mean in each direction. The standard deviation is a measure of how widely these scores are spread around the mean.

C   1. The two most important statistics for describing a normal probability distribution are the:

A. range and standard deviation
B. mean and mode
C. standard deviation and mean
D. mode and standard deviation

2. What is the best way to describe the range of individual differences in intelligence?

IV. HOW DO PSYCHOLOGISTS DEFINE AND DIAGNOSE MENTAL RETARDATION?

The American Association of Mental Deficiency defines mental retardation as a "significantly subaverage intellectual functioning existing concurrently with deficits in adaptive

behavior and manifested during the developmental period."
Three components of this definition include intellectual
functioning, adaptive behavior, and age of onset. The
traditional IQ cutoff for mental retardation is 70, but current
thinking places a reduced emphasis on IQ scores. Today
adaptive behavior (or the various duties and social roles
appropriate to age) is emphasized to determine the individual's
routine level of functioning in society. Finally, there is the
criterion that a diagnosis of mental retardation must be made
before the age of 18. (After 18 years of age a similar
constellation of symptoms is called dementia). As part of a
diagnosis, one refers to whether the symptoms reflect organ
retardation or cultural-familial retardation.

B   1. Which criteria are used to diagnose mental retardation?

     A. IQ score, etiology, and adaptive behavior level
     B. social competency, age, and IQ score
     C. IQ score and adaptive behavior level
     D. etiology and social competency

D   2. The age cutoff for mental retardation is _____ years and
        the IQ cutoff is _____.

     A. 15; 80
     B. 15; 70
     C. 18; 80
     D. 18; 70

     3. What are the three ways that psychologists diagnose mental
        retardation?

V.   WHAT IS GENIUS?   HOW DOES IT DIFFER FROM GIFTEDNESS AND
     CREATIVITY?

A genius is one who has evidence of public achievements, whose
activities have had a major impact on thinking within a field,
and who is considered a genius by qualified peers. Thus, a
genius has well-known public and observable behavioral acts who
is considered to be intellectually gifted. Not all gifted
individuals become geniuses however. Gifted individuals tend
to show considerable evidence of production, patents and
publications. Creativity reflects a quality of thought that
leads to novel and unexpected problem solving abilities. Two
separate abilities associated with creativity are divergent and
convergent thinking.

A   1. Which types of individuals are generally considered to have
        high intelligence levels as measured by IQ tests?

        A. genius and gifted
        B. gifted and creative
        C. creative and genius
        D. all of the above

     2. Discuss the similarities and differences between individuals
        who are geniuses, gifted, and creative.

VI. TO WHAT EXTENT ARE INDIVIDUAL DIFFERENCES IN INTELLECTUAL
     DEVELOPMENT DUE TO GENETICS VERSUS ENVIRONMENT? WHAT METHODS ARE
     AVAILABLE TO ANSWER THIS QUESTION?

     It is not possible to determine what extent an individual's
     intellectual development is due to genetic and environmental
     contributions. More generally, we talk about a genotype (or
     inherited genes) and phenotype (outward, visible expression of
     traits affected by the genes). One's genotype does not
     directly influence one's phenotype. Actually, one's phenotype
     falls within a "reaction range" which reflects, in addition to
     one's genotype, the type or quality of environmental
     experiences. An "enriched" environment will tend to facilitate
     an individual's full genotypic potential while a "restricted"
     environment will have the opposite effect. The goal is to
     determine a trait's heritability, a statistical measure of the
     contribution of heredity to a given population's trait in a
     certain environment. For example, some research suggests that
     70% of the variation in intelligence among individuals is due
     to genetic factors, thus implying high heritability for the
     intelligence trait. Current methods which are used to study
     the factors influencing intellectual development are twin,
     adoption, and family studies.

C   1. Which of the following statements is FALSE?

        A. enriched environments facilitate full genetic potential
        B. intelligence is said to have high heritability
        C. genotype determines phenotype
        D. phenotype falls within a reaction range

     2. Discuss how genetic and environmental factors influence the
        trait called "intelligence."

MULTIPLE-CHOICE QUESTIONS

INTRODUCTION: AUTISTIC SAVANTS--A PUZZLE UNSOLVED

B   1. A retarded child who can name the months during a particular
         year in which the 5th day will fall on a Thursday may be
         diagnosed as a(n):
         A. genius
         B. autistic savant
         C. intelligence genius
         D. schizophrenic

C   2. Autistic savants show a curious combination of what two
         characteristics?
         A. retardation and rapid physical growth
         B. genius and rapid physical maturity
         C. genius and retardation
         D. retardation and extroverted personalities

A   3. Which of the following is NOT a characteristic of autism?
         A. escape from reality with excessive sleeping
         B. noncommunicative
         C. often totally self-absorbed
         D. escape from reality with fantasy

D   4. "Savant" is a French term that means:
         A. showing unusual mental retardation
         B. showing unusual personality retardation
         C. a person of exceptional personality
         D. a person of exceptional learning

MEASUREMENT OF HUMAN INTELLIGENCE

D   5. The global capacity of an individual to act purposefully,
         think rationally, and deal effectively with his/her
         environment is known as:
         A. personality
         B. savy
         C. judgement
         D. intelligence

B   6. A useful model to have when viewing intelligence is to view
         it as a _____ ability with _____ mental abilities that
         are relatively independent of one another.
         A. general ; many
         B. general ; specific
         C. specific ; general
         D. specific ; many

HISTORY OF MENTAL TESTING

B   7. The first systematic study of human intelligence began
       approximately _____ years ago.
       A. 75
       B. 100
       C. 150
       D. over 500

A   8. Who was the American psychologist who expanded previous work
       on intelligence and coined the term "mental test?"
       A. Cattell
       B. Galton
       C. Wissler
       D. Rimland

C   9. The Frenchman who proposed that intelligence tests measure
       more than sensory and motor abilities, and who then
       developed his own test was:
       A. Wissler
       B. Scott
       C. Binet
       D. Galton

C 10. Binet's early intelligence test was originally used to
       evaluate those individuals who could:
       A. join the ruling class
       B. be good school teachers
       C. benefit from normal schooling
       D. respond well to mental therapy

A 11. When items on the Stanford-Binet intelligence test are
       grouped by age level, it is considered:
       A. age-standardized
       B. age-appropriate
       C. to be reliable
       D. to have validity

B 12. An age-standardized intelligence test has items grouped
       where approximately what percent of the children pass them?
       A. 50
       B. 75
       C. 90
       D. 100

D 13. An intelligence quotient is an index of the relation between
       one's:
       A. mental age and school performance
       B. chronological age and school performance
       C. mental age and test score
       D. mental and chronological age

D   14. A deviation IQ is an IQ defined by:
         A. how many persons fail to answer a particular test
            question
         B. MA divided by CA
         C. CA divided by MA
         D. one's relative standing among persons of the same age

C   15. Two of the best known Wechsler deviation IQ tests are the:
         A. WAIS and SAT
         B. SAT and WISC
         C. WAIS and WISC
         D. WISC and Army Alpha

A   16. Which of the following is a subtest of the verbal scale of
         the WAIS-R?
         A. digit span
         B. digit symbols
         C. picture completion
         D. block design

D   17. Which following verbal scale subtest of the WAIS-R requires
         that a problem such as "why should people pay taxes?" be
         explained?
         A. information
         B. picture completion
         C. vocabulary
         D. comprehension

B   18. The average of the verbal and performance IQs on the
         Wechsler tests is called the _____ IQ.
         A. final score
         B. full scale
         C. real valve
         D. combined

TYPES OF MENTAL TESTS

A   19. One major limitation of the Stanford-Binet and Wechsler
         intelligence tests is the fact they are:
         A. individually administered
         B. too long
         C. made up of too many French examples
         D. only scaled for children under 12

C   20. The Army Alpha and the Army Beta Tests are noteworthy
         because they are _____ tests.
         A. vocational
         B. aptitude
         C. group
         D. achievement

D   21. Achievement tests are designed to best measure:
         A. intelligence
         B. vocational choice
         C. school and work potential
         D. what individuals have previously learned

C   22. Aptitude tests are designed to measure one's:
         A. vocational choice
         B. past learning
         C. capacity to learn
         D. raw intelligence

D   23. An aptitude test familiar to most college students is the:
         A. WISC
         B. WAIS
         C. MMPI
         D. SAT

CHARACTERISTICS OF GOOD PSYCHOLOGICAL TESTS

B   24. Test reliability refers to a test's:
         A. content
         B. consistency
         C. predictive power
         D. validity

A   25. Which of the following is NOT a common method used to
         determine a test's reliability?
         A. repeat score
         B. test-retest
         C. split-half
         D. alternative forms

A   26. A test which has test validity is one that:
         A. actually measures what it claims to measure
         B. can be taken more than once with similar results
         C. generates similar scores when taken more than once
         D. has consistency of scores when different people take it

B   27. The term which refers to examining a test's content to
         determine whether it fairly represents the abilities being
         measured is called _____ validation.
         A. test
         B. content
         C. criterion-related
         D. construct

B   28. The extent to which a test is capable of measuring a
         psychological trait or construct refers to _____
         validation.
         A. trait
         B. construct
         C. content
         D. criterion-related

C   29. Traits refer to:
         A. one's attributes
         B. core elements of intelligence tests
         C. enduring characteristics of individuals
         D. one's aptitude

D   30. Construct validation is difficult because:
         A. tests are usually too long
         B. people sometimes "fake" their answers
         C. the "correct" content of a test varies
         D. traits cannot be observed directly

D   31. An advantage of standardizing a test is that it allows
         meaningful comparisons between:
         A. two individual scorers
         B. two parts of the same test
         C. different tests
         D. an individual test score with those of a norm group

A   32. Which of the following is a psychological trait?
         A. intelligence
         B. motivation level
         C. emotions
         D. all of the above

A   33. Which of the following is associated with the normal
         probability distribution?
         A. a symmetrical, bell-shaped curve
         B. a normal curve
         C. a mathematical ideal
         D. all of the above

C   34. With a normal probability distribution, the majority score
         in the:
         A. lower end
         B. higher end
         C. "average" range
         D. lower and higher ends

B   35. The two most important statistics for describing a
         distribution of test scores are the:
         A. mean and normal curve
         B. mean and standard deviation
         C. normal curve and standard deviation
         D. average score and content validation

C   36. An IQ score of 115 means that the individual is:
        A. 10 percentile above average
        B. 10 percentile below average
        C. one standard deviation above the mean
        D. one standard deviation below the mean

TESTING FOR INTELLIGENCE OVER THE LIFE SPAN

B   37. The Berkeley Growth Study of IQ stability found that our IQ
        score at age _____ is highly predictive of our score at
        age 17 to 18.
        A. 18 to 24 months
        B. 5 to 7 years
        C. 8 years
        D. 10 to 11 years

A   38. Gesell's test of intellectual processes which yields a
        developmental quotient is used with:
        A. infants
        B. children
        C. infants and children
        D. infants, children, and adolescents

D   39. Which of the following statements is FALSE?
        A. one's developmental quotient is related to later IQ test
           performance
        B. infant IQ scores do not correlate highly with later IQ
           scores
        C. cross sectional research data indicate an IQ decline with
           age
        D. longitudinal research data shows significant IQ decline
           with age

C   40. Which research design is used when periodic retesting of the
        same individuals is used?
        A. repeat measure
        B. cross-sectional
        C. longitudinal
        D. Berkeley

APPLICATION: TESTING YOUR OWN IQ

A   41. The name of the international high IQ society is:
        A. Mensa
        B. Zonix
        C. Top-Flight
        D. Top IQ

C   42. Membership in the international high IQ society is limited
         to those whose IQ scores are in the top _____ percent.
         A. 10
         B. 5
         C. 2
         D. 1

MENTAL RETARDATION

A   43. The traditional cutoff for mental retardation is an IQ score
         of:
         A. 70
         B. 75
         C. 80
         D. 85

B   44. What percentage of those with mental retardation are mildly
         retarded?
         A. 60
         B. 80
         C. 85
         D. 90

B   45. The term which refers to various duties and social roles
         appropriate to age is:
         A. social competency
         B. adaptive behavior
         C. behavioral competency
         D. socialization

D   46. A diagnosis of mental retardation is appropriate only for
         those who develop clinical symptoms before the age of:
         A. 8
         B. 12
         C. 15
         D. 18

C   47. Which of the following is NOT a criterion used to diagnose
         mental retardation?
         A. intellectual functioning
         B. adaptive behavior
         C. verbal skills
         D. age of onset

D   48. Dementia refers to:
         A. mental retardation
         B. mental and social retardation
         C. mental illness
         D. mental deterioration

A   49. Of the _____ children born each year who will be diagnosed
         as mentally retarded, most will be _____.
         A. 100,000 ; males
         B. 200,000 ; males
         C. 100,000 ; females
         D. 150,000 ; females

B   50. The most common cause(s) of organic retardation:
         A. is brain damage during birth
         B. are chromosomal and genetic abnormalities
         C. brain damage and genetic abnormalities
         D. accidental drug overdose during infancy

A   51. What percentage of mental retardation is due to organic
         factors?
         A. 25
         B. 40
         C. 50
         D. 65

D   52. Children with cases of cultural-familial retardation are
         usually _____ retarded.
         A. profoundly
         B. severely
         C. moderately
         D. mildly

C   53. Children with cultural-familial retardation usually are
         found in families:
         A. from the middle class
         B. living in urban areas
         C. from the lower IQ range
         D. with a normal IQ range

GENIUS, GIFTEDNESS, AND CREATIVITY

B   54. Francis Galton had an important influence on psychological
         thinking when he proposed that:
         A. mental retardation was primarily environmentally
            influenced
         B. one's mental abilities are inherited
         C. one's psychological abilities are primarily
            environmentally influenced
         D. personalities can be measured with tests

A   55. A person is defined as a genius on the basis of:
         A. public and observable behaviors
         B. IQ score
         C. degree of giftedness
         D. scientific contributions

C   56. Which of the following was NOT found in Terman's study of
         giftedness?
         A. many attended and graduated from college
         B. graduation honors were more numerous
         C. more than half became political leaders
         D. many wrote articles, books, and technical papers

D   57. The quality of thought that leads to novel and unexpected
         problem solving is called:
         A. convergent thinking
         B. originality
         C. giftedness
         D. creativity

D   58. Creative thinking is characterized by an ability to:
         A. be logical
         B. be a clear, but speedy thinker
         C. adjust traditional solutions to new problems
         D. examine alternative problem solutions

B   59. The type of thought where possibilities are narrowed so that
         the one best solution is attained is known as:
         A. divergent thinking
         B. convergent thinking
         C. focusing
         D. thought channelization

A   60. Standardized IQ tests typically require what type of
         thought?
         A. convergent
         B. divergent
         C. creative
         D. gifted

APPLICATION: IDENTIFYING CREATIVE TALENT

C   61. Creative people, as revealed by the California Personality
         Inventory, tend to be:
         A. submissive
         B. inhibited
         C. self-confident
         D. quiet

D   62. Guilford's Plot Titles Test is a _____ test to determine
         _____ .
         A. retrospective ; problem solving ability
         B. retrospective ; creativity
         C. prospective ; problem solving ability
         D. prospective ; creativity

B   63. What restricts creative thinking in children?
         A. the manipulation of objects and ideas
         B. eliminating fantasies from children's play
         C. under-emphasizing sex roles
         D. fostering curiosity

HUMAN BEHAVIORAL GENETICS

A   64. A rapidly growing field which studies the contribution of
         heredity to behavior is:
         A. human behavioral genetics
         B. scientific genetics
         C. applied genetics
         D. eugenics

C   65. Darwin's important contribution to the theory of evolution
         was the principle of:
         A. behavioral genetics
         B. eugenics
         C. natural selection
         D. the origin of species

C   66. Which of the following is NOT part of the principle of
         natural selection?
         A. individuals differ in various characteristics
         B. individual characteristics are partly determined by
            heredity
         C. characteristics vary between species
         D. characteristics associated with better fitness will
            become more frequent in later generations

D   67. Selective breeding of humans for desirable characteristics
         is known as:
         A. natural selection
         B. human behavioral genetics
         C. inbreeding
         D. eugenics

A   68. An environment which is _____ may limit one's _____ for
         intelligence.
         A. restricted ; reaction range
         B. restricted ; genotype
         C. enriched ; reaction range
         D. enriched ; genotype

B   69. Three methods used in human behavioral genetics include
         twin, adoption, and _____ studies.
         A. group
         B. family
         C. IQ test
         D. heritability

B   70. What term refers to the unique set of genes one inherits?
        A. phenotype
        B. genotype
        C. natural selection
        D. genetics

A   71. What term refers to the interaction of nature and nurture
        that causes observable trait variations?
        A. reaction range
        B. genotype
        C. phenotype
        D. behavioral genetics

C   72. Which type of twins would have the most similar IQs if the
        intelligence trait was entirely due to heredity?
        A. fraternal
        B. maternal
        C. monozygotic
        D. dizygotic

D   73. The most powerful estimate of the influence of heredity on
        behavior is obtained by studying:
        A. families
        B. adoptive siblings reared together
        C. fraternal twins adopted into the same foster family
        D. monozygotic twins reared apart

D   74. Adoption studies offer researchers a direct estimate of the
        relative influence of:
        A. heredity on intelligence
        B. genetics on twin development
        C. environment on genotypes
        D. environment on intellectual development

A   75. A summary of studies on family resemblances in measured
        intelligence found the two highest correlations to be in:
        A. identical twins reared both together and apart
        B. identical twins reared together and fraternal twins
           reared apart
        C. identical twins and fraternal twins reared together
        D. identical twins and fraternal twins reared apart

B   76. A statistical measure of the contribution of heredity to
        observed variations of a group trait in a certain
        environment is called:
        A. inheritance
        B. heritability
        C. genetic endowment
        D. genetic correlation

B   77. According to Bouchard's summary statement, approximately
        what percent of the variation in intelligence among
        individuals is due to genetic factors?
        A. 80
        B. 70
        C. 50
        D. 30

CONTROVERSIES IN BEHAVIORAL GENETICS

C   78. Socioeconomic status reflects a person's:
        A. education, occupation, intelligence
        B. occupation, intelligence, income
        C. income, education, occupation
        D. education, intelligence, income

D   79. Which of the following statements is FALSE?
        A. Jensen is America's foremost propopent of a hereditarian
           view of human intelligence
        B. Japanese outperform both white and Black Americans on IQ
           tests
        C. females score higher on verbal ability tests than do
           males
        D. there is a negative relationship between SES and IQ

FAMILY CONFIGURATION AND INTELLECTUAL DEVELOPMENT

A   81. One's family size, birth order, and sibling spacing define
        one's:
        A. family configuration
        B. intellectual potential
        C. family potential
        D. SES level

C   82. Zajonc's work with families' VIE is related to research
        which suggests that as _____, intellectual level in
        offspring generally _____.
        A. family size decreases ; declines
        B. sibling spacing declines ; increases
        C. family size and birth order increase ; declines
        D. birth order and sibling spacing increases ; increases

B   83. A criticism of Zajonc's family configuration theory is that
        it is:
        A. only relevant to American families
        B. based on cross-sectional studies
        C. true only for urban families
        D. does not account for sex differences

ENVIRONMENTAL ENRICHMENT PROGRAMS AND INTELLECTUAL DEVELOPMENT

D   84. Project Head Start does NOT seem to have a positive effect
         on children's:
         A. health
         B. academic achievement test scores
         C. social and emotional development
         D. measured IQ

A   85. Children who have participated in early enrichment programs
         generally:
         A. function better in regular school
         B. have fewer family problems
         C. have fewer psychological problems
         D. obtain better paying jobs as adults

APPLICATION: ENRICHMENT THROUGH NUTRITION

C   86. The name of the special "soft-drink" which some suggest
         would offer enrichment through nutrition is:
         A. Early Start
         B. Go
         C. Sampson
         D. Early-Sup

C   87. A test of Sampson's worth as a food supplement showed
         children who drank it:
         A. ate more "regular" food
         B. got better grades in school
         C. slept less in class
         D. were better in sports

ON THE HORIZON: ENGINEERING HUMAN INTELLIGENCE

B   88. The Graham project in California attempts to engineer human
         intelligence through:
         A. selective breeding
         B. artificial insemination
         C. racial isolation
         D. enrichment through nutrition

- CHAPTER 13 -

PERSONALITY THEORIES AND ASSESSMENT

OUTLINE

I. Introduction: "Three Faces of Eve" - a summary of Chris
    Sizemore and her 22 distinct personalities is used to introduce
    the importance of PERSONALITY; unlike many who view personality
    as social adroitness or effectiveness, psychologists define it
    as those personal characteristics that account for consistant
    and enduring patterns of response to various situations

II. Personality Theories

    A. Psychoanalytic Approach - the PSYCHOANALYTIC THEORY of Freud
       was the first modern theory; it incorporated terms such as
       the <u>ego, id, Freudian slip</u>, and <u>Oedipus conflict</u>
       1. Major assumptions - it is guided by the principle of
          <u>psychic determinism</u> while it also assumes <u>unconscious
          motivation</u>
       2. The processes of personality: Energy and Instincts -
          there were two types of biological <u>instincts</u> (<u>life
          instincts</u>, or eros, and <u>death instincts</u>, or thanatos);
          LIBIDO is the energy from the life instincts
       3. Personality structure - there are three interacting
          systems which generate maladjusted behavior if they are
          not in harmony
          a. ID - the part of the personality from which the
             instincts and instinctual energy are derived; it
             functions according to the <u>pleasure principle</u>

    b. EGO - that part of the personality which is attuned to the demands and opportunities of objective reality; it operates according to the <u>reality principle</u>

    c. SUPEREGO - the part which reflects those cultural values adopted by the child through the process of identifying with his or her parents; <u>anxiety</u> results from intrapsychic conflicts between the id, ego, and superego

4. Psychosexual stages of personality development - Freud's ideas form a theory of <u>psychosexual development</u> which states that a child passes through a series of <u>psychosexual stages</u> with each stage's libido being focused on a different <u>erogenous zone</u>; FIXATION refers to a portion of the libido being permanently invested in a particular psychosexual stage

    a. ORAL STAGE - occurs during the first year of life when sexual instinct seeks expression through oral stimulation; the two phases of this stage are <u>oral eroticism</u> and <u>oral sadism</u>

    b. ANAL STAGE - usually during the second year when the libido focus on the anal region with conflict centering on toilet training; the <u>anal-retentive personality</u> and the <u>anal-aggressive personality</u> result from different types of toilet training

    c. PHALLIC STAGE - occurs between three and five years of age when the libido focuses on the genitals; the OEDIPUS COMPLEX is the phenomenon where the male child experiences an unconscious longing for affection and sexual contact with the opposite-sexed parent; males experience <u>castration anxiety</u> and <u>identification with the aggressor</u> during this stage; females experience <u>penis envy</u>; the <u>Electra complex</u> is the female Oedipus complex

    d. LATENCY PERIOD is not actually a psychosexual stage, but occurs around age of five when a repression (until puberty) of sexual impulses takes place

    e. GENITAL STAGE is when sexual urges are renewed and libido is focused on the genitals, but self-gratification is replaced by desire to mate and display affection for someone of the opposite sex

5. Personal profile: Sigmund Freud (1856-1939) - Freud's theory was influenced by his own rearing experiences in the middle 1800's; his clinical activities developed into <u>psychoanalysis</u> in 1884

6. Neoanalytic approaches - most deemphasize the biological and sexual determinants of behavior

    a. Erikson proposed a sequence of <u>psychosocial</u> development stages

    b. Adler called his approach <u>individual psychology</u> with each of us having our own <u>style of life</u>

7. Evaluation of psychoanalytic approach - criticisms include the use of unverified data; an overemphasis on biological determinants; and too much concern with the disturbed side of human nature

B. Trait approach - the TRAIT APPROACH views personality in terms of how people differ on a <u>trait</u>
   1. Cattell - he distinguishes between <u>surface traits</u> and <u>source traits</u>; he measures personality with the <u>16 Personality Factor Inventory</u>
   2. Eysenck - he deals with basic dimensions or <u>types</u>; two major dimensions of personality are <u>introversion - extroversion</u>; people who are social and outgoing show EXTROVERSION; people who are quiet and reserved show INTROVERSION; people who are moody, touchy, and anxious show INSTABILITY; people who are stable, calm, and carefree show STABILITY
   3. Evaluation of trait approach - criticisms include the fact that people are inconsistent and that behavior is influenced by the situation

C. Humanistic approach - the HUMANISTIC APPROACH believes one should study human strengths and virtues, and what people are like at their best
   1. Rogers - he has a <u>self theory</u> which includes the innate motive of <u>self-actualization</u>; each person develops a SELF-CONCEPT or image of who they are, should be, or would like to be; one's self-concept is influenced by <u>organismic feeling</u> which may be <u>congruent</u> or <u>incongruent</u> with one's self experience; individuals seek <u>positive regard</u> from others, but sometimes <u>conditions of worth</u> are attached to positive regard; the treatment approach is to establish an <u>unconditional positive regard</u>
   2. Maslow - beliefs are similar to Rogers'; he studied historical figures who had achieved self-actualization
   3. Evaluation of humanistic approach - criticisms include limiting itself to the person's present, conscious, subjective experiences, being too narrow and simplistic, and being better able to describe than explain personality and behavior

D. Cognitive Approach - the COGNITIVE APPROACH is concerned with how thoughts and beliefs affect people's behavior
   1. Kelly - his theory focuses solely on the way in which we process information and control events in our life by forming, testing, and revising hypotheses about the world; we create PERSONAL CONSTRUCTS to predict events; constructs may be <u>validated</u> by success; the <u>Role Construct Repertory Test</u> measures constructs; Kelly's therapeutic approach is called <u>constructive alternativism</u>
   2. Evaluation of cognitive approach - two criticisms include essentially its ignoring of emotional or irrational influences and Kelly's ambiguity regarding the development or precise functioning of constructs

E. Behavioral approach - the BEHAVIORAL APPROACH focuses on behavior and environmental conditions that influence it; personality is the sum total of the individual's behavior; BEHAVIORAL SPECIFICITY refers to the notion that personal inconsistencies result when behavior changes to fit the circumstances; a new trend within the behavioral approach is the COGNITIVE-BEHAVIORAL APPROACH which emphasizes the study of covert as well as overt behavior
   1. Skinner - he urges us to do a FUNCTIONAL ANALYSIS OF BEHAVIOR, or an analysis of the causative or functional relationships between behavior and the environment
   2. Bandura - he suggests a social learning theory
      a. observational learning is important for one copies a model's behavior without the presence of rewards
      b. SELF-REGULATION refers to our ability to exercise influence over our own behavior; Bandura believes people are influenced by their environment, but they also influence it by choosing how to behave (i.e., RECIPROCAL DETERMINISM); we learn standards for expecting reinforcement; once learned, responses are regulated and maintained by general rules called EXPECTANCIES; one expectancy is SELF-EFFICACY which is the perceived ability to cope with specific situations; SELF-REINFORCEMENT is when individuals reinforce themselves for attaining personal goals or standards
   3. Rotter and Mischel - Rotter's theory says behavior will occur as a function of the individual's expectancies concerning response outcomes and the perceived values of those outcomes; to Rotter, GENERALIZED EXPECTANCIES pertaining to many situations are like learned traits; one generalized expectancy is LOCUS OF CONTROL which refers to whether an individual believes in internal control or external control; Mischel's cognitive social learning theory includes the notion that people respond to situations as they perceive them; Mischel's five person variables include competencies, encoding strategies and personal constructs, stimulus-outcome and behavior-outcome expectancies, subjective values of outcomes, and self-regulatory systems and plans
   4. Interactionism - the study of both individual differences and situation variables and how they interact is called INTERACTIONISM
   5. Evaluation of behavioral approach - criticisms include an undue emphasis on learning and too little attention given to psychological dispostions and people's subjective views of the environment

F. Application: Locus of control--Personality in action - Rotter's Locus of Control Scale evaluates internal-external orientation in individuals; internals, for example, try to control their environment more, are more motivated on the job, show greater academic achievement, and are more active in attempting to guard their health

III. Personality Assessment

    A. Psychoanalytic approach – interested in <u>indirectly</u> measuring unconscious influences on behavior through the formal assessment devices known as PROJECTIVE TECHNIQUES

        1. Projective techniques – based upon the <u>projective hypothesis</u> that individual needs are reflected in reactions to ambiguous stimuli

            a. the Rorschach – the Rorschach Inkblot technique scores responses to a series of ten inkblots

            b. the <u>Thematic Apperception Test</u> (TAT) consists of 29 cards each showing an ambiguous scene; evidence for the <u>reliability</u> and <u>validity</u> of projective techniques is lacking

    B. Trait approach – to measure traits psychologists use <u>self-report inventories</u> which are assumed to yield <u>signs</u> of underlying traits

        1. Self-report inventories – presentation of a large number of statements to which the subject responds in some manner

            a. construction of self-report inventories – some inventories are constructed by <u>content validation</u>, others by <u>criterion keying</u>; the <u>Minnesota Multiphasic Personality Inventory</u> used criterion keying

            b. Cattell's 16 Personality Factor Inventory – it has 187 items which measures personality in its entirety

            c. the Minnesota Multiphasic Personality Inventory is the most often used inventory; it contains 550 items dealing with a wide range of matters; it is used both in diagnosis and in research on normal personality traits

            d. the <u>California Psychological Inventory</u> (CPI) is a criterion keyed assessment device designed for use with normal populations

            e. critique – some argue that inventories are susceptible to biases; some people show <u>acquiescence</u> or <u>social desirability</u> in their answers, two examples of <u>RESPONSE SETS</u>

    C. Humanistic and cognitive approaches – these approaches favor self-report measures

        1. Interviews – they enable the humanistic psychologist to explore the subject's unique interpretations, perceptions, and meanings given to events; to overcome the problem with quantitative comparisons across interviews, CONTENT ANALYSIS involves establishing categories of verbal behavior that can be reliably rated by scorers

        2. Measures of the self-concept – the <u>Q-sort</u> technique is a structured method which requires the subject to sort cards with varying statements that may or may not apply to the subject

3. Critique – criticism focuses around the question as to whether subjects are both willing and able to accurately describe their subjective experiences

D. Behavioral approach – this approach emphasizes the direct assessment of <u>target behavior</u> in specific situations, though self-reports such as the <u>Fear Survey Schedule</u> are sometimes used

    1. Critique – two criticisms are that there is no standard technique for how one observes the target behavior or what precisely is observed, and there is the potential problem that a subject's behavior may be altered by the presence of the observer

E. Application: The MMPI in personnel selection – though not intended for this use, the MMPI is being used in industry to select future employees for the presence of emotional disturbance; criticisms of this activity center on the untrained people who administer the test, problems of confidentiality, right to privacy, and the accuracy of results

IV. On the Horizon: Personality Assessment in the Courtroom – the selection of jury members with the help of psychologists is growing; the goal is to select "good" jurors (i.e., ones who are neutral or favorable to the client); psychologists look for the trait called AUTHORITARIANISM which is typified by rigidity, dogmatism, resistance to change, intolerance and prejudice; authoritarianism is related to various behavioral characteristics in jurors; some well-known trials which have used personality assessment in the courtroom include the Harrisburg Seven conspiracy and the Wounded Knee trial with the American Indian Movement leaders

OBJECTIVES

I. WHAT IS PERSONALITY? HOW IS IT DEFINED?

According to psychologists, personality does not refer to social adroitness or effectiveness. In general, psychologists define personality as those personal characteristics that account for consistent and enduring patterns of response to various situations. This definition recognizes that people differ in a variety of characteristics and in their interpretations of, and responses to, situations. As a result, each person is unique and distinctive. Psychologists also consider personality to be enduring, consistent, and stable over time. Finally, in spite of how people differ, they are also similar. Personality therefore, represents those characteristics common to all individuals.

D   1. How do psychologists view personality?

   A. characteristics common to all people
   B. consistent and stable over time
   C. unique and distinctive for each individual
   D. all of the above

   2. What is personality and how do psychologists define this concept?

II.   LIST THE ESSENTIAL FEATURES OF THE FIVE MAJOR APPROACHES TO STUDYING PERSONALITY?

The psychoanalytic approach emphasizes unconscious forces, biologically-based urges for sex and aggression, and early-childhood conflicts as factors which shape personality. The trait theory views personality as being influenced by an individual's distinct, consistent personal qualities (i.e., traits), and its goal is to learn the traits of each person's traits, the origin of traits, and how they influence behavior. Humanistically-oriented psychologists believe one should study human strengths and virtues, and to study the best in people (not their worst). These psychologists emphasize human aspirations, their conscious experiences, free will, and the fulfillment of personal potential. The cognitive approach to personality is concerned with how thoughts and beliefs affect people's behavior, and an individuals own perspectives and unique interpretations of various situations. The behavioral approach to personality focuses on behavior and environmental conditions that influence it. To a behavioral psychologist, personality is the sum total of the individual's behavior.

B   1. Which approach to personality is concerned with personal aspirations, free will, and personal potential?

   A. psychoanalytic
   B. humanistic
   C. trait
   D. cognitive

C   2. An approach to personality which is concerned with an individual's distinct, consistent personal qualities is:

   A. psychoanalytic
   B. humanistic
   C. trait
   D. cognitive

3. Summarize the essential features of three of the five major approaches to studying personality.

III. NAME SOME CRITICISMS OF THE FIVE APPROACHES?

The psychoanalytic theory is criticized because it lacks experimental verification, it overemphasizes the biological determinants of behavior, and it is not sufficiently concerned with the healthy, mature individual. The trait theory is criticized because it does not deal enough with one's inconsistencies, especially as influenced by different situations. There are three criticisms of the humanistic approach. It is said to limit itself to the present, conscious, subjective experiences of the individual, to be too narrow and simplistic, and it is better at describing rather than explaining personality and behavior. Two problems with the cognitive approach is that it tends to ignore emotional or irrational influences and that it is not clear on the development or precise functioning of personal constructs. Some criticize the behavioral approach because it emphasizes learning at the expense of excluding genetic or biological influences on behavior, and because it pays too little attention to psychological dispositions and how people subjectively view the environment.

A   1. Which of the following is a criticism of the behavioral approach to personality?

A. it pays too little attention to psychological dispostions
B. it lacks experimental verification
C. it does not deal enough with individual's inconsistencies in behavior or emotions
D. it overemphasizes biological influences

2. What are the criticisms of three of the five major approaches to personality?

IV. WHAT ARE SOME OF THE MAJOR PERSONALITY ASSESSMENT DEVICES?

Projective tests, used primarily by psychoanalytically-oriented therapists, have been developed to probe unconscious impulses and attitudes through the presentation of ambiguous stimuli. Two well-known examples are the Rorschach inkblot test and the Thematic Apperception Test. Self-report inventories are paper-pencil tests that yield signs of an individual's underlying dispositions or traits. They are primarily used by those who adhere to a trait approach. Examples include the Minnesota Multiphasic Personality Inventory, the Cattell 16 Personality Factor Inventory, and the California Psychological Inventory. Interviews are commonly used by those who follow the cognitive and humanistic approach to personality, but more structured methods, such as the Q-sort, which involves card-sorting, are used to help the individual present accurate characterizations of himself or herself. Observing the individual behaving in one or more situations is a common method used by behaviorally-oriented psychologists.

B   1. Which of the following is NOT a major way of assessing personality?

        A. projective tests
        B. neurological workups
        C. self-report inventories
        D. interviews

A   2. Which of the following is NOT a self-report inventory?

        A. Q-sort Inventory
        B. Minnesota Multiphasic Personality Inventory
        C. California Psychological Inventory
        D. Cattell 16 Personality Factor Inventory

3. What are some of the major personality assessment devices?

V.   HOW DO PERSONALITY ASSESSMENT TECHNIQUES RELATE TO PERSONALITY THEORIES?

The personality assessment technique that one tends to favor or use is usually consistent with what type of information is provided by the assessment method. In turn, the type of information wanted is somewhat determined by the major personality approach that one supports or follows. Though any one therapist may use a variety of methods for any one particular individual, the following "match-ups" tend to occur: psychoanalytic - projective tests; trait - self-report inventories; humanistic and cognitive - interviews; behavioral - target behavior(s) in real situation(s).

1. How do various personality assessment techniques relate to particular personality theories? Give examples.

VI.   WHAT ARE SOME PROBLEMS ASSOCIATED WITH PERSONALITY ASSESSMENT?

There are many problems associated with personality assessment, with each method having its own weakness(es). The projective tests are lacking in both reliability and validity. The self-report inventories are susceptible to response sets or biases in the subject. Interviews are criticized for assuming that people are both willing and able to accurately describe their subjective experiences. The behavioral approach of observing behaviors in real situations is criticized on two points: there is no standard technique for what and how one observes and the individual's behavior may be altered by the presence of the observer.

C   1. Which personality assessment technique is criticized for
        assuming that subjects are willing and able to describe
        their subjective experiences?

        A. self-report inventories
        B. projective techniques
        C. interviews
        D. all of the above

     2. What are some problems with personality assessment
        techniques? Give examples.

MULTIPLE-CHOICE QUESTIONS

INTRODUCTION: "THE THREE FACES OF EVE"

C   1. The life experiences of Chris Sizemore demonstrated the case
        of:
        A. transsexualism
        B. amnesia
        C. multiple personalities
        D. schizophrenia

B   2. To the average person "on the street," the term
        "personality" refers to:
        A. enduring traits
        B. social effectiveness
        C. underlying traits
        D. behavioral tendencies

A   3. In general, psychologists refer to personality as:
        A. consistent or enduring patterns of response
        B. social adroitness or effectiveness
        C. the way we think, feel, and behave
        D. all of the above

D   4. In defining personality, psychologists recognize that
        people:
        A. differ in a variety of characteristics
        B. have enduring and stable traits over time
        C. are similar in spite of their differences
        D. all of the above

PSYCHOANALYTIC APPROACH

B   5. The first modern personality theory was _____ theory.
           A. trait
           B. psychoanalytic
           C. cognitive
           D. behavioral

D   6. Psychoanalytic theory is well-known for its emphasis on:
           A. unconscious forces
           B. biologically based urges for sex and aggression
           C. early childhood conflicts
           D. all of the above

C   7. Psychoanalytic theory is guided by the principle of:
           A. instincts
           B. unconscious motivation
           C. psychic determinism
           D. libido

A   8. Freud's term used to explain people's unawareness of the
           true motives underlying their behavior was:
           A. unconscious motivation
           B. psychic determinism
           C. life and death instincts
           D. Oedipus conflict

B   9. Which of the following is NOT associated with Freud's life
           instincts?
           A. survival needs
           B. inorganic state
           C. libido
           D. psychic energy

C   10. Which of the following is NOT associated with Freud's death
           instincts?
           A. destructive impulses
           B. Thanatos
           C. Eros
           D. aggression and suicidal tendencies

D   11. Libido refers to:
           A. a goal of returning the organism to an inorganic state
           B. conflict resolution at the unconscious level
           C. psychic energy from thanatos
           D. energy from the life instincts

A   12. The part of the personality from which the instincts and
           instinctual energy are derived is the:
           A. id
           B. ego
           C. superego
           D. libido

A   13. Which of the following is NOT relatd to id functioning
         according to Freud?
         A. delaying gratification
         B. the pleasure principle
         C. avoiding pain and seeking immediate pleasure
         D. all of the above

B   14. The part of the personality which is attuned to the demands
         and opportunities of objective reality is the:
         A. id
         B. ego
         C. superego
         D. libido

C   15. The goal of the ego is to:
         A. seek long-term satisfaction and pleasure
         B. evaluate and restrain behavior
         C. postpone the discharge of tension
         D. all of the above

D   16. Which statement is TRUE?
         A. the reality principle characterizes ego functioning
         B. the superego acts as an "internalized parent"
         C. a well-adjusted individual has an id, ego, and superego
            in harmony
         D. all of the above

C   17. The part of the personality which represents cultural values
         adopted by the child is the:
         A. id
         B. ego
         C. superego
         D. libido

B   18. Which part of the personality deals with reducing the
         anxiety created by intrapsychic conflicts?
         A. id
         B. ego
         C. superego
         D. libido

A   19. What time period according to Freud has a decisive effect on
         the development of the adult personality?
         A. the first five years
         B. ages 3 to 8
         C. the pre-adolescent years
         D. the adolescent years

D   20. During Freud's theory of psychosexual development, the child
       goes through psychosexual _____ where sexual energy is
       focused on a _____.
       A. periods ; intrapsychic conflict
       B. phases ; principles
       C. levels ; body part
       D. stages ; erogenous zone

D   21. When a portion of libido is permanently invested in a
       particular stage of development, it is called:
       A. instability
       B. stagnation
       C. displacement
       D. fixation

A   22. Freud believed that during the first year of life the child
       is in the _____ stage.
       A. oral
       B. anal
       C. phallic
       D. genital

C   23. According to Freud, fixation at the following phase leads to
       excessive pessimism, hostility, and aggression:
       A. penis envy
       B. oral eroticism
       C. oral sadism
       D. anal stage

B   24. In psychoanalytic theory, the conflict in the anal stage
       revolves around:
       A. the first spanking
       B. toilet training
       C. weaning
       D. conflicting impulses

B   25. The anal-retentive personality is thought to result from:
       A. weaning at too young of an age
       B. harsh toilet-training demands
       C. regular constipation
       D. fear of paternal spanking

A   26. Which is NOT a characteristic of the anal-aggressive
       personality?
       A. stubborn and stingy
       B. hostile and sadistic behavior
       C. temper tantrums
       D. cruelty and destructiveness

C   27. The Oedipus complex refers to the conflict in which Freudian psychosexual stage?
A. genital
B. latency
C. phallic
D. oedipal

D   28. During which stage of Freud's psychosexual stages is pleasure believed to come from masturbation and sex play?
A. anal
B. genital
C. latency
D. phallic

B   29. Which of the following statements is FALSE?
A. castration anxiety is an unconscious fear shown by males
B. penis envy is shown by females during the genital stage
C. the Electra complex is when the female identifies with the mother
D. all of the above

A   30. The resolution of the Oedipus complex occurs at around age:
A. 5
B. 6
C. 7
D. 8

C   31. Which is NOT a characteristic of the genital stage?
A. libido is focused on the genitals
B. it occurs around adolescence
C. sexual instincts for self-gratification
D. affection displayed for the opposite sex

C   32. The "father" of psychoanalysis was:
A. Alfred Adler
B. Erik Erikson
C. Sigmund Freud
D. Hans Eysenck

D   33. What characterizes the neoanalytic approaches to personality?
A. five psychosexual stages of development
B. more emphasis on emotional frustration
C. an emphasis on heterosexual relationships
D. a deemphasis on biological and sexual determinants of behavior

B   34. According to Adler, life was:
A. a sequence of psychosocial stages
B. a struggle against feelings of inferiority
C. centered around learning the "style of life" from our parents
D. all of the above

D   35. Which of the following is a criticism of Freudian theory?
         A. it is based on unverified data
         B. there was too strong of an emphasis on biological
            determinants of behavior
         C. there is little research to support the theory
         D. all of the above

TRAIT APPROACH

A   36. The trait approach to personality views people in terms of:
         A. how people differ
         B. unconscious events
         C. psychosocial influences
         D. behavioral consistency

A   37. Any distinct, consistent personal quality is a:
         A. trait
         B. characteristic
         C. dimension
         D. type

D   38. According to Cattell, surface traits:
         A. consist of visible response patterns
         B. include dimensions such as assertive-undecisive
         C. reflect underlying source traits
         D. all of the above

C   39. Cattell used a mathematical technique called _____ to
         analyze source traits.
         A. analysis of variance
         B. regression analysis
         C. factor analysis
         D. the t-test

B   40. According to Eysenck, one of the two major dimensions of
         personality is:
         A. dominant-submissive
         B. introversion-extroversion
         C. talkative-silent
         D. radical-conservative

A   41. The personality dimension of Eysenck which describes people
         as being quiet and reserved is:
         A. introversion
         B. extroversion
         C. instability
         D. stability

D   42. Which   dimension   of   personality   according   to   Eysenck
        describes   people   as   being   calm,   care-free,   and
        even-tempered?
        A. introversion
        B. extroversion
        C. instability
        D. stability

B   43. Which of the following statements is FALSE?
        A. extroverts are characterized by lower levels of
           physiological arousal
        B. a combination of high emotionality and high extroversion
           is thought to encourage strong anxiety
        C. behavioral theorists argue that there is too much
           inconsistency in behavior to warrant trait theories
        D. all of the above

HUMANISTIC APPROACH

D   44. The humanistic approach to personality:
        A. emphasizes human virtues and aspirations
        B. believes in studying human strengths and virtues
        C. emphasizes the fulfillment of personal potential
        D. all of the above

C   45. A basic assumption in _____ self theory is the notion of

        _____.
        A. Cattell's ; underlying dimensions
        B. Maslow's ; self-concept
        C. Roger's ; self-actualization
        D. Maslow's ; self-creativity

A   46. One's self-concept is the:
        A. image of who they are, should be, or might like to be
        B. amount of self-actualization
        C. organismic feeling one has about their emotions
        D. feeling that is opposite to their self-image

B   47. Roger's approach to treatment and prevention of maladaptive
        behavior is to establish:
        A. positive organismic feelings
        B. unconditional positive regard
        C. self-actualization
        D. conditions of worth

C   48. Which statement is TRUE according to Maslow?
        A. about 8% of the population are considered self-actualized
        B. maladjustment occurs when one's self-concept is
           threatened
        C. actualizing people tend to be virtuous and to work for
           an end to injustices
        D. all of the above

COGNITIVE APPROACH

C   49. Personality is concerned with how thoughts and beliefs affect people's behavior according to the _____ approach.
A. trait
B. humanistic
C. cognitive
D. emotional

D   50. According to Kelly, what are the expectations that guide our behavior and define our reality?
A. validated hypotheses
B. actualizing traits
C. actualizing hypotheses
D. personal constructs

A   51. Kelly's therapeutic approach which involves experimenting with new and altered construct systems is called:
A. constructive alternativism
B. modeling
C. validation synthesis
D. existentialism

BEHAVIORAL APPROACH

B   52. The behavioral approach to personality does NOT assume that:
A. behavior is influenced by environmental conditions
B. personality traits and dimensions influence overt behavior
C. personality is a hypothetical internal state
D. consistencies in behavior are cases of generalized learning

B   53. The behavioral approach deals with personal inconsistencies by suggesting that behavior changes to fit circumstances, an idea termed behavioral _____.
A. likelihood
B. specificity
C. flexibility
D. variation

C   54. An approach which emphasizes the study of the relationship between covert and overt behavior is the _____ approach.
A. reciprocal determinism
B. social learning
C. cognitive-behavioral
D. self-expectancy

D   55. Which of the following is a characteristic of behavioral
         theories?
         A. an interest in measurable behavior
         B. the use of research and scientific methods to test
            hypotheses
         C. an emphasis on environmental influences on behavior
         D. all of the above

A   56. The functional analysis of behavior approach to behavior is
         associated with:
         A. Skinner
         B. Bandura
         C. Cattell
         D. Erikson

A   57. An approach that analyzes the causative relationships
         between behavior and the environment is called a:
         A. functional analysis of behavior
         B. social learning theory
         C. cognitive approach
         D. humanistic approach

B   58. Bandura's social learning theory emphasizes the role of:
         A. validated responses by one's parents
         B. observational learning
         C. constructive alternativism
         D. personal constructs

C   59. Self-regulation according to Bandura's behavioral theory
         refers to our ability to:
         A. delay gratification
         B. reinforce ourselves for good behaviors
         C. exercise influence over our own behavior
         D. implement motives originating with the self-concept

A   60. The interaction between how the environment influences
         people and how people choose to behave is called:
         A. reciprocal determinism
         B. self-efficacy
         C. ego-interactionism
         D. interactionism

D   61. Bandura's theory says that once behaviors are learned, they
         are regulated and maintained by:
         A. locus of control
         B. observational learning
         C. self-reinforcement
         D. expectancies

B   62. According to Bandura, the expectation that one can bring
        about a desired outcome through personal effort is called:
        A. confidence
        B. self-efficacy
        C. generalized expectancy
        D. reciprocal determinism

C   63. Which concept is used by Bandura to emphasize that behavior
        is not governed solely through external reinforcers?
        A. observational learning
        B. standards for reinforcement
        C. self-reinforcement
        D. locus of control

D   64. Generalized expectancies are like:
        A. personal constructs
        B. Freud's superego
        C. internalized social standards
        D. learned traits

C   65. Believing reinforcements are due to oneself or to chance is
        an example of Rotter's generalized expectancy known as:
        A. reinforcement location
        B. egomania
        C. locus of control
        D. self-efficacy

A   66. The views of Rotter and Mischel which encourage the study of
        both individual differences and situation variables is known
        as:
        A. interactionism
        B. dualism
        C. the balance theory
        D. objective and subjective expectancies

APPLICATION: LOCUS OF CONTROL--PERSONALITY IN ACTION

B   67. Which test is used to determine one's locus of control?
        A. MMPI
        B. I-E Scale
        C. CPI
        D. TAT Scale

D   68. Which of the following is a characteristic of internally
        oriented individuals?
        A. they tend to be more motivated
        B. they engage in more precautionary health care
        C. they show greater academic achievement
        D. all of the above

PSYCHOANALYTIC APPROACH

D   69. Projective techniques in personality assessment are
        primarily used by _____ oriented therapists.
        A. humanistic
        B. trait
        C. behavioral
        D. psychoanalytic

C   70. Projective techniques utilize the person's response to:
        A. open-ended questions
        B. true-false types of statements
        C. an ambiguous or vague stimulus
        D. self-reported statements

B   71. Which of the following are projective tests?
        A. Rorschach and Q-Sort
        B. Rorschach and TAT
        C. Q-Sort and MMPI
        D. CPI and TAT

A   72. A criticism of projective tests is that they:
        A. lack reliability and validity
        B. are too long
        C. require an expertly trained administer
        D. all of the above

TRAIT APPROACH

C   73. The self-report inventories for personality assessment are
        designed to measure:
        A. emotions
        B. perceptions
        C. traits
        D. anxiety level

B   74. Which of the following is NOT a self-report inventory?
        A. MMPI
        B. Q-Sort
        C. CPI
        D. 16 P.F.

D   75. The Minnesota Multiphasic Personality Inventory:
        A. is the most often used personality inventory
        B. was constructed to aid in diagnosing psychiatric
           patients
        C. is relatively effective in predicting long-range
           behavior
        D. all of the above

A   76. A criticism of personality inventories and questionnaires is
       that people:
       A. have response sets which bias their scores
       B. lie on many questions
       C. frequently don't understand what is being asked
       D. with poor reading abilities can't take them

C   77. People who respond to items on a personality inventory in
       terms of their social desirability are demonstrating:
       A. situational determinism
       B. poor self-concepts
       C. response sets
       D. response codes

HUMANISTIC AND COGNITIVE APPROACHES

B   78. Which general type of assessment devices are favored by the
       humanistic and cognitive approaches?
       A. projective tests
       B. self-report measures
       C. personality inventories
       D. situation tests

D   79. A procedure in some interviews where categories of verbal
       behavior are established so that they can be reliably rated
       by scorers is called:
       A. item analysis
       B. self-efficacy
       C. personal constructs
       D. content analysis

A   80. Which of the following statements is TRUE?
       A. the interview technique is fallible and subject to error
          and bias
       B. the Q-sort is a modern version of the Rorschach inkblot
          test
       C. a criticism of humanistic psychologists is that they
          place too little emphasis on self-report data
       D. all of the above

BEHAVIORAL APPROACH

D   81. What statement would best describe the behavioral approach
       to assessment?
       A. an emphasis on direct assessment
       B. seeing how someone behaves in one or more situations
       C. linking specific responses to specific situations
       D. all of the above

C   82. One criticism of the behavioral approach to assessment is:
    A. there is too little emphasis on self-report data
    B. the patient's motives and emotions are not adequately evaluated
    C. the observer may cause the patient to alter his or her behavior
    D. there is only one standard technique for how target behaviors are observed

APPLICATION: THE MMPI IN PERSONNEL SELECTION

A   83. The MMPI is now being widely used in an area not originally intended. It is:
    A. personnel selection
    B. dating services
    C. premarital counseling
    D. athletic competition

D   84. A problem with using the MMPI in a manner not originally intended is:
    A. untrained individuals may administer the test
    B. the test results may not be correlated with actual behaviors
    C. an invasion of privacy may exist
    D. all of the above

ON THE HORIZON: PERSONALITY ASSESSMENT IN THE COURTROOM

B   85. In which setting may it be useful to assess the personality trait of authoritarianism?
    A. mental health
    B. courtroom
    C. industry
    D. education

C   86. The use of personality assessment techniques has been used on prospective jurors in order to measure their degree of:
    A. neutrality
    B. curiosity
    C. authoritarianism
    D. objectivism

— CHAPTER 14 —

STRESS AND COPING

OUTLINE

I. Introduction: Life's Little Hassles — an introduction to
    stress and what causes it; interestingly, "little hassles" are
    a better predictor of psychological and physical health than
    major life events; the difference between STRESS and ANXIETY

II. Sources of Stress — stress results when STRESSORS are imposed

   A. Frustration — blocking any goal-directed behavior results in
      FRUSTRATION
      1. Sources of frustration — five sources are presented
         a. delays — delays in obtaining a valued object cause
            frustrations
         b. lack of resources — lack of finances, education,
            skills or experience to obtain goals
         c. losses — losing something valued reduces the chances
            of obtaining some goal
         d. failure — real failures or those defined by
            individuals both cause frustration
         e. loneliness — a major source of frustration; most
            common in 18-25 year olds; lonely people are most
            often isolated, unattractive, aloof, shy, and with
            poor social skills

   B. Conflict — a CONFLICT arises when incompatible or opposing
      motives arise; four major conflict situations are presented

   a. APPROACH-AVOIDANCE CONFLICT exists when the same goal
      is both avoided and approached; GOAL GRADIENTS
      describe the strength of an approach or avoidance
      tendency; the avoidance gradient is steeper
   b. DOUBLE APPROACH-AVOIDANCE CONFLICT - a desire to both
      approach and avoid two different goals
   c. APPROACH-APPROACH CONFLICT exists when two goals are
      both desirable; these usually produce relatively
      little anxiety
   d. AVOIDANCE-AVOIDANCE CONFLICT exists when two or more
      choices are equally unattractive

C. Pressure - another source of stress originating from either
   external or internal origins

D. Life events - any event, desirable or undesirable, can cause
   stress if a change in life circumstances is involved; the
   Social Readjustment Rating Scale lists 43 life events which
   vary in perceived severity and time required for adjustment;
   this scale has shown that as life changes increase, so does
   the risk of illness within two years; negative events
   predict better than positive life changes

E. Environmental stressors - these include noise, heat,
   crowding, and urban settings

F. Application: Managing the frustration of a delay - research
   with children has shown that delays will be longer if the
   desired objects were not visible; elaborate self-distraction
   techniques were used during the delays to divert attention
   from the delayed reward; effective self-control may involve
   "transforming" something aversive into something pleasant

III. Physiological effects of stress - stress has a physiological as
     well as a psychological component

   A. The general adaptation syndrome - Selye first noticed that
      different stressors generate the GENERAL ADAPTATION SYNDROME
      (G.A.S.), a nonvarying general pattern of physical
      reactions; the G.A.S. occurs in potentially three sequential
      stages (alarm reaction, stage of resistance, and, with
      prolonged and severe stress, the stage of exhaustion)

   B. Psychosomatic disorders - three of the most common forms of
      PSYCHOSOMATIC DISORDERS are presented
      1. PEPTIC ULCER - a hole or lesion in the stomach lining
         frequently, but not always, due to stress; research with
         rats has shown unexpected shocks caused more ulcers than
         expected shocks

2. Migrane and tension headaches – most headaches are thought to be caused by stress; MIGRAINE HEADACHES are intense, headaches with deep throbbing pain on one side of the brain, the pain is due to dilation of the cranial arteries; the more common TENSION HEADACHES involve a sensation of tightness or pressure with a dull, steady pain around the entire head with the pain having a muscular origin

3. HYPERTENSION, or chronically high blood pressure, is usually caused by stress (especially emotions of anger and hostility)

C. General health – life stress serves to increase one's overall susceptibility to many illnesses; the life-stress relationship is best documented in men, but also is found in women; the validity of these conclusions must be determined by prospective research designs (rather than retrospective designs which are most common); the consequences of life stress may be attenuated by those with the personality trait called hardiness

D. Application: Relaxation and biofeedback – two strategies for coping with and preventing stress-related disorders are relaxation and biofeedback; progressive muscle relaxation facilitates relaxation; BIOFEEDBACK assumes that with proper learning, one can control biological processes to which one does not normally attend; headaches, high blood pressure, and increased heart rate are frequently treated with the aid of electromyographic biofeedback

IV. Coping With Stress

A. Cognitive appraisal – evaluations of a potentially stressful event are called COGNITIVE APPRAISALS; one may find something more threatening than someone else, or by cognitively reappraising an event, one may make it less threatening; a research study supporting this is discussed

B. Predictability – the severity of stressful events is reduced with predictability; one cause for this may be the safety signal hypothesis which says relaxation occurs during safe periods; another explanation is that we habituate faster to predictable events

C. Perceived control – the belief that one has the ability to influence an event's aversiveness is PERCEIVED CONTROL; we desire perceived control; consequences of actual or perceived control are an enhanced pain tolerance, reduced anxiety while anticipating, and improved self-image

D. Social supports – the presence of family and friends reduces the stress associated with stressful events; perceived social support can be as beneficial as actual support

E. Personality and health – two personality characteristics which influence how we respond to stress are <u>hardiness</u> and <u>Type A behavior</u>
    1. HARDINESS refers to those who can experience high degrees of stress without feeling ill; hardy individuals are characterized by commitment, control, and challenge
    2. TYPE A BEHAVIOR PATTERN is characterized by competition, high achievement, aggressiveness, impatience, harried sence of time urgency, and increased likelihood of heart attacks; Type B individuals are the opposite; this section discusses many differences between Type A and B individuals; one explantion for why Type A's have more heart attacks is a hyperactivity of the autonomic nervous system

F. Defense mechanisms – Freud theorized that DEFENSE MECHANISMS were <u>unconscious</u> psychological processes used to reduce or eliminate anxiety by distorting reality
    1. DENIAL – we pretend some unpleasant reality doesn't exist
    2. REPRESSION – keeping threatening and unacceptable thoughts out of consciousness
    3. REACTION FORMATION – the substitution in awareness of a socially acceptable desire opposite to one that is socially unacceptable
    4. RATIONALIZATION – finding "logical" and acceptable reasons to justify one's behavior
    5. PROJECTION – where we attribute or "project" our own unacceptable thoughts or behavior to other people or blame them for our faults; most often found in individuals with rigid moral codes
    6. REGRESSION – where long-outgrown behaviors are used to lessen a threat or anxiety
    7. COMPENSATION – counteracting an undesirable characteristic which makes a person feel anxious and inadequate by exaggerating an opposing trait
    8. Summing up – defense mechanisms are normal and useful unless they are overly used or become our sole strategy for dealing with stress; they do not help to solve the problem

G. Application: Breaking Type A habits – Type A individuals are hard to treat because they respond to stress with behaviors that produce more stress; strategies that can alleviate this cycle include <u>learn to relax</u>, <u>retrain your reactions</u>, <u>take control of your environment</u>, and <u>slow down</u>

V. On the Horizon: Community Stress Checks – Three Mile Island and Beyond – the accident at the Three Mile Island nuclear plant caused a great deal of stress; its start up potentially can induce more stress; a "psychological impact statement" (similar to an environmental impact statement) could determine the negative consequences of a start up at this plant; perhaps such psychological impact statements will be commonplace in the future

OBJECTIVES

I. HOW CAN FRUSTRATION LEAD TO STRESS? WHAT IS CONFLICT? IN WHAT
    WAYS MIGHT ONE EXPERIENCE CONFLICT?

    Frustration occurs when any goal directed behavior is blocked
    or perceived to be blocked. Common sources of delays include
    lack of resources, losses, failures, and loneliness. All of
    these can occur at anytime in our lives, but loneliness is most
    prevalent in 18-25 year olds. A conflict produces stress, but
    it also produces frustration. Incompatible or opposing motives
    result in conflict situations. Four common conflict situations
    involve: (1) "approach-avoidance" is when one goal is both
    approached and avoided; (2) "double approach-avoidance" is when
    two   goals   are   both   approached   and   avoided;   (3)
    "approach-approach" is where two goals are both approached; and
    (4) "avoidance-avoidance" is where two goals are both avoided.
    More than one goal object is involved in all but the
    approach-avoidance conflicts.

A   1. More than one goal object is present in all but _____
       conflict situations.

          A. approach-avoidance
          B. approach-approach
          C. double approach-avoidance
          D. avoidance-avoidance

    2. Discuss how conflict and frustrating situations occur to
       produce stress.

II. HOW DOES PRESSURE PRODUCE STRESS? WHAT ROLE DO LIFE EVENTS
    PLAY IN PRODUCING STRESS?

    Unrealistic assumptions about what we feel we should do or what
    others think we should do leads to pressure. Thus, pressure
    can have both internal and external origins. Common sources of
    external pressure include family, marriage, work, child-rearing
    problems, and financial concerns. Life events are major
    activities (e.g., marriage, divorce) which involve changing and
    adjusting to new demands. Many believe that any change,
    whether pleasant or unpleasant, is stressful. A scale used to
    quantify stress in terms of life changes (see Table 14-3) is
    the Social Readjustment Rating Scale.

C   1. Pressure results from:

          A. external sources such as parents
          B. internal sources such as our unrealistic assumptions
          C. both internal and external sources
          D. biological changes in the autonomic nervous system

B   2. Life events such as marriage and divorce are considered
       stressful because they require:

       A. emotional growth
       B. change
       C. some financial loss
       D. loss of personal status

    3. In what ways do pressure and life events cause stress?

III. WHAT IS THE GENERAL ADAPTATION SYNDROME?   HOW DOES IT HELP US
     UNDERSTAND THE OCCURRENCE OF STRESS-RELATED DISORDERS?

     The general adaptation syndrome (G.A.S.) is a nonvarying,
     general pattern of physical reactions to a stressor.   The
     G.A.S. consists of three sequential stages.   The alarm reaction
     works to defend the system by increasing heart rate,
     respiration, and adrenaline secretion.   Resistance to stress is
     actually diminished during this first stage.   During the stage
     of resistance, body reactions present in the first stage
     disappear and there is increased resistance to the stressor
     (but decreased resistance to other stressors).   A prolonged and
     severe stressor may cause one to enter the stage of exhaustion.
     During this final stage resistance weakens, alarm symptoms
     reappear, and "diseases of adaptation," such as heart disease
     or ulcers appear.

B   1. The second stage of the G.A.S., where our resistance to the
        stressor is increased, is the:

        A. alarm reaction
        B. stage of resistance
        C. stage of exhaustion
        D. fight-or-flight reaction

     2. What is the general adaptation syndrome and what three
        stages are potentially present during its occurance?

IV. LIST SOME COMMON PSYCHOSOMATIC REACTIONS.

Psychosomatic disorders are organic disorders which develop in response to stress and anxiety. The three most common forms are peptic ulcers, migraine and tension headaches, and hypertension. Peptic ulcers result when excess acid is secreted in the stomach when a person experiences stress and accompanying anxiety. Most headaches are thought to be due to stress. Migraine headaches are intense, recurrent deep throbbing pain on only one side of the head. Tension headaches involve a sensation of tightness or pressure with a dull, but steady pain around the entire head. Hypertension or chronically high blood pressure can result under chronically stressful conditions.

C   1. A psychosomatic disorder which involves throbbing pain, usually on one side of the head, is called a:

        A. hypertension headache
        B. tension headache
        C. migraine headache
        D. none of the above

     2. Present and discuss the three most common forms of psychosomatic disorders.

V.   WHAT IS THE ROLE OF COGNITIVE APPRAISAL IN MANAGING STRESS? WHY DO PREDICTABILITY AND PERCEIVED CONTROL AFFECT THE SEVERITY OF STRESS AND OUR ABILITY TO COPE WITH IT?

Cognitive appraisals pertain to how each individual reacts to a potentially stressful event based upon their evaluation of that event. We have the ability to interpret something as more or less threatening than someone else. Thus, the goal to manage stress would be to have people cognitively reappraise a stressful event as less threatening. The predictability of an aversive event, even if it can't be controlled, tends to reduce stress. Two explanations exist for this effect. One is that the organism can relax during the safe, no-stress period. The other is that the organism attends less to the stressful situation and then habituates faster. Perceived control is the "belief" that one can influence the occurrence or aversiveness of an event. One explanation is that this control allows us to know that a situation will not become so aversive that we cannot handle it.

A   1. Which of the following is NOT a way to reduce the stress in stressful events?

        A. physically ignoring the event
        B. cognitive appraisals
        C. perceiving control
        D. gaining predictability

D   2. An explanation as to why perceived or actual control over a
        stressful event lowers the stress one experiences is that:

        A. thinking about it makes it less threatening
        B. attention is diverted
        C. habituation occurs faster
        D. with control, we know we can apply it before a situation
           becomes too aversive; we can limit maximum future danger

     3. How do cognitive appraisals, predictability, and perceived
        control influence our ability to deal with stress?

VI. HOW ARE SOCIAL SUPPORT, PERSONALITY, AND DEFENSE MECHANISMS
     INVOLVED IN COPING WITH STRESS?

     Loneliness is a common source of anxiety. Thus, the social
     support of family and friends during stressful times offers not
     only help in coping with the stress, but also eliminates any
     anxiety which would be present if the person experienced the
     stress while alone. Two personality traits are correlated with
     above average abilities to cope with stress without developing
     other physical or mental disorders. These traits are known as
     hardiness and the Type B behavior pattern. Defense mechanisms,
     as theorized by Freud, are unconscious psychological processes
     which distort reality to bring about a reduction in anxiety.
     (The book talks about denial, repression, reaction formation,
     rationalization, projection, regression, and compensation).

     1. Discuss how personality or defense mechanisms are involved
        in coping with stress. Give appropriate examples.

                    MULTIPLE-CHOICE QUESTIONS

INTRODUCTION: LIFE'S LITTLE HASSLES

B   1. What did Lazarus' project with middle-aged persons find to
        be the best predictor of short term psychological and
        physical health?
        A. frequency of minor illness such as colds and the flu
        B. "little hassles"
        C. divorce
        D. death of a spouse

D   2. The hassles in our life become more damaging:
           A. the more often they occur
           B. the longer their duration
           C. the less effectively we cope with them
           D. all of the above

D   3. All stressful events, whether pleasant or unpleasant,
           require us to:
           A. slow down our mental activity
           B. slow down our physical activity
           C. decrease our adrenalin output
           D. adjust or adapt

A   4. A "healthy tension" is:
           A. a moderate level of stress
           B. tension without sickness
           C. actually damaging to us
           D. undesirable for optimum adjustment

A   5. A physical and psychological condition experienced whenever
           environmental demands are placed upon an organism is:
           A. stress
           B. anxiety
           C. trauma
           D. frustration

D   6. Anxiety is an emotion with unpleasant feelings of
           apprehension that accompanies:
           A. frustration
           B. conflict
           C. stress
           D. all of the above

SOURCES OF STRESS

B   7. Frustration and conflict are two major types of:
           A. anxiety
           B. stressors
           C. mental pressures
           D. adaptation syndromes

C   8. Stress arises when demands, called _____, are imposed on
           the person.
           A. conflicts
           B. delays
           C. stressors
           D. frustrations

FRUSTRATION

C   9. The blocking of any goal-directed behavior which prevents
       the satisfaction of some need is called:
       A. anxiety
       B. stressors
       C. frustration
       D. stress

D   10. Which of the following is NOT a common source of frustration
       according to Coleman?
       A. delays
       B. losses
       C. failure
       D. expectations

A   11. Shaver and Rubenstein (1980) report a number of specific
       reasons which adults give for feeling lonely. Which of the
       following is NOT among those reasons?
       A. having no pets
       B. having no spouse
       C. being far from home
       D. feeling different

B   12. Which type of frustration is difficult to understand because
       it actually is subjectively defined so often by the person?
       A. loneliness
       B. failure
       C. losses
       D. lack of resources

B   13. Loneliness is highest during which age span?
       A. 10-15 years
       B. 18-25 years
       C. 40-45 years
       D. 65 years and over

D   14. What is a quality or characteristic found in people
       susceptible to loneliness?
       A. their work keeps them socially isolated
       B. they are unattractive and aloof
       C. they are shy and have poor social skills
       D. all of the above

CONFLICT

C   15. What exists whenever a person has incompatible or opposing
       motives?
       A. frustration
       B. failure
       C. a conflict
       D. lack of resources

A   16. Frustration results from conflicts because:
        A. neither motive can be solved
        B. one motive is stronger than the other
        C. the motives represent biological drives
        D. the motives represent psychological drives

C   17. An approach-avoidance conflict exists when:
        A. a person is motivated to avoid two different goals
        B. the approach tendency is stronger than the avoidance
           tendency
        C. one wants to both approach and avoid the same goal
        D. all of the above

A   18. If you want to remain in school, but you also want to quit,
        you are having a(n) _____ conflict.
        A. approach-avoidance
        B. goal gradient
        C. double approach-avoidance
        D. approach-approach

B   19. What is the term which describes the strength of one's
        tendency to approach or avoid some goal object?
        A. stamina
        B. goal gradients
        C. goal expectations
        D. ego expectations

D   20. Compared to the approach gradient, the avoidance gradient
        is:
        A. weaker
        B. stronger far from the goal
        C. longer
        D. steeper

D   21. Generally, farthest from the goal the _____ gradient is
        _____.
        A. avoidance ; as strong as the approach gradient
        B. avoidance ; stronger than the approach gradient
        C. approach ; weaker than the avoidance gradient
        D. approach ; stronger than the avoidance gradient

C   22. What type of conflict results when one must choose between
        two new cars, both of which have positive and negative
        characteristics?
        A. approach-approach
        B. approach-avoidance
        C. double approach-avoidance
        D. multiple approach-avoidance

A   23. Which type of conflict produces the least amount of stress?
        A. approach-approach
        B. double approach-avoidance
        C. avoidance-avoidance
        D. approach-avoidance

B   24. Why do approach-approach conflicts tend to produce little
        stress?
        A. the motives are usually weak
        B. the motive not chosen can be satisfied later
        C. we convert them into other types of conflicts
        D. they are easier to rationalize

C   25. Which of the following terms best describes our behavior
        when we experience an avoidance-avoidance conflict?
        A. tranquility
        B. confidence
        C. vacillation
        D. none of the above

D   26. "Choosing the lesser of two evils" pertains to which
        conflict type?
        A. approach-approach
        B. double approach-avoidance
        C. multiple approach-avoidance
        D. avoidance-avoidance

B   27. What is a common solution to avoidance-avoidance conflicts?
        A. turn one into an attractive choice
        B. search for a way to avoid both
        C. turn both into attractive choice
        D. develop temporary amnesia

PRESSURE

D   28. Which is TRUE about pressure?
        A. it produces stress
        B. it has internal origins
        C. it has external origins
        D. all of the above

LIFE EVENTS

A   29. A way to quantify stress in terms of life changes is the:
        A. Social Readjustment Rating Scale
        B. Personal Stress Test
        C. Stressful Situation Impact Test
        D. Forced Life Change Scale

D   30. The Social Readjustment Rating Scale quantifies stress with
        events on the scale that vary in their:
        A. time required for adjustment
        B. degree of stress
        C. perceived severity
        D. all of the above

APPLICATION: MANAGING THE FRUSTRATION OF A DELAY

C   31. Mischel's work with children found that they could manage
        the frustration of a delay best when:
        A. the preferred object was in view
        B. the less desirable object was in view
        C. no rewards were visible
        D. both rewards were visible

C   32. Mischel's work with children found that those who managed
        their frustrating delay best:
        A. ate more candy while waiting
        B. chewed more gum while waiting
        C. devised self-distraction techniques
        D. concentrated on the physical aspects of the rewards

GENERAL ADAPTATION SYNDROME

A   33. The nonvarying, general pattern of physical reactions to a
        stressor is called:
        A. the general adaptation syndrome
        B. alarm syndrome
        C. anxiety
        D. frustration

C   34. The alarm reaction stage of the G.A.S. involves a(n):
        A. decreased adrenaline secretion
        B. increased resistance to stress
        C. increased heart rate and respiration
        D. all of the above

C   35. What is a characteristic of the resistance stage of the
        G.A.S.?
        A. increased heart rate and adrenaline secretion
        B. below normal resistance to the stressor
        C. increased resistance to the stressor
        D. exhaustion

B   36. The second stage of the G.A.S. is known as the:
        A. stage of exhaustion
        B. stage of resistance
        C. alarm reaction
        D. "fight-or-flight" reaction

A   37. If a stressor is prolonged and severe, the individual may
        eventually enter the third stage of the G.A.S., known as
        the:
        A. stage of exhaustion
        B. stage of resistance
        C. alarm reaction
        D. none of the above

PSYCHOSOMATIC DISORDERS

B   38. A psychosomatic disorder is one where:
     A. a mental stressor precedes a physical stressor
     B. actual tissue damage occurs in response to stress and
        anxiety
     C. a physical stressor preceeds a mental stressor
     D. an imagined stressor causes a real, physical disorder

C   39. Which of the following is NOT a common form of psychosomatic
         disorder?
     A. peptic ulcer
     B. hypertension
     C. tics
     D. migraine headache

A   40. Weiss' rat research on peptic ulcers found that FEWER ulcers
         developed when the:
     A. stressor was predictable
     B. stressor was presented infrequently
     C. rats were younger
     D. rats were older

D   41. Intense, recurrent headaches that are characterized by a
         deep throbbing pain are known as _____ headaches.
     A. arterial
     B. major
     C. tension
     D. migraine

D   42. Tension headaches differ from migraine headaches in the
         _____ of pain.
     A. degree
     B. origin
     C. location
     D. all of the above

B   43. Which of the following is NOT a characteristic of tension
         headaches?
     A. sensation of tightness or pressure
     B. dilation of cranial arteries
     C. dull, steady pain
     D. muscular in origin

C   44. Hypertension is believed to be most often caused by:
     A. kidney diseases
     B. a poor, salty diet
     C. stress
     D. obesity

A   45. Some researchers believe that chronic hypertension results
         from:
         A. anger and hostility
         B. excessive life stressors
         C. constant, minor "life hassles"
         D. high levels of frustration resulting from conflict
            situations

GENERAL HEALTH

D   46. Research has shown that life stress is related to:
         A. cancer in children
         B. mental depression
         C. sudden cardiac death
         D. all of the above

B   47. A major problem with life stress and general health studies
         is that they are often:
         A. prospective designs
         B. retrospective designs
         C. cross-sectional studies
         D. longitudinal studies

APPLICATION: RELAXATION AND BIOFEEDBACK

D   48. A technique to learn how to sense tenseness in our bodies
         and then to voluntarily control that tenseness is called:
         A. cognitive appraisals
         B. EMG biofeedback
         C. biofeedback
         D. progressive muscle relaxation

D   49. Progressive muscle relaxation has been reported effective in
         dealing with:
         A. some types of headaches
         B. high blood pressure
         C. physical symptoms of anxiety
         D. all of the above

B   50. Biofeedback assumes that individuals can _____ control
         normally imperceptible body functions.
         A. unconsciously
         B. learn to
         C. unintentionally
         D. not

C   51. Electromyographic (EMG) feedback is typically used for treating:
        A. peptic ulcers
        B. migraine headaches
        C. tension headaches
        D. psychosomatic disorders

A   52. One approach using biofeedback to treat migraine headaches has been to teach patients to:
        A. increase their finger temperature
        B. increase tension in the leg muscles
        C. lower their finger temperature
        D. lower tension in the leg muscles

COGNITIVE APPRAISAL

B   53. The evaluations or reactions to a potentially stressful event which depend on how we evaluate the situation are called:
        A. personal perceptions
        B. cognitive appraisals
        C. cognitive perceptions
        D. predictions

C   54. A study by Lazarus and his colleagues on the impact of cognitive appraisals showed that a film about Australian puberty rites causes the greatest stress when it:
        A. was in color
        B. had no soundtrack describing the events
        C. had a soundtrack which portrayed great suffering
        D. had a detached and scientific soundtrack

PREDICTABILITY

A   55. Research with humans and animals shows they would rather experience a _____ aversive stimulus rather than one that is _____.
        A. predictable ; unannounced
        B. larger ; predictable
        C. unannounced ; predictable
        D. predictable ; smaller

C   56. Predictability seems to have what effect on stressful events?
        A. it lowers their frequency
        B. it shortens their duration
        C. it reduces their severity
        D. it makes them more pronounced

B   57. The safety signal hypothesis says that predictable stressors
        are less stressful because they enable the organism to:
        A. lower its current anxiety level
        B. relax
        C. prepare physically for the upcoming stressor
        D. prepare emotionally for the upcoming stressor

PERCEIVED CONTROL

D   58. The belief that one has the ability to influence the
        aversiveness of an event is known as:
        A. cognitive appraisal
        B. social manipulation
        C. predictability
        D. perceived control

C   59. Perceived or actual control over an aversive event seems to
        actually:
        A. lower pain tolerance
        B. generalize pain
        C. enhance pain tolerance
        D. lower pain sensitivity

D   60. Perceived or actual control over an aversive event seems to:
        A. lessen chronic anxiety
        B. enhance pain tolerance
        C. positively reflect on one's self-image
        D. all of the above

SOCIAL SUPPORTS

A   61. An important way of making stressful situations less
        stressful is to have:
        A. social supports
        B. no understanding of the upcoming stressful event
        C. little control over them
        D. no knowledge as to when the stressful situations may
           occur

B   62. Perceived social support is nothing more than _____ one
        has the support of others.
        A. knowing
        B. believing
        C. hoping
        D. wishing

PERSONALITY AND HEALTH

C   63. Two personality characteristics which influence how we
         respond to stressful situations are:
         A. introversion-extroversion and hardiness
         B. Type A behavior and sociality
         C. hardiness and Type A behavior
         D. Type B behavior and introversion-extroversion

B   64. Hardiness, a personality trait, is NOT characterized by the
         term:
         A. control
         B. meticulous
         C. commitment
         D. challenge

A   65. Kobasa's study of executives with stressful life events
         found that those with greater hardiness showed greater:
         A. resistance to illness
         B. problem solving ability during stress
         C. creativity during stressful events
         D. social support systems

D   66. Which of the following does NOT characterize a Type A
         behavior pattern?
         A. impatience
         B. aggressiveness
         C. harried sense of time urgency
         D. less likelihood of heart attack

D   67. Those with Type A behavior patterns:
         A. tend to talk, move, and walk rapidly
         B. tend to feel guilty when they relax
         C. try to schedule more and more in less time
         D. all of the above

C   68. How do we currently explain the fact that Type A persons get
         more heart attacks?
         A. both are genetically inherited characteristics
         B. these people experience less stress
         C. hyperreactivity of the autonomic nervous system
         D. they are less able to predict stress

DEFENSE MECHANISMS

B   69. Freud believed defense mechanisms to be _____ processes
         used to protect people against _____.
         A. subconscious ; anxiety
         B. unconscious ; anxiety
         C. preconscious ; stressful events
         D. conscious ; stressful events

A   70. Which term would NOT typically be associated with Freud's
         explanation of defense mechanisms?
         A. frustration
         B. unconscious
         C. anxiety
         D. distorting reality

A   71. A defense mechanism whereby we pretend that some unpleasant
         reality does not exist is called:
         A. denial
         B. reaction formation
         C. rationalization
         D. projection

D   72. Someone who blocks unacceptable or inappropriate sexual
         feelings from their consciousness is using which defense
         mechanism?
         A. projection
         B. compensation
         C. rationalization
         D. repression

C   73. Substituting an extreme or excessive acceptable behavior for
         an unacceptable behavior is a defense mechanism called:
         A. denial
         B. regression
         C. reaction formation
         D. repression

B   74. Anxiety associated with not studying or failing at something
         important can be reduced through which defense mechanism?
         A. reaction formation
         B. rationalization
         C. repression
         D. compensation

B   75. The defense mechanism called projection is often found in
         persons with:
         A. Type B personalities
         B. rigid moral codes
         C. strong ethnic backgrounds
         D. higher education levels

A   76. A defense mechanism in which long-outgrown behaviors are
        used to reduce anxiety is called:
        A. regression
        B. compensation
        C. reaction formation
        D. repression

D   77. An extremely shy person may become overbearing and
        intimidating. This would exemplify which defense mechanism?
        A. rationalization
        B. projection
        C. reaction formation
        D. compensation

C   78. Which of the following statements is FALSE concerning
        defense mechanisms?
        A. they become a problem when we only use them to cope
        B. they serve to distort reality
        C. they help solve problems
        D. all of the above

APPLICATION: BREAKING TYPE A HABITS

B   79. Which of the following is NOT a suggestion offered by Suinn
        to change Type A behavior patterns?
        A. retrain reactions
        B. consume less cholesterol
        C. slow down
        D. learn to relax

ON THE HORIZON: COMMUNITY STRESS CHECKS--THREE MILE ISLAND
AND BEYOND

D   80. The fears and anxiety produced in residents about the start
        up of the Three Mile Island nuclear plant could be estimated
        through a:
        A. potential risk survey
        B. anxiety risk survey
        C. environmental impact statement
        D. psychological impact statement

– CHAPTER 15 –

ABNORMAL BEHAVIOR

OUTLINE

I.   Introduction: Schizophrenia and the Genain Quadruplets – a presentation of an ongoing longitudinal study of these quadruplets who all show schizophrenic symptoms in varying degrees; ABNORMAL BEHAVIOR is any behavior that has undesirable consequences for the individual or others

II. Classifying and Conceptualizing Abnormal Behavior

A. Issues in classification – psychology uses a <u>classification system</u> whereby observations are organized into reasonably similar groups; the current system has both advantages and disadvantages which are discussed; the value of any classification system is in its <u>reliability</u>, which is currently less than ideal due to the personal <u>judgment</u> involved in classifying people
1. DSM-III – the Diagnostic and Statistical Manual of Mental Disorders (DSM-III) is a set of guidelines for categorizing disorders on the basis of symptoms or <u>behaviors</u> and, when possible, the <u>potential</u> causes of disorders.
2. The labeling problem – there are dangers with <u>labeling</u>; many disadvantages are discussed, especially the problem of the <u>self-fulfilling prophecy</u>

B. Models of abnormality – there are seven broad, conceptual frameworks or models

1. The BIOLOGICAL MODEL OF ABNORMALITY (or medical model) views abnormal behavior as resulting from some organic or biological impairment
2. The PSYCHOANALYTIC MODEL OF ABNORMALITY views mental disorders as representing substitute expressions of repressed unconscious impulses which have their origin in early childhood
3. The BEHAVIOR MODEL OF ABNORMALITY contends that maladaptive behavior can be attributed to faulty learning processes; this behavior can be both learned and unlearned
4. The COGNITIVE MODEL OF ABNORMALITY views maladaptive behavior resulting from our <u>thinking</u> - the assumptions we make, the interpretations we place on our experiences, the meanings we give them, and the internal dialogue we carry on within ourselves
5. The HUMANISTIC MODEL OF ABNORMALITY presumes that abnormal behavior results from interference with the satisfaction of basic tendencies such as personal growth and the desire to fulfill one's potentials
6. The FAMILY INTERACTION MODEL OF ABNORMALITY holds that behavior results from faulty or disturbed relationships (e.g., communication patterns among family members)
7. The SOCIOCULTURAL MODEL OF ABNORMALITY sees the causes of abnormality as lying in the larger society where potential sources of maladaptive behavior include poverty, discrimination, and illiteracy

C. Application: Interpreting abnormality from different perspectives - the case of a college student who had excessive heterosexual anxiety is evaluated using the psychoanalytic, behavioral, cognitive, and humanistic views

III. Categories of Abnormal Behavior - six major disorders are presented

A. ANXIETY DISORDERS have as central features either high anxiety or the disruptive consequences of trying to avoid it or defend against it
1. GENERALIZED ANXIETY DISORDER - the individual displays a chronically high level of anxiety (at least one month duration) but is unaware of its source; it shows itself most notably in the following ways - <u>motor tension</u>, <u>autonomic hyperactivity</u>, <u>apprehensive expectation</u>, and <u>vigilance</u>
   a. causes that are discussed include the biological perspective which shows the influence of a genetic influence with a high CONCORDANCE RATE, and the psychological explanations which vary greatly

2. Phobic disorder - a PHOBIA is an irrational, persistent fear of some object, activity, or situation in which no real danger exists or the danger is unrealistically magnified; the three DSM-III subdivisions are AGORAPHOBIA (a marked fear of open spaces and unfamiliar settings), SOCIAL PHOBIA (a persistent, irrational fear of situations in which the individual may be scrutinized by others) and SIMPLE PHOBIA (a persistent, irrational fear of any object or situation other than those already described
   a. causes discussed are the psychoanalytic and the behavioral points of view
3. OBSESSIVE-COMPULSIVE DISORDER - where individuals feel compelled to think thoughts they do not want to think (OBSESSION) or to engage in some act they do not want to perform (COMPULSION); common obsessions and compulsions are discussed and a case history of a 15-year-old boy with compulsive behaviors is presented
   a. causes include a presentation of the psychoanalytic, behavioral, and cognitive viewpoints

B. Somatoform disorders - physical symptoms exist but without any known organic or physiological basis in the SOMATOFORM DISORDERS
   1. HYPOCHONDRIASIS is a preoccupation with the fear of having a serious disease
      a. causes reviewed include the biological and behavioral perspectives
   2. CONVERSION DISORDER - the central feature is a loss or alteration in physical functioning that has no physical basis and is not under voluntary control; symptoms such as paralyses are presented
      a. causes reviewed are the psychoanalytic and behavioral positions

C. Dissociative disorders - the DISSOCIATIVE DISORDERS involve a separation or alteration between an individual and his or her normal consciousness, identity, or motor behavior; these are relatively rare
   1. PSYCHOGENIC AMNESIA involves extensive but selective memory losses; four subtypes include localized (most common), selective, generalized amnesia, and continuous amnesia
   2. PSYCHOGENIC FUGUE involves a loss of memory with a sudden move away from home and work, a new identity, and no memory for one's former identity
   3. MULTIPLE PERSONALITY involves the presence of two or more distinct personalities within an individual
   4. Causes that are summarized are the psychoanalytic and behavioral interpretations

D. Affective disorders - everyone experiences normal periods of depression or "the blues" and new mothers may undergo postpartum depression; depression is the most prevalent mental health problem in the United States; an AFFECTIVE DISORDER is a major disturbance of mood or emotions involving depression or mania; two basic types of affective disorders are MAJOR DEPRESSIVE DISORDER (a persistent and pronounced dysphoric mood state) and BIPOLAR DISORDER (a persistent mood disturbance in which both depressive and manic symptoms are prominent); manic refers to a highly excited or irritable mood state

1. Major depressive disorder - the most common major affective disorder with considerable variability between individuals; in severe forms there are DELUSIONS and HALLUCINATIONS

2. Bipolar disorder - a case history of an individual is provided

3. Causes are discussed in more detail than in previous sections of this chapter

   a. biological model - emphasizes the possibility of a hereditary predisposition; the CATECHOLAMINE HYPOTHESIS suggests that depression results from low levels of catecholamines while the SEROTONIN HYPOTHESIS suggests that low levels of serotonin is the explanation

   b. psychoanalytic model emphasizes the real or imagined loss of a significant person in childhood as the source of the problem

   c. behavioral model stresses a history of too little reinforcement

   d. cognitive model views depression as resulting from a distorted, irrational, negative way of thinking; Beck refers to a thinking pattern called OVERGENERALIZATION; Seligman emphasizes feelings of helplessness as being externally caused, specific, and temporary or internally caused, global, and stable

E. Schizophrenic disorders - the SCHIZOPHRENIC DISORDERS are a group of disorders involving disturbances in thought and perceptual processes, inappropriate affect or emotion, disturbances in motor activity, a withdrawal from social relationships, and a loss of contact with reality; the term schizophrenia is used; these disorders are the most commonly diagnosed ones in the United States

1. Characteristics of schizophrenia - one can distinguish between process and reactive schizophrenia; there are four general characteristics associated with these disorders

   a. thought - bizarre, disorganized, and illogical thinking; neologisms (newly-coined words) may be present; delusions of presecution, control, and grandeur occur

   b. perception - hallucinations, expecially auditory, are common

      c. emotion - affect is characterized by blunting, flattening, or inappropriateness

      d. motor activity - a range from agitated to catatonic-like postures

  2. Types of schizophrenia - there are four main categories

      a. DISORGANIZED SCHIZOPHRENIA is characterized by marked incoherence and flat, incongruous, or silly affect

      b. CATATONIC SCHIZOPHRENIA shows a disturbance in motor activity, either of an excited or a stuporous type

      c. PARANOID SCHIZOPHRENIA shows a primary disturbance in thought pattern, expecially with persecutory delusions and ideas of reference; a dialogue between a patient and doctor is provided

      d. UNDIFFERENTIATED SCHIZOPHRENIA includes symptoms of incoherence, prominent delusions, hallucinations, and grossly disorganized behavior

  3. Causes

      a. biological model - a biochemical cause is advanced by the DOPAMINE HYPOTHESIS which emphasizes an excess of dopamine

      b. psychoanalytic model believes there is a regression to an earlier phase of the oral stage

      c. behavioral model stresses reinforcers which increase the schizophrenic symptoms

      d. family interaction model emphasizes the presence of a schizophrenogenic mother and/or a DOUBLE-BIND PATTERN where parents give children incompatible and contradictory messages

      e. sociocultural model offers an explanation that the disorder results from a low socioeconomic status; however, some believe the SOCIAL DRIFT HYPOTHESIS accounts for this correlation

F. Personality disorders - inflexible and maladaptive patterns of relating to, and interacting with, others (i.e., the presence of maladaptive personality traits) are called PERSONALITY DISORDERS

  1. Common features of personality disorders - of the many mentioned, the most prominent is the difficulty in establishing positive interpersonal relationships

  2. Types of personality disorders - paranoid, schizoid, and schizotypal disorders seem "odd" or different; histrionic, narcissistic, antisocial, and borderline disorders show dramatic, emotional, or erratic behavior; dependent, compulsive, and passive-aggressive disorders are often associated with anxiety

  3. Causes

      a. biological model - speculates that an autonomic nervous system functions at a low level of arousal

      b. family interaction model - stresses an adult who was neglected and emotionally deprived as a child

      c. sociocultural model - lower socioeconomic status fosters antisocial personalities

G. Application: Warning signs for student suicide - statistics on attempted and successful suicides with a presentation of behaviors which suggest when an attempt will be made; the precipitating factors are also discussed

IV. On the Horizon: Diagnosing Abnormal Behavior with the PET Scanner - the PET scanner provides a metabolic picture of how the brain tissue consumes biochemicals; the Genain sisters are shown to provide different brain activity relating to the degree of their schizophrenic symptoms; the PET scanner promises to be an additional diagnostic tool in the future

OBJECTIVES

I.   WHAT IS ABNORMAL BEHAVIOR?

Abnormal behavior is any behavior that has undesirable consequences for the individual or others. Behavior is abnormal when it is maladaptive and self-defeating, when it impairs optimal functioning, causes personal distress, or causes others distress or harm. Not all abnormal behavior is "strange" or "bizarre", some "ordinary" behaviors are also quite maladaptive. Abnormal behavior is not defined in terms of its statistical frequency.

D   1. Behavior is considered abnormal if it:

     A. impairs optimal functioning
     B. causes personal distress
     C. causes others distress or harm
     D. all of the above

     2. What is psychology's view of abnormal behavior?

II. LIST SOME ADVANTAGES AND DISADVANTAGES IN CLASSIFYING ABNORMAL BEHAVIOR INTO SPECIFIC CATEGORIES.

A classification system is advantageous for a number of reasons. It allows researchers and clinicians to efficiently communicate about the behavior, it suggests possible causes of problems, it provides us with behaviors that might be expected, and it suggests possible treatments. Disadvantages include its current reliability which is not perfect due to the many personal judgments involved in classifying abnormality. Furthermore, with classification comes labeling. Labeling does not mean that all people in a category behave in the same way.

Sometimes when a label is given, there is a tendency to no longer question that label and to adjust current treatment on a label made in the past. Both clients and clinicians tend to view the label as a name for the person rather than for the person's behavior. Finally, there is the problem of the self-fulfilling prophecy whereby one behaves according to what is expected for one with that particular label.

C   1. Which of the following is NOT an advantage of classifying abnormal behavior?

     A. communication is facilitated
     B. possible treatments are suggested
     C. people tend to behave more similarly
     D. causes of problems are suggested

C   2. Which of the following is NOT a disadvantage of classifying abnormal behavior?

     A. the self-fulfilling prophecy
     B. we tend to view the label as a name for the person
     C. it includes potential causes of the behavior(s)
     D. it may influence future treatment(s)

     3. Present the advantages and disadvantages of classifying abnormal behavior.

III. WHAT ARE THE MOST USEFUL CURRENT MODELS OF ABNORMALITY?

There are seven current models of abnormality. The biological (or medical) model views abnormal behavior as resulting from some organic or biological impairment. It is the basis of much current research. The psychoanalytic model views mental disorders as representing substitute expressions of repressed unconscious impulses. The behavioral model says that maladaptive behavior can be attributed to faulty learning processes. The cognitive model views abnormal behavior as resulting from our thinking - the assumptions we make, the interpretations we place on our experiences, the meanings we give them, and the internal dialogue we carry on within ourselves. The humanistic model views maladaptive behavior as resulting from interference with the individual's striving for personal growth and fulfillment of his or her potentials. The family interaction model stresses faulty or disturbed relationships among family members as the cause of abnormal behavior. Finally, the sociocultural model see abnormality as resulting from the society. Poverty, discrimination and illiteracy contribute to maladaptive behavior.

B   1. Which model of maladaptive behavior emphasizes personal
           interpretations of one's situations?

           A. sociocultural
           B. cognitive
           C. psychoanalytic
           D. behavioral

A   2. What model of abnormal behavior does NOT emphasize an
           external source as the major influence or cause?

           A. biological
           B. behavioral
           C. humanistic
           D. family interaction

        3. There are seven models of maladaptive or abnormal behavior.
           Discuss five of them in some detail.

IV.   HOW DO THE MODELS OF ABNORMALITY DIFFER IN   THEIR   EXPLANATIONS
      OF MENTAL DISORDERS?

      The models of abnormality differ in the locus of influence
      (internal vs. external) and whether the cause is primarily
      physical, mental or environmental in origin. Internal models
      would include the biological, psychoanalytic, and cognitive
      while externally-oriented models would include family
      interaction, sociocultural, humanistic, and behavioral.
      Another viewpoint is to group the causes as physical (i.e.,
      biological or medical model), mental (i.e., cognitive and
      psychoanalytic models), or environmental (i.e., family
      interaction, sociocultural, humanistic, or behavioral models).

A   1. Which of the following models of abnormal behavior
           emphasizes the person's internal state as causing his or her
           problem(s)?

           A. psychoanalytic
           B. humanistic
           C. sociocultural
           D. behavioral

B   2. A physically based explanation for maladaptive behavior
           would be found in which model?

           A. cognitive
           B. biological
           C. psychoanalytic
           D. sociocultural

3. What different types of explanations for maladaptive behavior are offered by the various models of abnormality?

V.   NAME THE MAJOR CHARACTERISTICS OF EACH OF THE CATEGORIES OF ABNORMAL BEHAVIOR.

The central feature in anxiety disorders is either high anxiety or the disruptive consequences of trying to avoid it or defend against it. Somatoform disorders describe those individuals who have physical symptoms without any known organic or physiological basis. Major disturbances of mood or emotion characterize the affective disorders. Schizophrenic disorders are a group or cluster of behaviors involving disturbances in thought and perceptual processes, inappropriate affect or emotion, disturbances in motor activity, a withdrawal from social relationships, and a loss of contact with reality. Personality disorders are characterized by inflexible and maladaptive patterns of relating to and interacting with others.

D   1. Which category of abnormal behavior has the most and widest-range of major characteristics associated with it?

A. anxiety disorders
B. somatoform disorders
C. affective disorders
D. schizophrenic disorders

C   2. Anxiety disorders are associated with:

A. mood or emotional problems
B. physical symptoms without an organic basis
C. disruptive consequences of trying to reduce or defend against internal tension
D. all of the above

3. Present the dominant characteristics that are associated with each of the five major categories of abnormal behavior.

VI. WHAT ARE SOME OF THE SPECIFIC FACTORS THAT HAVE BEEN CITED AS CAUSES OF THE DIFFERENT PSYCHOLOGICAL DISORDERS?

(Since the authors devote considerable space to the range of potential and/or known causes of the 5 major categories of psychological disorders discussed in this chapter, it is difficult to provide an answer to this question which would be similar to "the" answer which would be expected from the majority of students; i.e., there is no "correct" answer. The instructor is referred to the chapter for the full range of specific factors which could be included in a "correct" answer.)

1. Discuss some of the specific factors that have been presented in the text as being causes of at least two different psychological disorders.

MULTIPLE-CHOICE QUESTIONS

INTRODUCTION: SCHIZOPHRENIA AND THE GENAIN QUADRUPLETS

C   1. The longitudinal study of the Genain quadruplets is concerned with:
A. neurosis
B. affective disorders
C. schizophrenia
D. somatoform disorders

C   2. The study of the Genain quadruplets suggests that their disorder may be:
A. genetically determined
B. environmentally determined
C. influenced by both genetic and nongenetic factors
D. easily treated if it is environmentally determined

A   3. Any behavior that has undesirable consequences for the individual or others is called _____ behavior.
A. abnormal
B. deviant
C. neurotic
D. unproductive

D   4. A behavior is considered abnormal if it:
A. is maladaptive or self-defeating
B. impairs optimal functioning
C. causes others distress or harm
D. all of the above

ISSUES IN CLASSIFICATION

B   5. In order to communicate efficiently about abnormal behavior, psychologists have developed a:
A. way of understanding the causes of it
B. classification system
C. way of predicting the results of it
D. behavioral check-list of symptoms

A 6. A current set of guidelines for categorizing disorders on the basis of symptoms or behaviors is the:
A. DSM-III
B. Labeling Check-list
C. Psychological Assessment Inventory
D. all of the above

D 7. DSM-III has improved classification by:
A. emphasizing causes of abnormality
B. including optimum treatment procedures
C. listing more diagnostic categories
D. providing detailed discriptions of each disorder

C 8. One problem with the labeling of abnormal behaviors is that:
A. everyone with that label acts the same
B. it is too difficult to be reliable
C. of the self-fulfilling prophecy
D. it is impossible to use with the majority of patients

MODELS OF ABNORMALITY

D 9. The biological model for abnormal behavior is sometimes referred to as the _____ model.
A. genetic
B. physical
C. biochemical
D. medical

B 10. Which model of abnormality views the behavior as resulting from some organic or biological impairment?
A. cognitive
B. biological
C. behavioral
D. psychoanalytic

B 11. The model which views abnormal behavior as a "symptom" is the:
A. behavioral
B. psychoanalytic
C. family interaction
D. sociocultural

A 12. The behavioral model of maladaptive behavior emphasizes:
A. faulty learning processes
B. substitute expressions of impulses
C. the blocking of basic tendencies
D. faulty or disturbed relationships

D   13. The cognitive model of abnormality assumes that the basic problem is in our:
    A. unconscious area
    B. faulty learning
    C. poor self-concepts
    D. thinking

C   14. Which model of abnormality stresses the unfulfillment of personal growth and potentials?
    A. family interaction
    B. cognitive
    C. humanistic
    D. sociocultural

B   15. Faulty communication patterns between related individuals is considered a factor leading to maladaptive behavior in which model?
    A. sociocultural
    B. family interaction
    C. humanistic
    D. behavioral

A   16. The sociocultural model of abnormality emphasizes such contributing factors as:
    A. poverty, discrimination, and illiteracy
    B. the breakdown in nuclear family communication
    C. unhappiness and failure to self-actualize
    D. negative and self-critical statements

APPLICATION: INTERPRETING ABNORMALITY FROM DIFFERENT PERSPECTIVES

C   17. The text presented an example of George who was anxious when women were present. Which type of theorist might explain his problem on the basis of him saying to himself that "No woman is going to be satisfied with me?"
    A. psychoanalytic
    B. humanistic
    C. cognitive
    D. sociocultural

ANXIETY DISORDERS

A   18. Anxiety disorders affect what percent of the population at some time or another?
    A. 2 - 4
    B. 7 - 10
    C. 10 - 15
    D. 25 - 30

A   19. The category of anxiety disorders does NOT include which disorder?
A. affective disorders
B. generalized anxiety disorders
C. phobic disorders
D. obsessive-compulsive disorders

A   20. The characteristics of motor tension, autonomic hyperactivity, apprehensive expectation, and vigilance are found in the _____ disorder.
A. generalized anxiety
B. phobic
C. obsessive-compulsive
D. dissociative

B   21. The concordance rate for generalized anxiety disorder is _____ percent.
A. 40
B. 49
C. 55
D. 82

D   22. What characterizes a phobia?
A. a high degree of free-floating anxiety
B. apprehensive expectation
C. motor tension and autonomic hypoactivity
D. irrational, persistent fear without a basis in reality

C   23. The most general and severe type of phobia is the _____ while the most common is the _____ phobia.
A. simple ; agoraphobia
B. social ; simple
C. agoraphobia ; simple
D. social ; agoraphobia

A   24. A marked fear of open spaces and unfamiliar settings is called a(n):
A. agoraphobia
B. simple phobia
C. claustrophobia
D. social phobia

D   25. A persistent, irrational fear of situations in which the individual may be scrutinized by others is called a(n):
A. agoraphobia
B. simple phobia
C. claustrophobia
D. social phobia

B   26. Claustrophobia and acrophobia are two examples of:
A. agoraphobia
B. simple phobia
C. claustrophobia
D. social phobia

D   27. The most common obsessions involve thoughts of:
          A. violence
          B. contamination
          C. doubt
          D. all of the above

C   28. The text's example of a boy who touched a glass 16 times
          before drinking from it exemplified a(n):
          A. phobia
          B. obsession
          C. compulsion
          D. anxiety neurosis

SOMATOFORM DISORDERS

B   29. In somatoform disorders a:
          A. large degree of tissue damage actually occurs
          B. symptom occurs without a physiological basis
          C. free-floating anxiety is turned outward
          D. physical ailment causes excessive anxiety

A   30. Which of the following is NOT a characteristic of
          hypochondriasis?
          A. realistic fears of disease
          B. preoccuption with the fear of having a disease
          C. numerous physical complaints
          D. morbid concern with health

D   31. Which of the following is NOT a text example of symptoms
          shown in conversion disorders?
          A. paralyzed legs in combat soldiers
          B. night blindness in night flying fighter pilots
          C. foot paralysis when traveling against the wishes of one's
             mother'
          D. sexual impotence in older males

DISSOCIATIVE DISORDERS

C   32. The abnormal behavior which involves a separation or
          alteration between an individual and his or her normal
          consciousness, identity, or motor behavior is called a
          _____ disorder.
          A. anxiety
          B. affective
          C. dissociative
          D. somatoform

B   33. Which statement about dissociative disorders is FALSE?
    A. the most common type is psychogenic amnesia
    B. they are relatively common
    C. the most common type of psychogenic amnesia is localized
       amnesia
    D. all of the above

A   34. The least common form of psychogenic amnesia is _____
    amnesia.
    A. generalized
    B. localized
    C. selective
    D. fugue

A   35. The failure to recall events from a particular point in the
    past, up to and including the present, is known as _____
    amnesia.
    A. continuous
    B. psychogenic
    C. selective
    D. generalized

D   36. What is a major difference between psychogenic fugue and
    psychogenic amnesia?
    A. age of onset
    B. gender of those who develop each disorder
    C. degree of paralysis
    D. there is no assumption of a new identity in psychogenic
       amenesia

C   37. Which of the following is NOT characteristic of psychogenic
    fugue?
    A. sudden movement away from home
    B. assumption of a new identity
    C. unable to recall specific places or people
    D. the establishment of a "new life"

B   38. The presence of two or more distinct personalities within an
    individual is called a(n) _____ personality.
    A. affective
    B. multiple
    C. duo
    D. conversion

AFFECTIVE DISORDERS

D   39. Following the birth of a child mothers, and sometimes
    fathers, may undergo a brief period of:
    A. fugue
    B. major affective depression
    C. "the blues"
    D. postpartum depression

D   40. Which is the most prevalent mental health problem in the United States today?
    A. somatoform disorders
    B. anxiety neurosis
    C. schizophrenia
    D. depression

C   41. A major disturbance of mood or emotions is called a(n):
    A. schizophrenia
    B. psychosomatic disorder
    C. affective disorder
    D. phobia

B   42. Affective disorders usually involve _____, but also at times _____.
    A. mania ; fugue states
    B. depression ; mania
    C. mania ; depression
    D. depression ; fugue states

A   43. A persistent and pronounced dysphoric mood state is called a _____ disorder.
    A. major depressive
    B. bipolar
    C. manic
    D. delusional

D   44. The major depressive disorder is characterized by:
    A. attempted suicide
    B. loss of job
    C. heightened interest in normally pleasurable activities
    D. concentration and sleep disturbances

A   45. Thoughts that have no basis in reality are called:
    A. delusions
    B. obsessions
    C. hallucinations
    D. compulsions

C   46. When one hears voices that ridicule the person for his or her sins and faults, it is said they are suffering from a(n):
    A. delusion
    B. obsession
    C. hallucination
    D. compulsion

B   47. Which of the following is NOT characteristic of the bipolar disorder with manic symptoms?
    A. very physically active
    B. moody and mute
    C. rapidly changing thoughts
    D. easily irritated

D   48. When discussing causes of the affective disorders, the
         biological model would favor a(n):
         A. origin early in childhood
         B. history of too little positive reinforcement
         C. negative way of thinking
         D. hereditary predisposition

A   49. A biochemical explanation for the affective disorders is
         based on the:
         A. role played by neurotransmitters
         B. cell's axon and its dendrites
         C. enkephalins and endorphins
         D. lower blood supply to the brain

C   50. Which explanation suggestion that depression results from a
         low level of norepinephrine?
         A. medical model
         B. serotonin hypothesis
         C. catecholamine hypothesis
         D. neurotransmitter theory

B   51. The serotonin hypothesis suggests that depression results
         from:
         A. high levels of serotonin
         B. low levels of serotonin
         C. excessive catecholamines
         D. too little catecholamines

D   52. The psychoanalytic model of depression views it as:
         A. a regression to an earlier way of coping
         B. an excessive build-up of unconscious anxiety
         C. unconsciously wishing oneself was a different person
         D. turning one's unconscious aggressive impulses inward

B   53. Someone who reaches a general conclusion about his or her
         ability or worth on the basis of only one event is showing:
         A. narrow thinking
         B. overgeneralization
         C. irrational thinking
         D. schizophrenic conclusions

C   54. The cognitive view of depression according to Beck
         emphasizes:
         A. early thought patterns that have become habitual
         B. excessive use of delusions
         C. overgeneralization
         D. childhood fantasies

B   55. A cognitive theory by Seligman states that depression is
         likely to occur if one views their helplessness as:
         A. temporary yet specific
         B. global and stable
         C. externally caused and global
         D. internally caused and temporary

SCHIZOPHRENIC DISORDERS

A   56. The most commonly diagnosed disorder in the United States
          is:
          A. schizophrenia
          B. depression
          C. affective disorders
          D. anxiety disorders

C   57. Of those admitted to mental hospitals each year, how many
          are diagnosed as schizophrenic?
          A. one-half
          B. two-thirds
          C. one-fourth
          D. three-fifths

B   58. Which of the following is NOT characteristic of a
          schizophrenic disorder?
          A. inappropriate affect
          B. amnesia
          C. withdrawal from social relationships
          D. loss of contact with reality

D   59. Which type of schizophrenia shows gradual symptom onset and
          a long history of poor adjustment and emotional blunting?
          A. prolong
          B. terminal
          C. reactive
          D. process

C   60. The prognosis for improvement is much better for which form
          of schizophrenia?
          A. prolong
          B. terminal
          C. reactive
          D. process

A   61. Neologisms are an example of schizophrenic:
          A. thinking
          B. perception
          C. emotion
          D. motor activity

D   62. A neologism is a schizophrenic's:
          A. advanced delusion
          B. way of feeling emotion
          C. pattern of rhyming words in a sentence
          D. newly-coined word

B   63. Emotion or affect in schizophrenics is characterized by:
A. shallow and spontaneous
B. blunting, flattening, and inappropriate
C. spontaneous, energetic, and sharp
D. shallow, uneven, and recurrent

A   64. The terms "odd" or "bizarre" commonly describe the _____ schizophrenic.
A. disorganized
B. catatonic
C. paranoid
D. undifferentiated

B   65. The disorganized schizophrenic shows:
A. excited or stuporous motor activity
B. childish disregard for social conventions
C. persistent, extreme suspiciousness
D. all of the above

C   66. A schizophrenic who is disturbed in motor activity, negativistic, and possibly violent is likely to be a _____ schizophrenic.
A. disorganized
B. undifferentiated
C. catatonic
D. paranoid

D   67. A common schizophrenic delusion that involves their thoughts being broadcast to others is the delusion of:
A. projection
B. grandeur
C. ideation
D. control

C   68. The typical schizophrenic hallucinations are _____ in form.
A. tactual
B. visual
C. auditory
D. olfactory

D   69. The primary disturbance of paranoid schizophrenics is in:
A. the range of hallucinations
B. the type of hallucinations
C. emotional reactivity
D. thought patterns

A   70. What type of delusions are most common in the paranoid schizophrenic?
A. persecution
B. control
C. grandeur
D. ideation

C   71. Someone is classified as an undifferentiated schizophrenic
        if they:
        A. show exaggerated symptoms in 3 of 5 areas
        B. show exaggerated symptoms in all 5 areas
        C. do not meet the criteria for the other classifications
        D. have known brain damage in addition to their behavioral
           symptoms

B   72. The average concordance rate for schizophrenia is about
        _____ percent for identical twins compared to _____
        percent for fraternal twins.
        A. 75 ; 14
        B. 50 ; 9
        C. 60 ; 25
        D. 83 ; 12

A   73. The most prominent biochemical theory today that attempts to
        explain schizophrenia is the _____ hypothesis.
        A. dopamine
        B. epinephrine
        C. serotonin
        D. transmethylene

D   74. Indirect support for the dopamine hypothesis for
        schizophrenia comes from:
        A. the results of twin studies
        B. chromosomal analyses of schizophrenics
        C. the high amount of dopamine in the blood
        D. the activity of amphetamines

C   75. The family interaction model of schizophrenia often
        emphasizes the role that a _____ plays in the development
        of this disorder.
        A. inherited recessive gene
        B. emotionally charged and unloving family
        C. schizophrenogenic mother
        D. schizophrenogenic father

C   76. A schizophrenogenic mother is said to produce schizophrenia
        by acting in a _____ manner.
        A. aloof, yet oversensitive
        B. inconsistent (loving vs. cool)
        C. cold, rejecting, insensitive
        D. none of the above

B   77. A family pattern which is said to contribute to
        schizophrenia in children by presenting incompatible and
        contradictory messages is called the:
        A. yes-no syndrome
        B. double-bind pattern
        C. social drift hypothesis
        D. constellation factor

A   78. The social drift hypothesis helps to explain why more
         schizophrenics are:
         A. found in the lower class
         B. located near large cities
         C. located near our coastal areas
         D. all of the above

PERSONALITY DISORDERS

D   79. Personality disorders are defined by the presence of:
         A. an overdeveloped Id
         B. those behaviors also found in other family members
         C. excessive use of defense mechanisms
         D. maladaptive personality traits

C   80. The most prominent feature of personality disorders is the:
         A. degree of observable anxiety
         B. receptivity to therapy
         C. difficulty in establishing positive interpersonal
            relationships
         D. flexibility when relating to others

A   81. In which personality disorder does the individual tend to be
         dramatic, emotional, or erratic?
         A. histrionic
         B. schizoid
         C. compulsive
         D. paranoid

D   82. The dependent personality disorder tends to:
         A. seem odd or "different"
         B. be erratic and aloof
         C. be dramatic and emotional
         D. often exhibit anxiety

APPLICATION: WARNING SIGNS FOR STUDENT SUICIDE

B   83. Which characteristic about suicides is FALSE?
         A. one in ten suicide attempts is successful
         B. more men than women attempt suicide
         C. men tend to commit suicide with more violent means than
            women
         D. a change in one's mood and behavior is a significant
            warning of possible suicide

C   84. For most suicidal students, both male and female, the major
        precipitating stressor appears to revolve around:
        A. poor grades
        B. unrealistic family expectations
        C. close interpersonal relationships
        D. part- or full-time work assignments

ON THE HORIZON: DIAGNOSING ABNORMAL BEHAVIOR WITH THE PET SCANNER

A   85. Which technique offers promise as a diagnostic tool for
        schizophrenia?
        A. PET scanner
        B. chromosomal analysis
        C. epinephrine analysis
        D. serotonin analysis

D   86. A promising future diagnostic tool for predicting or
        determining schizophrenia is based on:
        A. hemispheric dominance
        B. family pathology
        C. determining true social class level
        D. brain glucose consumption

— CHAPTER 16 —

TREATMENT OF ABNORMAL BEHAVIOR

OUTLINE

I. Introduction: A Helpful Dose of Disgust - the authors intentionally present a disgusting description of part of a treatment program called COVERT SENSITIZATION where clients image highly aversive events to help reduce their attraction to troublesome behaviors; there are many different therapies; some therapists use only one while others are eclectic and use many

II. Psychological Therapies - psychological approaches differ from physical or medical; PSYCHOTHERAPY involves pairing a therapist with a client with the two of them communicating in an attempt to alter the client's disordered feelings, beliefs, or actions

A. Freudian psychoanalysis - the goal of Freudian PSYCHOANALYSIS is to help the patient gain insight into buried conflicts and impulses, to become aware of them; one strategy in psychoanalysis is FREE ASSOCIATION whereby the patient is told to say anything that comes to mind, regardless of how meaningless, embarrassing, or illogical it may seem; RESISTANCES reflect unconscious efforts to repress sensitive topics; through INTERPRETATION of what the patient says, the therapist identifies the patient's defenses, repressed conflicts, and wishes; an avenue to self-insight is TRANSFERENCE whereby patients display attitudes, feelings, and behaviors toward the therapist similar to those they displayed toward important people in their lives

1. Evaluation of Freudian psychoanalysis - it is open to
many criticisms involving not only the theoretical
approach and techniques of therapy, but also involving
its cost and time

B. Humanistic therapies - they, like psychoanalysis, are
insight therapies, but they have many differences as well
1. Client-centered therapy - developed by Carl Rogers,
CLIENT-CENTERED THERAPY aims to establish a warm,
accepting, and non-judgmental atmosphere in which
clients explore their true feelings and desires; an
UNCONDITIONAL POSITIVE REGARD is displayed by the
therapist who maintains a totally accepting and
non-judgemental attitude; the therapist must have
empathetic understanding and he/she, during therapy,
reflects what the client is feeling; a client-therapist
dialogue is presented
2. Personal profile: Carl Rogers (1902-   ) - an American;
he was trained in theology and psychology, and he has
received considerable professional recognition for his
achievements in psychology
3. Gestalt therapy - developed by Fritz Perls, GESTALT
THERAPY attempts to have clients deal with problems by
helping them achieve full awareness of their experiences
and needs; Gestalt refers to an emphasis on one's entire
experiences; a client-therapist dialogue is presented
4. Evaluation of humanistic therapies - client-centered
therapy is widely used, but it cannot be easily
evaluated; strengths and weaknesses are presented

C. Behavioral therapies - the BEHAVIORAL THERAPIES attempt
to directly alter problem behaviors through learning
principles; behavioral therapy is the same as behavior
modification
1. Counterconditioning - one response to a stimulus is
substituted for another in COUNTERCONDITIONING
a. systematic desensitization - involves substituting
relaxation for such maladaptive responses as anxiety
or fear; patients imagine anxiety-arousing stimuli
while relaxed and work through a hierarchy of stronger
fears; a case of a mail carrier with a fear of
criticism is presented using an anxiety hierarchy
b. ASSERTION TRAINING is used for fears with a rational
basis; it attempts to increase the client's ability to
express both negative and positive feelings, and to do
so in an honest, socially acceptable manner; behavior
rehearsal is used; a client-therapist dialogue is
presented
c. AVERSIVE CONDITIONING seeks to make negative feelings
the response to a particular stimulus; this is a
reversal of desensitization
2. Operant conditioning

    a. reinforcement and shaping - these are used to increase
       the frequency of a behavior; TOKEN ECONOMY uses tokens
       to   reinforce   adaptive   behaviors,   usually   in   an
       institutional setting
    b. withholding   rewards   (extinction)   -   both   withdrawing
       rewards   and   time-out   procedures   are   effective   at
       reducing the frequency of behaviors
    c. SATIATION   means   that   a   reinforcer   is   no   longer
       reinforcing   when   it   occurs   with   high   regularity   or
       frequency; a towel hoarding case is presented
    d. punishment - is effective with some behaviors under
       certain circumstances; examples are given
 3. Modeling - VICARIOUS EXTINCTION refers to the process
    where a client observes a model approach feared objects
    without any aversive consequences; an adjunct to modeling
    is guided participation
    a. self-efficacy   -   perceived self-efficacy   seems   to
       increase as does the effectiveness of a treatment
    Evaluation   of   behavioral   therapies   -   all   behavioral
 4. therapies   which   have   been   discussed   have   empirical
    support,   though   valid   criticisms   exist;   SYMPTOM
    SUBSTITUTION whereby behavioral symptoms are eliminated
    without removing their cause is rare in behavior therapy
    cause is rare in behavior therapy
D. Cognitive-behavioral   therapies   -   the   COGNITIVE-BEHAVIORAL
   THERAPIES   emphasize   techniques   that   directly   alter
   troublesome cognitions, but they also attempt to alter overt
   behavior
   1. Rational-emotive therapy - according to Ellis, the goal
      of RATIONAL-EMOTIVE THERAPY is to rid clients of their
      irrational beliefs so that they can behave logically and
      rationally,   and   experience   appropriate   and   adaptive
      emotions; a client-therapist dialogue is presented
   2. Cognitive   therapy   -   in   Beck's   COGNITIVE   THERAPY,   the
      strategy   is   to   emphasize   the   importance   of   undoing
      negative   thinking   and   faulty   reasoning   to   overcome
      emotional disorders, especially depression for which it
      was developed; a client-therapist dialogue is presented
   3. Evaluation   of   cognitive-behavioral   therapies   -   even
      though the techniques are too new to properly evaluate, a
      1983 study reached four general conclusions which are
      presented

E. Group therapy - several people are treated simultaneously
   in GROUP THERAPY; many therapies discussed so far can use
   this approach
   1. Psychodrama - developed by Moreno, PSYCHODRAMA attempts
      to have individuals gain insight into problems by acting
      out   feelings   in   emotionally   significant   events   or
      situations, as if they were in a play

2. Family and marital therapy - family members are treated as a group rather than individually in FAMILY THERAPY; a case is discussed; MARITAL THERAPY is a form of family therapy involving treatment for couples having marital problems

3. **Evaluation of group therapy - there is little evidence available to support its effectiveness**

F. Application: On selecting a therapist - the authors discuss the training, interests, and therapies of a <u>psychologist</u>, a <u>psychiatrist</u>, a <u>psychoanalyst</u>, a <u>psychiatric social worker</u>, and <u>pastoral counselors</u>; how to find and evaluate a therapist is also covered in this section

III. Medical Therapies - MEDICAL THERAPIES involve physical alteration or manipulation of the body for the purpose of treating maladaptive behavior

A. Chemical therapy - the use of drugs to treat maladaptive behavior is CHEMICAL THERAPY; drugs are often classified according to their therapeutic application

1. Neuroleptics - a class of drugs to treat and control extreme psychological disturbances (hallucinations, severe agitation, confusion) are the NEUROLEPTICS; examples are <u>chlorpromazine</u>, <u>phenothiazines</u>, <u>haloperidol</u>, <u>butyrophenones</u>

2. Anxiolytics - the minor tranquilizers or antianxiety agents are known as ANXIOLYTICS and they treat mild anxiety and tension; examples are <u>benzodiazepines</u>, <u>chlordiazepoxide</u>, <u>diazepam</u>, <u>glycerol derivatives</u>

3. Antidepressants - the ANTIDEPRESSANTS are used to treat severe depression and its symptoms; examples are <u>tricyclics</u>, <u>monoamine oxidase inhibitors</u>, <u>imipramine</u>, and <u>amitriptyline</u>; a new generation of antidepressants with fewer toxic side effects are <u>trimipramine</u>, <u>amoxapine</u>, <u>malprotiline</u>, and <u>trazodone</u>

4. Antimanics - drugs used in treating the mania associated with a bipolar disorder are the ANTIMANICS; the only effective one is <u>**lithium carbonate**</u>

B. Electroconvulsive therapy - ELECTROCONVULSIVE THERAPY involves passing a brief electric current of about 70-130 volts through the brain; effective for fairly rapid alleviation of symptoms of depression; an important side effect is memory loss

C. Psychosurgery - the most ethically extreme medical therapy is PSYCHOSURGERY which involves any form of surgery in which part of the brain is removed or made nonfunctional; used in severe disorders such as schizophrenia or severe depression; traditionally known as <u>lobotomy</u>; a rare procedure

D. Application: Drug therapy in action - a case history of the symptoms and chemical treatment of a woman with a severe case of bipolar disorder

IV. General Evaluation of Therapies

A. Methodological issues in evaluating therapies - the authors discuss the assumptions involved when one evaluates therapies; controlled research is needed, with the use of both an attention-placebo group and an alternative treatment group; the PLACEBO EFFECT refers to any improvement in the client that is due to elements of hope and an expectation of improvement rather than to specific therapeutic procedures; the double-blind procedure should be used; evaluation problems apply to both psychotherapy and medical therapy

B. An evaluation of psychological therapies - generally, therapy does help, it is more effective than being ministered to by a sympathetic listener, and psychotherapies are roughly equivalent in their effectiveness

C. An evaluation of medical therapies - the authors present evaluations of a number of different drugs and electroconvulsive therapy

D. Application: "You're on the air" -- the new radio psychologists - a discussion as to whether offering professional advice over the radio to phone callers is good, legitimate, and ethical; advantages and disadvantages are presented

V. On the Horizon: The Future of Psychotherapy - a poll of 36 experts published in 1982 predicted that self-change approaches to maladaptive behaviors will increase, psychotherapy will become more cognitive-behavioral in orientation, that family and marital therapy will become more popular, and that drug therapy will increase at the expense of psychotherapy

OBJECTIVES

I. WHAT ARE THE CORE PRINCIPLES OF THE VARIOUS PSYCHOLOGICAL THERAPIES?

The psychological therapies, in contrast to the physical or medical, each pairs a therapist with a client and these two then communicate in an attempt to alter the client's disordered feelings, beliefs, or actions. The thrust of psychoanalysis is to help the patient gain insight into buried conflicts and impulses, to become aware of them. Humanistic therapy involves structuring environments and therapeutic relationships in which people who are inherently good and striving for personal growth can, without inhibition, realize their potentials and work towards self-enhancement. Those using behavioral therapy assume that maladaptive behavior is learned, and that this behavior can be unlearned or more adaptive behavior can be learned in its place. Cognitive-behavioral therapies assume that faulty, irrational, or pessimistic cognitions cause us to distort our interpretations of events in our environment and thus negatively influence our behavior.

B   1. Which type of psychotherapy emphasizes the inherent good of humans and their striving for personal growth?

   A. Freudian psychoanalysis
   B. humanistic
   C. behavior
   D. cognitive-behavioral

   2. Discuss the core principles of the four major psychological therapies.

II. WHAT BASIC DIFFERENCES DISTINGUISH THE PSYCHOANALYTIC, HUMANISTIC, AND BEHAVIORAL APPROACHES?

The differences between these approaches reflect the differences in how they view maladaptive behavior. For the psychoanalyst, behavior is a result of unconscious, instinctual forces and the individual's attempt to control them. The humanistic therapist assumes that people are inherently good and will naturally strive for personal growth, but exhibit maladaptive behavior when their environments and therapeutic relationships are not supportive. The behavioral approach does not incorporate non-supportive environments or underlying instincts, conflicts, or motives into an explanation of maladaptive behavior. In contrast, it views behavior as being learned through such principles as reinforcement, extinction, shaping, and modeling. As a result, what is actually attempted during therapy differs among the three therapies. In Freudian psychoanalysis, the patient's problems are dealt with indirectly and resolution of problems relies on gaining insight and self-understanding. This process takes place over a long time period. The humanistic approach involves less time. In one type, called client-centered therapy, the aim is to establish a warm, accepting, and non-judgmental atmosphere during which clients can explore their true feelings and desires. In contrast to the two insight therapies (psychoanalysis and humanistic therapy), the behavioral approach works on changing maladaptive behavior or having more adaptive behavior take its place. Generally, behavior therapy does not extend over long periods of time.

A   1. In what area is the basic difference between psychological therapies the greatest?

   A. interpretation of maladaptive behavior
   B. length of treatment
   C. success rate
   D. cost

   2. Discuss some basic differences between psychoanalytic, humanistic, and behavioral approaches to therapy.

III. HOW DO THE BEHAVIORAL AND COGNITIVE-BEHAVIORAL APPROACHES DIFFER?

Many behavior therapists have realized that changes in behavior are mediated by altered thoughts or conditions. For example, the things we tell ourselves, our beliefs and expectations, and especially the meaning we place on events greatly affect behavior. As a result, the cognitive-behavioral therapies emphasize techniques that directly alter troublesome cognitions because they are often faulty, irrational or pessimistic. Two such therapies are Albert Ellis' rational-emotive therapy and Aaron Beck's cognitive therapy. These approaches attempt to reeducate clients by either pointing out, or helping them recognize, their irrational and illogical ways of thinking by having discussions with the individual. In contrast, the strict behavior modification approaches attempt to directly alter problem behaviors with various learning principles.

D   1. Cognitive-behavioral therapeutic approaches differ from strict behavioral methods in their:

   A. emphasis on how we interpret our environments
   B. attempt to point out irrational or illogical ways of thinking
   C. use of an open communication or dialogue between the client and therapist
   D. all of the above

   2. How do behavioral and cognitive-behavioral therapies differ?

IV. WHAT ARE MEDICAL THERAPIES? WHEN ARE THEY USED?

The medical therapies involve a physical alteration or manipulation of the body for the purpose of treating maladaptive behavior. These take different forms and include chemical therapy (which is the use of drugs to treat maladaptive behavior), electroconvulsive therapy (which is when a brief electric shock of approximately 70 to 130 volts is passed through the brain), and psychosurgery (which is any form of surgery in which part of the brain is removed or made nonfuctional). The medical therapies have tended to be used when a mental disorder is severe or does not respond to psychological therapy; however, the recent widespread use of chemical therapy both in conjunction with psychotherapy and even without it tends to negate this general statement. Chemical therapy involves many different kinds of drugs which are effective at treating schizophrenia, depression, manic-depressive bipolar reactions, as well as mild anxiety and tension. Electroconvulsive therapy is primarily used to treat cases of depression when a change is needed faster than drugs could create. Psychosurgery is not common and is used only in the most severe cases in which patients present a danger to themselves or others and when all other forms of treatment have failed.

C   1. Which of the following is NOT a medical therapy?

         A. chemical therapy
         B. electroconvulsive shock
         C. physioadaption
         D. psychosurgery

A   2. Which medical therapy tends to treat the widest range of maladaptive behaviors?

         A. chemical therapy
         B. electroconvulsive shock
         C. physioadaption
         D. psychosurgery

       3. What are the medical therapies, what do they involve, and when are they used?

V.   IS THERAPY GENERALLY EFFECTIVE?   ARE SOME THERAPIES MORE EFFECTIVE THAN OTHERS?

Generally, therapy does help. Though when, for whom, and under what circumstances is not perfectly understood. Reviews of research on psychotherapy has lead to some general conclusions. Not only does therapy help, but it seems to help more than patients that have received placebo treatment (or that "therapy" being ministered to by a sympathetic listener). Psychotherapies are roughly equivalent in their effectiveness, but the behavioral and cognitive therapies may be modestly superior to all others.

C   1. Which of the following statements about psychotherapy is TRUE?

         A. psychoanalysis appears to be superior to the cognitive or behavioral approaches
         B. more often than not, placebo treatments are better than behavior modification
         C. generally, therapy does help
         D. all of the above

2. Is therapy effective in general, and are some therapies more effective than others?

VI. WHAT PROCESSES DO PSYCHOTHERAPIES HAVE IN COMMON?

Since psychotherapies tend to have uniformly positive results, many have wondered if there is some common component to all therapies to account for their effectiveness. Some researchers have suggested that each therapy instigates and persuades clients to confront feared situations and to actually behave in more adaptive ways. It may be that all effective approaches engender strong feelings of perceived self-efficacy.

B   1. Perceived self-efficacy is used to explain why:

A. some patients improve with psychotherapy but others do not
B. all therapies have uniformly positive results
C. therapies are not even better than they are
D. short-term therapy is more productive than long-term therapy

2. What processes do psychotherapies have in common?

MULTIPLE-CHOICE QUESTIONS

INTRODUCTION: A HELPFUL DOSE OF DISGUST

B   1. Covert sensitization is a **behavioral** therapy which incorporates the patient's _____ into the treatment procedure.
A. conscious wishes
B. imagination
C. family and friends
D. learned behaviors

D   2. Which of the following statements is TRUE?
A. covert sensitization matches highly aversive events with troublesome behaviors
B. prior to the twentieth century abnormality was often attributed to supernatural causes
C. treatment methods typically reflect each therapist's view of how maladaptive behavior develops
D. all of the above

C   3. Therapists who may use a variety of methods to treat the
            same problem are considered:
            A. universal
            B. unusual
            C. eclectic
            D. multi-optioned

PSYCHOLOGICAL THERAPIES

A   4. The one thing that psychotherapies have in common is their
            _____ approach.
            A. psychological
            B. physical
            C. medical
            D. behavioral

C   5. The pairing of a client with a therapist for the purpose of
            communication to alter the patient's state is called:
            A. bibliotherapy
            B. medical therapy
            C. psychotherapy
            D. behavior modification

D   6. Psychotherapists disagree on:
            A. how maladaptive behavior should be treated
            B. what is the origin of maladaptive behavior
            C. the focus of treatment - feelings, thinking, or behavior
            D. all of the above

FREUDIAN PSYCHOANALYSIS

B   7. The goal of Freudian psychoanalysis is to help **patients:**
            A. change the reasons for their maladaptive behavior
            B. gain insight into buried conflicts and impulses
            C. better understand the true, unconscious feelings of
               others
            D. all of the above

A   8. Which of the following is NOT used in psychoanalysis to
            bring unconscious material to the surface and understand it?
            A. empathetic understanding
            B. free association
            C. interpretation
            D. transference

B   9. Which of the following is NOT characteristic of free
        association?
        A. the patient is relaxed
        B. meaningless or illogical information is discouraged
        C. unconscious material surfaces in disguised or symbolic
           form
        D. all of the above

C   10. Freud believed that patients are often unwilling to discuss
        or explore sensitive topics during free association due to:
        A. cultural expectations
        B. cultural norms
        C. resistances
        D. transference

A   11. A   consequence   of   interpretation   during   Freudian
        psychoanalysis is that the patients:
        A. learn the "true" meaning of their symptoms
        B. show more transference
        C. are more relaxed and susceptible to the therapist's
           treatment suggestions
        D. begin to interpret their own dreams

D   12. During psychoanalysis, transference:
        A. reflects the **patients showing feelings toward the**
           therapist that are similar to those once directed to
           other important people in their lives
        B. is thought to give insight into the patient's unconscious
           conflicts
        C. is used to reveal patient feelings and the origin of
           those feelings
        D. all of the above

D   13. In psychoanalysis, the patient's problems are dealt with:
        A. indirectly
        B. through insight
        C. through self-understanding
        D. all of the above

B   14. Which of the following is NOT a criticism of Freudian
        psychoanalysis? It is:
        A. both time-consuming and expensive
        B. less effective than other therapies
        C. impossible to test empirically
        D. difficult to tell if transference has actually **occurred**

HUMANISTIC THERAPIES

C   15. Freudian psychoanalysis and humanistic therapies share what
        view in common?
        A. unconscious forces must be dealt with
        B. people are inherently good
        C. people must gain insight into their problems
        D. none of the above

A   16. Humanistic therapies strive to create favorable:
        A. environments and therapeutic relationships
        B. patient insight into unconscious problems
        C. personal and professional goals
        D. feelings toward the therapist

A   17. What are two types of humanistic therapies?
        A. client-centered and Gestalt
        B. client-centered and rational
        C. implosive and rational
        D. Gestalt and rational-emotive

B   18. What person is primarily associated with client-centered
        therapy?
        A. Fritz Perls
        B. Carl Rogers
        C. David Rimm
        D. Albert Ellis

D   19. Which therapy attempts to establish a warm and accepting
        atmosphere so that individuals can explore their true
        feelings and desires?
        A. cognitive
        B. family
        C. Gestalt
        D. client-centered

C   20. To facilitate self-acceptance during client-centered
        therapy, the therapist should display:
        A. high reflective abilities
        B. a high judgmental attitude
        C. unconditional positive regard
        D. insight and strong self-respect

C   21. Gestalt therapy, as developed by Perls, places an emphasis
        on awareness of one's _____ experiences.
        A. personal
        B. emotional
        C. entire
        D. cognitive

A   22. Which of the following statements about Gestalt therapy is
         FALSE?
         A. the basic strategy is to focus on the past, not the
            here-and-now
         B. it assumes maladaptive behavior stems from being unaware
            of various aspects of oneself
         C. the therapist attempts to create situations in which the
            client faces unpleasant experiences
         D. none of the above

D   23. One criticism of the humanistic therapies is that they are:
         A. not too cost-effective
         B. based more on experimentation than on clinical
            experiences
         C. difficult to do in groups
         D. inappropriate for individuals with severe psychological
            disorders

BEHAVIORAL THERAPIES

B   24. Behavioral therapy attempts to help patients by dealing with
         their:
         A. underlying instincts
         B. problem behaviors
         C. conflicting motives
         D. all of the above

B   25. Behavioral therapy:
         A. is not the same as behavior modification
         B. assumes that problem behaviors can be unlearned
         C. questions whether adaptive behaviors can be learned
            in the place of maladaptive behavior
         D. all of the above

C   26. A number of behavioral therapy techniques involve replacing
         one response with another. This approach is known as:
         A. substitution
         B. response exchange
         C. counterconditioning
         D. satiation

D   27. Systematic desensitization involves substituting anxiety or
         fear with:
         A. real adaptive behaviors
         B. imagined adaptive behaviors
         C. more desirable thoughts
         D. relaxation

A   28. Which of the following is NOT part of systematic
        desensitization?
        A. relaxation is paired with the real object whenever
           possible
        B. relaxation is paired with imagined stimuli
        C. a hierarchy of fears is used
        D. learning to approach feared objects or situations

D   29. Systematic desensitization has effectively treated:
        A. phobias
        B. social withdrawal
        C. sexual difficulties
        D. all of the above

B   30. **Assertion** training may be a more appropriate treatment for
        fear than systematic desensitization if the fear:
        A. deals with animate objects
        B. has a rational basis
        C. involves an object regularly confronted
        D. involves a situation regularly experienced

C   31. The goal of **assertion** training is to _____ the client's
        ability to· _____.
        A. decrease ; express anxiety verbally
        B. decrease ; take criticism passively
        C. increase ; express feelings in an honest manner
        D. increase ; take control of the situation

A   32. **Assertion** training is mainly carried out through:
        A. behavior rehearsal
        B. practice at home
        C. vicarious extinction
        D. satiation

B   33. Aversive conditioning seeks to have a particular response:
        A. replaced by positive emotional feelings
        B. associated with negative feelings
        C. increase in frequency with the use of pain or disgust
        D. extinguished

C   34. The best known therapeutic application of reinforcement and
        shaping is with:
        A. counterconditioning
        B. vicarious extinction
        C. token economy
        D. **assertion** training

D   35. Which of the following is TRUE about token economy?
        A. reinforcers are given immediately after the desired
           behavior occurs
        B. adaptive behaviors are rewarded
        C. frequently used in institutional settings
        D. all of the above

A   36. A socially inappropriate behavior may be decreased in frequency by either extinction or:
A. time out
B. response sampling
C. response pyramiding
D. assertive training

C   37. Ayllon (1963) successfully treated a female schizophrenic who hoarded 20 to 30 towels at a given time through:
A. symptom substitution
B. the withholding of rewards
C. satiation
D. response sampling

B   38. Vicarious extinction is a behavioral therapy that relies on:
A. punishment
B. modeling
C. counterconditioning
D. generalization

A   39. Guided participation, an adjunct to vicarious extinction, is believed to be so effective because it:
A. increases perceived self-efficacy
B. gets the patient physically as well as emotionally involved in the treatment
C. reduces the length of treatment
D. all of the above

D   40. Behavioral therapies are positively evaluated because they:
A. have some empirical support for their effectiveness
B. are effective with a wide range of client populations
C. can be implemented by individuals with varying degrees and types of training
D. all of the above

COGNITIVE-BEHAVIORAL THERAPIES

B   41. Cognitive-behavioral therapies emphasize techniques that alter:
A. behaviors the client doesn't understand
B. troublesome cognitions
C. behaviors which in turn improve one's thoughts and feelings about those behaviors
D. none of the above

A   42. Rational-emotive therapy is a type of _____ therapy.
A. cognitive-behavioral
B. Gestalt
C. marital
D. family

C   43. It is the goal of which therapy to rid clients of irrational beliefs so that they can logically experience adaptive emotions?
A. group
B. social-learning
C. rational-emotive
D. client-centered

D   44. What does Albert Ellis advocate in rational-emotive therapy?
A. to challenge and dispute the client's belief system
B. an active, direct confrontation with the client
C. homework assignments
D. all of the above

B   45. Beck suggests that cognitive therapy:
A. deemphasize the importance of undoing negative thinking during the actual therapy session
B. encourage clients to examine their ideas about their behavior
C. persuade clients that their thinking is faulty
D. all of the above

A   46. Cognitive therapy was originally developed to treat:
A. depression
B. schizophrenia
C. neurosis
D. psychosis

C   47. The best evaluative statement of the cognitive-behavioral therapies is that they are:
A. quite effective with a wide range depressive individuals
B. very good, but too costly for most individuals
C. too new for a definitive assessment of their effectiveness
D. actually better than the behavioral therapies they are said to complement

GROUP THERAPY

C   48. Which of the following is NOT characteristic of group therapy?
A. several people are treated simultaneously
B. it makes more efficient use of the therapist's time
C. too often, members of the group still function as if they are experiencing individual therapy
D. it gives clients an opportunity to acquire new skills from others

B   49. Which of the following is NOT an example of a group therapy?
        A. psychodrama
        B. Gestalt therapy
        C. family therapy
        D. marital therapy

A   50. Individuals gain insight into their problems during psychodrama by:
        A. acting out their feelings in emotionally significant events
        B. observing a professional actor mimic their maladaptive behaviors
        C. observing other clients mimic their maladaptive behaviors
        D. taking acting lessons and participating in local plays

D   51. The goal of family therapy is to:
        A. improve lines of communication
        B. clarify expectations that family members have of each other
        C. aid family members in working toward satisfying interactions
        D. all of the above

APPLICATION: ON SELECTING A THERAPIST

D   52. Psychologists and psychiatrists typically differ in their:
        A. training
        B. orientation
        C. use of medical therapy
        D. all of the above

A   53. Which of the following statements is FALSE?
        A. psychiatrists typically are prepared to use a variety of therapeutic approaches
        B. a psychoanalyst is a psychotherapist who specializes in psychoanalysis
        C. pastoral counselors may practice psychotherapy
        D. psychologists have advanced training and degrees in clinical psychology or counseling psychology

C   54. Answers to which of the following questions should NOT typically be sought during the first session with a therapist?
        A. does the therapist think therapy will help you?
        B. what treatment approach will the therapist use?
        C. how often does the therapist have unsuccessful cases?
        D. what are the therapist's fees?

MEDICAL THERAPIES

B   55. Medical therapies may be utilized when the mental disorder
          is:
          A. severe or unusual
          B. severe or does not respond to psychological therapy
          C. unusual or occurs with another physical disorder
          D. does not respond to psychotherapy or the patient has a
             history of physical disorders

B   56. Which of the following is NOT considered a medical therapy?
          A. chemical therapy
          B. placebo therapy
          C. electroconvulsive therapy
          D. psychosurgery

CHEMICAL THERAPY

A   57. In chemical therapy, drugs are often classified according to
          their:
          A. therapeutic application
          B. degree of action
          C. addictive qualities
          D. type of side effects

C   58. Which is a class of drugs used to treat and control extreme
          psychological disturbances, such as schizophrenia?
          A. anxiolytics
          B. antimanics
          C. neuroleptics
          D. antidepressants

D   59. Which of the following is NOT a neuroleptic type of drug?
          A. chlorpromazine
          B. phenothiazine
          C. haloperidol
          D. tricyclics

A   60. The most widely prescribed drugs today are the:
          A. anxiolytics
          B. antimanics
          C. neuroleptics
          D. antidepressants

B   61. The class of drugs known as anxiolytics:
          A. treat hallucinations and severe agitation
          B. may lead to physical dependence and rather severe
             withdrawal symptoms
          C. block the activity of dopamine receptors
          D. all of the above

D   62. Which of the following statements is TRUE?
         A. valium and librium are anxiolytics which make the user
            feel relaxed and less anxious
         B. antidepressants, such as imipramine (Tofranil), are used
            to elevate the person's mood
         C. some antidepressants are fairly toxic and have numerous
            side effects
         D. all of the above

C   63. Antimanic drugs, such as lithium carbonate, are used to
         treat individuals with:
         A. severe suicidal tendencies
         B. manic psychotics
         C. episodes of mania and depression
         D. severe depression

B   64. In general, it appears that the psychoactive drugs are
         effective because they influence:
         A. axonal conduction
         B. neurotransmitter activity
         C. blood flow to various brain areas
         D. oxygen supply to individual neurons

ELECTROCONVULSIVE THERAPY

C   65. Electroconvulsive therapy:
         A. involves passing a brief electric current of about 180
            volts through the brain
         B. is increasing in frequency as a substitute for the toxic
            antidepressant drugs
         C. is used because it acts faster than chemical agents
         D. all of the above

A   66. What is an undesirable side effect of ECT?
         A. memory impairment
         B. emotional leveling
         C. increased aggressive and competitive tendencies
         D. listlessness which can last for months or years

PSYCHOSURGERY

B   67. Historically, psychosurgery was used to treat:
         A. neuroses
         B. schizophrenia or severe depression
         C. violent behavior
         D. all of the above

D   68. Unlike psychosurgery in the past, today it:
    A. is more sophisticated and precise
    B. involves relatively small areas of the brain
    C. limited to severe cases who are dangerous to themselves
       and who can't benefit from other treatments
    D. all of the above

APPLICATION: DRUG THERAPY IN ACTION

C   69. The text illustrates the use of lithium carbonate, in
       combination with Thorazine and Elavil, to treat a
       30-year-old housewife who:
    A. regressed to a childish way of behaving
    B. had regularly threatened, and recently attempted, to
       commit suicide
    C. was euphoric, but who had a history of depressive
       episodes
    D. exhibited something like a multiple personality

METHODOLOGICAL ISSUES IN EVALUATING THERAPIES

D   70. Methodological issues in evaluating therapies include use
       of:
    A. controlled research studies
    B. attention-placebo group
    C. alternative treatment group
    D. all of the above

A   71. Any improvement in a client that is due to the elements of
       hope and expectations, rather than to specific therapeutic
       procedures is called:
    A. the placebo effect
    B. transient improvement
    C. artificial improvement
    D. apparent change

AN EVALUATION OF PSYCHOLOGICAL THERAPIES

A   72. What research method is used when evaluating therapies to
       control for the therapist's expectations biasing the
       results?
    A. double-blind method
    B. alternative-treatment group
    C. attention group
    D. attention-placebo method

C   73. Which of the following evaluative statements about
        psychological therapies is FALSE?
        A. psychotherapy is more effective than being ministered to
           by a sympathetic listener
        B. psychotherapy is better than no treatment at all
        C. behavioral and cognitive therapies are vastly superior to
           other approaches
        D. none of the above

B   74. Psychotherapies tend to have uniformly positive results
        because they:
        A. all involve open communication
        B. may increase perceived self-efficacy
        C. involve active involvement on the part of the patient
           to solve his or her problem
        D. are not being evaluated scientifically as yet

AN EVALUATION OF MEDICAL THERAPIES

D   75. Which evaluative statement about medical therapy is TRUE?
        A. the phenothiazines are effective in the treatment of
           schizophrenia
        B. the antianxiety drugs tend to be overprescribed and may
           not be that effective in the first place
        C. antidepressants do work, but frequently psychotherapy and
           drugs together work better when treating depression
        D. all of the above.

B   76. Antidepressants may require _____ or more days to take
        effect while with ECT, improvement occurs by the _____
        day.
        A. 15 ; 5th to 6th
        B. 10 ; 3rd to 4th
        C. 4 to 5 ; 6th
        D. 2 to 3 ; 8th

APPLICATION: "YOU'RE ON THE AIR" -- THE NEW RADIO PSYCHOLOGISTS

C   77. Recently, a few psychologists have begun to offer advice:
        A. violation of APA ethical guidelines
        B. without proper training
        C. on radio talk shows
        D. during special house-call visits

D   78. A problem with psychologists offering advice "on the air" is
        that:
        A. too little information is known about the client's back-
           ground
        B. other listeners may inappropriately apply the same advice
           to their own situations
        C. it is difficult to make accurate diagnoses and judgments
        D. all of the above

A   79. What is the best approach for a therapist to offer to a
        listener "over the air?"
        A. suggest the caller seek direct contact with a therapist
        B. ask the caller to return the call after the show is over
        C. offer two or three remedies that the caller may try
           before seeking direct contact with a therapist
        D. all of the above

ON THE HORIZON: THE FUTURE OF PSYCHOTHERAPY

D   80. A poll by Prochaska and Norcross (1982) conducted on the
        future of psychotherapy reported that there will be an
        increase in:
        A. self-change approaches
        B. family and marital therapy
        C. **cognitive-behavioral orientation**
        D. all of the above

B   81. Which statment is FALSE concerning some predictions about
        the future of psychotherapy?
        A. drug therapy will increase at the expense of
           psychotherapy
        B. **psychotherapists will become less specialized to meet the**
           changing cultural needs
        C. "brand name" approaches such as Gestalt therapy will fall
           by the wayside
        D. none of the above

- CHAPTER 17 -

HUMAN SEXUALITY

OUTLINE

I. Introduction: "Dear Ann Landers" - a letter to Ann Landers questioning the difference between nudists, strippers, and exhibitionists; GENDER, rather than the ambiguous term sex, refers to the state of being male or female

II. The Development of Gender

A. Biological differences - PRIMARY SEXUAL CHARACTERISTICS include the sexual and reproductive organs of males and females; PRENATAL SEXUAL DIFFERENTIATION is the process determined by genetic materials which leads to specific physical differences between females and males during the prenatal period; the GONADS (reproductive glands) are undifferentiated during the first few weeks after conception; by the eighth week after conception, the newly formed testes in the males produce "male" hormones called ANDROGENS, of which TESTOSTERONE is most important; during puberty, testosterone for males and ESTROGENS or "female" hormones in females contribute to the development of SECONDARY SEXUAL CHARACTERISTICS; the biological development of gender has much to do with the development of GENDER IDENTITY or one's personal sense of maleness or femaleness; John Money says that 5 things determine an individual's gender (genetic sex, hormonal sex, gonadal sex, genital sex, internal reproduction organs); when these five are not consistent, a HERMAPHRODITE occurs; the adrenogenital syndrome may contribute to hemaphroditism due to a malfunctioning adrenal gland which produces too much androgens; a TRANSSEXUAL is someone who is psychologically uncomfortable with his or her anatomical sex (e.g., Dr. Renee Richards who plays professional tennis)

B. Gender roles - a GENDER ROLE is society's expectations regarding how individuals of a particular gender are to behave; gender roles are actually stereotypes or fixed ways of thinking about a particular group of people; stereotypes contribute to the formation of our gender identity; gender roles are communicated to children through parental messages, school expectations, and role models

C. Application: Gender roles and sexuality - a traditional male role involves the desire to achieve and be successful, aggressiveness and power of control, not showing emotion, initiator of sex; a traditional female role involves a passive role, noninitiator of sexual activity, slow to become sexually aroused as compared to the male

III. Researching Human Sexual Behavior

A. Surveys of sexual behavior and attitudes toward sex - sexual surveys by Kinsey (1948, 1953) and by Hunt (1974) evaluated sexual behaviors; in spite of these surveys' limitations, they provide information about attitudes and behaviors and how they have changed
  1. Sexual behaviors - incidence refers to the percentage of individuals who have experienced a particular behavior while frequency refers to how often they engage in the behavior
     a. MASTURBATION refers to self-stimulation of the genitals; about 95% of all adult males and 67% of all adult females have masturbated to ORGASM; the incidence of masturbation has not increased while the age of onset is lowering
     b. PETTING refers to physical, sexual contact between individuals that does not include sexual intercourse; almost all adults have engaged in petting; oral-genital contact is becoming more prevalent, petting seems to be occurring at an earlier age
     c. premarital intercourse - traditionally males but not females can engage in this; its incidence is increasing for both males and females
     d. marital intercourse - the frequency of intercourse is increasing in every age group and the frequency of COITUS (another term for sexual intercourse) is decreasing with age; oral sex is increasing; Hunt's study reports 90% of married couples under twenty-five have practiced both FELLATIO (oral stimulation of the male genitals) and CUNNILINGUS (oral stimulation of the female genitals)

e. extramarital intercourse - nearly half of all married men and 20% of married women have engaged in extramarital intercourse, but the incidence for women is rising rapidly

2. Sexual attitudes - attitudes have changed; attitudes on both masturbation and premarital sex have become more positive since earlier this century; attitudes toward extramarital sex remain strongly negative

3. Personal profile: Alfred C. Kinsey (1894-1956) - the most famous American investigator of human sexual behavior; began the Institute for Sex Research at Indiana University

B. Physiology of sexual behavior: Laboratory observations of the sexual response cycle - laboratory investigations, primarily by Masters and Johnson, can assess the body's response to sexual stimulation; the four-phase process of physiological responses of sexuality is called the SEXUAL RESPONSE CYCLE; the first or EXCITEMENT PHASE shows an increased blood flow to the genital area brought on by sexual stimulation; the PLATEAU PHASE involves a continuing, increasingly higher level of sexual arousal; the ORGASM PHASE occurs when sexual arousal reaches a peak with a psychological experience of intense pleasure; the RESOLUTION PHASE occurs when bodily functions return to prearousal state; only males undergo a REFRACTORY PERIOD when, during the resolution phase, they are unresponsive to sexual stimulation; females can receive additional sexual stimulation during the resolution phase and may experience multiple orgasms

C. Experimental studies of sexual behavior - psychologists have experimentally studied PORNOGRAPHY (any written, visual, or verbal material that is considered sexually arousing); pornography leads to arousal in both females and males; males who observe aggressive pornography show more aggression toward women and alter their perceptions of both rape and rape victims; sexual behavior such as masturbation and intercourse are not readily influenced by pornography

D. Application: Adolescent sex and the problem of contraception - teens use few contraceptives because it appears that they lack accurate information about sex and contraception; the problem may be reduced by more sex education and open discussions on teen values

IV. Sexual Variations, Sexual Dysfunctions, and Homosexuality

A. Variations in sexual behavior - SEXUAL VARIATIONS refer to sexual behaviors that deviate from conventional norms and that are maladaptive

1. Variations in object choice - where the object is not an adult of the opposite gender

      a. FETISHISM refers to attaching sexual significance to objects that are not necessarily sexual in nature (e.g., animate parts of the body or inanimate objects such as clothing or shoes); shown almost only in men

      B. RAPE is an act of aggression in which one persn forces another, nonconsenting person to engage in a sexual act; rape is viewed as an act of violence and attempt to exert power

  2. Variations in sexual aim - those behaviors that do not seek sexual intercourse

      a. VOYEURISM refers to deriving pleasure from secretly watching others undress or have sexual intercourse

      b. EXHIBITIONISM occurs when sexual gratification is derived from exposing one's genitals to unsuspecting and unwilling strangers; a behavior almost totally shown by men

      c. TRANSVESTISM refers to receiving sexual gratification by dressing in the clothing of the opposite gender; almost always found in men; a <u>transvestite</u> is not a <u>transsexual</u>

B. Gender identity disturbance: Transsexualism - transsexuals have a gender identity which is at odds with their anatomy; we have treated some with change-of-sex surgery since 1953, though sex reassignment is anatomical

C. Homosexuality - HOMOSEXUALITY can be defined as having sexual attraction toward or, engaging in sexual behavior with, a member of the same gender; about 2% of men and 1% of women are exclusively homosexual; those attracted to or who engage in sexual activity with members of the opposite gender are HETEROSEXUAL; about 75% of men and 85% of women are exclusively heterosexual; homosexualtiy is not currently considered an abnormal behavior but just someone with a different sexual preference; a discussion of the genetic, psychoanalytic, and learning theory positions on homosexuality is presented

D. Sexual dysfunctions refer to sexual difficulties or impairments in sexual functioning - at least half of American marriages may be affected by some type of dysfunction

  1. Sexual dysfunction in men - ERECTILE DYSFUNCTION (preferred over <u>impotence</u>) is the inability to have or to maintain an erection; it typically has a psychological origin; PREMATURE EJACULATION occurs when the male ejaculates too soon for his partner to experience orgasm through intercourse; psychological factors such as performance anxiety are relevant causes; RETARDED EJACULATION is where a man is unable to ejaculate into a women's vagina even is he has an erection; there are many psychological causes; treatment procedures are discussed after the presentation of each of these dysfunctions

2. Sexual dysfunction in women - ORGASMIC DYSFUNCTION
(preferred over frigidity) is the inability to have an
orgasm; some question if this is really a dysfunction
since 10% of all women have never had an orgasm during
intercourse; psychological explanations are offered;
VAGINISMUS involves an involuntary contraction of the
muscles surrounding the vaginal entrance, sometimes
leading to pain and making intercourse impossible;
treatments are offered for each of these dysfunctions

E. Application: Preventing sexual dysfunctions - the five
include (1) open communication, (2) don't view sex as a
performance to be evaluated, (3) don't think there is a
"correct" way to behave sexually, (4) trust one's partner,
and (5) don't ignore sexual problems when they occur

V. On the Horizon: Society's Reactions to the Rape Victim -
presents the story of a female who was raped while others
watched and cheered; the authors present and discuss a number
of typical attitudes and assumptions made by the police,
lawyers, and jurors concerning the victim's behavior, dress,
and intentions prior to the rape

OBJECTIVES

I. FROM A BIOLOGICAL PERSPECTIVE, WHAT IS INVOLVED IN GENDER
DEVELOPMENT?

Biological factors which include genetic and hormonal
mechanisms determine sexual differentiation. Embryos that
become females receive an X chromosome from each parent while
embryos that become males receive an X chromosome from their
mother and a Y chromosome from their father. Regardless of
their genetic makeup, all embryos are anatomically identical
during the first few weeks of development because the gonads
are undifferentiated. About the seventh week, the presence of
the Y chromosome causes a chemical release which transforms the
gonads into testes; gonads develop into ovaries about the 12th
week if just X chromosomes are present. Sexual differentiation
is basically controlled by hormones after these gonadal
changes. The testes produce androgens (e.g., testosterone)
which cause further masculinization both internally and
externally. At the same time, the testes release a chemical
which retards the growth of structures that would eventually
form female internal sex organs. In contrast, female sexual
differentiation does not depend on hormones. Usually, by the

14th week of development there is a clear difference in the internal and external structures of a male and female fetus. Hormonal influences on gender development reappear at puberty when the testes and ovaries produce testosterone and estrogens, respectively, to influence masculine or feminine secondary sexual characteristics.

D   1. By what age does the fetus typically become a male or female with appropriate internal and external structures?

       A. 6-8 weeks
       B. 8-10 weeks
       C. 10-12 weeks
       D. 12-14 weeks

B   2. For which gender are hormones NOT necessary for prenatal sexual differentiation?

       A. male
       B. female

      3. What are the genetic and hormonal influences on gender development?

II.   WHAT ROLE DOES SOCIALIZATION PLAY IN GENDER DEVELOPMENT?

Early in life we are taught a gender role or our society's expectations regarding how individuals of a particular gender are to behave. It is this gender role that is said to be "appropriate" behaviors. Gender roles are actually stereotypes, and these expectations about how one should behave contribute to the formation of our gender identity. We communicate gender roles in various ways. Both parents and schools communicate gender differences. Children also learn gender roles through observing others. The importance of socialization is demonstrated by John Money's studies of hermaphrodites who can develop either male or female gender identities simply on the basis of being "assigned" to either a "male" or "female" role.

D   1. Socialization influences gender development because:

       A. parents and schools communicate stereotypes
       B. children observe others behaving in particular ways
       C. little boys and girls are "assigned" roles about how
          they should behave
       D. all of the above

      2. In what ways does socialization influence gender development?

III. HOW IS THE SURVEY APPROACH USED TO STUDY SEXUAL BEHAVIOR?   WHAT IS THE NATURE OF CURRENT SEXUAL PRACTICES AND ATTITUDES?   HAVE THEY CHANGED FROM EARLIER TIMES?

Large numbers of males and females are asked questions about their sexual behavior. Kinsey pioneered sex surveys in the late 1940's, and Hunt has conducted another one in the early 1970's.   Unfortunately, both surveys have some problems. Neither sampled accurately the nation's population.   Rural dwellers and poorly educated people were underrepresented in Kinsey's survey and Hunt's survey (only 20% of the original sample agreed to participate) polled those with mostly liberal attitudes and behavior.   About 95% of adult males and 67% of adult females masturbate.   Almost all adults have engaged in petting.   Both petting and masturbation are currently occurring at an earlier age compared to earlier surveys.   Premarital intercourse has increased in frequency for both males and females. Marital intercourse is more common now than before at all ages.   Oral sex, both fellatio and cunnilingus, is increasing with 90% of those under 25 years old in the Hunt survey having practiced both.   Extramarital intercourse is reported by almost 50% of the men and about 20% of the women, with the women increasing in frequency more rapidly than the men.   Over the years, our culture's attitudes toward masturbation and premarital sex have become more positive, but attitudes toward extramarital sex have remained strongly negative.

C   1. Which of the following sexual behaviors has NOT increased in frequency over the last 30-40 years?

A. extramarital intercourse in females
B. oral sex
C. masturbation
D. premarital intercourse

A   2. The sexual attitude which has remained negative over the years concerns:

A. extramarital sex
B. premarital sex
C. oral sex
D. petting

3. Summarize the results of the Hunt and Kinsey surveys on sexual behaviors and attitudes.

IV. WHY IS SEXUAL BEHAVIOR ALSO STUDIED THROUGH DIRECT OBSERVATION AND EXPERIMENTS? WHAT IS KNOWN ABOUT THE PHYSIOLOGY OF SEXUAL RESPONSE?   WHAT HAS EXPERIMENTATION TAUGHT US ABOUT PORNOGRAPHY?

Laboratory investigations on sexual behavior have an advantage in that they avoid the problem of potential distortion in the self-report sex surveys. In the laboratory, the body's responses to sexual stimulation can be readily recorded. Masters and Johnson, leading laboratory sex researchers, describe the sexual response cycle as falling into four phases of physiological responsivity: excitement, plateau, orgasm, and resolution. The excitement phase shows increased blood flow to the genital area. The plateau phase shows a continuing, increasingly higher level of sexual arousal that precedes orgasm. The orgasm phase occurs when sexual arousal reaches a peak and it is characterized by the involuntary contraction of muscles, especially in the genital region. Following orgasm, a resolution phase occurs during which bodily functions return to their prearousal state. Only males go through a refractory period which is a period of time following orgasm when they are unresponsive to sexual stimulation. Females however, if they experience additional sexual stimulation during the resolution phase, may show an increase in sexual arousal and potentially experience multiple orgasms before the end of the resolution phase.

Pornography leads to both self-reported and physiologically measurable arousal in both males and females. There is an interest in aggressive pornography since it involves physical force being used, or threatened, to coerce a woman to engage in sexual acts such as rape. Research has shown that in college students, males who view rape films later exhibit a higher level of aggression toward women and tend to view women as enjoying a rape. In contrast, exposure to pornography in general has very little effect on such sexual behavior as intercourse or masturbation.

B   1. Which of the following sexual states or phases is NOT shown by females?

    A. plateau
    B. refractory
    C. excitement
    D. resolution

    2. What are the characteristics of the four phases of physiological responses during sexual activity and how are they similar or different between the genders?

A   3. Research has shown that college students who view aggressive pornography are likely to:

    A. show more aggression toward women
    B. perform fewer future rapes
    C. consider it primarily a behavior in criminals
    D. show an increase in compassion for actual rape victims

4. What has experimentation taught us about pornography?

V.   LIST THE MOST COMMON VARIATIONS IN SEXUAL BEHAVIOR.   WHAT HAVE PSYCHOLOGICAL STUDIES REVEALED ABOUT HOMOSEXUALITY?

Sexual variations refer to sexual behaviors that deviate from conventional norms and that are maladaptive. The behaviors revolve around variations in object choice, variations in sexual aim, and gender identity disturbances. The variations in object choice include fetishism and rape. Variations in sexual aim include voyeurism, exhibitionism, and transvestism. Transsexualism is a gender identity disturbance. Psychological studies have concluded that when homosexuals were satisfied and not distressed with their sexual preference they were as psychologically well-adjusted as were heterosexuals. If they do show signs of abnormality, homosexuals do not differ in type or degree than that seen in heterosexuals. Furthermore, maladaptive behavior in homosexuals is believed due to the social stigma attached to homosexuality rather than to the homosexuality per se.

C   1. Research on homosexuals has shown that, compared to heterosexuals, they:

   A. show more sexual variations
   B. are more likely to develop non-sexual abnormal behaviors
   C. are as well-adjusted if they are satisfied with their sexual preference
   D. show a stronger desire to change their sexual preference

   2. Discuss some of the most common variations in sexual behavior?

VI.   WHAT ARE THE MAJOR SEXUAL DYSFUNCTIONS OF MEN AND WOMEN? WHAT ARE SOME OF THE ORIGINS OF SUCH DYSFUNCTIONS?   HOW CAN THE DYSFUNCTIONS BE TREATED?

Males exhibit erectile dysfunction (impotence, or the inability to have or to maintain an erection), premature ejaculation (when one ejaculates to soon for his partner to experience orgasm through intercourse), and retarded ejaculation (the man with an erection is unable to ejaculate into the woman's vagina). Females show orgasmic dysfunction (frigidity, or the inability to have an orgasm) and vaginismus (an involuntary contraction of the muscles surrounding the vaginal entrance). Anxiety associated with one's performance contributes to erectile dysfunction and premature ejaculation. Retarded ejaculation may stem from a fear of impregnation or anger over the partner's infidelity. Orgasmic dysfunctions in females may result from emotions of shame, guilt, or fear and/or the expectation of pain during coitus. Many of the treatments involve increasing the individual's ability to focus on the physical sensations associated with the sexual excitement while going through a shaping procedure to reach the desired behavior.

1. Discuss the characteristics, causes, and treatments involved in two of the five sexual dysfunctions found in males or females.

MULTIPLE-CHOICE QUESTIONS

INTRODUCTION: "DEAR ANN LANDERS"

C   1. The "Dear Ann Landers" letter in the introduction of the chapter on human sexuality dealt with:
A. extramarital intercourse
B. homosexuality
C. exhibitionism
D. transsexuals

D   2. Which of the following is a false belief or myth about sexual behavior?
A. alcohol is a sexual stimulant
B. people are either totally homosexual or totally heterosexual
C. masturbation is a practice restricted almost exclusively to men
D. all of the above

A   3. Why is the term "gender" used instead of the term "sex?"
A. it does not refer to sexual behavior or reproduction
B. it is medically correct
C. it does not have negative connotations
D. all of the above

BIOLOGICAL DIFFERENCES

B   4. One's sexual and reproductive organs are known as:
A. gender role
B. primary sexual characteristics
C. gonads
D. sex organs

B   5. Following conception, the process that leads to specific
        physical differences between males and females is called:
        A. primary sexual classification
        B. prenatal sexual differentiation
        C. gender differences
        D. gonad differentiation

C   6. During the first few weeks of development after conception
        the _____ are _____.
        A. testes ; one-third their normal size
        B. gonads ; already differentiated
        C. gonads ; undifferentiated
        D. ovaries ; absent

A   7. The female's ovaries and the male's testes are called:
        A. gonads
        B. androgens
        C. secondary sexual characteristics
        D. reproductive differences

D   8. The "male" hormones that cause masculinization are known as:
        A. progesterone
        B. estrogens
        C. testosterone
        D. androgens

D   9. Testosterone:
        A. is the most important androgen
        B. stimulates development of internal male sex structures
        C. stimulates development of external male sex structures
        D. all of the above

C   10. Which of the following statements is FALSE?
        A. embryos that become female have two X chromosomes
        B. by the 14th week of development the fetus is clearly
           male or female
        C. only males produce androgens
        D. the main source of androgens in males is the testes

A   11. Estrogens:
        A. are "female" hormones
        B. determine one's gender identity
        C. are "turned on" by the Y chromosome
        D. all of the above

B   12. Secondary sexual characteristics:
        A. appear by the 16th week of pregnancy
        B. signal readiness for reproduction
        C. are only evident in males
        D. result from one's gender identity

B   13. One's personal sense of maleness or femaleness is known as one's:
    A. secondary sexual orientation
    B. gender identity
    C. primary sexual orientation
    D. sexual responsiveness

C   14. Which of the following statements is FALSE?
    A. genital sex refers to the external sex organs
    B. genital sex refers to one's chromosomal make-up
    C. gonadal sex refers to internal reproductive organs
    D. hormonal sex refers to estrogen and androgen levels

D   15. A hermaphrodite is one whose:
    A. secondary sexual characteristics are incomplete
    B. birth label is incorrect
    C. external sex organs are incomplete
    D. gender is biologically ambiguous

A   16. The adrenogenital syndrome causes:
    A. a hermaphrodite
    B. multiple orgasms
    C. homosexuality
    D. retarded ejaculation

A   17. A transsexual is one who is:
    A. psychologically uncomfortable with his or her anatomical sex
    B. actually a transvestite
    C. lacking androgens
    D. lacking estrogens

B   18. The case of Dr. Renee Richards demonstrates:
    A. transvestism
    B. transsexualism
    C. exhibitionism
    D. homosexuality

B   19. What does John Money consider to be the most crucial in the determination of gender identity?
    A. heredity
    B. learning
    C. androgen level
    D. estrogen level

GENDER ROLES

C   20. Our society's expectation regarding how an individual of a
         particular gender is to behave is one's:
         A. stereotype
         B. gender identity
         C. gender role
         D. secondary sexual characteristics

D   21. Research by Broverman and others on gender role stereotypes
         found that positively valued male traits revolved around the
         general characteristic of _____ while those for females
         revolved around _____.
         A. adventureness ; love
         B. dominance ; submissiveness
         C. aggression ; passiveness
         D. competence ; warmth-expressiveness

D   22. Which of the following was an example in the text of how
         gender roles are communicated to young children?
         A. messages from parents
         B. observing others
         C. school teachers and counselors
         D. all of the above

APPLICATION: GENDER ROLES AND SEXUALITY

B   23. Which of the following is NOT part of a traditional American
         gender role in sexuality?
         A. males are responsible for initiating sex
         B. the female is easy to arouse
         C. males refrain from being tender and emotional
         D. females are more passive

SURVEYS OF SEXUAL BEHAVIOR AND ATTITUDES TOWARD SEX

A   24. The pioneer in the use of surveys for studying sexual
         behavior was:
         A. Alfred Kinsey
         B. John Money
         C. Sigmund Freud
         D. John Hunt

C   25. A criticism of Hunt's sexual survey in 1974 was that its
         respondents were _____ than average.
         A. more rural
         B. less well-educated
         C. more liberal
         D. more conservative

B   26. Self-stimulation of the genitals is called:
       A. orgasm
       B. masturbation
       C. petting
       D. fellatio

D   27. Surveys reveal that _____ percent of males and about
       _____ percent of females have masturbated to orgasm.
       A. 80 ; 75
       B. 85 ; 67
       C. 90 ; 75
       D. 95 ; 67

A   28. The pleasurable release of sexual tension and the climax of
       sexual arousal is known as a(n):
       A. orgasm
       B. sexual response cycle
       C. plateau phase
       D. peak experience

C   29. Physical or sexual contact between individuals that does not
       include sexual intercourse is called:
       A. masturbation
       B. coitus
       C. petting
       D. heterosexuality

D   30. Which statement about the results of the sex surveys by
       Kinsey and Hunt is TRUE?
       A. the incidence of masturbation has not increased
       B. masturbation and petting is occurring at a younger age
       C. premarital sex is increasing
       D. all of the above

B   31. Surveys have shown that _____ (another name for sexual
       intercourse) _____ with age.
       A. coitus ; increases
       B. coitus ; decreases
       C. orgasm ; decreases
       D. orgasm ; increases

A   32. Oral stimulation of the male genitals is called _____
       while oral stimulation of the female genitals is called
       _____.
       A. fellatio ; cunnilingus
       B. fellatio ; coitus
       C. cunnilingus ; coitus
       D. cunnilingus ; vaginasmus

A   33. What percentage of the married couples under twenty-five in
       the Hunt survey reported engaging in both forms of oral sex?
       A. 90%
       B. 80%
       C. 75%
       D. 70%

C   34. Sexual attitudes have become more positive about which two
       behaviors over the last 50 years?
       A. masturbation and coitus
       B. premarital sex and extramarital sex
       C. masturbation and premarital sex
       D. extramarital sex and masturbation

PHYSIOLOGY OF SEXUAL BEHAVIOR: LABORATORY OBSERVATIONS OF THE
SEXUAL RESPONSE CYCLE

C   35. The primary limitation of self-report data or surveys on
       sexual behavior is the area of:
       A. sample size
       B. changing attitudes
       C. accuracy
       D. replication

B   36. Masters and Johnson's laboratory research has identified
       _____ phases of physiological responses of sexuality.
       A. 3
       B. 4
       C. 5
       D. 6

D   37. Which of the following is NOT a phase of the sexual response
       cycle?
       A. excitement
       B. resolution
       C. plateau
       D. completion

A   38. The part of the sexual response cycle which involves an
       increased flow of blood to the genital areas following
       stimulation is the _____ phase.
       A. excitement
       B. plateau
       C. orgasm
       D. resolution

C   39. The psychological experience of intense pleasure is associated with the _____ phase of the sexual response cycle.
    A. excitement
    B. resolution
    C. orgasm
    D. plateau

A   40. Unlike males, females are capable of increased sexual arousal during the _____ phase of the sexual response cycle.
    A. resolution
    B. excitement
    C. refractory
    D. plateau

B   41. A period of time following orgasm when males are unresponsive to sexual stimulation is the _____ period.
    A. excitement
    B. refractory
    C. absolute
    D. dysfunction

D   42. Which of the following statements about the sexual response cycle is FALSE?
    A. females can have multiple orgasms during the resolution phase
    B. sexual arousal reaches a peak during the orgasm phase
    C. all female orgasms occur as a result of stimulation of the clitoris
    D. the plateau phase follows the orgasm phase

D   43. Multiple orgasms are:
    A. two or more successive orgasms prior to the end of the resolution phase
    B. possible in females during the resolution period
    C. possible but not necessary for female sexual satisfaction
    D. all of the above

EXPERIMENTAL STUDIES OF SEXUAL BEHAVIOR

C   44. One of the most significant issues concerning sexual behavior which has been experimentally investigated recently is the issue of:
    A. sexual dysfunction
    B. sexual response cycles
    C. pornography
    D. sexual variations

A   45. Which of the following statements about pornography is
         FALSE?
         A. it leads to measurable arousal in males but not usually
            in females
         B. it refers to any written, verbal, or visual material
            that is sexually arousing
         C. exposure to it has little effect on intercourse
            frequency
         D. exposure to it has little effect on masturbation
            frequency

B   46. Research on aggressive pornography has shown that:
         A. females are more susceptible than males
         B. viewing sexual violence can have antisocial effects
         C. children are victimized more often than adults
         D. viewers of rape films actually show more homosexual
            behavior

APPLICATION: ADOLESCENT SEX AND THE PROBLEM OF CONTRACEPTION

C   47. One suggested way to counteract the teenage pregnancy
         epidemic is to:
         A. encourage sterilization
         B. eliminate sex education
         C. provide more information about contraceptives
         D. have fewer educational films on contraceptive devices

D   48. The teenage pregnancy epidemic is said to result from:
         A. insufficient knowledge about contraceptives
         B. a lack of models of contraceptive behavior in the
            mass media
         C. the association of sex with feelings of anxiety
         D. all of the above

VARIATIONS IN SEXUAL BEHAVIOR

A   49. Sexual behaviors that deviate from conventional norms and
         that are maladaptive are called sexual:
         A. variations
         B. handicaps
         C. dysfunctions
         D. peculiarities

B   50. Which statement about fetishism is TRUE?
         A. only inanimate objects
         B. it occurs primarily in males
         C. it is where someone attaches sexual significance to
            objects that are long or round
         D. all of the above

A   51. Attaching sexual significance to objects that are not
        necessarily sexual in nature is known as:
        A. fetishism
        B. voyeurism
        C. tranvestism
        D. exhibitionism

D   52. Which statement about rape is TRUE?
        A. it is an act of aggression, usually directed toward a
           female
        B. sexual arousal plays a minor role in this behavior
        C. most rapes are planned
        D. all of the above

C   53. Which of the following is NOT a variation in sexual aim?
        A. voyeurism
        B. exhibitionism
        C. transsexualism
        D. transvestism

B   54. A voyeur derives sexual pleasure from:
        A. inflicting pain on other people
        B. secretly watching others undress or have sexual
           intercourse
        C. receiving pain from other people
        D. exposing one's genital's to unsuspecting strangers

D   55. One who receives sexual gratification by dressing in the
        clothing of the opposite sex is showing:
        A. fetishism
        B. voyeurism
        C. exhibitionism
        D. transvestism

A   56. Which of the following statements is FALSE?
        A. transsexuals crossdress with the same intent as do
           transvestites
        B. most exhibitionists are men
        C. transvestites engage in crossdressing
        D. tranvestites have no desire to change their gender

GENDER IDENTITY DISTURBANCE: TRANSSEXUALISM

C   57. Someone who is "trapped in the wrong body" is likely to
        exhibit:
        A. sexual dysfunctions
        B. orgasmic dysfunctions
        C. transsexualism
        D. transvestism

D   58. Transsexuals:
         A. are psychologically uncomfortable with their anatomical
            sex
         B. usually are males who feel they are females
         C. often undergo change-of-sex surgery
         D. all of the above

HOMOSEXUALITY

B   59. Having a sexual attraction toward, or engaging in, sexual
         behavior with a member of the same gender is termed:
         A. heterosexuality
         B. homosexuality
         C. transsexualism
         D. sexual variation

B   60. Exclusive homosexuality is found in about _____ percent of
         men and _____ percent of females.
         A. 5 ; 4
         B. 2 ; 1
         C. 10 ; 20
         D. 2 ; 10

A   61. Those that are sexually attracted to, or engage in sexual
         activity with, members of the opposite gender are known as:
         A. heterosexuals
         B. homosexuals
         C. cross-gender individuals
         D. transsexuals

C   62. Sexual surveys have reported that about _____ percent of
         men and _____ percent of women are exclusively
         heterosexual.
         A. 50 ; 75
         B. 75 ; 100
         C. 75 ; 85
         D. 50 ; 50

A   63. Which of the following statements is TRUE?
         A. homosexuality is not considered to be a mental disorder
         B. all but about 2% of men and women are exclusively
            homosexual or heterosexual
         C. researchers have recently found a biological cause
            for homosexuality
         D. all of the above

D   64. Psychoanalytic studies have found homosexuality to be
         related to a _____ mother and a _____ father.
         A. passive, affectionate ; dominant, intimate
         B. passive, hostile ; dominant, hostile
         C. dominant, unaffectionate ; passive, overprotective
         D. dominant, overprotective ; passive, unaffectionate

SEXUAL DYSFUNCTIONS

B   65. Sexual dysfunctions refer to:
         A. abnormal or deviant sexual behaviors shown primarily
            by males
         B. sexual difficulties or impairments in sexual functioning
         C. psychological impairments leading to an inability to
            become sexually aroused
         D. all of the above

B   66. What percent of American marriages may be affected by some
         type of sexual dysfunction?
         A. 10
         B. 50
         C. 75
         D. 95

C   67. An inability to have or to maintain an erection is called
         a(n):
         A. premature ejaculation
         B. sexual variation
         C. erectile dysfunction
         D. orgasmic dysfunction

A   68. Masters and Johnson define an erectile dysfunction as
         existing when it results in unsuccessful intercourse
         approximately _____ percent of the time or more.
         A. 25
         B. 10
         C. 50
         D. 75

B   69. Which of the following statements is FALSE?
         A. impotence also refers to erectile dysfunction
         B. erectile dysfunction typically has a physical origin
         C. sensate focus exercises are suggested to overcome
            erectile dysfunction
         D. all of the above

C   70. When the male ejaculates too soon for his partner to
         experience orgasm through intercourse, it is called:
         A. orgasmic dysfunction
         B. erectile dysfunction
         C. premature ejaculation
         D. impotence

D   71. The Seman's start-stop method is used to treat:
        A. erectile dysfunction
        B. retarded ejaculation
        C. vaginismus
        D. premature ejaculation

C   72. Retarded ejaculation refers to the man's:
        A. orgasm occurring after the females
        B. inability to experience emotional pleasure concurrent
           with physical ejaculation
        C. inability to ejaculate into the woman's vagina
        D. ejaculation after intercourse has ended

A   73. Which of the following is NOT a male sexual dysfunction?
        A. orgasmic dysfunction
        B. retarded ejaculation
        C. premature ejaculation
        D. erectile dysfunction

B   74. An inability to have an orgasm is referred to as:
        A. vaginismus
        B. orgasmic dysfunction
        C. orgasm phase
        D. retarded orgasm

D   75. Some studies report that about _____ percent of all women
        have never experienced orgasm during intercourse.
        A. 1
        B. 20
        C. 50
        D. 10

C   76. What two characteristics are considered necessary for one to
        classify one's condition as an orgasmic dysfunction?
        A. premature ejaculation and vaginismus
        B. pain and high anxiety experienced during intercourse
        C. no or infrequent orgasms and resulting distress
        D. feelings of guilt and premature sexual response

D   77. Which of the following is NOT associated with the
        dysfunction known as vaginismus?
        A. contraction of the muscles surrounding the vaginal
           entrance
        B. the vaginal spasms may be very painful
        C. sexual intercourse may become impossible
        D. premature orgasms occur about 35% of the time

APPLICATION: PREVENTING SEXUAL DYSFUNCTIONS

A   78. What according to noted sex therapists is the first important step in preventing sexual dysfunctions from occuring?
    A. for parents to establish a positive family atmosphere for sexual attitudes and questions
    B. early sexual education prior to grade six
    C. an open dialogue between female and male
    D. a decrease in performance anxiety on the part of the male

D   79. What according to noted sex therapists can lead to the occurance of sexual dysfunctions?
    A. a lack of trust in one's partner
    B. believing there is a correct way to behave sexually
    C. grading and evaluating sexual performances
    D. all of the above

ON THE HORIZON: SOCIETY'S REACTIONS TO THE RAPE VICTIM

B   80. Frequently during testimony in rape trials:
    A. there is no opportunity for the victim to tell her side of the story
    B. it appears the victim is "on trial"
    C. the judge places more emphasis on the victim's age
    D. all of the above

C   81. When does the rape victim NOT tend to be given responsibility for the attack?
    A. if she was drunk at the time of the rape
    B. if she is dating the attacker
    C. when she is physically attractive rather than unattractive
    D. when she is wearing a particular or suggestive style of dress

— CHAPTER 18 —

SOCIAL PSYCHOLOGY

OUTLINE

I. Introduction: Thirty-Eight Witnesses - the true story of how a
    woman in New York City is stabbed three times over a period of
    35-minutes and is killed, yet none of the 38 witnesses called
    the police; SOCIAL PSYCHOLOGY is the field that studies the
    manner in which the behavior, feelings, or thoughts of one
    individual are influenced or determined by the behavior and/or
    characteristics of others

II. Person Perception - the process of making judgments about
    others, particularly their abilities, motives, interests, or
    traits is called PERSON PERCEPTION

    A. Appearance and impressions - underlying many judgments of
       others are STEREOTYPES, preconceived images of what most
       members of a particular group are like; stereotypes are
       oversimplifications,   rigidly   resistance   to   change,   and
       highly evaluative; stereotypes apply strongly to concepts of
       <u>physical attractiveness</u>; many characteristics assigned to
       attractive and unattractive people are presented
       1. The   self-fulfilling   nature   of   stereotypes - it   is
          difficult to shed preconceptions and stereotypes due to
          the   SELF-FULFILLING   PROPHECY,   when   persons   act   in
          accordance with the treatment they get from others so
          that the "expected" behavior actually occurs

B. Attribution process – ATTRIBUTION is when we infer the causes of someone's behavior as well as their traits, motives, and intentions merely by observing their behavior; we make attributions about stable, internal characteristics
   1. Searching for the internal causes of others' behavior – we are more likely to seek internal causes when the behavior is unusual or unpopular and when it has noncommon effects
   2. Distinguishing between internal and external causes – a CASUAL ATTRIBUTION is where one determines whether an actor's behavior is due to internal or external reasons; to make internal and external attributions, we use three types of information – CONSISTENCY (how stable or general the person's behavior is over time, modality, or context), DISTINCTIVENESS (whether the same behavior or liking occurs in other situations), and CONSENSUS (how others behave in the same situation)

C. Forming impressions – IMPRESSION FORMATION is when we take separate bits of information and combine them into some coherent picture of a person
   1. First impressions – the first information presented exerts the most influence on an impression – the primacy effect
   2. Combining information in forming impressions – the WEIGHTED-AVERAGE MODEL says that our final impression of someone is a weighted average of all the available information about that person

D. Biases in person perception – getting to know someone is a subjective process, based upon one's IMPLICIT PERSONALITY THEORY (our beliefs about what traits tend to occur together) and influenced by the HALO EFFECT (when we tend to see good traits as going with good traits and bad traits with bad traits)
   1. Actor-observer difference – the tendency to see one's own behavior as due to situational or external factors and others' behavior as due to personal characteristics is the ACTOR-OBSERVER DIFFERENCE; this results because actors and observers have different types of information available to them as well as a different focus of attention; this actor-observer bias is very evident in prisons
   2. Self-serving bias – while we ascribe responsibility for our negative outcomes, we tend to take more credit for our positive outcomes, a tendency called the SELF-SERVING BIAS; this bias allows us to maintain a positive self-image

E. Application: Attribution therapy for college students – behavior can be attributed to <u>stable</u> causes that are permanent and unchangeable or to <u>unstable</u> causes that are temporary and likely to change; a recent study using "attribution therapy" with college freshman was effective at convincing them that their academic problems were due to unstable causes

III. Changing Attitudes and Influencing Behavior

A. Attitude formation and change – an ATTIDUE represents a relatively enduring predisposition to feel, think, and respond in particular ways toward some object, person, group, or issue; attitudes are made up of <u>affective</u>, <u>cognitive</u>, and <u>behavioral</u> components
  1. The process of learning attitudes – attitudes are learned by means of <u>classical conditioning</u>, <u>instrumental or operant conditioning</u>, and <u>observational</u> learning
  2. Attitude change through persuasion – factors relevant to persuasion include the communication's <u>source</u> (who said it), <u>message</u> (what is said), and <u>audience</u> (who hears it)
    a. the source – the greater the CREDIBILITY (how believable the source is) of the source the greater the attitude change; attractiveness and similarity also are important in the source
    b. the message – <u>one-sided vs. two-sided arguments</u> and "fear-inducing" advertisements influence the effectiveness of a message
    c. the audience – women (sometimes), individuals with low self-esteem, and individuals not committed to an attitude are more easily persuaded
  3. Attitude change through dissonance reduction – when we behave in a manner inconsistent with our attitudes, we are showing ATTITUDE-DISCREPANT behavior; such behavior is commonplace; COGNITIVE DISSONANCE refers to an unpleasant emotional state experienced when an inconsistency occurs between one's attitudes or one's attitude and behavior; various ways to reduce dissonance are presented; however, little or no dissonance occurs if there is <u>sufficient justification</u> for one's behavior, a lack of choice in behaving, or when the behavior does not lead to aversive consequences

B. Conformity – we attempt to behave in accord with SOCIAL NORMS, or explicit and implicit rules within a group regarding what kind of behavior is important; we display CONFORMITY when our behavior is consistent with these norms and we behave like others in the group
  1. When do we conform? – the classic studies by Asch on group pressures on line estimation with the use of <u>confederates</u> are summarized and interpreted; a difference exists between <u>public compliance</u> and <u>private acceptance</u>

2. Why do we conform? - in NORMATIVE SOCIAL INFLUENCE we conform in order to be socially accepted while with INFORMATIONAL SOCIAL INFLUENCE we conform because we believe the information provided is correct

C. Compliance - COMPLIANCE, a subtle means of influencing people, occurs when behavior is carried out in accordance with a request from someone; techniques for obtaining compliance include the FOOT-IN-THE-DOOR TECHNIQUE (which involves making a small request and then a large request), the DOOR-IN-THE-FACE TECHNIQUE (where the small and desired request is made after a large, likely to be refused request is made), and LOW-BALLING (where an individual reaches a decision, but then the reasons for making the decision are changed or removed with the hope that the original decision will remain)

D. Obedience - behavior carried out in accordance with an order from an authority figure is called OBEDIENCE; this is the most direct and obvious form of influence presented in the text; DESTRUCTIVE OBEDIENCE refers to the phenomenon where we still obey even though we disapprove of the orders given us; this type of obedience may explain the treatment of innocent people in Nazi Germany; Milgram's classic studies on destructive obedience in the laboratory using "shock" are presented and then interpreted for variables which enhance or decrease such obedience

E. Application: Jumping on the charity bandwagon - two research studies are presented which attempted to enhance charitable donations; one was to legitimize small donations which then increased the number of donations, the other showed a list of previous contributors to prospective donors

IV. Liking, Helping, and Hurting Others

A. Attraction - the evaluation of another individual in a positive or negative manner, in essence an attitude held toward another individual, is called an ATTRACTION
1. Theories of attraction - the BALANCE THEORY emphasizes the importance of consistency among one's thoughts and assumes that we like to perceive a balance or consistency in a network of liking relationships; balance is a pleasant state while imbalance is the opposite; the REINFORCEMENT-AFFECT MODEL assumes that most stimuli in our environment are either rewarding or punishing and that our evaluations of objects or persons are based on the positive or negative emotions we associate with them
2. Determinants of attraction
a. similarity - attraction increases as attitude similarity increases
b. reciprocal liking - we are attracted to people that like and evaluate us positively

      c. proximity - attraction increases as physical closeness decreases; based on the <u>familiarity effect</u>

      d. affect - people tend to elicit the feelings that one experienced in their presence

B. Prosocial behavior - Voluntary acts that have positive consequences for others is PROSOCIAL BEHAVIOR

    1. Theories of prosocial behavior - both <u>learning</u> and <u>cognitive</u> explanations of prosocial behavior are offered; prosocial acts are affected by our <u>expectations</u> about being rewarded or punished and our observations of others; Latané and Darley say helping in an emergency depends on one's perceptions and judgments as the emergency unfolds

    2. Helping in emergencies - we must work our way up a decision tree; <u>notice</u> something is happening, <u>interpret</u> it as an emergency, accept <u>responsibility</u> for helping, decide <u>how to intervene</u>, and finally <u>implement</u> the behavior; two factors working against prosocial behavior are the SOCIAL INFLUENCE PROCESS, whereby bystanders inhibit each other from helping through each person's lack of action or apparent concern, and the DIFFUSION OF RESPONSIBILITY, where bystanders share responsibility with others present and then feel reduced responsibility for helping; an important variable in helping behavior is <u>group size</u>; studies and real-life situations are presented where people did and did not help in emergencies; acceptance of responsibility for another is affected by the bystander's EMPATHY, or understanding of the victim's feelings and plight

C. Aggression - behavior whose intent is to inflict harm or injury on another living being is called AGGRESSION

    1. Theories of aggression - there are three categories of theoretical perspectives on the origins of aggression

      a. instincts - Freud and Lorenz suggested that aggression is instinctive

      b. frustration - the FRUSTRATION-AGGRESSION HYPOTHESIS states, in part, that frustration always leads to some form of aggression

      c. <u>a social learning approach</u> - it views aggression as being acquired and maintained through rewards and modeled behavior

    2. Determinants of aggression

      a. <u>frustration and the role of aggressive cues</u> - frustration is especially likely to lead to aggression when there are AGGRESSIVE CUES (stimuli associated with aggression) present in the situation

      b. <u>attack: insult and assault</u> - physical provocation often leads to aggression

       c. <u>other aversive stimulation</u> - these forms include heat,
          impleasant odors, and physical pain
       d. <u>models of aggression</u> - children acquire aggressive
          responses by observing the actions of an aggressive
          model; an extensive review of the literature on
          modeled aggression along the lines of the classic
          Bandura studies is presented; in general, watching
          filmed or televised aggression increases the
          likelihood of the observers engaging in similar
          aggressive acts

D. Application: Increasing helpfulness and reducing aggression
- suggestions for increasing prosocial behavior include more
reinforcement for those who do help, providing more models
of helping behavior, and familiarizing people with the
research on prosocial behavior; strategies for controlling
aggression include fostering incompatible responses such as
empathy and humor, exposure to nonaggressive models,
reducing an emphasis on the masculine values of aggression,
not rewarding or expecting aggressive behavior in boys

V.   On the Horizon: Television Violence and the Future - social
psychologists in the future must convince the producers and
consumers of television violence that it doesn't help the
ratings and that televised violence can contribute to real-life
aggression; this is especially important because television
viewing is increasing in our society

OBJECTIVES

I.   WHAT ARE STEREOTYPES?   HOW DO THEY AFFECT OUR IMPRESSIONS OF
PEOPLE?

Stereotypes are preconceived images of what most members of a
particular group are like. They are oversimplified, rigidly
resistant to change, often highly evaluative, and they negate
the uniqueness of individuals. Stereotypes apply strongly to
concepts of physical attractiveness, with attractive
individuals (both children and adults) usually being responded

to more favorably and being helped more often. Attractive people tend to be perceived differently in a number of ways, e.g., more pleasant, more socially at ease, having a higher self-esteem, being of a higher occupational status, more sensitive, more modest, kinder, more happy and well-adjusted. However, sometimes they are viewed as being vain and egotistical. One research project found that attractive people were judged less harshly for crimes of burglary but more harshly when the crime was a swindle.

C   1. Which of the following is NOT typically associated with the stereotype of an attractive person?

      A. happy and well-adjusted
      B. vain and egotistical
      C. aloof and distant
      D. pleasant and socially at ease

     2. What is a stereotype and discuss what characteristics are associated with the physical attractiveness stereotype?

II.   HOW DO WE MAKE ATTRIBUTIONS AND FORM IMPRESSIONS? IN WHAT WAYS ARE OUR PERCEPTIONS OF OTHERS AND OURSELVES SOMETIMES BIASED?

Probably the most crucial basis for making attributions and forming impressions about others is by observing their behavior. Through observations we infer causes of behavior as well as the individual's traits, motives, and intentions. Frequently, our first contact with an individual is more influential than repeated contacts. Once we gather bits of information, they are treated unequally - we "weight" or put more emphasis on certain types of information as suggested by the weighted-average model. Our impressions of others may be biased, on the basis of the physical attractiveness stereotype and stereotypes of what personality traits correlate with other traits (e.g., the implicit personality theory, and the halo effect).

A   1. What is the most important way that we make attributions and form impressions?

      A. observing someone's behavior
      B. talking to someone directly
      C. talking about someone with others
      D. socially interacting with the person in a group setting

D   2. In which way are our perceptions of others and ourselves sometimes biased?

      A. stereotypes
      B. the halo effect
      C. one's implicit personality theory
      D. all of the above

3. In what ways are our perceptions of others and ourselves sometimes biased?

III. WHAT ARE ATTITUDES? HOW ARE THEY FORMED? HOW DO THEY CHANGE?

An attitude is a relatively enduring predisposition to feel, think, and respond in particular ways toward some object, person, group, or issue. Attitudes have effective, cognitive, and behavioral components. Many theorists think that attitudes are learned, like any other behavior, by means of classical and instrumental conditioning and observation. Attitudes are changed through persuasion in the form of communications from parents, peers, the mass media, or whomever. Three factors relevant to the degree of persuasiveness in a communication is its source (who says it), its message or content (what is said), and the audience or recipient (who hears it).

B   1. Attitudes are changed through persuasive communications. Such communications are influenced by "who says it," "what is said" and:

       A. "where it is said"
       B. "who hears it"
       C. "how it is said"
       D. "when it is heard"

    2. What are attitudes and how are they formed?

IV. HOW DO CONFORMITY, COMPLIANCE, AND OBEDIENCE DIFFER? WHAT FACTORS AFFECT EACH?

Conformity is displayed when people's behavior is consistent with social norms and they behave like others in the group. Conformity is influenced by our need to be socially accepted (normative social influence) and because we accept the information or behavior of others as being correct (informational social influence). Much of our conformity is unintentional and only becomes evident when someone breaks the current norms. Compliance, in contrast, is carried out in accordance with a request from someone, and, therefore, it is less subtle. Compliance is commonly achieved in the retail sales world through the "foot-in-the-door" and "door-in-the-face" techniques and by low-balling. Obedience is the least subtle form of attitude and behavior change. It is behavior carried out in accordance with an order from an authority figure. Obedience is influenced by proximity to the figure, behavior in other members of the social group, and whether the individual has responsibility for the consequences of the order or command

C   1. Which type of social influence is the most direct and
       obvious?

       A. conformity
       B. compliance
       C. obedience
       D. instruction

    2. How are conformity, compliance, and obedience both different
       and the same?

V.   WHAT ARE THE MAJOR THEORIES AND FINDINGS ABOUT ATTRACTION?

    The two major theories which explain attraction are the balance
    theory and the reinforcement-affect model. The balance theory
    emphasizes the importance of consistency among one's thoughts
    and assumes that we like to perceive a balance or consistency
    (i.e., a pleasant state) in a network of liking relationships.
    Balance results when two people like each other and agree about
    some object of communication. The reinforcement-affect model
    states that our evaluations of objects or persons are based on
    the positive or negative emotions we associate with them.
    These emotions, in turn, result from whether we experienced
    rewarding or punishing stimuli in the presence of objects or
    persons. Most research has focused on the specific
    determinants of attraction. These include similarity between
    individuals, reciprocal liking, proximity, and affect. Our
    attraction to people is increased if we are similar to them, if
    we both like each other, and when we come into physical
    closeness. We tend to like someone if good feelings in us have
    occurred while in their presence (irrespective of whether the
    other individual caused the feelings or not).

A   1. Of the specific determinants of attraction which have been
       studied systematically, which one has more to do with the
       physical environment?

       A. proximity
       B. similarity
       C. affect
       D. reciprocal liking

    2. What are the two major theories of attraction?

MULTIPLE-CHOICE QUESTIONS

INTRODUCTION: THIRTY-EIGHT WITNESSES

D   1. To   demonstrate   something   of   interest   to   social
        psychologists, the text discusses a murder in New York to
        which there were _____ witnesses but no phone calls to
        police for help.
        A. 5
        B. 11
        C. 23
        D. 38

B   2. Which area of psychology is interested in how we are
        influenced by the presence and characteristics of those
        around us?
        A. environmental
        B. social
        C. group
        D. interpersonal

PERSON PERCEPTION

A   3. Person perception is the process of making _____ about
        others.
        A. judgments
        B. statements
        C. recommendations
        D. excuses

D   4. Person perception is the process of making judgments about
        other's:
        A. abilities
        B. motives
        C. traits
        D. all of the above

APPEARANCE AND IMPRESSIONS

C   5. Underlying many of our judgments of others are:
        A. social norms
        B. their abilities and motives
        C. stereotypes
        D. self-serving biases

B   6. A preconceived image of what most members of a particular
        group are like is called a(n):
        A. halo effect
        B. stereotype
        C. attitude
        D. consensus

A   7. Which of the following is NOT characteristic of stereotypes?
        A. unique qualities
        B. oversimplifications
        C. rigidly resistant to change
        D. highly evaluative

C   8. Which of the following best describes the physical
        attractiveness stereotype?
        A. what is beautiful is often mean and spiteful
        B. what is beautiful is miserable
        C. what is beautiful is good
        D. what is beautiful is not worth having

D   9. According to the notion of a self-fulfilling prophecy,
        people:
        A. change their stereotypes as they get older
        B. overachieve in front of others in a social setting
        C. have attitudes shift to match their overt behavior
        D. act in accordance with the treatment others give them

B   10. It is difficult to shed stereotypes and preconceptions
        because of:
        A. mass communications
        B. self-fulfilling prophecies
        C. parental training
        D. peer pressure

ATTRIBUTION PROCESS

A   11. The process whereby we infer the causes of peoples' behavior
        as well as their traits and intentions is known as:
        A. attribution
        B. the halo effect
        C. conformity
        D. catharsis

C   12. Making attributions is made easier when the observer looks
        for:
        A. socially desirable behavior
        B. social norms
        C. noncommon effects
        D. common effects

B   13. In causal attribution, one determines whether an
        individual's behavior is due to:
        A. past or current experiences
        B. internal or external reasons
        C. cognitive or emotional factors
        D. all of the above

A   14. Which of the following is NOT a type of information used to
        make a causal attribution?
        A. credibility
        B. consistency
        C. distinctiveness
        D. consensus

D   15. The stability of one's behavior over time is called _____
        while how others behave in the same situation is called

        _____.
        A. credibility ; distinctiveness
        B. consensus ; credibility
        C. distinctiveness ; consensus
        D. consistency ; consensus

C   16. Distinctiveness is said to be low for Dave if he liked:
        A. a John Denver song regardless of where or when he hears
           it
        B. a John Denver song that no one else likes
        C. all John Denver songs he hears
        D. this, but not other John Denver songs

FORMING IMPRESSIONS

B   17. Taking separate bits of information about a person and
        combining them into some coherent picture is known as:
        A. the weighted-averaging method
        B. impression formation
        C. compiling
        D. information grouping

A   18. The primacy effect is influential in impression formation
        because it is believed to:
        A. change the meaning of later information
        B. cause one to lose interest sooner
        C. make later information more important
        D. all of the above

D   19. Which model suggests that we put more emphasis on some types
        of information when we form an impression?
        A. irregular grouping
        B. attraction
        C. bias
        D. weighted-average

D   20. Which type of information tends to be more heavily weighted
         by individuals?
         A. highly negative traits
         B. information from highly credible people
         C. information particularly relevant to the current
            judgment
         D. all of the above

BIASES IN PERSON PERCEPTION

C   21. The implicit personality theory refers to one's beliefs
         about:
         A. how behaviors match certain attitudes
         B. what unconscious factors influence our evaluation of
            others
         C. what traits tend to occur together
         D. what predispositions are found in certain groups of
            people

B   22. Once we form an impression of someone, we tend to assume
         that that person has other characteristics consistent with
         that impression. This is known as the:
         A. Cattell effect
         B. halo effect
         C. diffusion phenomenon
         D. consistency phenomenon

A   23. The tendency to see one's own behavior as due to situational
         factors   but   others'   behavior   as   due   to   personal
         characteristics is called the:
         A. actor-observer difference
         B. internal-external orientation
         C. normative social influence phenomenon
         D. credibility hypothesis

A   24. The actor-observer difference says that one tends to see
         their own behavior as due to _____ factors and others'
         behavior as due to _____ characteristics.
         A. situational ; personal
         B. motivational ; emotional
         C. personal ; situational
         D. cognitive ; motivational

C   25. Two   factors   which   are   believed   to   influence   the
         actor-observer difference are:
         A. stereotypes and degree of empathy
         B. the halo effect and attribution
         C. types of information available and focus of attention
         D. interpersonal attraction and degree of conformity

C   26. Ascribing positive experiences to our credit but negative
        experiences to situational factors is known as:
        A. extrapolation
        B. projection
        C. self-serving bias
        D. causal attribution

D   27. The common interpretation of the self-serving bias is that
        it allows us to maintain a:
        A. consensus with others
        B. low level of cognitive dissonance
        C. positive outlook on life
        D. positive self-image

APPLICATION: ATTRIBUTION THERAPY FOR COLLEGE STUDENTS

B   28. Wilson and Linville (1982) reported a use of "attribution
        therapy" with college students to:
        A. decrease dating problems
        B. improve grades and decrease dropping out of school
        C. increase contact with individual faculty members
        D. decrease vandalism and suicide threats

A   29. The "attribution therapy" used by Wilson and Linville (1982)
        with college freshmen attempted to stress their difficulties
        as being due to:
        A. unstable, nonpermanent factors
        B. emotional unstability
        C. poor habits learned in high school
        D. all of the above

ATTITUDE FORMATION AND CHANGE

C   30. A relatively enduring predisposition to feel, think, and
        respond in particular ways is called a(n):
        A. attribution
        B. trait
        C. attitude
        D. stereotype

B   31. Which of the following is NOT a component of an attitude?
        A. emotions or feelings
        B. sensations or perceptions
        C. thoughts or beliefs
        D. responses or behavior

D   32. Which of the following is considered a process of learning
        attitudes?
        A. classical conditioning
        B. operant conditioning
        C. observational learning
        D. all of the above

A   33. Credibility in persuasion attempts pertains to:
        A. how believable the source is
        B. the effectiveness of the source
        C. the realistic nature of the communication
        D. all of the above

D   34. A factor influencing the credibility of a source is:
        A. attractiveness
        B. similarity to the receiver
        C. ability to argue against their own best interest
        D. all of the above

C   35. Which of the following is NOT a common persuasion technique
        discussed in the text?
        A. one-sided messages
        B. two-sided messages
        C. interpersonal confrontations
        D. "fear-inducing" advertisements

B   36. Which is NOT a common audience characteristic that might
        influence the effects of persuasion attempts?
        A. one's gender
        B. one's marital status
        C. our knowledge about the topic
        D. personality factors such as self-esteem level

B   37. Research has shown that attitudes are changed by persuasion
        and:
        A. guilt
        B. attitude-discrepant behavior
        C. a willingness on the part of the individual
        D. all of the above

A   38. When we exhibit attitude-discrepant behavior:
        A. our attitudes tend to become consistent with our behavior
        B. our behaviors tend to shift toward our attitudes
        C. those around us are made to feel uneasy
        D. we base more of our decisions on emotionality

D   39. The unpleasant emotional state experienced when attitudes
        and behaviors are inconsistent is called:
        A. actor-observer difference
        B. behavioral imbalance
        C. anxiety
        D. cognitive dissonance

C   40. Which characteristic of one's attitude-discrepant behavior
will NOT produce cognitive dissonance?
A. produces aversive consequences
B. small reinforcement
C. sufficient justification
D. freedom of choice

CONFORMITY

B   41. We say that individuals are displaying _____ when they act
in accordance with _____.
A. consensus ; internal expectations
B. conformity ; social norms
C. consistency ; attitudes
D. credibility ; group pressures

C   42. Explicit and implicit behavioral rules within a group are
called:
A. social standards
B. behavioral expectations
C. social norms
D. group norms

A   43. When we act according to the rules of our group, we are
showing:
A. conformity
B. dependence
C. obedience
D. empathy

D   44. The Asch studies which used confederates and line estimation
found that _____ of the experimental subjects conformed to
the group's incorrect choice on at least one trial.
A. almost half
B. none
C. all
D. three-fourths

C   45. The Asch studies with line estimation reported that there
was less conformity when the experimental subjects:
A. were questioned last
B. merely had to use a hand signal
C. gave a private response
D. were questioned near the end

B   46. The line estimation studies conducted by Asch suggested a
difference between:
A. conformity in each gender
B. public compliance and private acceptance
C. social and individual norms
D. consensus and conformity

A 47. When we conform in order to be socially accepted we are
        showing:
        A. normative social influence
        B. informational social influence
        C. social diffusion
        D. social attraction

D 48. Informational social influence is when we conform because:
        A. we give up resisting
        B. of cognitive dissonance
        C. of a self-serving bias
        D. we accept the information from others as being correct

COMPLIANCE

D 49. Behavior carried out in accordance with a request from
        someone is referred to as:
        A. consensus
        B. obedience
        C. conformity
        D. compliance

B 50. When one signs a petition or donates to a charity after
        being asked, they are showing:
        A. consensus
        B. compliance
        C. conformity
        D. obedience

C 51. Which compliance technique is traditionally used by
        salespersons?
        A. halo effect
        B. compliance
        C. foot-in-the-door technique
        D. door-in-the-face technique

A 52. The foot-in-the-door technique involves:
        A. making a small request before making a larger one
        B. having the purchaser physically touch the product
        C. having the purchaser say a good thing about the product
        D. all of the above

A 53. Which technique is opposite that of the door-in-the-face
        technique?
        A. foot-in-the-door technique
        B. low-balling
        C. request gradation
        D. informational social influence

B   54. Which strategy involves making a large request first with
        the hope that a smaller request will actually be accepted?
        A. foot-in-the-door technique
        B. door-in-the-face technique
        C. request gradation
        D. request flexibility

C   55. Which technique, often used by automobile salespersons,
        involves agreeing on a sale and then increasing the price of
        the product?
        A. door-in-the-mouth technique
        B. foot-in-the-door technique
        C. low-balling
        D. compliance

D   56. Which of the following is a strategy for obtaining
        compliance?
        A. foot-in-the-door technique
        B. door-in-the-face technique
        C. low-balling
        D. all of the above

OBEDIENCE

C   57. Behavior carried out in accordance with an order from an
        authority figure is called:
        A. consensus
        B. conformity
        C. obedience
        D. compliance

A   58. Which of the following forms of influence is the most direct
        and obvious?
        A. obedience
        B. conformity
        C. compliance
        D. aggression

B   59. Destructive obedience is said to occur when:
        A. peer pressure results in property damage
        B. we obey even though we disapprove of the orders
        C. aggression is induced by someone else
        D. all of the above

C   60. In Milgram's (1974) study on obedience, what percent of the
        subjects continued to deliver shocks up to 450 volts?
        A. 35
        B. 50
        C. 65
        D. 80

D   61. The enlightening finding in the Milgram (1974) study on obedience was that:
A. few people actually delivered the shocks
B. obedience was lower than expected
C. women actually delivered more shocks than men
D. the subjects' behavior wasn't expected by most people

D   62. Which of the following statements about Milgram's research on obedience is TRUE?
A. our tendency to obey the commands of authority figures is strong
B. obedience is increased when the authority figure is close by
C. obedience is reduced if the subject believes he is responsible for the victim
D. all of the above

APPLICATION: JUMPING ON THE CHARITY BANDWAGON

A   63. Research by Cialdini and Schroeder (1976) found that charity donations in a door-to-door drive could be increased by:
A. legitimizing small donations
B. making both written and oral requests
C. having both female and male solicitors
D. using children as solicitors

B   64. A study by Reingen (1982) showed that donations increased among college students when:
A. a group of solicitors was present
B. a list of previous contributors was shown
C. the request was made on weekends
D. all of the above

ATTRACTION

C   65. An evaluation of another individual in a positive or negative manner is a(n):
A. stereotype
B. feeling
C. attraction
D. catharsis

D   66. The balance theory of attraction emphasizes the importance of:
A. equal status between individuals
B. open communication
C. interpersonal feelings
D. consistency among one's thoughts

A   67. A pleasant state which exists when two people like each
          other and agree about some object of communication is the
          focus of the _____ theory of attraction.
          A. balance
          B. reinforcement
          C. emotional
          D. valence

B   68. Which of the following is NOT a characteristic or assumption
          of the reinforcement-affect model of attraction?
          A. attraction is a learned response
          B. classical conditioning accounts for almost all responses
             of attraction
          C. we associate positive or negative emotions with objects
             or people
          D. rewarding stimuli elicit positive feelings

C   69. The statement "birds of a feather flock together" reflects
          what determinant of attraction?
          A. reciprocal liking
          B. proximity
          C. similarity
          D. affect

D   70. The effects of proximity as a determinant of attraction are
          explained by the:
          A. diffusion process
          B. social influence process
          C. catharsis hypothesis
          D. familiarity effect

PROSOCIAL BEHAVIOR

A   71. A voluntary act which has positive consequences for the
          recipient is a _____ behavior.
          A. prosocial
          B. altruistic
          C. credible
          D. emphatic

B   72. The cognitive explanation of prosocial behavior by Latane
          and Darley (1970) emphasizes:
          A. the degree of danger involved
          B. a "decision tree"
          C. "reading" other bystanders' feelings
          D. rationalization and projection

C   73. According to Latané and Darley, bystanders may inhibit each
        other from helping in an emergency through the _____
        process.
        A. familiarity
        B. social norm
        C. social influence
        D. attitude-discrepant behavior

A   74. The process called diffusion of responsibility accounts for
        _____ by bystanders during emergency situations.
        A. less help offered
        B. more help offered
        C. the great concern shown
        D. all of the above

D   75. The study by Darley and Latané (1968) which demonstrated the
        diffusion of responsibility process so well was the:
        A. football crowd experiment
        B. old man experiment
        C. library accident study
        D. seizure study

B   76. The real-life situation of where Lenny Skutnik rescued the
        drowning Priscilla Tirado following a plane crash
        demonstrated his _____ for the victim.
        A. attitude
        B. empathy
        C. feelings of guilt
        D. feelings of attraction

C   77. Understanding for a victim's feelings and plight is called:
        A. diffusion
        B. condolence
        C. empathy
        D. apathy

A   78. Empathy is said to positively influence what behavior?
        A. rescue attempts
        B. studying
        C. aggression
        D. compliance

AGGRESSION

B   79. Which of the following is NOT a theoretical perspective on
        the origin of aggression?
        A. instincts
        B. cognitions
        C. frustration
        D. learning factors

B   80. Freud and Lorenz are associated with a(n) _____
        interpretation of aggression.
        A. learning
        B. instinctive
        C. motivational
        D. cognitive

D   81. Frustration is most likely to lead to aggression when the
        frustration is:
        A. weak
        B. strong
        C. illegitimate
        D. both B and C

A   82. The frustration-aggression hypothesis states, in part, that:
        A. frustration leads to some form of aggression
        B. frustration and aggression are learned emotions
        C. aggression cannot be extinguished
        D. aggressive behavior produces frustration

D   83. A social-learning approach to aggression emphasizes:
        A. environmental influences
        B. the previous reward of aggressive behaviors
        C. the role of modeling
        D. all of the above

C   84. Some suggest that frustration is especially likely to lead
        to aggression when there is also the presence of:
        A. a lower intelligence level
        B. a social group
        C. aggressive cues in the environment
        D. an innate aggressive drive

C   85. A common aggressive cue would be a:
        A. tennis racquet
        B. television set
        C. gun
        D. darkness

D   86. Which of the following is a common form of aversive
        stimulation according to Berkowitz?
        A. frustration
        B. personal insults
        C. physical attacks
        D. all of the above

A   87. The best general statement about imitation, aggression, and
         television viewing is:
         A. television violence is one cause of aggression
         B. aggression in children would be stopped if television
            cartoon viewing was stopped
         C. aggression increases when the model is similar to the
            viewer
         D. there is a positive correlation between the amount of
            television viewing and the amount of aggression shown

D   88. Viewing aggression on television may:
         A. teach new ways of being aggressive
         B. reduce restraints against aggressive behavior
         C. result in an emotional desensitization to aggression
         D. all of the above

A   89. Which of the following has the LEAST support as a way of
         controlling aggression?
         A. catharsis
         B. exposure to nonagressive models
         C. engaging in incompatible responses
         D. empathy

C   90. Catharsis is based on the assumption that aggression will
         decrease when _____ is/are decreased.
         A. frustration
         B. drives
         C. anger
         D. opportunities

APPLICATION: INCREASING HELPFULNESS AND REDUCING AGGRESSION

B   91. Which of the following ways of increasing prosocial behavior
         in our society was NOT suggested in the text?
         A. reinforce helping behavior more often
         B. legally require helping behavior when it is necessary
         C. teach specific helping skills
         D. make people aware of the research findings

C   92. Which of the following ways of controlling aggression was
         suggested by Eron in the text?
         A. provide fewer aggressive cues
         B. heighten frustration levels
         C. socialize boys like we do girls
         D. show more situation comedies on television

ON THE HORIZON: TELEVISION VIOLENCE AND THE FUTURE

D   93. Violence on television is disturbing to social psychologists
       because:
       A. we spend considerable time watching television
       B. much violence occurs on television
       C. television violence has been shown to influence
          aggression
       D. all of the above

– CHAPTER 19 –

ENVIRONMENTAL PSYCHOLOGY

OUTLINE

I. Introduction: The Urban Environment – a news report about
    Houston, Texas, its rapid growth, and how the urban environment
    influences people; ENVIRONMENTAL PSYCHOLOGY is the study of
    interrelationships between behavior and the physical
    environment; the PHYSICAL ENVIRONMENT is anything of a physical
    nature that surrounds us

II. Spatial Behavior – two forms of spatial behavior are personal
    space and territoriality

    A. Personal space – an area surrounding the body defined by an
       invisible boundary which may not be trespassed is PERSONAL
       SPACE, and the particular amount of personal space one
       requires in a given situation is referred to as one's
       personal space bubble; a personal space bubble functions for
       self-protection and communication
       1. How much space do you need? – one's space increases with
          age, anxiety level, the American culture and decreases if
          you are a female and if you are similar to other person
       2. When you have too little or too much space – PROXEMICS is
          the study of interpersonal distancing; interacting at an
          inappropriate distance constitutes a negative
          communication; Hall suggests North Americans use four
          ranges of personal space: INTIMATE DISTANCE (0-1.5 feet
          and reserved for intimate contacts or close contacts),
          PERSONAL DISTANCE (1.5-4.0 feet and used for

conversations between acquaintances or close friends), SOCIAL DISTANCE (4.0-12.0 feet and used for impersonal, formal, and businesslike contacts), and PUBLIC DISTANCE (more than 12.0 feet and reserved for one-way communications such as public speaking); EQUILIBRIUM THEORY deals with the variety of actions an individual engages in to regain equilibrium when optimum physical distance is not maintained

3. Personal space invasions - intrusions upon the personal space of others are referred to as PERSONAL SPACE INVASIONS; research which investigated invasions into one's personal space is presented

B. Territoriality - "keep out" and "no trespassing" statements are familiar expressions of territoriality; TERRITORIAL BEHAVIOR refers to acts that are carried out in an attempt to claim space and exclude members of one's own species

  1. Types of territories - Altman distinguished three types; a PRIMARY TERRITORY is one that is perceived as "owned" and that is used and controlled on a relatively permanent basis; a SECONDARY TERRITORY is used regularly by some individual or group but the area is not "owned," and the people involved have less control over it; a PUBLIC TERRITORY is an area that is occupied only temporarily and one that is available to anyone, thus making it difficult to own

  2. Evidence for territorial behavior in humans - individuals use a variety of techniques to claim a territory; TERRITORIAL MARKERS are possessions we place in an area to retain that territory; numerous territorial markers are discussed as well as in what locations they are effective

    a. dealing with territorial intrusions - people generally go to great lengths to defend a territory

C. Application: Designing responsive environments - environments that allow easy shifts from separateness to togetherness are called RESPONSIVE ENVIRONMENTS (e.g., Japanese homes); we should, and can, design buildings and housing projects to control social interaction and access

III. Environmental Determinants of Behavior - these include crowding, noise, temperature, and the urban environment

A. Crowding - psychologists define CROWDING as a stressful psychological state, and a personal, subjective reaction to insufficient space; POPULATION DENSITY refers to the number of people or animals per unit of space; crowding seems to result from a lack of personal control

  1. Negative effects of crowding - these include increases in heart rate, blood pressure, and physical illness and decreases in social interactions and the quality of task performances

    2. Reducing the perception of crowding and its effects – studies are discussed which suggest that crowding results from a sense of a loss of control; thus, increasing actual or perceived control will decrease crowding

B. Noise – an unwanted sound is NOISE
    1. Performance effects – whether or not noise adversely affects task performance depends upon the type of task and the predictability, controllability, and intensity of the noise; noise also produces a variety of <u>aftereffects</u> which can reduce performance levels
    2. Social effects – noise increases aggression in angry but not in nonangered subjects; it can also decrease prosocial or helping behavior; various research studies are discussed

C. Temperature – heat may adversely affect attraction toward total strangers but not with others; available research data suggests a curvilinear relationship between temperature and aggression with aggression increasing as heat increases but then declining as heat increases further; summer riots are more likely to occur during moderate rather than high temperatures

D. Urban environment – many of the negative beliefs regarding cities may be misperceptions
    1. Social effects – urban dwellers desire less interaction with strangers, they show less eye contact, and provide less helping behavior; Milgram believes that urban OVERLOAD, (an excess of stimulation from many varied sources which impinges upon residents) contributes to the behavior shown by urban dwellers; research on helping behavior is discussed

E. Application: Reducing crowding stress in a dormitory – a study by Baum and Davis (1980) manipulated the "length" of long-corridors in a dormitory without reducing the population density in order to generate more interaction and less withdrawal in the students; this study alleviated crowding architecturally

V.   Environmental Design and Environmental Behavior Change

A. Environmental design – Osmond classifies environments as SOCIOPETAL SPACES (those arrangements which encourage social interaction) and SOCIOFUGAL SPACES (arrangements that reduce the level of social interaction); a discussion of research and examples of various types of spaces and arrangements is presented; airport lounges, any side-by-side seating, and many modern low-income housing complexes are examples of sociofugal spaces; a DEFENSIBLE SPACE is a physical space that is characterized by a high level of social responsibility and personal safety; more housing units should be built so as to maximize defensible space

B. Changing environmental behavior – two successful approaches are reinforcement techniques and prompts
   1. Reinforcement techniques – positive reinforcement has been used to pick up litter; a variation of this technique is the marked item technique; energy conservation has been manipulated with rewards in "mastered-metered" apartment complexes; FEEDBACK involves informing people "how they are doing" by giving information about their performance and has been used to reduce energy consumption; research results are discussed
   2. Prompts – cues that convey messages are called PROMPTS (e.g., signs, the state of the environment); research results are discussed

C. Application: Reducing air conditioning usage – a novel project by Becker and Seligman (1978) incorporated a signaling device that was activated whenever the air conditioner was in use when the outside temperature was 60 degrees F or less; electricity usage was reduced by about 16%

V. On the Horizon: Crowding Research and the Future of Prisons – a discussion of the negative effects of crowding in prisons and some ways to negate these effects

OBJECTIVES

I.   WHAT ARE THE FUNCTIONS OF PERSONAL SPACE AND TERRITORIALITY?

Personal space is an area surrounding the body defined by an invisible boundary which may not be trespassed. This boundary may expand or contract, depending on the situation and individual needs. The amount of personal space one requires is referred to as one's personal space bubble. Self-protection and communication are two functions of the personal space bubble. Territorial behavior refers to acts that are carried out in an attempt to claim space and exclude members of one's own species. Territories regulate with whom we interact while personal space influences the distances that are maintained in interactions. The functions of territories in humans are to regulate privacy, aid in our sense of identity, and lend order and continuity to our life.

C   1. Which of the following is a function of one!s personal space bubble?

   A. lends order and continuity to life
   B. regulate with whom we interact
   C. influences the distance of interactions
   D. aids in our sense of identity

2. What are the differences between, and functions of, personal space and territoriality?

II. **LIST SOME CONSEQUENCES OF INTERACTING AT INAPPROPRIATE DISTANCES. LIST THE CONSEQUENCES OF PERSONAL SPACE INVASIONS.**

Interacting at an inappropriate distance (e.g., too close or too far) constitutes a negative communication which leads to negative assumptions about the other person and negative feelings. There are four ranges of personal space typically used by Americans as a function of the type of communication involved: intimate distance, personal distance, social distance, and public distance. Research has found that invasions of one's personal space by strangers are uncomfortable, aversive, and stressful, and depending on the situation, people react in different ways. Common reactions are to leave, avoid eye contact, and engage in defensive behaviors. Negative impressions are also found about the invader. In contrast, invasion of one's personal space by friends, lovers, or attractive people may actually lead to positive reactions.

D   1. Invasions of one's personal space can lead to:

   A. negative impressions being formed about the invader
   B. an uncomfortable and stressful situation
   C. positive reactions
   D. all of the above

2. Discuss the consequences when one interacts at an inappropriate distance and when one's personal space is invaded.

III. HOW DO CROWDING, NOISE, AND HEAT EFFECT BEHAVIOR?   HOW ARE
THESE EFFECTS EXPLAINED?

Crowding is a stressful state. As a result, there are negative
consequences of crowding. These include stress-related
physiological consequences such as increases in heart rate,
blood pressure, and physical illness. Furthermore, many
negative feelings and negative social behaviors are associated
with crowding (e.g., social withdrawal, fewer interactions,
less group activities). Finally, crowding lowers performance
on various complex tasks. Noise also has a negative effect on
performance, but the degree of the effect is influenced by the
predictability, controllability, and intensity of the noise and
the type of task. Noise also produces a variety of negative
aftereffects on performance which some believe reflects a sense
of helplessness in the individual. There are also negative
effects on social behavior as a result of noise in that it can
increase aggression in angered subjects, decrease helping
responses, and lessen attention to peripheral cues of a
situation. Heat tends to reduce attraction to strangers but it
has minimal effects on our interactions with those experiencing
the heat with us. The relationship between heat and aggression
is curvilinear whereby aggression first increases, then
declines as heat increases.

B   1. The relationship between heat and aggressive behavior is
        stated as:

        A. the higher the heat the more aggression
        B. aggression first increases, then declines as heat
           increases
        C. aggression is low at low and moderate heat levels, but
           is high at high heat levels
        D. surprisingly, research has found no relationship between
           heat and aggression

     2. How do crowding, noise, and heat affect behavior?

IV. WHAT ARE THE PSYCHOLOGICAL CONSEQUENCES OF LIVING IN AN URBAN
     ENVIRONMENT?

     Research suggests that urban residents do not have more mental
     health or psychological problems, and they seem to feel as
     happy as rural residents. However, their social behavior is
     different in some ways. City dwellers desire less interaction
     with strangers, they do not make eye contact as often, they are
     less likely to be friendly in response to friendly gestures by
     strangers, and they are less likely to help people (even when
     children are in need of assistance).

A   1. Which of the following characteristics is FALSE about the behavior of people residing in urban areas? They:

A. show more psychological problems
B. help others less often
C. desire fewer social interactions
D. are less friendly to friendly strangers

V.   IN WHAT WAYS CAN THE ENVIRONMENT BE DESIGNED TO MATCH THE NEEDS OF ITS USERS?

Osmond has classified environments as those arrangements which encourage social interaction (sociopetal spaces) or which reduce the level of social interaction (sociofugal spaces). These arrangements may include furniture, walls of a room, and hallways in buildings. For example, furniture lined up in a way that individuals sit side-by-side or back to back (as in airport lounges and institutions) do not facilitate interaction, whereas chairs placed around small tables does. Likewise, modern "open offices" that have few walls favor a high level of interaction but they do not favor close interpersonal relationships. The designs of some low-income housing units favored vandalism, rapes, and robberies because they had too many pieces of public territory (in contrast to defensible space that is characterized by a high level of social responsibility and personal safety).

1. In what ways can the environment be designed to best match the needs of its users?

VI.   HOW CAN BEHAVIOR BE ALTERED TO MAINTAIN ENVIRONMENTAL QUALITY?

Two approaches that have had some success in modifying environmental behaviors are reinforcement techniques and prompts. Positive reinforcement has been used to increase constructive environmental behaviors such as littering. A variation in picking up litter is the marked item technique where rewards are provided for picking up items marked in an undetectable manner. Thus, all items are picked up with the hope that the "good" ones are retrieved. Positive reinforcement has also been used in energy conservation, especially in "master-metered appartments" where groups of appartment dwellers compete against each other for the money reward that is given to the group consuming the least amount of energy. A positive reinforcement technique known as feedback gives no tangible rewards, but does inform people "how they are doing." Thus, those interested in changing their behavior (e.g., reduce energy consumption) can know immediately that their efforts are or are not successful. Prompts are cues that convey messages. Common prompts are signs (e.g., "do not litter," "keep off the grass"), but just the state of the environment (e.g., a clean room as compared to a cluttered room) can influence behavior.

B   1. Which positive reinforcement technique that does not use a tangible reward has been used successfully to reduce energy consumption?

   A. prompts
   B. feedback
   C. fading
   D. stimulus discrimination

A   2. Techniques used to increase constructive environmental behavior have been reported for energy consumption and _____.

   A. littering
   B. jaywalking
   C. helping others
   D. interpersonal aggression

3. How can behavior be altered to maintain environmental quality?

MULTIPLE-CHOICE QUESTIONS

INTRODUCTION: THE URBAN ENVIRONMENT

D   1. The story in the text of Houston's growing population and resulting problems is of interest to environmental psychologists who study:
   A. Sun-Belt development
   B. southern racial issues
   C. industrial growth
   D. the urban environment and its effects

B   2. Environmental psychology is the study of interrelationships between _____ and the _____.
   A. actions ; individual's motivations
   B. behavior ; physical environment
   C. emotions ; climatic changes
   D. motives ; environment

C   3. Which of the following is NOT typically considered part of
        the physical environment by environmental psychologists?
        A. a city
        B. a work space
        C. neighbors
        D. the weather

SPATIAL BEHAVIOR

D   4. Personal space and territoriality are forms of _____
        behavior.
        A. congruent
        B. individual
        C. social
        D. spatial

PERSONAL SPACE

B   5. An area surrounding the body defined by an invisible
        boundary which may not be trespassed is known as one's:
        A. buffer zone
        B. personal space
        C. social bubble
        D. primary territory

C   6. The particular amount of personal space one requires in a
        given situation is often referred to as one's:
        A. primary territory
        B. halo zone
        C. personal space bubble
        D. personal territory

A   7. What are two functions of the personal space bubble?
        A. communication and self-protection
        B. identification and esteem maintenance
        C. relaxation and image conveyance
        D. terrioriality and defense

D   8. Which of the following influences on the size of one's
        personal space was NOT discussed in the text?
        A. gender
        B. anxiety
        C. age
        D. body size

D   9. One's personal space tends to be smaller if one is:
        A. female
        B. younger
        C. relaxed
        D. all of the above

B   10. Proxemics is the study of:
        A. the psychological effects of using artifical limbs
        B. interpersonal distancing
        C. industrial pressures on psychological well-being
        D. temperature as it influences motivation level

A   11. Hall suggests that a negative communication results when
        people:
        A. interact at inappropriate distances
        B. do not appreciate each other's social motives
        C. underestimate the size of their personal bubble
        D. overestimate the size of their personal bubble

A   12. Which of the following distances is the smallest for North
        Americans?
        A. intimate
        B. personal
        C. social
        D. public

C   13. One's social distance typically extends from:
        A. 0-1.5 feet
        B. 1.5-4.0 feet
        C. 4.0-12.0 feet
        D. 12.0 feet and up

B   14. Which statement is FALSE?
        A. comforting behaviors take place within one's intimate
           distance
        B. one's personal distance is the smallest in terms of feet
        C. social distance includes formal and business-like
           contacts
        D. conversations between close friends occur within one's
           personal distance

D   15. Which is a characteristic of one's public distance?
        A. it extends more than 12 feet
        B. reserved for formal public speaking
        C. one-way communications
        D. all of the above

C   16. When optimal physical distance is not maintained between
        individuals, they engage in a variety of actions to regain
        closeness. This refers to:
        A. social distancing
        B. social jockeying
        C. equilibrium theory
        D. personal space adjustments

D   17. According to equilibrium theory, the level of immediacy in an interaction is affected by:
   A. physical distance
   B. eye contact
   C. body orientation
   D. all of the above

B   18. Intrusions upon the personal space of others is referred to as:
   A. bubble-breakers
   B. personal space invasions
   C. primary territory intrusions
   D. personal distance intrusions

C   19. The effect of personal space invasions:
   A. is usually negative
   B. is evident more in males
   C. depends on the actions and characteristics of the invader
   D. all of the above

TERRITORIALITY

A   20. Acts that are carried out in an attempt to claim space and exclude members of one's own species are called _____ behavior.
   A. territorial
   B. protective
   C. self-serving
   D. defiance

D   21. Human territoriality:
   A. regulates privacy
   B. aids in a sense of identity
   C. lends order to life
   D. all of the above

C   22. Which statement is FALSE?
   A. territorial behavior regulates with whom we interact
   B. personal space maintains distances in interactions
   C. personal space has fixed boundaries whereas territories have flexible boundaries
   D. all of the above

3   23. A space that is used regularly by some individual or group, but is not "owned" is a _____ territory.
   A. primary
   B. secondary
   C. public
   D. shared

D   24. An example of a primary territory is one's:
      A. seat at the dining room table
      B. spot on a beach
      C. classroom seat
      D. office space

C   25. Objects or behaviors which communicate that a certain
      territory is "taken" are called:
      A. proxemics
      B. behavioral markers
      C. territorial markers
      D. prompts

A   26. What types of territorial markers are used in situations
      where it is difficult to use physical markers?
      A. actions
      B. valuable belongings
      C. personal belongings
      D. signs

D   27. People who have intruders enter their territories typically:
      A. use more territorial markers
      B. modify their territorial attitudes
      C. alter their territories, but remain close by
      D. defend them verbally or physically

APPLICATION: DESIGNING RESPONSIVE ENVIRONMENTS

B   28. Environments which allow easy shifts from separateness to
      togetherness are called:
      A. sociofugal spaces
      B. responsive environments
      C. modal environments
      D. multi-purpose spaces

B   29. Which culture tends to have responsive environments for
      living quarters?
      A. English
      B. Japanese
      C. German
      D. French

C   30. In which type of situation have the markers for secondary
      territories been absent so that these areas have become
      public territories?
      A. park benches
      B. bus stops
      C. urban housing developments
      D. "home" and "away" sides to a football field

CROWDING

D   31. A stressful psychological state in reaction to insufficient
         space is called:
         A. claustrophobia
         B. space anxiety
         C. population density
         D. crowding

A   32. The number of people or animals per unit of space is
         referred to as:
         A. population density
         B. crowding
         C. spatial distance
         D. sociopetal space

A   33. In terms of environmental determinants of behavior, density
         is a _____ term while crowding is a _____ term.
         A. physical ; psychological
         B. natural ; scientific
         C. psychological ; scientific
         D. natural ; physical

B   34. Crowding is most likely to be experienced when a person:
         A. has lost use of his or her primary territory
         B. feels a lack of personal control in the setting
         C. has two or more individuals within his or her intimate
            distance
         D. all of the above

D   35. Which of the following has been reported as a negative
         effect of crowding in humans?
         A. increases in blood pressure and heart rate
         B. social withdrawal
         C. decreased performance on complex tasks
         D. all of the above

C   36. One way to reduce the effects of crowding on task
         performance is to:
         A. spread the tasks out over a period of time
         B. require that the tasks have a high attention level
         C. inform people about the effects of crowding
         D. all of the above

B   37. Baum and Valins' (1977) study with college dormitory
         residents found that crowding was influenced by:
         A. class level in school
         B. corridor or suite-style room arrangements
         C. whether it was or wasn't a mixed-gender dormitory
         D. the length of evening "study hours"

NOISE

C   38. Noise is defined as:
        A. sounds that physically damage the auditory system
        B. psychologically disruptive sounds
        C. unwanted sound
        D. sounds that increase blood pressure and heart rate 80%
           of the time

A   39. Which factor does NOT influence whether noise adversely
        affects task performance?
        A. meaning
        B. predictability
        C. controllability
        D. intensity

D   40. The variety of aftereffects of noise are attributed to:
        A. lowered auditory pain thresholds
        B. excessive fatigue
        C. overcompensation after the noise is removed
        D. a sense of helplessness

D   41. Research on noise suggests that with the passage of time and
        an opportunity to adjust, noise:
        A. is still attended to
        B. causes negative effects
        C. is still perceived as annoying
        D. all of the above

C   42. Research on the social effects of noise has found that it:
        A. decreases acts of anger
        B. shifts attention to peripheral cues in the situation
        C. decreases helping responses
        D. all of the above

TEMPERATURE

B   43. Which weather condition has received considerable research
        attention by environmental psychologists?
        A. the winter months
        B. the temperature
        C. rainy weather
        D. hurricane and tornado conditions

A   44. Research has found that heat adversely affects attraction
        toward:
        A. total strangers
        B. the elderly
        C. the same gender
        D. the opposite gender

C   45. The available research on how heat influences aggression
         suggests that high temperatures:
         A. increase aggressive behaviors
         B. increase aggressive responses, but only in young people
         C. do not necessarily facilitate aggression
         D. actually have no effect on aggressive behavior

URBAN ENVIRONMENT

D   46. Compared to rural living, which is a negative social effect
         of urban living?
         A. less eye contact
         B. less helping behavior
         C. less interaction with strangers
         D. all of the above

B   47. Milgram has described the problem of urban _____, where
         excess stimulation from many varied sources impinges upon
         residents.
         A. trauma
         B. overload
         C. noise
         D. decay

APPLICATION: REDUCING CROWDING STRESS IN A DORMITORY

A   48. Research by Baum and Davis (1980) with college students
         living in dormitiories found that crowding could be
         alleviated with:
         A. architectural intervention
         B. staggering classloads and classtimes
         C. sensitivity group sessions
         D. hall posters listing the causes of crowding

B   49. The purpose of the Baum and Davis (1980) study to alleviate
         crowding in college student dormitory living was to:
         A. educate the students about past research findings
         B. increase the likelihood of small group formation
         C. create less eye contact among residents
         D. all of the above

ENVIRONMENTAL DESIGN

C   50. According to Osmond, environmental arrangements which
    encourage social interaction are called _____ spaces while
    those that reduce the level of social interaction are called
    _____ spaces.
    A. sociofugal ; sociopetal
    B. expanding ; restricting
    C. sociopetal ; sociofugal
    D. sociofugal ; restricting

D   51. Arrangements of furniture which tend to encourage social
    interaction are called _____ spaces.
    A. expanding
    B. sociofugal
    C. responsive
    D. sociopetal

A   52. Research by Sommer and Ross (1958) found that social
    interactions increased significantly in a hospital geriatric
    ward when the furniture was:
    A. placed around small tables
    B. lined up in rows
    C. arranged for side-by-side sitting
    D. arranged for back-to-back sitting

C   53. A good example of a typical sociofugal seating arrangement
    is:
    A. in offices of dentists or doctors
    B. small tables in cocktail lounges
    C. lounge areas of airports
    D. circular banquet tables

B   54. Defensible space is a physical space characterized by a high
    level of social responsibility and:
    A. social interaction
    B. personal safety
    C. physical markers
    D. one's primary territory

A   55. The Pruitt-Igoe housing project in St. Louis was a failure
    because it did not have _____ space.
    A. defensible
    B. sociopetal
    C. sociofugal
    D. personal

D   56. An answer to reducing urban crime may lie in designing
    physical settings that encourage people to:
    A. use them more often
    B. personalize them
    C. take responsibility for them
    D. all of the above

A   57. What is the central characteristic of defensible space?
        A. natural surveillance
        B. enclosed areas
        C. an area less than 144 square feet
        D. primary territory

CHANGING ENVIRONMENTAL BEHAVIOR

C   58. Two approaches that have had some success in modifying
        environmental behaviors are reinforcement techniques and:
        A. natural surveillance
        B. feedback
        C. prompts
        D. group planning

B   59. Which type of reinforcement approach has NOT been shown to
        be effective at increasing constructive environmental
        behavior?
        A. positive reinforcment
        B. token economies
        C. the marked item technique
        D. monetary reward programs

D   60. Reinforcement techniques have been effective at reducing
        _____ and increasing _____.
        A. jay-walking ; obeying of traffic signals
        B. illegal parking ; helping behavior
        C. speeding ; charitable donations
        D. littering ; energy conservation

C   61. An approach related to positive reinforcement that involves
        informing people "how they are doing" is called:
        A. scheduling
        B. prompting
        C. feedback
        D. fading

A   62. Prompts are defined as:
        A. cues that convey messages
        B. verbal supports to helping behaviors
        C. reinforcements used with prosocial behavior
        D. physical suggestions for verbal actions

D   63. Common prompts that are used to discourage environmentally
        destructive behavior are:
        A. authority figures
        B. feedback
        C. newspaper ads
        D. signs

B   64. Research by Krauss et al. (1978) on the disposal of used
    tissues found that littering was reduced by:
    A. positive reinforcement
    B. the state of the environment
    C. specific anti-littering signs
    D. general anti-littering signs

APPLICATION: REDUCING AIR CONDITIONING USAGE

A   65. Becker and Seligman (1978) cut energy consumption in air
    conditioned homes by:
    A. using a blue light to signal when it was wasteful to
       use one's air conditioner
    B. having individuals insulate their homes better
    C. having individuals monitor someone else's energy
       consumption and wastefulness
    D. training children to check the thermostat 3 to 4 times
       per day

ON THE HORIZON: CROWDING RESEARCH AND THE FUTURE OF PRISONS

B   66. One of the most important future applications of crowding
    research will be in the area of:
    A. urban housing
    B. prison policy
    C. mass transportation
    D. office management

D   67. Which of the following consequences of crowded conditions in
    prisons is believed to be TRUE?
    A. illness increases
    B. disciplinary problems increase
    C. life-expectancy decreases
    D. all of the above

– CHAPTER 20 –

APPLIED PSYCHOLOGY

OUTLINE

I.   Introduction: Unemployment--A National Crisis - the
     consequences of unemployment in Detroit and how psychologists
     are dealing with it; APPLIED PSYCHOLOGY is concerned with
     solving real-life problems; VOCATIONAL PSYCHOLOGY is concerned
     with vocational choice and adjustment

II. Vocational Psychology

     A. Vocational choice - in our vocational choice we choose a way
        of life and largely determine our social status

     B. Career development - CAREER DEVELOPMENT deals with
        adjustment to work that takes place throughout one's work
        life; Super suggests five stages of career development -
        growth, exploration, establishment, maintenance, and
        occupational decline

     C. Career counseling - the field of CAREER COUNSELING is
        concerned principally with occupational choice; career
        counselors clients make career decisions
        1. Occupations - they are classified by level, field, and
           enterprise
        2. Abilities and worker requirements - a career counselor
           evaluates the client's aptitudes and abilities; common
           measures are the Differential Aptitude Test and the
           Scholastic Apptitude Test

   3. Vocational interests - information about <u>vocational interests</u> helps clients to make career decisions
   4. Trends in career counseling - many tests and inventories (e.g., <u>Strong-Campbell Interest Inventory</u>) are used

D. Application: Assessing vocational interests - the STRONG-CAMPBELL INTEREST INVENTORY measures vocational interests to aid occupational decision making by recording clients' "likes" and "dislikes" or relative preference for many kinds of activities, people, and objects; an individual can be described in terms of one or more of six occupational-interest themes (<u>R-theme</u>, <u>I-theme</u>, <u>A-theme</u>, <u>S-theme</u>, <u>E-theme</u>, and <u>C-theme</u>)

III. Psychology In Industrial and Organizational Settings - INDUSTRIAL-ORGANIZATIONAL PSYCHOLOGY, a fast growing applied area in psychology, is concerned with behavior in the world of work; it encompases <u>personnel selection</u>, <u>personnel development</u>, <u>consumer psychology</u>, and <u>psychology of advertising</u>

A. PERSONNEL SELECTION - the art and science of choosing the best person for a given job
   1. Job characteristics - during a JOB ANALYSIS, psychologists identify the duties required of the employee and behaviors necessary for successful job performance
   2. Person characteristics - those applicants most qualified to meet specific job requirements are then identified using as many as 20 personality dimensions; research has shown that successful and nonsuccessful excutives differ on some personality dimensions (e.g., ability to understand other people's perspectives)
   3. Prediction - persons making personnel selection decisions must demonstrate the accuracy of their assessments, for example, in the form of <u>Expectancy Charts</u>
   4. Assessment centers - the ASSESSMENT CENTER APPROACH involves inviting a small number of candidates for the same type of job to an <u>assessment center</u> where they undergo two to three days of multiple assessment procedures, including <u>situational tests</u>; the <u>Management Progress Study</u> positively evaluated the worth of assessment centers

B. Personnel development - four STAGES OF PROFESSIONAL CAREERS are presented (<u>apprentice</u>, <u>colleague</u>, <u>mentor</u>, and <u>sponsor</u>) that involve different developmental tasks, relationships, and psychological adjustments; all stages are discussed; the sponsor stage fulfills one or more of the roles of <u>manager</u>, <u>internal enterpreneur</u>, and <u>idea innovator</u>; <u>mentor relationships</u> are important for several reasons; a MENTOR refers to an advisor, teacher, or protector who is to support, foster, and facilitate the young adult's career development

C. Application: Consumer psychology and the psychology of advertising – CONSUMER PSYCHOLOGY is the scientific study of consumer behavior which encompases the acquisition, use, and disposition of products, services, and ideas; the PSYCHOLOGY OF ADVERTISING is a field that attempts to determine how advertising motivates consumers and why consumers choose and use particular products and services; two areas of advertising research include characteristics of ads and characteristics of consumers
   1. Characteristics of ads – size, repetition, color, (or color psychology), position and illustrations all influence ad readership
   2. Characteristics of consumers – attempts to understand consumer needs are made with opinion surveys
   3. Conclusion – the positive effects of advertising are generally small

IV. Psychology In Other Professions

A. Psychology and medicine – BEHAVIORAL HEALTH refers to the new interdisciplinary subspecialty concerned with health maintenance and the prevention of illness
   1. Diagnosis – the Minnesota Multiphasic Personality Inventory is used as a clinical assessment tool
   2. Prevention of health problems – psychologists are making a contribution in reducing the number of cigarette smokers; behavioral health specialists are fostering individual responsibility for maintaining health and preventing illness

B. Psychology and Law – FORENSIC PSYCHOLOGY is concerned with applying psychological knowledge and principles to law and the judicial process (e.g., police departments); correctional psychologists deal with problems of juvenile delinquency and crime; court psychologists are involved in an expanding variety of roles that center on diagnostic evaluation of the individual using a variety of testing and interviewing techniques

C. Psychology and education – SCHOOL PSYCHOLOGY is a specialty that interfaces education with clinical and counseling psychology; school psychologists work as consultants to educational administrators and teachers, and as counselors for students; EDUCATIONAL PSYCHOLOGY is the application of psychology to education; educational psychologists are most likely to be involved in teacher training or research; the subfield of instructional psychology is involved in programmed instruction and computer assisted instruction

D. Application: Educational and psychological testing – formal testing permeates and will likely increase in the future

1. Admission testing – ADMISSIONS TESTING attempts to select those applicants most likely to succeed in educational programs and colleges; the Educational Testing Service is responsible for the administering, scoring, and interpreting of over 300 testing programs (including the Graduate Record Exam, the Graduate Management Admission Test, the Law School Admission Test, and the Multi-State Bar Exam)
2. The case of Larry P. vs. Wilson Riles – a lawsuit filed in California over the placement of students in special classes (frequently blacks) based on IQ test results which it was argued were culturally biased
3. Nader's raid on testing – a report in 1980 sponsored by Ralph Nader charged that admissions tests have undue influence on admissions to higher education and that tests have little value in predicting future performance
4. The Bakke case – it dealt with reverse discrimination whereby an eligible medical school applicant was denied admission but less qualified minority groups were accepted

V. On the Horizon: The future of admissions testing – some states are passing laws which curtail the use of admissions tests; the pressure to make test items public will increase the cost of exams and may lower quality; the shrinking college enrollment during the future will encourage more systematic admissions, something similar to personnel selection

OBJECTIVES

I. WHAT SERVICES ARE OFFERED BY VOCATIONAL PSYCHOLOGISTS?

The field of career counseling is concerned principally with occupational choice. Career counselors help people of all ages to make career decisions, but they don't make them for the client. Career counselors try to improve each client's decision making capabilities by providing information about alternative courses of action. The role of the career counselor is to acquaint clients with available occupations and to help clients determine occupations for which they are best suited.

D   1. What is one thing that career counselors do NOT do?

   A. advise people as to available vocations
   B. help clients make career choices
   C. improve their client's decision making capabilities
   D. select appropriate careers for clients

2. What general services are offered by vocational psychologists?

II. IF YOU WERE DOING CAREER COUNSELING, WHAT STEPS WOULD YOU TAKE TO HELP YOUR CLIENT IMPROVE DECISION MAKING CAPABILITIES?

Effective career decisions require knowledge about occupations, abilities, and interests. Counselors acquaint clients with available occupations so that they can determine which occupations best suit them. Aptitude tests, such as the Differential Aptitude Test (DAT) and to some extent the Scholastic Aptitude Test (SAT), are administered and interpreted to aid in matching clients with occupations. Vocational interets are commonly measured by the Strong-Campbell Interest Inventory. After acquiring information about the client's aptitudes, interests, and relevant and suitable occupation alternatives, the career counselor would work with the client in his or her decision making process.

1. What steps would you as a career counselor take to help your client improve his or her decision making?

III. HOW DO PROFESSIONALS IN INDUSTRIAL AND ORGANIZATIONAL SETTINGS ACHIEVE THE GOALS OF PERSONNEL SELECTION?

To choose the best person for a given job, psychologists carry out a job analysis in which they identify the duties required of the employee and behaviors necessary for successful job performance. This analysis must identify specific behaviors that lead to either success or failure on the job as well as describing the job duties that are involved. Then, the professional identifies those applicants most qualified to meet specific job requirements by evaluating as many as 20 personality dimensions. The most favored procedure for matching jobs with personnel today is the assessment center approach. Typically, a small number of candidates for the same type of job are brought to an assessment center where they undergo evaluation for two or three days. Multiple assessment procedures and multiple assessors are used to predict the candidates' likelihood of success. These include ability tests, personality and interest inventories, structured interviews, and job-related situational tests.

B   1. What process in the procedure of personnel selection in industry is used to identify the duties required of the employee and behaviors necessary for successful job performance?

A. ability testing
B. a job analysis
C. administering interest inventories
D. a structured inventory

2. How do professionals in industrial and organizational settings achieve the goals of personnel selection?

IV. HOW HAS PSYCHOLOGY BEEN APPLIED TO ADVERTISING AND THE STUDY OF CONSUMER BEHAVIOR?

Consumer psychology is the scientific study of consumer behavior which encompasses how products, services, and ideas are acquired and used. The psychology of advertising attempts to determine how advertising motivates consumers and why consumers choose and use particular products and services. Research has been conducted on ad characteristics and characteristics of consumers. This research has found that advertisement readership can be increased with larger size, more repitition, more color, position (e.g., inside front and back covers are best), and illustration highlights. Through the use of opinion surveys, research in consumer psychology has provided information about what typical customers like and dislike about specific products, what characteristics of products lead to a change of brands, and how particular products are utilized.

D   1. What has research found that increases advertisement readership?

   A. color
   B. position
   C. repitition
   D. all of the above

2. What contributions has psychology made to our understanding of consumer behavior and advertisement readership?

V. HOW HAS PSYCHOLOGY BEEN APPLIED TO MEDICINE AND LAW?

Behavioral health is the new interdiciplinary subspecialty that is concerned with health maintenance and the prevention of illness. More physicians are relying on nonphysician specialists to improve the accuracy of diagnosis. One of the most significant contributions has been the development of the Minnesota Multiphasic Personality Inventory. In addition, psychologists have begun to apply behavioral principles to the prevention and/or treatment of both physical and mental dysfunctions. Cigarette smoking is one of several areas in which psychologists are making a contribution. Forensic psychology is concerned with applying psychological knowledge and principles to law and the judicial process. Psychologists work in police departments to assess applicant qualifications and to counsel officers exposed to emotional trauma. Correctional psychologists deal with problems of juvenile delinquency and crime both from a diagnostic and treatment view point. Court psychologists identify personal characteristics of offenders that may influence their motives and attitudes both toward crimes and rehabilitation.

A   1. In which area of medicine has psychology made a particularly
        important contribution?

        A. prevention of cigarette smoking
        B. treatment of heart disease
        C. diagnosis of personality characteristics
        D. selection of applicants for medical school

D   2. Forensic psychologists work in:

        A. police departments
        B. correctional programs
        C. legal courtrooms
        D. all of the above

     3. How has psychology been applied to law and medicine?

VI. DESCRIBE   THE   USE   OF   PSYCHOLOGICAL   TESTS   IN   EDUCATIONAL
     SETTINGS. WHAT ARE THE ARGUMENTS FOR AND AGAINST THEIR USE?

     Standardized educational and psychological tests are widely
     used to aid in selecting, classifying, assigning, or promoting
     students and employees. Admissions testing attempts to select
     those applicants most likely to succeed in educational programs
     and colleges.   Today, a college entrance examination board
     oversees the placement of students in over 3000 colleges
     annually and contracts with the Educational Testing Service
     (ETS) for assistance in developing and administering admissions
     tests.   The ETS administers the Scholastic Aptitude Test, the
     Graduate Record Exam, the Graduate Management Admission Test,
     and the Law School Admission Test among others.   Arguments
     against admissions tests include the belief that they have an
     undue influence on admissions to higher education and that
     tests have little value in predicting future performance.

     1. Describe the use of psychological tests in educational
        settings.

MULTIPLE-CHOICE QUESTIONS

INTRODUCTION: UNEMPLOYMENT--A NATIONAL CRISIS

B   1. That branch of psychology which is concerned with solving
          real-life problems is called _____ psychology.
          A. clinical
          B. applied
          C. vocational
          D. industrial

D   2. Mental health professionals who create programs specifically
          designed to aid the unemployed and their families would be
          called _____ psychologists.
          A. practical
          B. personnel
          C. vocational
          D. applied

A   3. A specialty area concerned with vocational choice and
          adjustment to work is known as _____ psychology.
          A. vocational
          B. personnel
          C. applied
          D. industrial

D   4. How many members of the American Psychological Association
          work in applied settings?
          A. just over 25%
          B. about 40%
          C. almost 50%
          D. the majority

VOCATIONAL CHOICE

C   5. Which of the following is NOT a consequence of one's
          vocational choice?
          A. it influences our way of life
          B. it largely determines our social status
          C. it influences the type of counseling one seeks
          D. it often determines income and living style

CAREER DEVELOPMENT

B   6. One's adjustment to work that takes place throughout one's
        work life is referred to as:
        A. job satisfaction
        B. career development
        C. vocational choice
        D. vocational counseling

C   7. How many stages are there in career development according to
        Super?
        A. 3
        B. 4
        C. 5
        D. 6

A   8. The stage of career development where initial educational
        decisions are made and career goals are examined is the
        _____ stage.
        A. exploration
        B. establishment
        C. growth
        D. maintenance

D   9. Which of the following is NOT a characteristic of the
        establishment stage of career development?
        A. tendency to settle down
        B. stabilize in a chosen field of work
        C. advance in a chosen field of work
        D. maintain satisfactory performance

B   10. The notion of "trial-and-error" in career development is
        associated with the _____ stage.
        A. growth
        B. exploration
        C. establishment
        D. maintenance

C   11. Conceptualizing career development as an extended process
        implies the importance of:
        A. the growth stage
        B. the exploration stage
        C. life-span counseling
        D. an extended work life for men and women

CAREER COUNSELING

A   12. The field of career counseling is concerned primarily with:
         A. occupational choice
         B. developing a positive self-image
         C. educational decisions as they influence future job
            activity
         D. all of the above

A   13. Career counselors try to:
         A. improve a client's decision making capabilities
         B. make wise career decisions for clients
         C. primarily reeducate clients for new or different
            vocations
         D. improve the psychological and social support in the
            client's family

B   14. Which is NOT a way of classifying occupations?
         A. level
         B. flexibility
         C. field
         D. enterprise

D   15. One's work setting defines the _____ of their occupation.
         A. level
         B. flexibility
         C. field
         D. enterprise

C   16. To be effective, a career counselor should know about a
         client's:
         A. skill level and abilities
         B. aptitudes and intelligence level
         C. aptitudes, abilities, and interests
         D. traits and preferences

C   17. One of the most widely used aptitude tests given by
         counselors today is the:
         A. Scholastic Aptitude Test
         B. Strong-Campbell Interest Inventory
         C. Differential Aptitude Test
         D. Lambert Aptitude Scale

B   18. What information is of greatest interest to career
         counselors?
         A. results from standardized achievement tests
         B. vocational interests and client abilities
         C. aptitude test results
         D. general ability for a particular vocation

APPLICATION: ASSESSING VOCATIONAL INTERESTS

A   19. Which of the following is a FALSE statement about the
         Strong-Campbell Interest Inventory?
         A. it reflects abilities, not interests
         B. it is a self-report inventory
         C. it has been standardized for over 125 different
            occupations
         D. it scores a client's likes, dislikes or preferences for
            an activity

A   20. The Strong-Campbell Interest Inventory provides information
         about the _____ occupational-interest themes proposed by
         Holland.
         A. 6
         B. 7
         C. 8
         D. 9

C   21. Occupations such as design engineer, biologist, physicist,
         and technical writer are preferred by individuals with high
         scores on the:
         A. R-Theme
         B. A-Theme
         C. I-Theme
         D. C-Theme

D   22. Which of the following is a characteristic of the
         "enterprising" or E-Theme?
         A. a great talent for words
         B. impatient with precise work
         C. enjoys power, status, and material wealth
         D. all of the above

B   23. Which type of person tends to score highest on the "social"
         or S-Theme?
         A. scientist
         B. clinical psychologist
         C. clerk typist
         D. all of the above

A   24. Which characteristic is NOT associated with the "artistic"
         or A-Theme?
         A. a liking of problems that require physical skills
         B. more emotional and sensitive
         C. original and creative thinker
         D. likes tasks of self-expression

PSYCHOLOGY IN INDUSTRIAL AND ORGANIZATIONAL SETTINGS

D   25. The area that is concerned with behavior in the world of
        work is called _____ psychology.
        A. counseling
        B. personnel
        C. vocational
        D. industrial-organizational

D   26. Which is an area of interest for the industrial-
        organizational psychologist?
        A. organization development
        B. improving employee motivation
        C. career and vocational development
        D. all of the above

PERSONNEL SELECTION

B   27. The art and science of choosing the best person for a given
        job is involved in:
        A. job analysis
        B. personnel selection
        C. career counseling
        D. vocational counseling

A   28. What is the first step in successful personnel selection?
        A. study the job characteristics
        B. evaluate the applicant's aptitudes
        C. evaluate the applicant's abilities
        D. widespread advertising of the position

D   29. A key component in a job analysis is:
        A. a simple description of the job duties
        B. a rank-ordering of the various duties of the job
        C. to differentiate as to whether it is a female or male
           type of position
        D. an identification of specific behaviors that lead to
           success or failure on the job

C   30. Research by McCall and Lombardo (1983) found that the most
        glaring differences between successful and nonsuccessful
        executives was:
        A. overmanaging
        B. inability to boss with different styles
        C. inability to understand other people's perspectives
        D. betrayal of trust

A   31. Expectancy charts are used in what phase of personnel selection?
A. prediction
B. job characteristics
C. person characteristics
D. assessment

B   32. The importance of predictive accuracy in personnel selection was first demonstrated with:
A. executive selection for IBM
B. pilot training schools during WWII
C. applicants for college
D. professional race car drivers in the early 1950's

D   33. Which of the following is a characteristic of the assessment center approach in personnel selection?
A. it was first developed during WWII
B. they work with a small number of canditates brought to an assessment center
C. they use multiple assessment procedures and multiple assessors
D. all of the above

C   34. What is the distinctive feature of the assessment center approach to personnel selection?
A. personality and interest inventories
B. on the job evaluations
C. situational tests
D. intelligence and motivational tests

A   35. The longitudinal investigation called the Management Progress Study found that managerial success is highly:
A. predictable
B. predictable for males but not females
C. predictable for females but not males
D. predictable for the first 10 years on the job

PERSONNEL DEVELOPMENT

B   36. Dalton, Thompson, and Price (1977) have described _____ stages of professional careers.
A. 3
B. 4
C. 5
D. 6

B   37. Which is the final stage of professional careers according to Dalton, Thompson, and Price (1977)?
A. apprentice
B. sponsor
C. colleague
D. mentor

D   38. Which of the following is a characteristic of the colleague
         stage of professional careers?
         A. developing a reputation as a competent professional
            with a speciality
         B. peer relationships are of paramount importance
         C. establishing close ties with competent colleagues in
            the same area
         D. all of the above

C   39. In which stage of professional careers do individuals
         influence and shape organizational development and
         direction?
         A. apprentice
         B. colleague
         C. sponsor
         D. mentor

D   40. Which of the following is NOT a role fulfilled in the final
         stage of professional careers?
         A. manager
         B. internal enterpreneur
         C. idea innovator
         D. consultant

A   41. According to Levinson, the presence or absence of a
         mentoring relationship is an important element of
         professional life during the:
         A. 20's and 30's
         B. 30's and 40's
         C. 40's and 50's
         D. 50's and early 60's

A   42. The most crucial function of a mentor according to Levinson
         is to support, foster, and facilitate the:
         A. young adult's development
         B. growth of the company
         C. productivity of his or her peers
         D. functioning of his or her sponsors

APPLICATION: CONSUMER PSYCHOLOGY AND THE PSYCHOLOGY OF ADVERTISING

C   43. The scientific study of the acquisition, use, and
         disposition of products and services is:
         A. consumer focus
         B. the psychology of advertising
         C. consumer psychology
         D. forensic psychology

D   44. The psychology of advertising is concerned with:
         A. how advertising motivates consumers
         B. why consumers choose products and services
         C. why consumers use products and services
         D. all of the above

B   45. Which of the following statements about characteristics of
         ads is FALSE?
         A. the larger the size of ads the greater their readership
         B. generally, ad repetition tends to make us react
            negatively to the product and decreases readership
         C. ads appearing on the inside of the front and back
            covers of a magazine have greater readership
         D. illustrations, such as the presence of people, highlight
            ad messages

C   46. Research on "sexy" illustrations in ads suggests that:
         A. sexy males were as effective as sexy females
         B. blonds were judged more effective than brunettes
         C. "sexy" illustrations may actually distract consumers from
            the sponsor's message
         D. all of the above

A   47. What have those interested in the psychology of advertising
         used to determine consumer characteristics?
         A. opinion surveys
         B. projective techniques
         C. personality inventories
         D. none of the above

D   48. The general conclusion about the effects of advertising is
         that it:
         A. decreases sales in about 15% of the products
         B. decreases sales in about 40% of the products
         C. leads to rather large increases in sales
         D. leads to rather small increases in sales

PSYCHOLOGY AND MEDICINE

B   49. Behavioral health psychology is the new interdisciplinary
         subspecialty concerned with:
         A. medicine and dietary influences
         B. health maintenance and illness prevention
         C. medicine and psychiatry
         D. learning principles applied to health and dietary
            restrictions

A   50. Two areas where behavioral health psychologists are likely
        to make contributions include the prevention of health
        problem's as well as the problem's:
        A. diagnosis
        B. classification
        C. medical course
        D. all of the above

PSYCHOLOGY AND LAW

B   51. The area of psychology concerned with applying psychological
        knowledge and principles to law and the judicial process is
        called _____ psychology.
        A. court
        B. forensic
        C. correctional
        D. none of the above

D   52. Which of the following activities is associated with
        forensic psychology?
        A. developing and evaluating selection procedures for new
           police officers
        B. retraining or counseling of police officers exposed to
           the emotional trauma of their job
        C. diagnosing and setting up treatment programs for
           offenders
        D. all of the above

PSYCHOLOGY AND EDUCATION

C   53. Which specialty interfaces education with clinical and
        counseling?
        A. psychometricians
        B. clinical psychology
        C. school psychology
        D. community psychology

C   54. Which of the following activities is NOT typically
        associated with school psychologists?
        A. counseling students
        B. administering achievement and interest tests
        C. classroom instruction
        D. insuring smooth transitions for students between grades

A   55. The application of psychology to education is known as
        _____ psychology.
        A. educational
        B. instructional
        C. school
        D. academic

B   56. Educational psychologists most often have specialty areas in
         either learning or:
         A. career counseling
         B. measurement and test development
         C. career planning
         D. none of the above

B   57. Programmed instruction and computer assisted instruction
         were developed through research in _____ psychology.
         A. school
         B. instructional
         C. academic
         D. psychometric

APPLICATION: EDUCATIONAL AND PSYCHOLOGICAL TESTING

D   58. The most controversial issue in educational psychology today
         is:
         A. forced busing
         B. repeating a grade level
         C. grade skipping or grade promotion
         D. testing

C   59. Attempts to select those applicants most likely to succeed
         in educational programs and colleges is accomplished by:
         A. career counselors
         B. school psychologists
         C. admissions testing
         D. instructional psychologists

C   60. The   important   court   case   Larry P. vs. Wilson Riles   in
         California resulted in the barring of:
         A. admissions tests in private high schools
         B. admissions tests in private colleges
         C. language tests for minority students
         D. intelligence tests for the placement of educable
            mentally retarded children

A   61. The Allen Bakke case of reverse discrimination dealt with
         the use of admissions tests in:
         A. medical school
         B. law school
         C. private colleges
         D. graduate school

B   62. Ralph Nader and associates in 1980 argued:
         A. for standardized admissions testing in colleges
         B. against standardized admissions testing in colleges
         C. for intelligence testing following admission into the
            armed services
         D. against intelligence testing following admission into
            the armed services

ON THE HORIZON: THE FUTURE OF ADMISSIONS TESTING

D   63. The future of college admissions testing is likely to
         include:
         A. a decline in the use of admissions tests as the sole
            predictor
         B. higher costs to take less valid tests
         C. selections based on who is most likely to remain in
            college for four years
         D. all of the above

FURTHER READING SUGGESTIONS

Anastasi, A. (1979). Fields of applied psychology. (2nd edition).
    New York: McGraw-Hill.

Campbell, D. P. (1974). If you don't know where you are going,
    you'll probably end up somewhere else. Niles, Illinois:
    Argus Communications.

Dunnette, M. D. (1966). Personnel selection and placement.
    Belmont, CA: Wadsworth.

Dunnette, M. D. (Ed.) (1976). Handbook of industrial and
    organizational psychology. Chicago: Rand McNally.

McCormick, E. J., and Sanders, M. S. (1982). Human factors in
    engineering and design. (5th edition). New York: McGraw-Hill.

Schulz, D. P. (1979). Psychology in use: An introduction to
    applied psychology. New York: Macmillan.

†